D1601354

GENDER POLITICS
IN THE WESTERN BALKANS

Post-Communist Cultural Studies
Thomas Cushman, General Editor

The Culture of Lies
Antipolitical Essays
Dubravka Ugrešić

Burden of Dreams
History and Identity in
Post-Soviet Ukraine
Catherine Wanner

Gender Politics in the Western Balkans
Women and Society in
Yugoslavia and the Yugoslav
Successor States
Sabrina P. Ramet

WOMEN AND SOCIETY
IN YUGOSLAVIA
AND THE YUGOSLAV
SUCCESSOR STATES

EDITED BY
SABRINA P. RAMET
AFTERWORD BY
BRANKA MAGAŠ

GENDER POLITICS
IN THE WESTERN BALKANS

THE PENNSYLVANIA STATE UNIVERSITY PRESS
UNIVERSITY PARK, PENNSYLVANIA

Library of Congress Cataloging-in-Publication Data

Gender politics in the Western Balkans : women and society in Yugoslavia and the
    Yugoslav successor states / edited by Sabrina P. Ramet.
        p.   cm.—(Post-Communist cultural studies)
        Includes bibliographical references and index.
        ISBN 0–271–01801–1 (cloth : alk. paper)
        ISBN 0–271–01802-X (pbk. : alk. paper)
        1. Women—Yugoslavia—History.   2. Women—Former Yugoslav
    republics—History.   3. Feminism—Yugoslavia—History.   4. Feminism—
    Former Yugoslav republics—History.
    I. Ramet, Sabrina P., 1949–   . II. Series.
    HQ1715.5.G46 1999
    305.4'09497—dc21   98-20732
                                                                           CIP

It is the policy of The Pennsylvania State University Press to use acid-free paper
for the first printing of all clothbound books. Publications on uncoated stock
satisfy the minimum requirements of American National Standard for Information Sciences—Permanence of Paper for Printed Library Materials, ANSI
Z39.48–1992.

CONTENTS

PREFACE AND ACKNOWLEDGMENTS

As always happens with edited projects, the final product corresponds only in part to the original scheme. One of the original contributors disappeared without a trace during work on this book, while another contributor, who had been contracted to compose a chapter on women in interwar Croatia, offered a product which diverged by a wide margin from the contracted topic. Because this occurred late in the life of this project, it proved to be impossible to obtain a replacement chapter on this subject within an acceptable time frame.

I am deeply grateful to Tom Cushman and to the anonymous reader contracted by Penn State Press for helpful comments on an earlier draft of this manuscript. I also wish to thank *Ethos* for permission to reprint Andrei Simić's chapter; *War Report* for permission to publish an expanded and updated version of Žarana Papić's essay, which originally appeared in its pages; The Johns Hopkins University Press for permission to reprint the chapter by Dorothy Thomas and Regan Ralph, originally published in *The SAIS Review* under the title, "Rape in War: Challenging the Tradition of Impunity"; and Ute Gerhard for permission to print Vlasta Jalušič's chapter on women in interwar Slovenia. I am also deeply grateful to my spouse, Christine Hassenstab, for preparing the index for this book, and to Patty Mitchell for her hard work throughout the production process.

SABRINA P. RAMET
SEATTLE, WASHINGTON

To Jere Bacharach, friend

OVERVIEW

PART ONE

1

Sabrina P. Ramet

Feminism is born with the realization that the structure of social reality is not neutral, is not opaque, but assumes the form of patriarchy.[1] One well-established definition holds:

> Patriarchy is the power of the fathers: a familial-social, ideological, political system in which men—by force, direct pressure, or through ritual, tradition, law and language, customs, etiquette, education and the division of labor—determine what part women shall or shall not play, and in which the female is everywhere subsumed under the male.[2]

The mere realization that society is patriarchal does not, however, in and of itself constitute a feminist conversion or even a sufficient impetus to action. An intervening variable, namely, political ideology or tradition, is necessary to translate the apprehension of the reality of patriarchy into a disposition with regard to that patriarchy; in particular, the assessment that patriarchy is unjust requires political presuppositions derived from an overarching ideological orientation.

In the twentieth century, there have been five ideologies which have been developed to a highly articulate degree, all of them having roots earlier in history. These five are *liberalism* (in the sense of the tradition beginning with Machiavelli, Hobbes, Locke, Kant, and J. S. Mill, but also including Herbert Spencer, among others), *socialism* (above all, in its Marxist variant), *fascism* (under which we may subsume also Naziism), *anarchism* (which had its heyday in the doomed Spanish Republic of the interwar era and which has all but expired in the meantime), and *clericalism* (by which I understand the effort to legislate or otherwise compel mass conformity with a system centered on the supremacy of Church and family, the subservience of women to their husbands, and the equation of womanhood with motherhood). That there are also hybrid formations should be self-evident: one need only think, for example, of social democracy (a hybrid of liberalism and Marxist socialism) or of the American Christian Right in the 1980s and 1990s (a hybrid of fascism and clericalism).

To identify these traditions is also to realize that neither fascism nor clericalism can provide a hearth for feminist activity, the Marija feminist movement of the Soviet Union in the 1970s, notwithstanding. In fact, both traditions see women's "purpose" as consisting in the bearing and rearing of *men*! Hitler put it this way at a 1935 Nazi Party rally: "The reward which National Socialism bestows on woman in return for her labour is that it once more rears men, real men, decent men who stand erect, who are courageous, who love honor."[3]

Having excluded fascism and clericalism, we see that the remaining three political traditions, in fact, give rise to five alternative forms of feminism: *socialist feminism* (the position of Zillah Eisenstein, but also the position adopted by Tito and the Titoists), *liberal feminism* (the position adopted by Betty Friedan and the National Organization for Women), *social-democratic feminism* (the position of the Zagreb-based Woman and Society group, formed in 1979, and of sociologists such as Rada Iveković), *anarcho-feminism* (a position adopted, at best, by isolated intellectuals lacking real influence), and *radical feminism*, which breaks with both liberalism and socialism by rejecting their suppositions that women's rights can be subsumed within a broader and more general agenda but which insists, on the contrary, that women's rights be made the object of a specific struggle. As Shulamith Firestone put it in 1970,

The contemporary radical feminist position . . . sees feminist issues not only as *women's* first priority, but as central to any larger revolutionary analysis. It refuses to accept the existing leftist analysis not because it is too radical, but because *it is not radical enough*: it sees the current leftist analysis as outdated and superficial, because this analysis does not relate the structure of the economic class system to its origins in the sexual class system, the model for all other exploitative systems, and thus the tapeworm that must be eliminated first by any true revolution.[4]

The history of South Slav women in the twentieth century is, in part, the history of their struggles within the frameworks of these rival ideologies. But, it should be stressed, the struggle for human dignity, for equality, for an end to oppression, can also be waged in the absence of a conscious confrontation with broader political concepts, though not without a conscious assessment that certain institutions or practices, if not the entire system, must be seen as unjust to women; such a struggle, shorn of political conceptualization, will of necessity assume mundane forms.

This book aims to provide an overview of the social and political history of South Slav women in the twentieth century, focusing, above all, on the experiences of women in Slovenia, Serbia, Croatia, Kosovo, and Bosnia. This book takes it for granted that culture, in all its senses, is a vital and central element in politics, and that a political history must, of necessity, take up cultural questions.

In the course of the twentieth century, Yugoslav women have lived under six different systems: *dynastic monarchy* (in the years up to 1918), *constitutional monarchy* (most of the years between 1918 and 1941), *fascist occupation* (1941–45), *communist one-party rule* (1945–90), *flawed democracy* (Slovenia and Macedonia since 1990), and *nationalism* (Croatia, Serbia, and Bosnia since 1990). Although politicians in all of these systems developed elaborate notions as to what was best for women and for gender relations, only Tito's system actually adopted gender equality as a central and explicit goal of policy.

Was Tito, then, a feminist? The simple answer is that he was *not* a feminist, both because Tito declined to give women's equality a priority above or outside the development of self-managing socialism and because he and the Titoists rejected the term "feminist" which they equated with *bourgeois* activism and, hence, antisocialist thinking. But to be entirely fair to Tito and the self-management project, one must concede that gender equality was, all the same, *part* of the socialist program that Tito envisioned, and that although he did not use the term "feminist" in referring to himself, he was nonetheless engaged in the same project, albeit set in a socialist context. Moreover, I am unaware of any important differences between Tito and Eisenstein when it comes to their assessments of the relationship between socialism and gender equality, and Eisenstein calls herself a feminist.

During the rest of this century, the women of the Yugoslav area were told that there were more important things to which it was necessary to attend, and that gender equality could wait. In some systems (for example, the fascist and nationalist systems) even this formulation could be seen as too "radical"; for fascists and nationalists alike, gender inequality is natural and any effort to overthrow the natural hierarchy in social relations is an assault on sacred traditions.

This book is, among other things, about the concern for social justice in Yugoslavia, about the demand that democracy be not just for men but for all citizens. In the age of politicized nationalism, the self-proclaimed defenders of "the Nation" reinterpret the community in folk-mythological terms, reducing women to "womenfolk" who need men's protection[5] and construing feminists who dare to challenge the patriarchal agenda of the nationalists *as witches*.[6] For the nationalists, so it seems, women should be seen and not heard, as the phrase goes. But the women of Slovenia, Serbia, Croatia, and Bosnia include among their number sufficient numbers of politically aware women committed to social justice. They are not content staying at home, knitting, washing the dishes, cooking the meals, and waiting for their husbands to explain the world to them. What they want is simple: dignity and equality. As Marina Blagojević put it at a symposium organized by the Center for Women's Studies in Belgrade,

> We were hoping for democracy, but the "democracy" realized is a democracy without women. There are less women than ever in all the bodies that make decisions. We were hoping for freedom, but it happened to be a freedom without safety and security. . . . We were hoping for true equality, not [an] ideological one, but that new equality turned [out] to be equality of poverty. . . . [The nationalists' version of] equality turned out to be self-sacrifice for women, and, paradoxically, this sacrifice strengthened the imbalance between genders.[7]

The chapters in this book are organized into four parts. In Chapter 2 of Part I, Andrei Simić outlines traditional gender-linked behaviors among the South Slavs, arguing that, although the interaction between husband and wife is purely patriarchal, the typical relationship between aged mother and adult son reveals strong traditions of maternal influence, sufficient to permit one to describe the resultant gender system as a crypto-matriarchy.[8] Simić finds unifying trends in both rural and urban settings.

Part II traces the struggle to overcome the injustices of patriarchal society in the western Balkans, from the eve of the founding of the Kingdom of Serbs, Croats, and Slovenes (in 1918) to the historical experience of the communist federation of Yugoslavia after 1945. In the early twentieth century, the relations between the sexes in the Balkans were not so different from those reflected in the account offered by E. M. Forster in his *A Room with a View*. "It was not that ladies were inferior to men," he wrote there, appealing to notions of propriety,

> it was that they were different. Their mission was to inspire others to achievement rather than to achieve themselves. Indirectly, by means of tact and a spotless name, a lady could accomplish much. But if she rushed into the fray herself, she would be first censured, then despised, and finally ignored. Poems had been written to illustrate this point.[9]

Thomas Emmert (Chapter 3) and Vlasta Jalušič (Chapter 4) trace the emergence of feminist organizations in interwar Serbia and Slovenia, respectively. Emmert notes that Svetozar Pribićević and Stjepan Radić were among the interwar politicians to address the subject of gender equality. But, as Emmert notes, the rhetoric of male politicians notwithstanding, many bourgeois feminists soon found themselves in agreement with socialist women that the emancipation of women would depend on the radical transformation of society. Jalušič begins her story in Habsburg-ruled Slovenia, recounting liberal fears (c. 1902) that female suffrage would augment the vote for conservative parties. As she notes, the first Slovenian feminist organization, the Feminist Alliance, was established as early as 1923.

Barbara Jancar-Webster (Chapter 5) discusses the rise of socialist organizations for women. The Anti-Fascist Women's Front, formally established in 1942, figures in both accounts. Jancar-Webster is concerned with women's experience in the Yugoslav partisan struggle of 1941–45.

As she notes, women's participation in the war transformed gender relations in some significant ways, including opening up new jobs for women and assuring them of positions in the postwar political apparatus.

Part II closes with my own study of the Titoist era (Chapter 6). As I note there, Yugoslavia's communist authorities identified the problems entailed in gender inequality frankly and insightfully and outlined the appropriate remedies without equivocation; their failure was twofold—in that they believed that the problems of gender inequality could be solved without treating them as constituting an autonomous sphere of policy and in that they did not adopt the remedies which they had themselves prescribed. But, as I argue, "By its very failure, socialism showed that the reduction of the question of gender equality to some more general question risks not merely the subordination of women's inequality to other concerns but its scuttling."

Part III is devoted to the experiences of women in the Yugoslav successor states, with separate chapters devoted to Slovenia, Croatia, Serbia, Kosovo, and Bosnia. Vlasta Jalušič, in Chapter 7 on post-socialist Slovenia, observes ruefully that "conservatives always find 'more important issues' than social justice and human dignity." In the process of political demonopolization, thus, women have been marginalized, in Slovenia as elsewhere, and the representation of women in the parliament has dropped precipitously.

Tatjana Pavlović (Chapter 8) confirms the syndrome noted by Jalušič but, in the course of examining the Croatian case, adds some interesting details. The post-communist elites in Croatia, she finds, are not only misogynist but homophobic. Inspired by partially atavistic, partially solipsistic notions of "the traditional family," Croatia's media moguls conjure up fantasies of the ideal Croatian family—heterosexual, ethnically Croat parents and four children, all smiling in joy at having Franjo Tudjman as their president. Contemporary Croatian films replicate this image in dramatic form, promulgating reverence for women *as mothers*.

Žarana Papić (Chapter 9) extends the analysis to Serbia, characterizing Milošević's regime as a personal despotism in which the reconstruction of the gender system has figured as an essential element and exploring the role of the Serbian Orthodox Church in stirring up paranoia about the declining birth rate in Serbia. The toughening of the law on abortion (in 1993) was a natural accompaniment of the more intense patriarchalism characteristic of the Milošević years.

The situation of Albanian women in Kosovo is the subject of

Chapter 10. Here, Julie Mertus examines the interaction of gender identities and national identities. Thanks to Milošević's hard-fisted rule, "Albanian" is translated as "victim" in today's Kosovo, but the experience of being victimized is different for the men and women of Kosovo. As Mertus notes, "A man who is beaten on his genitals can say 'I knew I was a man [and] they could not take that from me. . . .' In contrast, women have little support in their community as women. A woman who is raped or sexually assaulted would not say, 'I knew I was a woman.'"

Chapters 11 and 12 offer contrasting views of rape warfare in Bosnia. In Obrad Kesić's view (Chapter 11), women in Bosnia have figured not merely as victims but also as the perpetrators of atrocities. Indeed, he suggests that they "probably differ little from the men who commit" these same atrocities. Warning that the promulgation of images of women as "amazons, sluts, victims, witches, and wombs" figures as a central instrument in the systematic erosion of women's rights and status, Kesić criticizes the "attempt to single out Serb-committed rape as being uniquely evil and horrible" and warns against naïvely accepting inflated estimates of the number of rapes in Bosnia. Kesić shows how discussions about the ethnicity of rape victims inflamed controversy between alternative feminist groups in the Yugoslav successor states. Indeed, he highlights this as a significant side effect of rape warfare in Bosnia.

Dorothy Thomas and Regan Ralph (Chapter 12) place the emphasis elsewhere, documenting the systematic rape of Bosnian Muslim women in Serb-run detention camps. They present the high incidence of rape in Bosnia as an integral tool embraced by Serbian forces loyal to Radovan Karadžić for the purpose of terrorizing non-Serbs and driving them to take flight. Their interpretation corroborates the European Council's finding that the widespread "rape [in Bosnia] cannot be seen as incidental to the main purpose of the aggression but as serving a strategic purpose in itself."[10]

Part IV looks at the cultural sphere, focusing on women in literature and religion. Gordana P. Crnković examines the literary sphere from two perspectives—women writers in South Slav literature (Chapter 13) and women as constructed by men writers in literature of the same region (Chapter 14). Crnković concludes the latter chapter by noting that female characters in Yugoslav fiction "seem to have been constructed mostly, though not exclusively, as projections of male desires or fears, rather than as known fellow human beings. . . . Also common is the creation of female characters as types—fatal women, woman martyrs, giving mothers." In affirming the creation of female stereotypes, Crnković finds herself in agreement with part of Kesić's argument.

In Chapter 15, Mart Bax examines instances of female hysteria at Medjugorje, site of alleged appearances of the Madonna. As he notes, the intense religiosity associated with the apparitions found a kind of counterbalance in an escalating series of reports of demons in the vicinity. Bax adds that female hysteria in Medjugorje seemed to intensify as a by-product of the spread of the war to southern Herzegovina.

Finally, in a special afterword written for this volume, Branka Magaš, the noted author of *The Destruction of Yugoslavia* (1993), shares her thoughts on the subject of women in the lands of the southern Slavs.

2

MACHISMO AND CRYPTOMATRIARCHY: POWER, AFFECT, AND AUTHORITY IN THE TRADITIONAL YUGOSLAV FAMILY

Andrei Simić

> *Majku i Bog ima.*
> Even God has a mother.
>
> *Čovek je dete dok je živ; drži ga na prsima*
> *i uvek će biti zadovoljan.*
> A man is a child as long as he lives; keep
> him at your breast and he will always be
> satisfied.
>
> —SERBIAN FOLK APHORISMS

PROLOGUE

It is always problematic to generalize about entire cultures, especially those of complex societies such as the areas that once comprised socialist Yugoslavia, a country which exhibited a broad spectrum of regional and ethnic variation, as well as distinct rural-urban and social-class differences. However, in this regard, the following discussion does not attempt to portray the entire range of South Slav family types but merely to illuminate what I have found to be a widespread pattern of familial and kinship relationships. Also, it should be noted that a large part of the data upon which this chapter is based was derived from personal experience and fieldwork conducted among Serbs, and thus may not be as typical of other ethnic groups. More-

Originally published under the same title in Ethos *11, nos. 1–2 (spring–summer 1983): 66–86. Reprinted by permission of the author and the journal. Research during 1973–74 was sponsored by Grant #G1-ERP 72–03496 under the Exploratory Research and Problem Assessment Component of the Research Applied to National Needs Program of the National Science Foundation.*

over, some critics have raised the question as to whether my findings represent a rural rather than an urban variant. My response to this observation is that a significant component of Yugoslav urban populations in the twentieth century has consisted of rural migrants or their children, while the civil war of 1991–95 further inundated cities such as Belgrade and Sarajevo with masses of refugees from the countryside.

Although field research for this chapter was carried out over twenty years ago, subsequent trips to Yugoslavia in 1988, and to Yugoslav successor states in 1993, 1996, and 1997, as well as continued interaction with Serbs in America, strongly suggest that my characterization of family structure and relationships is still valid for a significant number of Yugoslavs. Nevertheless, the conflict waged during 1991–95 raises many new questions. For instance, What will be the result of the separation of family members, premature deaths out of "natural" sequence, and the uprooting of entire villages and communities? What will become of hundreds of thousands of mixed marriages in a nationalistic and emotionally charged atmosphere in which it is generally no longer tenable to categorize oneself in terms of a hyphenated ethnicity or a generalized Yugoslav identity? What will be the effect on family life in cities such as Belgrade and Sarajevo which have accommodated masses of refugees while large segments of their own populations have been reduced to poverty by the almost complete economic collapse of the society? In this context, one may well ask if there will emerge the same kind of familial anomie associated with the "culture of poverty" in many other parts of the world. Or will the traditional South Slav kinship ethos prove sufficiently strong to overcome this present adversity?

The chapter which follows was originally published in 1983, and is reprinted here with slight revisions in the conviction that it remains useful in illuminating some aspects of traditional family life in the South Slav region.

THE ROLE OF MOTHERS IN THE EXTENDED FAMILY

On the northern Adriatic island of Krk, as elsewhere in Yugoslavia, elderly women constitute an influential social category. Grandmothers, swathed from head to foot in the black of mourning, are seemingly everywhere. The islanders sometimes refer to themselves humorously as "black crows," since, like these omnipresent fixtures of Krk's rocky landscape, "they see and know everything." What remains unsaid but implied is their salient role in the control and manipulation of interpersonal relationships and in the safeguarding of community mores. For instance, it was rumored that a recent marriage resulted from the conspiratorial intercession of two grandmothers who engineered periods of prolonged privacy for the young couple so that the faltering romance could be rekindled and expedited by the prospective bride's anticipated pregnancy.

The power of older women is equally evident in the western Serbian village of Borina, where adult male informants, some of advanced age, casually relate that, while they frequently make important decisions without consulting their wives, they almost always seek the opinions of their mothers. Similar behavior is depicted in the Yugoslav feature film *Skupljači perja* (The feather gatherers), set in the region of Vojvodina on the rich Pannonian plain. The Gypsy protagonist, who publicly beats his wife and spends his money with wild abandon in drinking bouts which include the self-infliction of wounds with broken glasses he has smashed on the café table in a demonstration of machistic prowess, is also depicted as meekly acquiescing to his mother's demands and seeking her advice in both business and love.

In the light of such behavior, it is not surprising that mothers provide one of the most pervasive themes in South Slav popular culture. For instance, in the analysis of the lyrics of seventy-one contemporary folk songs dealing with courtship,[1] mothers assume a central role in twenty-one. In these lively commentaries on contemporary Yugoslav life (not unlike the American country-western tradition), mothers encourage their sons to marry (sometimes even selecting their brides), caution them about the dangers of nightlong carousing and the wiles of "inappropriate" women, protect their daughters' virginity and reputations, and act in general as confidantes to their children in unhappy love relationships. In other songs, parents, particularly mothers, emerge as the focus of intense emotional attachments. The cultural significance and emotional power of these sentiments is indicated by the fact that such lyrics are capable of moving even burly truck drivers and grizzled peasants to bouts of tearful sentimentality.

Given the overtly machistic and male-oriented nature of Yugoslav culture, the preceding examples pose a number of apparent paradoxes and evoke questions regarding the relationship between formal ideology and social structure on the one hand, and social process and the quality of interpersonal ties on the other. Specifically, the authoritative and influential positions occupied by older women appear anomalous in the light of a social charter stressing patrilineality, patrilocality, and male dominance. However, this apparent contradiction can be resolved if viewed in terms of a system typified by the complementary distribution of sexually and generationally specific roles. In other words, traditional Yugoslav society is one in which the modes of behavior associated with men and women, as well as with the old and the young, are not generally interchangeable, and the kinds of power and authority associated with these are appropriate exclusively within the contexts of certain restricted social arenas and sets of relationships.

In order to further explain these seemingly contradictory variants, I shall focus on three basic characteristics of native family life. First, in contrast to the West European and North American variants, the South Slav family is not as isolated in regard to kinship ties or patterns of residence, and thus family processes must be viewed within a framework transcending the nuclear household. Second, the apparent patriarchal nature of the family and society as a whole is more a public than a private fact and, because of this, the important affectual power of women is obscured. And third, women achieve this power not by virtue of being wives but as the result of becoming mothers and, eventually, grandmothers. In this way, I shall demonstrate, women legitimate their status within their husbands' kinship groups by giving birth to sons and through the influence they exert over their children in general.

STRUCTURE AND PROCESS IN THE CONTEMPORARY YUGOSLAV FAMILY

One of the hallmarks of anthropological research has been the study of social phenomena in the simplest and most basic contexts possible. In this respect, the family provides an optimum medium for the analysis of sex-role behavior. However, in the Yugoslav case, the observer should take care not to be unduly influenced by apparent structural similarities between the contemporary South Slav household, particularly its urban variant, and its middle-class American counterpart. For example, in the analysis of authority within the American family there is generally little need to leave the confines of the nuclear family or even the husband-wife dyad. In contrast, although many modern Yugoslav households also consist of nuclear families, the nature of interaction with other kin suggests that a larger unit of study is more appropriate. Here, the division of labor, the exercise of power, and the flow of affect can be best understood when placed in the perspective of broader sets of relationships, in particular those linking the generations, that is, grandparents, parents, and children.

In this discussion of the South Slav family, the model employed has been derived from a study of more than two hundred households, both rural and urban, spanning the gamut from peasants and unskilled workers at one end of the spectrum to professionals and highly placed bureaucrats at the other. Materials were collected during five field trips spanning the period from 1966 through 1978. Research was carried out in such varied localities as the northern Adriatic coast (Hrvatsko Primorje), Bosnia, and Serbia. The sample included Catholics, Orthodox, and Muslims, and was supplemented by data gathered from among Yugoslav-Americans in California. However, in spite of this diversity, in no case did the rural-urban dichotomy or regional, ethnic, or religious differences reveal any significant or widespread variations in cultural patterns in regard to family life, though a range of behavior, much of it situationally determined, could be discerned everywhere. Similarly, superficial differences in cultural styles tended to mask a deeper level of ideological and structural homogeneity underlying the ethnic and historical heterogeneity of the Yugoslav population.[2] At the same time, this analysis does not attempt to demonstrate the statistical distribution or modality of certain traits but rather to simply elucidate and explain behavior which not only appears to occur with great frequency but is also widely accepted as "normal" and even desirable by present-day Yugoslav standards.

A number of factors can account for contemporary attitudes about kinship and family life in Yugoslavia. Though urbanization and social mobility have diminished the importance of the large, corporate, patrilocally extended households (*zadruge*) that formerly typified much of rural life in this part of the Balkans, and the emergence over the last century of a strong central government has virtually eliminated the political functions of the tribal society that once dominated the Dinaric Highlands, the mentality associated with these earlier forms of social organization has survived essentially intact.[3] Moreover, the generally particularistic and personalistic nature of Balkan culture did not significantly diminish under the impact of Marxism, economic development, and modernization. Thus, the system of intense reciprocal ties linking family members and kin (and, by extension of the same principle, fictive kin and close friends) continues to provide the individual in today's Yugoslavia with what is probably his or her most vital resource in the struggle for success or simple survival.[4] In this respect, many educated Yugoslavs interested in the rapid modernization of their country view this fixation on kinship and personal relationships as a kind of "national vice" inhibiting the development of more rational (in the Weberian sense), large-scale social and economic institutions.[5]

As the product of a long history of corporate and anti-individualistic ideology, the contemporary Yugoslav family thus stands in sharp opposition to the ideal of the independent nuclear household so familiar to most Americans. This contrast is not necessarily one of form and composition (though it may be), but rather one of conceptualization. Stated succinctly, the Yugoslav tends to view the family not as an entity isolated at one moment in time but rather diachronically as one stretching endlessly backward and forward, the generations flowing almost imperceptibly one into the next without sharp ruptures or discontinuities. Therefore, regardless of the actual composition of a given household at any moment in time, ideologically and conceptually its developmental cycle is a very long one, one that is, in fact, theoretically infinite. In this way, for example, households may *symbolically* contain members who are physically absent, even dead.

The ramifications of this cognitive view of the family are numerous. For instance, the postmarital neolocality that typifies much of the Western world is not in harmony with the imperatives of a multigenerational, corporate family ethic. In much of the Yugoslav countryside, patrilocality is still the rule, and in the city, both patrilocality and matrilocality are encouraged not only by traditional norms but also by an acute housing shortage as well. As Barić has observed, modernization has simply resulted in the extension of the rules governing kinship to matrilateral as well as patrilateral links.[6] Moreover, where married couples (with living parents) form new households, the nature of ritual, material, and affectual reciprocity between the generations indicates that social and psychological separation has not been complete. Needless to say, the premarital neolocality so common in the United States is utterly alien to the South Slav mentality. Even when children do leave their natal homes to attend school or accept employment elsewhere, such individuals usually continue to consider their parental households their "real" loci of residence. For example, the response of a twenty-two-year-old university student is typical of attitudes observed among fifty-six young adults interviewed in Belgrade. When asked if she would like to have her own apartment, she replied simply, after some perturbation, "What a strange idea! It would be lonely without my parents." In a similar vein, a number of married adult informants related that they did not hold a celebration in honor of their patriline saint (the *slava*) in their Belgrade apartments because their fathers performed this ritual for them "at home" in the village.

Another reflection of the multigenerational nature of the Yugoslav family is dual or even multiple residence on the part of older persons. For instance, the Belgrade sample revealed a large number of cases where elderly persons spent the cold winter months in their children's urban apartments, the men typically idling away the daytime hours or indulging in leisurely shopping for the family at the open market, and the women performing household chores and caring for their grandchildren. With the coming of spring, these same elderly people returned to their villages, frequently with urban grandchildren in tow. In every case recorded, the presence of grandparents in either rural or urban homes was regarded as a *positive* asset. Thus, even though parents and children may live spatially apart (sometimes even in different countries), conceptually their residences can be regarded as separate loci of a single household.

Even the dead continue to cast their aura on family life, and generational continuity is symbolically assured through elaborate funerary practices, regular graveside memorial feasts (*daće*), and other observances in honor of the dead. Lifelong mourning is not unusual, particularly on the part of older women who are the arbiters of ritual propriety. Mourning may be symbolized in a number of ways, including the relinquishment of most forms of recreation and pleasure. Such behavior may be manifested at any age; for example, a Dalmatian Catholic informant donned black and gave up his favorite pastimes upon the death of his mother when he was in his early forties, and, a dozen years later, he was still commemorating his loss in this manner.

In spite of the emotional trauma associated with a parent's death, especially that of a mother, the event represents a major marker in the developmental sequence of an individual. It conforms closely to van Gennep's classic interpretation of rites of passage.[7] Children, frequently in advanced middle age, are separated from their old status of social, economic, and psychological dependence and from those who define it (their parents); they pass through a stage of transition embodied in elaborate funerary rituals and a prolonged period of mourning, and then emerge as full adults. In this respect, feasts in honor of the dead and other commemorative practices can be interpreted as overt signs of newly achieved adulthood regardless of what other social and psychological functions they may also fulfill. To adequately interpret this *extended childhood*, it is necessary not only to examine the relationships of power and affect that bind children and parents together in a system of intense emotional and substantive reciprocity but also to make explicit the underlying ideological basis which structures all social relationships among the South Slavs. In essence, the ethic of individualism and the belief in self-determination which constitute core values in much of contemporary American thought are notably lacking; rather, family corporacy and interpersonal dependence provide central themes. This orientation is expressed by the strong attachment of children to their siblings, parents, and other kin in preference to extrafamilial peers. Moreover, family roles are conceived as interdependent, reciprocal, and complementary rather than replicative.

At the same time, the family constitutes an almost closed universe, and is the focus of a double moral standard in a society which functions, even in the public sector, largely in terms of particularism and personalism. In other words, strict moral standards are applied in dealings among family members, extended kin, fictive kin, and a few close friends, but to a very few outside this circle. One significance of this is that marriage, particularly in rural settings, is essentially an alliance between competitive and potentially antagonistic kinship groups.[8] Thus, a wife initially enters her husband's home as an outsider, and during the first years of marriage she is, in effect, *unprotected* by children of her own who, upon their birth, will be full members of their father's lineage.

In most cultures, marriage is a logical point of departure for describing family processes. Where neolocality is the rule, this event signifies the beginning of a new and independent social entity. In other societies, such as Yugoslavia, marriage contributes a new member to an existing social unit, a member who initially occupies an inferior position and must accommodate him- or herself to the existing social order. During the traditional period in the Balkans, which lasted well into modern times, marriages in most areas were arranged, and the bride and groom may have scarcely spoken to each other before the ceremony. Even after marriage, there was little expectation of communication, positive affect, or companionship. Essentially, the conjugal pair constituted an exclusive relationship only in the realm of sexuality and procreation, a relationship which was otherwise subsumed in the context of a larger kinship group. Moreover, the open expression of affection and other overt signs of solidarity between a husband and wife were perceived as a threat to the unity of the household. Vera St. Erlich, for instance, in her study of three hundred Yugoslav villages, made use of questionnaires distributed by school-teachers throughout the country between 1937 and 1941, and notes, inter alia, cases in Macedonia where men between fifty and sixty years of age would not speak with their wives or call their wives by their given names in front of their own fathers. In Serbian villages, she found that men, when in the presence of their own parents, commonly avoided looking at their wives.[9]

Similarly, Halpern, in a 1958 study, calls attention to similar restrained behavior in the Serbian village of Orasac, which he had studied in 1953 and 1954.

> Although a great deal of affection is shown to children, and from children to parents and grandparents, parents are never openly demonstrative toward one another. In fact, it is still common for couples to refer to each other as He and She or My Husband and My Wife. Even in addressing one another directly, they rarely use proper names. If a man calls to his wife, for example, he shouts "Ženo! Odi 'vamo!" (Wife! Come here!)[10]

Even in contemporary Yugoslavia, with the increased freedom to choose one's own mate, the anonymity of urban life, the advent of dating-like behavior, and a growing ideology of sexual freedom, there appears to have been little concomitant increase in the communicative aspects of marriage. In fact, the stylized ritual and romantic idealizations which typify South Slav courtship quickly give way to emotional indifference in marriage. While the nature of private behavior between husbands and wives is difficult to verify and can only be indirectly inferred, the statements of informants and the observation of public behavior suggest that deep affection and communicative empathy are relatively rare phenomena between husbands and wives, especially during the earlier years of marriage. In contrast, the open expression of affection between parents and children (and even between more distant kin) continues to be the rule as in the past, and the following example is not atypical.

> A twenty-eight-year-old urban Muslim woman was greeted by her father, mother, aunt, and husband as she left the hospital after a prolonged stay. She rushed to her parents and aunt, kissing and warmly embracing each in turn, and then turned to her husband, and formally shook hands.[11]

The relationship between husbands and wives conforms to the generally sex-segregated nature of Yugoslav society, especially in those regions which were longest under Turkish domination. For instance, most married informants reported that they spent little or no leisure time alone with their spouses, but rather each chose to socialize with other family members, kin, or friends of the same sex.[12] In this respect, a Yugoslav professor visiting at a California university, impressed by laundromats, unconsciously revealed his view of the role of wives in the Balkans: "In America, you don't need a wife, just a pocketful of quarters!" In another case, a forty-two-year-old married informant underscored the relative lack of emotional attachment in marriage when he observed, upon the death of a friend's wife, that "a man can always find household help, but he has only one mother." Similarly, a twenty-nine-year-old Belgrade woman with three children replied with great surprise when questioned if she missed her husband who had been working in Libya for almost two years. "Why should I? I have my children and my mother and father." Moreover, her statement should not be considered in any way a sign of an unsuccessful marriage but as an indication that husband and wife were respectively fulfilling their proper roles—he by providing an economic base and "giving her children," and she (safely chaperoned by her parents) by maintaining the home and rearing the children.

Another example is provided by a middle-aged informant employed by a Belgrade construction firm who returned only once a year to visit his wife and three children who lived with his parents in a village in southern Serbia. Neither he nor any other informants found this the slightest bit unusual or distressing, nor was such behavior a class-specific phenomenon. For example, intellectuals, who might be expected to hold a more Western view of marriage, were fully as tolerant of long separations from their spouses as were working-class informants. The major difference distinguishing the two poles of the social spectrum was that professional women enjoyed greater freedom and autonomy than their less-educated counterparts but apparently with only slightly higher levels of mutual affect and communication in their marriages. However, what emerges as a crucial variable for the understanding of male-female relationships within the family is the interplay of sex and age. As men grow older, they lose much of the aggressiveness and vitality that is so valued in machistic societies, and women experience a parallel decline in sexual attractiveness. It is at this point in life that many husbands and wives grow emotionally closer, with the wife not infrequently stepping into the power vacuum left by her husband in his declining years. Thus, as men and women age, their relationships toward each other are transformed little by little, and the overt power the man enjoys in the larger society as often as not becomes, at least in part, a façade masking the locus of other kinds of authority and control. Moreover, this metamorphosis is tacitly recognized also in public life, where older women enjoy a latitude of behavior unconstrained by the strict rules enforced against them in their youth. As Halpern notes,

> As they advance in years, women approach a status more respected than at an earlier period and which more nearly resembles the status enjoyed by males. They are permitted a greater degree of freedom of conduct, hedged in by none of the restrictions imposed on them in their younger days. For example, old women may usually go where they please, whenever they wish. They can go alone to market, social gatherings, and weddings. In the company of their cronies, they can dance, drink, tell jokes, and "whoop it up" at a gathering of relatives and neighbors without being condemned for their behavior.[13]

What is clearly reflected here is that males and females experience different life trajectories with the power of men peaking in middle age, and women gradually accruing greater and greater authority, influence, and prestige as they grow older.[14] Nevertheless, this is not the product of sex and seniority alone but also stems from events tied to the developmental cycle of the family itself. Of particular cogency in this respect is the nature of the relationship between mothers and sons.

MOTHERS AND SONS

Dynamics within the Yugoslav family can be modeled quite succinctly in terms of three dyadic relationships: husband/wife, mother/son, and daughter-in-law/mother-in-law. In the absence of an affectual tie to her husband, and as a reaction to the dominance of her mother-in-law, the young wife cultivates unusually strong reciprocal links with her children, validating these attachments through the inculcation of supportive moral imperatives and appeals to her children's sense of guilt, phrased in the idiom of her own ostensible dedication to parental duty, self-sacrifice, and martyrdom. As St. Erlich has stated quite simply, on the basis of her observations in rural Serbia, "Because love between married couples is poorly developed, the mother attaches herself to her children." However, since daughters, especially in the countryside, almost always marry into other households and even other communities, sons usually become a mother's primary focus. Regarding this, St. Erlich notes that "a mother ties herself to her son in the battle against the dominance of his father."[15] Nevertheless, as true as this may be, the real threat to a woman's position in the family stems not so much from her husband as from her mother-in-law, against whom a daughter-in-law's principal weapon is the status and pride which results from grandparenthood. An almost identical situation has been described by Cornelisen in her eloquent and moving account of the lives of women in southern Italy.

> Once a woman has power, however slight her influence appears to be outside the family, she consolidates it into a hold over her sons stronger than that famous boast of the Jesuits. Only death will loosen it, but already her daughter-in-law has learned the art of day-by-day living and day-by-day power and has tied her sons to her as firmly as though they were still swaddled.[16]

Thus, in the traditional South Slav family, the son as a member of his father's lineage and the inheritor of a share of his father's property provides the validation of his mother's position in what is after marriage initially, for her, a "household of strangers." Moreover, as a son becomes an adult, he gradually assumes, within the limitations of his family's reputation and his own attributes, the prestigious and authoritative position which society formally bestows on a man, and it is through him that his aging mother can exert influence and power both within the family and in the external world, drawing on the affectual and moral levers that are not only condoned but overtly encouraged by the culture. At the same time, the young daughter-in-law must be patient until she too has succeeded in creating a similar position through the medium of her own sons. In the contemporary Yugoslav region, the tenacity of such behavior is revealed in the fact that even the tremendous social and spatial mobility which occurred after World War II did not significantly erode the established pattern.

For instance, a mother's manipulation of her married sons does not seem to be dependent upon her residing with them, and even in urban settings characterized by nuclear families the age-old process continues. With regard to this pattern, sociologist Olivera Burić once commented that she was familiar with a case where "a mother had gone from household to household and [had] ruined the marriages of [each of] her sons in turn."[17] Though such a situation is undoubtedly quite rare, it nevertheless reflects the fact that the success of a marriage depends to a great degree on the ability of a daughter-in-law to get along with her husband's mother, who is, in the final analysis, the arbiter of her excellence as a wife. This powerful influence of mothers in the marital affairs of their sons is widely reflected in popular folklore and, for example, a composed folk song of some years ago ("*Svadbena pesma*" ["The Wedding Song"]) proclaimed, "I am getting married, and there is joyous music and drinking, but happiest of all is my old mother because she is getting a bride."

Another variant of the parent-child relationship is what may be termed the *sacrificial-child syndrome*.[18] Here, reference is made to an unmarried adult son or daughter who remains with his or her parents until they have passed away. Probably the most common expression of this behavior is the situation in which a son renounces marriage in order to attend to his mother's material and psychological needs. Although this clearly occurs in other cultures, including in American society, it is considered among South Slavs to be well within the realm of expected behavior and to be an essentially normal expediency. In some cases, an older sibling may assume responsibility for an aging parent so as to "liberate" younger brothers and sisters. However, family histories collected in both Yugoslavia and among Yugoslav-Americans indicate that in many cases mothers deliberately select a particular child to be socialized for this role. As a California Serbian Orthodox priest commented, "What wife could ever make such a man feel like a king from the moment he enters the door when in reality he is only a common laborer or peasant?"

The incidence of the sacrificial-child syndrome may be more frequent among Yugoslav-Americans than in Yugoslavia. In part, this can be explained by a reduced need for this kind of behavior in Yugoslavia because of the presence of greater numbers of extended households which include married children, and because of the fact that the American-born children of immigrants are frequently called upon to act as culture brokers negotiating relationships between the home and the outside world, and in this way playing the role of interpreters of American life styles. The frequency of this phenomenon among American Yugoslavs is suggested by my 1976 census of a California Serbian Orthodox parish. Of 119 households surveyed, there were 57 married couples or individuals with living adult children. In 24 of these cases, an unmarried son or daughter (a number of them middle-aged) lived with his or her parent or parents. In one case, a married daughter and her husband lived with her parents. In another case, an adult grandchild lived with his paternal grandmother and great aunt. Thus, in almost half of the situations in the parish where it was possible, the sacrificial-child syndrome occurred. Moreover, this fails to take account of those who lived in close proximity to their parents, and probably carried out many of the functions of the sacrificial-child except for co-residence.

As I previously indicated, the power of mothers is accrued slowly over the years through the medium of their sons who occupy positions of prestige and authority in an overtly patriarchal society. This power is not only derived from the structural legitimacy bestowed by the birth of a son in a system of patrilineal descent but also from the more subtle affectual and moral dominance exercised by mothers, a dominance which is both the product of widely accepted cultural values and a long and careful process of socialization and indoctrination. Among the most important messages conveyed to sons are those concerning sex and procreation. These imperatives are rooted in a sexual and moral double-standard. On the one hand, the mother surrounds herself with an aura of martyrdom and virginal purity, giving visible expression of the "pain" associated with sexuality and childbirth. At the same time, a mother sometimes tacitly encourages her sons to associate with "profane" women outside the home. The implicit message is that women other than family members and kin enjoy lower status. Moreover, while sexual exploits are entirely excluded from acceptable household conversation, they are, at the same time, clearly taken for granted. Such attitudes are evident even in present-day urban areas in the western Balkans, where young men and women generally conceal contacts with the other sex from their parents, and introduce only prospective mates into their households.

Probably closely associated with the dominance of mothers and the sexual and moral double-standard are the extravagant demonstrations and dramatizations of masculinity which can be observed with much frequency in many parts of the region which once comprised the Socialist Federated Republic of Yugoslavia (S.F.R.Y.).[19] This machistic behavior almost always takes place in public settings such as bars or cafés. A number of core elements are usually present in a generalized atmosphere of carousing, and include, inter alia, open-handed hospitality and the seemingly heedless outlay of money, heavy drinking (usually in the company of a small group of male friends but sometimes including also prostitutes, bar girls, or female singers), the destruction of property (most often of glasses, tableware, and bottles, but occasionally also of tables, chairs, and other barroom fixtures as well), trancelike, ecstatic behavior induced by a combination of alcohol and the performance of erotic love songs, and, not infrequently, brawling and more serious forms of physical violence. Significantly, however, these dramatic exhibitions of male prowess almost never occur within the household or in any other arena typified by the interaction of family members or kin. In this way, the illusion of total male dominance is maintained through the segregation of activities that might otherwise demand the resolution of the paradox posed by the ascendancy of the mother. Similar observations have been made by Halley in a 1980 essay dealing with the Yugoslav family in America.

> A mother's continuing control, coupled with interior distress at one's own dependency and bondage (which undercuts one's honor), and deep resentment at the perpetual and unpayable debt (including the deeply felt obligation to support one's mother in all her conflicts, even in conflicts between her and one's wife) could at times provoke outbursts of rage.[20]

In effect, the culture chooses to *consciously* ignore the disparity posed by the authoritative position of older women and the principle of patriarchy, and, indeed, the actors appear to perceive no anomaly in the exalted and authoritative positions accorded mothers. This juxtaposition of conceptually irresolvable imperatives within South Slav culture seems to confirm Weber's view of society as "an equilibrium between opposing forces."[21]

As is the case in most of the Mediterranean, the semi-sacred aura surrounding mothers in the Balkans is probably very ancient. For example, the theme of the martyred and self-sacrificing mother appears repeatedly in South Slav epic poetry. A dramatic example of this is found in the epic "The Building of Skadar" (*Zidanje Skadra*). King Vukašin with his two brothers orders the building of the city of Skadar but they are thwarted by the constant destruction of their work by female nature spirits (*vile*). To appease these spirits, the wife of one of the brothers is entombed in the city walls, leaving behind a small child in the cradle. However, on her pleas, openings are made in the masonry so that her breasts are left free to nourish her small son, and even after she dies, the milk continues to flow until the child has grown up. Later, a spring of "miraculous and healing water" appears at the site.

A similar stereotyping of mothers, in terms of sacredness, devotion, sublime altruism, and martyrdom, was frequently expressed by informants within the context of dichotomous sets opposing mothers and fathers.

> Mothers earn love and devotion, fathers our respect!
> Our mothers are angels, our fathers devils.
> Mothers advise and console, fathers command.
> Mothers suffer for their children, fathers fight for them.

Thus, the South Slav mother provides a perfect conceptual counterpart to the image of the aggressive and heroic male. The power of this maternal image is rooted in a moral superiority derived from self-abnegation and suffering phrased in a mother's devotion to the well-being of her children at the expense of other forms of self-realization. In this way, "maternal sacrifice" provides the keystone for the support of a structure of guilt on the part of children, especially sons, assuring the perpetuation of a mother's influence and power throughout her lifetime. As Halley insightfully comments, the mother has created a debt which can never be fully repaid, and "the mother's capacity for mobilizing the support of all her children against anyone who opposes her is a sort of 'calling in the chips.' "[22]

The roles that mothers frequently play vis-à-vis their sons in Yugoslav society would certainly be considered emotionally debilitating by most middle-class Americans, as well as by contemporary psychologists. However, the question may be raised as to whether it is, at least in part, a conceptual error to attribute negative psychological ramifications, ethnocentrically, to behavior considered entirely normal in another culture. For example, the Serbian mother who proclaimed at a large social gathering that her married, forty-six-year-old son was "his mama's spoiled darling" (*mamina maza*) did so not only with pride, but also with the total assurance of the appropriateness of her words and with the approbation of her audience. Moreover, it is not at all surprising in a society where sexuality and positive affect are virtually disassociated from each other that a strongly dependent and emotion-laden relationship flourishes in the overtly asexual content of the mother-son tie. Thus, in contrast to the common American model of the family, with its focus on the husband-wife dyad, the flow of affect and authority within the Yugoslav family underwrites and perpetuates its multigenerational structure.

The seemingly paradoxical relationship between the subordination of men to their mothers and the machistic role assigned to them by Yugoslav culture can also be explained with reference to ideas regarding the contrasting nature of men and women, and the behavior appropriate to each. In this regard, South Slav culture clearly demonstrates its affinity with that of other Mediterranean and Middle Eastern societies in that males and females are viewed as "separate orders of creation," each with particular abilities, predilections, predispositions, and innate knowledge and with attributes which are different but nevertheless mutually interdependent and reciprocal.[23] Similarly, the generations are typified by the same kind of complementarity, and underlying the reciprocity between those of different age and sex is the general rule that *only likes may compete or occupy identical niches in a given social arena.*[24] Therefore, in traditional South Slav culture, children do not vie with adults, nor do women openly "usurp" the roles of men, although, as noted above, there are variations in levels of social tolerance and expectation with regard to female behavior, depending upon the woman's age and status and the given social context. Even in contemporary urban settings where the majority of women are employed outside the home, wives and mothers continue to manage the family arena, setting and maintaining the moral tone of the home while, at the same time, exerting a certain influence on their sons even outside the context of family life. Thus, it is that the strict segregation of incompatible roles and behavior makes it mandatory for a man, who may spend large sums of money brawling in the local honky-tonk, to act only with the greatest decorum in the quasi-sacred context of his mother's home, respecting the fact that he may never openly compete with his mother, toward whom he is prohibited from expressing any form of open hostility or antagonism.

The Yugoslav family also exhibits what may be termed *long-term dynamics* related to different male and female life trajectories.[25] Mothers eventually grow old and die, wives become mothers, and finally, mothers-in-law and grandmothers. In old age, men also experience profound changes, with a decline in the physical strength and aggressiveness so valued in males by the culture. Moreover, the death of a mother leaves the son with an affectual and authoritative void which must somehow be filled. Thus, a middle-aged wife is frequently able to assume the role previously occupied by her mother-in-law, and in this way, the asymmetrical power relationship which typifies a young husband and wife is subsequently reversed in later life. In this way, in a society that accords a woman little public power, a female can accrue great prestige and even authority. Moreover, the transference of dependency on the part of the husband from his mother to his aging wife is made possible by her symbolic loss of what the culture considers a dangerous and potentially defiling sexuality incompatible with a status of autonomy.

CONCLUSION

The model of family process and sex roles elucidated in this chapter, like all models, is an abstraction conforming only approximately to reality, and glossing over very real differences in individual experience. Nevertheless, among the many informants interviewed and families studied, not a single case was totally counterindicative of the behavior and values identified here. In essence, what I have described in this chapter is a set of pervasive ideas prevalent in the western Balkans. Moreover, these are ideas which appear to have important consequences for the structure of family life as well as for the molding of sex-role behavior. The South Slav case also has implications which transcend this particular context, and suggests that models of sex-role behavior which speak simplistically of male dominance and female submissiveness obscure the intricacies and subtleties of the sociocultural process everywhere.

The characterization of Yugoslav society as a *cryptomatriarchy* is not intended to deny the patriarchal core of that culture, but to call attention to the pitfalls inherent in the cross-cultural study of power and authority, as well as to nuances in the social construction of patriarchy. One problem in this respect is conceptual and is related to the opposition commonly drawn between *patriarchy* and *matriarchy* as mutually exclusive categories, with the latter all too often defined as merely a reversed mirror image of the former. For example, Margaret Mead, in her classic study of sex roles, *Male and Female*, has defined matriarchy as follows: "A matriarchal society," she writes, "is one in which some, if not all, of the legal powers relating to the ordering and governing of the family—power over property, over inheritance, over marriage, over the house—are lodged in women rather than in men."[26]

There has clearly been a tendency in anthropology (and elsewhere as well) to look at differential power between the sexes in terms of formal institutional organization, that is, in the context of ideological and social structures which may or may not be the actual loci of the moral and affectual order. For example, Fisher, in a recent feminist critique of traditional anthropology, points out with some justification that the typical "male cosmology" evident in the work of many famous ethnographers is based largely on the analysis of formal structural characteristics, and thus, there is a failure to consider the more subtle conceptual and qualitative aspects of male-female relationships.[27] Her contention is, to a large degree, validated by the evidence from Yugoslavia. As this chapter has indicated, power may assume diverse forms, some formal and overt, others informal and veiled. Power may be reflected in concrete instrumental action or shrouded in symbol, innuendo, and quasi-mysticism. It may be intentionally or situationally determined, permanent or transitory, contractual or manipulative, ascribed or achieved. In Yugoslav culture, it stems from a variety of sources including the very structure of the family itself. At the same time, power and affect in South Slav society are not only closely interrelated but are also inherent in, and restricted by, the nature of the various arenas in which individuals act out their lives.

PART TWO

THE INTERWAR ERA, WORLD WAR II, AND THE SOCIALIST ERA

3

ŽENSKI POKRET: THE FEMINIST
MOVEMENT IN SERBIA IN THE 1920S

Thomas A. Emmert

World War I not only brought untold suffering to Serbia but it also pro-
pelled it dramatically into the twentieth century. The old Serbian patriarchal society was bombarded with new ideas and new social forces which
demanded change with a compelling urgency. Among the voices advocating reform in the early years after the war were those of progressive Serb
women. Legally and by custom, Serb women were among the most oppressed of European women. Some of them hoped that the opportunities
and the challenges of the 1920s would provide the incentive for the building of a new society which would recognize the equality of the sexes.

   The tireless and often effective work of many Serbian women's organizations was not given careful attention by scholars during the period of
Tito's Yugoslavia. What publications there were on the subject tended to
emphasize the activities of socialist women in the interwar period and
gave far too little attention to nonsocialist women's organizations, which

*Research on this subject was first presented in a paper under this same title at the 1986 annual conference
of the Association for the Advancement of Slavic Studies in New Orleans.*

they labeled as "bourgeois." Jovanka Kecman, in her 1978 study, *Žene Jugoslavije u radničkom pokretu i ženskim organizacijama* (Women of Yugoslavia in the workers' movement and in women's organizations), divided the organizations of the period into two categories: feminist and proletarian. Under the feminist label, Kecman included various middle-class organizations whose philosophy and activities, according to her, only encouraged the partial liberation of women. In her view, the organization which developed within the framework of the socialist workers' movement was the only women's force which understood that complete emancipation could only result from the destruction of capitalist society and the creation of a new classless society.[1]

The philosophical confinement which results from this categorization of women's societies inhibited scholars like Kecman from seeing the true nature, philosophy, and contributions of some nonsocialist women's organizations. While it is true that many women's organizations limited their activities to education and humanitarian work, such limitations did not characterize all of them; and, more important, certain accomplishments, however limited in their scope, should not be underestimated. The fragile society of the postwar Kingdom of Serbs, Croats, and Slovenes benefited immensely from the humanitarian efforts of its women. Furthermore, no matter what the character of the organization, the very effort of organizing women for work in society carried with it a certain politicization of those women. No one expressed it better than Zorka Kasnar-Karadžić in an article in 1922.

> The only way to enlighten women is to create women's organizations from that small number of cultured women whom we have who can then draw others into their public work. . . . Why do we not look at our world the way it is today and not the way it was one hundred years ago. . . . Remember that historical moment when Serbia fell in 1915. . . . The woman was left alone to protect the homeland, the children, and to await the enemy. With lightning speed she found herself in new circumstances. Within a year . . . the whole economy was in her hands . . . the fertile fields were abloom with her work. . . . Does not that woman have the talent for public work? Does she not have the right to seek schools for her village, to participate in the administration of the opština, to seek a limekiln for the village so that her house can be light and clean, to seek new wells for good water, to seek better roads, and

to advocate that villagers distill less brandy and produce more milk? The conditions for feminism present themselves when a country becomes conscious of the fact that it is of value to the land when women no longer live in ignorance and darkness and when their energy is not wasted.[2]

When war broke out in 1914, the organizing efforts of Serb women already enjoyed a half-century of history. Inspired by the words of Dositej Obradović, who once remarked that "no enlightenment will ever come to a people who leave their women in ignorance and barbarism,"[3] Serb women took their first steps in 1864 with the founding of a women's organization in Novi Sad, in the Hungarian-controlled Vojvodina. The first women's organization in Serbia-proper was Žensko Društvo (The Women's Society), founded in Belgrade in 1875. This was followed in 1899 with Društvo "Kneginja Ljubica" (The Society of Princess Ljubica); and, in 1903, with the largest of the prewar organizations, Kolo Srpskih Sestara (The Circle of Serbian Sisters).

By 1906, the number of independent Serbian women's organizations was large enough so that a national organization, Srpski Ženski Savez (Serbian Women's Alliance), was founded in order to coordinate some of their efforts. In 1914, there were thirty-two organizations in the alliance, which by then had become a member of the International Women's League and the International Alliance for Women's Right to Vote.[4]

Having worked so hard to sustain the nation and support its effort during the four-year nightmare of World War I, many Serb women were ready to direct new postwar efforts to the rebuilding of their shattered society. While many of the prewar societies revived their activities after the war, many new societies sprang up every month not only in Serbia but also in other parts of the Kingdom. In Belgrade alone, the early post-war years saw the founding of Ženski hrišćanski pokret (The Women's Christian Movement), Udruženje nastavnica srednjih i stručnih skola (Association of Women Teachers of Middle and Technical Schools), Organizacija učiteljica (Organization of Women Teachers), Udruženje ženskih lekara (Association of Women Doctors), Udruženje studenkinja (Association of Women Students), Udruženje prijatelja umetnosti "Cvijeta Zuzorić" (Cvijeta Zuzorić Association of Friends of the Arts), Matica naprednih žena (Cultural Society of Progressive Women), Udruženje za obrazovanje domaćice i matere (Association for the Education of Housewives and Mothers), Društvo Srpkinja "Kneginja Zorka" (Princess Zorka

Society of Serb Women), Društvo zaštita devojaka (Society for the Protection of Girls), Odbor gospodja za zaštitu slepih devojaka (Ladies' Committee for the Protection of Blind Girls), and many others.[5]

Encouraged by the Serbian Women's Alliance, representatives of women's organizations from all over the Kingdom met in Belgrade in August 1919 and founded the National Women's Alliance of Serbs, Croats, and Slovenes (Narodni ženski savez Srba, Hrvata, and Slovenaca). The organizations within the new alliance retained their individual autonomy, but the alliance represented them at international conferences and in certain domestic forums. By the end of 1921, 205 organizations, representing more than fifty thousand women were a part of the national alliance.[6] At the third conference of the alliance held in Ljubljana in July 1922, the members reiterated their primary goals: national unity, equality of women and men in private and public law, equal pay for equal work, the protection of women, the protection of children and youth, equal educational opportunities for boys and girls at home and in school, a single moral code for women and men, a war against prostitution, and a war against alcohol.[7]

Not every women's organization was comfortable with these broad-ranging goals, however. Some conservative groups remained so opposed to the struggle for equal rights that a number of them finally left the alliance in 1926 and created the Narodna ženska zajednica (National Women's Union). By 1927, this Union enjoyed the support of eighty-five women's organizations. A smaller number of feminist organizations, on the other hand, remained supportive of the work of the National Women's Alliance but went much further in their struggle for the political rights of women. Here it is important to observe that only a few of the so-called bourgeois women's organizations were feminist, contrary to Jovanka Kecman's categorization. In 1924, Alojzija Štebi, a leading feminist from Slovenia, estimated that of the 250 women's organizations in the National Women's Alliance only about 12 accepted feminist ideas without any reservations or qualifications.[8] Feminists insisted on struggling for women's suffrage, for they believed that it was only through the vote that women could ever hope for a better life.

The most important of these feminist groups was the Društvo za prosvećivanje žene i zaštitu njenih prava (Society for the Enlightenment of Woman and the Defense of Her Rights). Founded in April 1919 in Belgrade, and in September 1919 in Sarajevo, this society became a leading voice in the slow-moving struggle for women's rights in Serbia, Bosnia, and the whole country. Its journal, *Ženski Pokret*, which began publication in April 1920, would eventually give its name to the organization. This chapter focuses its attention on the philosophy and activities of this first feminist organization in Yugoslavia during the first critical years of its life.

The struggle for political rights was a particularly difficult one in Serbia. In the 1920s, Serbian society still functioned according to the Serbian civil code of 1844. This law essentially sanctioned the inequality of the sexes. A married woman had no right to govern her own property; she could not be guardian for her own children; she could not undertake any legal matter that concerned inheritance without the consent of her husband; if a husband had any other legal heir, a wife inherited nothing; and, among many other things, the law forbade paternity investigations.[9]

It was particularly difficult to guarantee the protection of women when they had no legal stature as individuals. Inheritance laws designed to protect the *zadruga* (the rural institution of the multiple-family collective) were hopelessly out of date in the twentieth century. According to the Serbian code, inheritance rights passed from the husband through several degrees of kinship on his paternal side and six degrees of kinship on his maternal side before his wife could inherit anything. As one woman suggested in a discussion of the civil code in Serbia, "For a wife to inherit anything, her husband would have to have dropped from the sky like a meteor."[10] Marriage, in fact, took important rights away from women. Adult women (at least twenty-one years of age) had the right to administer their own property. But Law 920 of the civil code forbade certain adults to take care of their own property, among them the insane, the good-for-nothings (*propalice*), those heavily in debt, and married women while their husbands were still alive.[11]

The elimination of such laws and many others like them became a primary objective of Ženski Pokret. In the spring of 1921, as the government held discussions concerning the project for a new constitution, Ženski Pokret agitated for a constitution which would include political and civil rights for women. Calling a meeting for 8 May 1921 in Belgrade to appeal for equal rights, the organization printed posters which included the following:

Women of Belgrade! Soon the Constitutional Assembly will make a decision concerning the political and civil rights of women. The

Government's proposed constitution which has emerged from the constitutional committee denies us both [political and civil] rights.

According to the proposed constitution once again we would be cast into a terrible slavery. Again . . . women would remain without the right to vote and without basic civil rights. . . . We will continue to be banned from making decisions . . . even though we have to bear the consequences of bad political [decisions] and even though we with our children suffer more than anyone else from the terrible light, diet, water, dust, and diseases which choke our city.

They will continue to take our sons from us and chase them into terrible wars while they deny us the rights to make decisions about war.

They will continue to place terrible state debts on our shoulders and on the shoulder of our families and to apportion taxes without our participation [in the decisions]. . . .

We have no rights to speak about, to vote on, or to make decisions concerning the things that concern our lives and the lives of our families.

We are condemned to remain silent, like dumb slaves, and to put up with everything that is forced on us. . . .

It is our obligation to rise up with all our strength against this barbarism.

It is our obligation to cast off decisively this insult to Yugoslav women.

[We] earned our rights in the course of the terrible war.

[We] showed our talents in the worst horrors of the war, the occupation, and the slavery. . . . If women were capable of fulfilling their responsibilities in the darkest days and under the most terrible circumstances, then they have the talent to possess political rights.[12]

While the new constitution ultimately denied women basic political and civil rights, the members of Ženski Pokret continued to fight for equality in marriage, society, and the political life of the state. The struggle would not be easy, of course, since it would clearly necessitate a change in Serbian men's views toward women. The argument was made in one of the first issues of *Ženski Pokret* that men, even if they are followers of the most extreme socialist views, underestimate the value of women and look at them as opponents. The author admonished her readers to remember, however, that modern science had already demonstrated that men and women may have differences but that they are not higher and lower forms of human life; rather they complete one another and are only fulfilled when they both leave their mark in society.[13] Ženski Pokret believed that by educating women and raising the consciousness of women and men to the inequalities of life in Serbia, the foundation would be laid for a transformation of society. And while they had no illusions about any quick success, they believed that month after month of working diligently to create solidarity would ultimately pay off.

The movement encouraged an intelligent and serious concern for the enormous problems of postwar Serbia and the new Kingdom. The middle-class readers of *Ženski Pokret* were compelled to confront themselves, their attitudes, and the contemporary realities of their society. They held meetings to protest the lack of progress in legislation for equal rights, to complain about the high costs of living, and to draw attention to what they considered to be the corruption and the wasteful extravagances of the upper class. In Sarajevo, for example, the organization pledged itself to refrain from the use of all luxury goods. "What can I say about luxury?" asked a feminist in the Bosnian capital.

I don't envy those dressed in silk from head to toe, who drink champagne all night in our cabarets, who adorn their homes with Persian carpets, Venetian mirrors, and Japanese vases. . . . I pity them because they will not look around them to see their poor neighbors. They will not look one day ahead, and they cannot even imagine what can eventually come out of this inequality.[14]

A concern for the poor and oppressed led the organization to take special interest in the protection of war orphans, unwed mothers and their children, women and child workers, prostitutes, and delinquent youth. Article after article in *Ženski Pokret* detailed the horrible conditions these groups experienced. In 1924, for example, Draga Stefanović painted a Dickensian picture of parts of Belgrade society. She argued that the suffering began in the womb because many pregnant women worked in the factories where they breathed terrible fumes and worked themselves too hard. Once the children were born they continued to suffer from the cramped, dirty conditions of the capital and their woefully inadequate diets.[15]

In order to refute those who might think that she was prejudiced because she came from the working class herself, Stefanović quoted from an article published in *Politika* on 26 March 1923 in which a pediatrician in the Belgrade city clinic examined over two thousand infants and children and found that 80 percent suffered from various internal illnesses. The main causes were hunger, poverty, and damp apartments. One of the biggest problems appeared to be bottle feeding, especially during the summer months when the so-called child's cholera was so prevalent. According to this pediatrician, 88 percent of infants in Belgrade who were not breast-fed died.[16] If the children survived infancy, they often ended up in the factories in spite of laws forbidding child labor. Stefanović claimed that children as young as ten, eleven, and twelve years old were working nine-hour shifts for four to six dinars per day. She quoted advertisements from *Politika* in which women offered their children for adoption because they could not afford to feed them.

Stefanović saved her most critical attack for what she perceived to be the government's lack of concern for its war orphans. Quoting the government's own statistics, she observed that in 1923 there were 103,320 war orphans of whom 94,820 were not cared for. According to the budget of the Ministry for Social Politics, 36 para per day were allotted for the care of orphans in families, colonies, or private institutions. At the same time the budget allowed 27.40 dinars per day for police horses and 5.65 dinars per day for police dogs. Who, she wondered, was going to pay for an orphan's food when bread was 5 dinars a kilogram and milk was 5 dinars a liter, especially when the 36 para per day was supposed to take care of the orphan's education as well? She concluded by appealing to parliament: "Don't increase the budget for the feeding of police dogs. Make the feeding and protection of children and youth a first priority."[17]

Appeals and petitions to the government were the organization's main avenue for seeking solutions to problems and injustices. Members waited long hours in the halls of ministries and parliament to confront the Kingdom's political leaders. While legislation to provide equal rights for women was not achieved, the government did begin to support some of the organization's voluntary efforts. The ministries of health, buildings, trade and industry, social politics, transportation, even forests and mines assisted in one way or another in the humanitarian projects of Ženski Pokret and several other women's organizations.[18]

This limited cooperation from the government ministries, however, certainly did not inhibit the organization from criticizing the government and its politicians. In March 1922, Jovanka Šiljak pondered the absence of government leaders who could serve as true apostles to organize the new state and educate the people. Who arrived instead, she asked? Unscrupulous partisans, whose first concern was for their pocket, then their party, and only after that the state. She chided them for their poisonous work among the people, promising land to slaves, promising Greater Croatia from Soća to the Vardar, or Greater Serbia from the Vardar to Soća, promising to release the people from taxes and to create heaven on earth. Šiljak observed, however, that none of the promises was fulfilled after the elections. Instead corruption prevailed. With all of this, she sadly concluded, how could anyone have any confidence in the government?[19]

Such critiques of the contemporary scene were not frequent in the pages of *Ženski Pokret*. Nevertheless, for a largely middle-class organization in a very conservative state the range of views expressed in its journal demonstrates a remarkable tolerance for wide-ranging dialogue. After the government banned communist organizations in 1920, several communist women found their way into Ženski Pokret and expressed their own perspectives in the pages of the journal.

From many articles in *Ženski Pokret*, it also appears that feminists from all over the new state worked together more easily and more successfully than did the country's male leaders. The feminist movement cut across national, economic, and confessional boundaries, and one sees very little indication of divisive partisan perspectives. As one woman commented in 1926,

A good part of the credit for the democratization of our people goes to those meetings and conferences where women from different levels of society exchanged ideas. In our united country there is not that separation among women as there is among men—by faith, ethnic group, region, or party. . . . Historians and sociologists of future generations will extol this fact and give women credit for their work for the general good.[20]

A number of articles, for example, were devoted to the particular concerns of the nation's Muslim women. In 1920, at a congress of women from the whole country held in Zagreb, the delegates "were pleasantly surprised" to discover that for the first time the contingency from Sarajevo included "a Muslim sister."[21] This woman, Rasema Bisić, became the object of great concern for the other women at the congress because of threats she received from Sarajevo promising harm to her upon her return to the Bosnian city if she participated in the sessions of the women's congress. Considered a woman of great courage, Bisić was the first Muslim woman to move into the public arena in the Yugoslav state. As such, she became a symbol for Ženski Pokret; the organization continually stressed the importance of struggling on behalf of its Muslim sisters.

There was disagreement among the members of the movement concerning the appropriate kind of political participation for women. Many argued that the changes they sought would not come about simply by filling the Skupština with women or by creating a women's political party. As one critic put it, "We do not need to add our cries to the ridiculous debates and the trivial party struggles which characterize the Skupština today."[22] Ironically, when many male politicians were arguing that women were not ready for political activity, many feminists were suggesting that it was the men who were not prepared. Alojzija Štebi observed:

Our political parties will have to undergo an evolution before they change their views to approach the questions raised by feminists. They will have to evolve from trivial political interests to the politics of ideas and principles. With the exception of the Social Democratic Party and the Independent Workers' Party of Yugoslavia, which are too weak to have any influence on our political life, no single political party encompasses the whole country. All the important political parties which play a decisive role . . . have an ethnic or religious complexion. . . . The reorganization of parties on the basis of socioeconomic principles will have rich consequences for feminist evolution.[23]

While the movement in its early years encouraged a political neutrality, by 1925 a majority of the membership began to support the idea of women's participation in existing political parties. Alojzija Štebi offered a justification for such participation in an article in *Ženski Pokret*:

> Events during and after the last elections demonstrate that our views concerning political freedom, the equality of all citizens, and the inflexibility of political principles estrange us from the healthy, moral advancement of the people and characterize us before the court of the world as Balkan types, reactionaries, and political adventurers. Do not these events awaken the desire of all . . . to help end the demoralization of the people? A true love for our country and for our people, and solidarity with all those who struggle throughout the world for justice, truth, and freedom—these should require that a woman cannot be a neutral observer in this great struggle of ideas. Her position in society, in the state, and in the family depends on the outcome of this battle.[24]

To encourage that political participation, representatives of a number of parties were invited to address the members in a series of lectures in the first half of 1926. Radosav Agatonović of the Democratic Party, Svetozar Pribičević of the Independent Democratic Party, Josip Hohnjec of the Slovene People's Party, Uroš Stajić of the Alliance of Agrarian Workers, Stjepan Radić of the Croat People's Peasant Party, Lazar Marković of the Radical Party, Nedeljko Divac of the Socialists, and Jaša Prodanović of the Republican Party—each appeared at the Women's Club in Belgrade and presented a brief address with discussion on the issue of the question of gender equality.[25] With the exception of the small and insignificant Republican Party, most perspectives on equal rights for women were predictable. In a patronizing way, each of them assured his listeners of his party's enormous respect for women and suggested that everyone was eager to provide new opportunities for women. Stjepan Radić, for example, began his lecture with the observation: "I was fortunate to have a good and intelligent mother, and even more fortunate to have a good and intelligent wife. In all my life I have never met a single bad woman, and I emphasize that with satisfaction."[26]

When it came to the crucial question of women's right to vote, however, Radić and most of the other party leaders were unwilling to support immediate women's suffrage. There was concern that suffrage might be too revolutionary, that women were not ready for the vote, and that women did not really need the vote to do many of the social and humanitarian things they were already doing. The Radical Party, in typical form, argued that there was little time to worry about women's rights when Parliament had to secure the very unity of the country and deal with problems like Mr. Radić.[27] Only Jaša Prodanović expressed views which echoed the philosophy of his audience. He suggested that all of the arguments given for denying women the vote were sophisms, and he supported women's rights by railing against all inequalities: "For us no single man shall have more rights than the whole people, no tribe shall rule over another, no faith over other, and no social class will exploit others."[28] Prodanović actually argued more convincingly against the myths of gender-based characteristics than did some of the feminists themselves.[29] Indeed, not a few articles in *Ženski Pokret* accepted the stereotypes of physical and psychological differences between men and women while still arguing for the equality of the sexes.

The nurturing aspect of women's traditional role was, in fact, important to these feminists. They were concerned that social and humanitarian work would never be a priority of the men who held power. And the statistics appeared to support their view. A conference of women organized by the movement, and held at the University of Belgrade on 16 May 1926, focused its attention on existing health conditions in Belgrade. The capital, which endured the reputation as the dirtiest and most unhealthy city in all of Europe, took first place in the number of deaths from tuberculosis and in the number of cases of communicable diseases. In the early years of the century, more than one-third of all deaths in the city were attributable to tuberculosis, a statistic which fell only slightly to one-quarter of all deaths in 1923. In 1925, 625 people in Belgrade fell ill from scarlet fever, typhus, diphtheria, tetanus, or dysentery.[30]

Papers delivered at the congress told of dust everywhere that made breathing difficult, of humid apartments, unhealthy schools, muddy streets, and a lack of parks. Flies and rats infested the marketplaces. Politicians argued that Belgrade grew too quickly and that money was unavailable to solve all of the problems. The real reason for the disaster according to some of the women, however, was the original method of health service practiced in Belgrade.

Take street cleaning, for example. In the middle of the day, workers simply pushed the dust from one side of the street to the other and from one end of town to the other. Half of the garbage ended up in the street.

There was little control of food markets where meat full of parasites and milk that was half water were allowed to be sold.[31] Housing was totally inadequate. Since the war, the Belgrade opština had built three apartment buildings while Vienna in the same period had built nineteen thousand apartment buildings. In Belgrade, the sewage system was not complete and water was woefully inadequate so that every hour some part of the city was without water.[32]

What was most lacking, argued the feminists, was an intelligent and well-organized plan for the development and modernization of Belgrade. Instead, every administration seemed to do whatever seemed appropriate at the moment which only led to chaos and little progress. Women were encouraged to struggle together against the situation and defend their views on the principles of modern hygiene rather than party interests. It was argued that a well-run opština would see that there was adequate and healthy water, clean and inexpensive markets, and apartment buildings which satisfied the need for hygiene and aesthetic beauty.[33] The conference admonished the nation's leaders to quit arguing that these are the problems of an "oriental" people and to realize that all they need to do is to hire some experts to tackle the problems instead of relying on the party hacks who only create a worse situation.[34]

As bad as things were in Belgrade, the members of Ženski Pokret did not limit their attention to the cities. Life in the villages and mining communities was indescribably primitive. In a survey taken in Šumadija shortly before the war, it was discovered that 75 percent of the men and 99 percent of the women were illiterate; 95 percent were without healthy water; 38 percent had no beds; 70 percent had no dishes; 14 percent had no windows in their homes; 37 percent ate no meat; 92 percent did not buy books and 97 percent did not buy magazines; and infant mortality was 50 percent.[35] In some mines, there was no decent drinking water, no ventilation for the removal of dust, no adequate toilets, and no showers. Ninety percent of the miners' homes in Senjski Rudnik were considered unhealthy; as many as ten people might occupy a space of only fifty square meters. The laws to protect women and children in the mines were blatantly ignored.[36]

Some believed that the traditional moral order had been destroyed in the war. One woman offered alarming examples of family discord in rural areas and suggested that all of life there had taken on the appearance of an animal den. Throwing out one's wife, for example, and bringing in a young girl seemed to be a simpler proposition that "choosing a stud for one's stock."[37] A Mostar doctor argued that morality had disappeared so dramatically in some mining towns that parents were having children simply to get the 150 dinars that was allowed them from the mine for each birth. Then they were letting them die so that they could collect the 150 dinars which was provided for each funeral.[38]

In the firm belief that education in the countryside could help to change this and advance the whole country, the society organized courses in home economics for the largely illiterate peasant girls of the villages. In one- or two-month courses, the girls learned how to cook, clean, and care for a house. And some of them were given rudimentary reading lessons. The first of these courses began in January 1922, in the village of Požega for twenty young girls, none of whom had ever even seen a toothbrush. The organization declared its responsibility "to raise up the peasant woman, develop in her a conscious, working being, and encourage in her a consciousness for her own worth as a human being and the importance of her role in life."[39] Within a year, scores of villages requested these domestic courses.

In addition to these courses in the countryside, Ženski Pokret also concerned itself with the education of women in the city. In the early 1920s, the members organized literacy courses for female and male railroad workers; they provided courses in hat making, tailoring, and dressmaking for hundreds of women. Serious lectures for the enlightenment of women were held in the Women's Club of Belgrade, located at 18 Karadjićeva. The club was founded by the feminist movement so that young women workers and students would have a place to read and meet one another without tobacco smoke and the smell of alcohol. It also offered meals at a reasonable price and provided a place for the society's meetings and evening lectures.[40] The club opened on 19 January 1922, and each of the guests at the afternoon celebration that day received a souvenir on which was written, "A new life for humanity is born by the partnership of a new man and a new woman."[41]

The Women's Club sponsored a large number of lectures in the first years of its existence. Most of them dealt with the basic issues of the society's interest—women's rights and the defense of women. Lecturers discussed such topics as the pathetic position of women teachers, efforts in the women's movement around the globe, the history of the women's movement, marriage, illegitimate children, the particular problems of Muslim women, and prostitution.[42]

Illegitimacy was a concern for Ženski Pokret from the early days of its founding. In 1920, Ruža Stojanović, one of its members, committed suicide after becoming pregnant by Mladen Berić, a mathematician who refused to accept responsibility for his paternity. Belgrade society placed all of the blame on Stojanović and "left her alone to face a life in which she would lose her position and reputation."[43] The organization became resolved to return again and again to sexual questions and the issue of the double standard in society. How is it, observed Sima Marković in *Ženski Pokret*, that a man is allowed to be a cad, a good-for-nothing, a criminal with a woman and suffer no ill from it?[44] There was only one solution. The laws would have to change in order to save the Ružas of their world.

For the members of Ženski Pokret, prostitution represented the most glaring symbol of women's oppression in history and contemporary society. A number of lectures were given on the topic at the Women's Club, and frequent articles on the problem filled the pages of the organization's journal. In an impassioned article in the spring of 1922, Vasa Knezević expressed her outrage at the Belgrade newspapers which were so quick to blame the victim of prostitution and the victim's family. When a hungry nine-year-old is offered a plate of cakes and then sexually attacked, Knezević pondered, what good would the most wonderful family have done for the child in that situation? Something is wrong in society when somehow a child of nine or even fourteen years old is responsible for the evil and not the forty-year-old perpetrator of the crime.

Unfortunately, old ideas would not disappear overnight, and these feminists were not so naïve to assume that there would be any easy solutions to the problem of prostitution or to any of the other serious problems facing women. Knezević cited a *Politika* article in which Dr. Djordje Djordjević, head of the clinic for skin and venereal diseases in Belgrade, absolved the city's male population of some responsibility when he informed his readers that venereal disease is transferred only from women to men and not vice versa.[45] With such attitudes in society, Knezević argued, it was obvious that simply reducing the number of prostitutes or establishing homes for these women would not begin to solve the problem. The solution would be found rather in the basic struggle of women for political and other civil rights. In Knezević's words, the success of that struggle would "raise women to the position of equal societal members, whose offended private interests would represent, as they do for men, offenses to the very legal system."[46]

While the Serb feminist movement made very little progress in its struggle for equal rights, affiliations with feminist groups in other parts of Yugoslavia and international feminist organizations helped the Serb movement to see itself as part of a much larger and more important force in the contemporary world. On 22 and 23 September 1923, a meeting of feminist societies in Ljubljana resulted in the creation of the Aliancija Feminističkih Društava u Državi S.H.S. (Alliance of Feminist Societies in the State of Serbs, Croats, and Slovenes). Founding societies of the new alliance were Ženski Pokret from Belgrade and Sarajevo, Udruženje Jugoslovenskih Žena (Association of Yugoslav Women) from Zagreb and Splošno Žensko Društvo from Ljubljana. This alliance was affiliated with the International Alliance for Women's Right to Vote, and delegates from the alliance participated in the annual conferences of this international group.[47]

In 1923, Yugoslav feminists also joined in the creation of Mala Ženska Antanta (Women's Little Entente), a regional organization consisting of Yugoslavia, Czechoslovakia, Romania, Bulgaria, Greece, and Poland. Annual conferences brought women together from these countries to monitor progress on women's issues in each country and encourage common action on a number of important issues, including the elimination of all inequalities which relate to women, the right to vote, the protection of children and minorities, a reform in the treatment of children born out of wedlock, the end to the death penalty, and the teaching of civilization rather than war in history classes.[48]

How successful was Ženski Pokret? Government ministries supported some of their humanitarian and social projects, but many of the more fundamental issues of concern to the membership were not discussed widely outside the pages of the organization's journal. Most of the basic laws which were the targets of their struggle were not changed during the years of their activities. Still, however, the organization forced many people to ask new questions and consider bold solutions to some very old problems. More important, the organization should be remembered for the impact it had on the lives of countless women and children in Serbia and in other parts of the Kingdom of Serbs, Croats, and Slovenes. At a time when the government showed too little concern for the health and welfare of its citizens, especially its women and children, Ženski Pokret refused to sit idly by. Literacy courses, domestic courses, orphanages and maternity centers, an employment bureau for women, lectures and evenings of entertainment for women workers in Belgrade, and unselfish crusades on behalf of individual women who found themselves the victims of society and its patriarchal values and laws—these and more made a difference in the lives of those they touched.

Many of the feminists probably agreed with the socialist women that the complete emancipation of women could not be achieved without a rather radical transformation of society as a whole. But the dedicated members of Ženski Pokret would take issue with the critique of their work offered by some later observers who suggested that the feminist circle remained too narrow and simply did not pay enough attention to the specific problems of workers and peasants. Ženski Pokret did not settle for words and the hope for meaningful change which would come within the framework of a workers' movement. Its members devoted time and money to raise the consciousness of society about women's issues and also to do what was possible within the framework of the existing social order.

This was a delicate time of transition for awakened Serb women. If Pokret activists sometimes accepted old ideas, such as the legendary Kosovska Devojka (The Maiden of Kosovo) as one model of the ideal woman, it was because they wanted to transform the narrow, nurturing role of woman into a force which would help to change all of society. To do that they had to struggle against the Serb male's image of the Kosovska Devojka which, though full of respect, was patronizing and discriminatory and which inhibited the possibility of an equal partnership for men and women in society.

4

WOMEN IN INTERWAR SLOVENIA

Vlasta Jalušič

The emergence of the modern state as a certain political space has been—together with the citizenship concept, providing all individuals living in one country with an equal political status—an extremely important source of and motive for the legitimization of women's claims. In a way, it is even possible to argue that, without the state and "stateness," feminism and its articulation are impossible. The specific political nature of feminism is especially related to the emergence of the (nation-)state. Since the first declarations of women's rights, modern feminism has emerged, so to speak, simultaneously with the state-building process, relating to it as a critique, correction, redefinition, and so on.

This fact has presented a great problem for women's movements within all stateless national and traditional communities, as well as for women's movements in ex-communist countries where the concept of

This essay is a revised version of a paper presented at the conference "Feminism and Democracy: European Women's Movements in the Interwar Period," and will be published in a volume edited by Ute Gerhard (Central European Press). Published here with the consent of Professor Gerhard.

citizenship was not put into the foreground. In such nonpolitically organized communities, the national, cultural, or other traditional integrative
factors always dominate, prevailing over the concept of equality. This is
also the main reason for the non-simultaneousness and unevenness of
women's movements and their claims in different countries and communities.[1]

The history of women's movements and feminist claims in Slovenia
might help to highlight this question. It is interesting precisely because
of the radical changes connected to the rise, existence, and disintegration
of the states that have been—with more or less continuity—the political
framework, the space of appearance for these movements. Women "made
it through," survived these changes and have been active in different circumstances: within the Austro-Hungarian empire (1861–1918), in the
State of Serbs, Croats, and Slovenes and the Kingdom Yugoslavia (the
so-called first Yugoslavia, 1918–41), in the battles of World War II
(1941–45), within the Socialist Federative Republic of Yugoslavia (the
second Yugoslavia, 1945–91) and, finally, Slovenia.

Already at the beginning of this century, the women's movements in
the region of Slovenia represented an element within the movement for
political equality and democracy. Simultaneously (however paradoxical
this might seem from the contemporary point of view), they automatically supported the nation-state–building process. This paradox is connected to the nature of modern democratic institutions, namely, to the
fact that democracy as a form of political government and citizenship as
an individual status can only be established within a certain political
space: the state.[2]

THE WOMAN QUESTION AND THE NATIONAL QUESTION

The elements of modern women's movement in the region of Slovenia
emerged at a certain historical moment. The organized movement is—at
least partly—connected to the crisis and disintegration of the Austro-
Hungarian empire, and with the rise of the political aspirations of the
(south) Slavic part of the monarchy respectively.

Within the nineteenth-century monarchy, the movement only took
flight—above all in the attempts of some individuals to make claims for
women's rights.[3] The most radical defender of women's rights was the
writer Zofka Kveder (1879–1926), whose early, frequently attacked mas-

terpiece was *Misterijžene* (The woman's mystery) (Prague, 1900). However, the actual raising of consciousness concerning the position of women in society was connected to the appearance of women's societies (the first one, the Slovene Teacher's Society, was founded in 1887) and women's presses. In 1897, *Slovenka* (The Slovene woman), the first women's magazine with feminist ideas, was launched in Trieste.

In 1901, the General Woman's Society (Splošno žensko društvo) was founded, the only society which existed without interruption in the first few decades of the century. It survived the disintegration of the Austro-Hungarian empire and continued its work in the newly established South-Slavic state after the World War I. Nataša Budna, one of the younger historians dealing with the history of women's movement in Slovenia, points out that "the General Women's Society was the foundation out of which the whole feminist movement before World War II emerged."[4] Alojzija Štebi, one of the founders and a member of the society, wrote in 1926 that it showed "a clear feminist and social orientation."[5] Thus, it could in fact serve "as the basis and the model for all other bourgeois and socialist women's organizations"[6] in the region of Slovenia. In some regards, its concept and its model of work and development could be compared to a few other European liberal-bourgeois women's societies in the nineteenth century, especially the work of a group within the General Women's Society which, between the two world wars, corresponded to the radical (liberal) wing of the German Women's Societies Alliance (Bund der Deutschen Frauenvereine).[7]

The existing sources reveal that it was not easy to establish an independent women's society in the region of Slovenia at the turn of the century. Minka Govekar, one of the "founding mothers," complained about the difficulties connected with the attempt to establish a separate women's organization: "It has not been so easy to found an independent women's society, to start preparing the ground for women to stand on their own feet, to use their own brains and to work for their own interests."[8] It was virtually impossible to establish an independent women's organization without linking it to the main concern in this area at the turn of the century, and to the general national issue, too. The whole female population within the region of Slovenia, as part of the Austro-Hungarian monarchy, lived under conditions of specific sociopolitical and national discrimination. The claim and assumption that the women's issue should represent an important part of the national liberation issue (a part of the general and national progress as well) was thus an important source of legitimacy and support for the appearance of the first Slovene women's organizations. Hence, the General Slovenian Women's Society (GSWS) was, formally speaking, founded by the "nationally conscious womanhood of Ljubljana, prepared for self-sacrifice."[9] Its first plans and ideology were connected with the cultural, social, and educational work for women. Within this framework, some socialist ideas and goals were developed as well. But the woman question was not regarded only as a part of other important social questions. The GSWS members argued that its solving would also contribute to national progress.

In the already-mentioned magazine *Slovenka*, one of the members of the society, Minka Govekar, expressed the wish that "every woman and girl, *interested in the progress of Slovene people* should become a member of this society."[10] In turn, national emancipation should bring more freedom to women, too; inasmuch as they would be recognized as equal members of their own nation, of course. Minka Govekarjeva wrote that the founding members of the society were "aware that educated, independent womanhood is the best support of the nation, that only a massive, healthy and strong organization is powerful." But this nation-supporting statement represents only one side of the coin. It was quite apparent, on the other hand, that "the conscious" women at the beginning of the century were not prepared "to stand in the first lines of the national manifestations, to go anywhere men told them, to go receive guests from other Slavic nations, to sell bunches of flowers and lottery-tickets . . . to play and dance for 'the welfare of the nation' "[11] anymore, but wanted to participate actively in the political and social life, too.

Slovene social thinkers at the turn of the century started to connect the national to social question to a great extent.[12] The defenders of women's rights did something similar at the beginning of the twentieth century: they linked the national and women's issue by somehow "using" the national liberation argument "for their own purpose." That is to say, they could not effectively express their political aspirations (equal participation in public life) without referring to the national issue. The result of the amalgamation of national and women's goals was, however, paradoxical: it seems that the national issue gained many more benefits from it than women themselves.

THE GENERAL SLOVENIAN WOMEN'S SOCIETY

The society kept the name General Slovenian Women's Society (GSWS) until 1922.[13] It was active within the Austro-Hungarian monarchy in its first period. It established a formal connection with the Austrian women's movements (a member of the Bund der Österreichischen Frauenvereine but particularly close to Croatian and Czech women's associations) and became a member of the International Women's League as well.

The members of the society came from different backgrounds: there were many writers, teachers, employees, physicians, and also wives of important Slovene male intelligentsia. Although active at all levels of the society, they emphasized educational work above all—they worked particularly on the general education of poor women and on education in the so-called social sciences, meaning the education about the importance of the woman question. This was the issue some of them referred to as the "feminist" activity. They founded libraries (the Slavic Library in Ljubljana in the 1930s, the first public library in the region of Slovenia) and organized exhibitions about women's achievements in all areas of their work and activities. Last, but not least, not only did they carry out a lot of humanitarian work during World War I but they also demonstrated against the war.

Politically speaking, their activities focused on two main issues. First and foremost, their program displayed a general progressive and national educational tendency which could unite many women; it represented a kind of a general cultural program. Second, the society put some important collective feminist demands on the political agenda—above all the demand for equal citizenship, for suffrage. This was the most important among the feminist issues of the GWS, although the members were not united in their arguments for it.

In this context, the struggle for the right to vote is particularly interesting. It reveals the relationship among women, the state or nation, and the position of women's organizations within what we could call a (potential) "political unit." The struggle for suffrage can be considered a standard for "measuring" the relationship between women's organizations and the state at that time or, to put it differently, it shows to what extent women can consider the existing political organizations, the state and nation, as "theirs," and to what extent they are treated as "equals" and are able to participate in social and political life as active members of the political unit.

It is therefore interesting to examine both how political representatives reacted to women's claims and how women reacted to the attempts by political representatives to ignore their demands. On the other hand, the struggle and arguments for suffrage reveal the sources of legitimacy which women used for their cause and the different ways which they considered appropriate for improving their conditions. This was usually the point where the opinions differed to the highest degree. One of the main characteristics of the entire period up to World War II was, despite many common activities, the many differences in the society member's convictions. The differences were particularly linked to the question of how to argue and how to struggle for women's rights. The whole spectrum of opinions and convictions was represented within a single society—from radical-feminist and social-liberal ideas to liberal-conservative arguments.

THE FIGHT FOR THE RIGHT TO VOTE

The first demand for the right to vote can be found in the demands of the Slovene Teachers' Society (the first society that struggled for women's rights, founded in 1897) at the turn of the century. [14] After that first demand, the GSWS took the initiative over. In 1911 (after the abolishment of the paragraph forbidding women to act and organize themselves politically), the demand was directed to the National Council. Namely, in the Austro-Hungarian empire only men obtained the right to vote in 1907.

The GSWS supported many other international actions for women's right to vote, particularly of Czech women, among others. Together with Czech women the members petitioned against sections 30 and 7 of the general law (section 30 prevented women from becoming members of political societies, whereas section 7 excluded them from the general right to vote). In 1912, the GSWS (as a member of the Austrian League of Women's Societies) took part in a large demonstration for women's right to vote in Vienna. Like in the rest of Europe the demands for the right to vote became more and more intense in the time before World War I.

Most of the existing Slovene parties did not support the struggle for female suffrage before World War I, however. The Catholic-oriented parties did not support it because of their principles (women should play the role of God's servants and mothers and stay in the background in the private, they should use "other means," not politics, to influence public matters). Liberals did not oppose it at first, but they were afraid that later women would vote for conservatives. When women in the GWSW realized early in 1902 that they would not get any positive support for women's suffrage from the liberal party, they stated stoically: "Even though the 'liberal' party is not enthusiastic about our ideas it seems that it does not oppose them. This is giving us hope that in some time we could get some support from it."

It was, above all, the Social Democrats who first supported the general women's vote in the region of Slovenia. In spite the factual similarities between the goals of the GSWS and the Social Democratic program, as well as the socialist orientation of some women from the GSWS, the interests of Social Democrats and the GSWS never really met. Social Democrats in the region of Slovenia were a part of the Austrian Social Democratic Movement which sacrificed women's vote in 1907 in favor of more "general" goals. As did democrats in Germany and Austria, Slovene Social Democrats kept constantly repeating that women's suffrage was actually a liberal demand which the liberals did not dare take into their program. They emphasized the social instead of the political dimension of the woman question. Besides, women from Slovenian society did not trust the capabilities of the Social Democrats. They argued that "if this work (the organization of women) was taken over by them—as they alluded in their program—they would do more harm than good to the present state of affairs."[15]

This was probably one of the reasons why—in spite of the presence of social democracy—there was no social-democratic or proletarian women's movement in the region of Slovenia before World War I. There were some elements which anticipated the later split between the bourgeois and the proletarian movements, which became the two streams in the GSWS: the social-feminist and the conservative-liberal. One of the "founding mothers" of the GSWS, Alojzija Štebi, claimed in 1907 that, judging by experience, "it seems easier to carry out the feminist work which has to be done in the country . . . outside the GWS." In 1913, she started to edit the first journal of Slovene socialist women, *Ženski list* (Women's newsletter). But since the Social Democratic Party did not support it, *Ženski list* ceased to exist after six issues.[16]

However, the differences within the GSWS did not become unbridgeable until the 1920s and 1930s, when some members left because, in their view, the society was not radical enough.[17] Alojzija Štebi left the society in 1924, but she founded and joined the independent Feminist Alliance and not the proletarian women's movement. Some years later, she declared that in that part of the world the time to work with a mass of women on feminist principles had not come yet.

The existing link between national and women's liberation issues brought another important consequence for the further development of women's political demands. At the decline of Habsburg rule, women had great expectations connected with the emergence of the potential new political unit of the South Slavic nations, in spite of the ambiguous relationship of Slovene political organizations toward the demands for women's rights. In 1917–18, women in Slovenia and especially in the GSWS campaigned for Yugoslav unity within the Austro-Hungarian Empire. They collected signatures in support of the so-called May Declaration, proposed by the South Slavic deputies in the Austrian parliament. The May Declaration espoused the union of the South Slavic nationalities (Slovenes, Croats, and Serbs) under the Austro-Hungarian Empire. The South Slavic union would be a third unit in the empire, in addition to Austria and Hungary (Dualism); hence the name Trialism.

Reports about the action spoke of the "seven thick books of collected signatures." The action was interpreted as "proof of women's national consciousness during the World War I."[18] The hopes that women had to unite the Slovene people with the other South Slavic nations were underlined in many estimations of the time. Erna Muser wrote, for example, that "the May declaration . . . regardless of the Austrian monarchic framework . . . has brought two high expectations not only for the Slovene nation but also for women." What they expected was actually a new, democratic state—not only the "national emancipation and reunion of all Slovenes, and their union with other Slavic nations but also a socially just state—just towards the female population, too."[19]

But the final result, the new state (not the expected new State of Slovenes, Croats, and Serbs existing under Habsburg rule or independently but the union with the Kingdom Serbia), was not very promising. Although women

> rightly expected that the new state would recognize their humane and civil equality that did not happen. On the contrary, Slovene women in Austria had a better social and legal position—even some citizenship rights—than women in Serbia, Montenegro, Macedonia and Bosnia and Herzegovina. The Old Yugoslavia[20] never harmonized the legislation it had inherited from its various parts—above all, differences in women's legal position. Besides, the danger that the Serbian civil code would be extended to other parts of the state always loomed.[21]

UNITED AND SEPARATED AGAINST THE NEW STATE

Above all, the right to vote was not introduced in the new South Slav state. Meanwhile, women in Austria and the Czech Republic (the empire successor states) had acquired the right to vote after 1918. Some strata of women, already having gained the local vote in Austria before World War I, even lost it again with the creation of the Kingdom of Serbs, Croats, and Slovenes in 1918. The disappointment was profound. However, in the first few years of the Kingdom of Serbs, Croats, and Slovenes (during the "consolidation time") the old hope that the state might incorporate women's political equality continued to exist.

How did women argue for the right to vote during the time of the formation of the new state? How did they legitimize their demands for equal citizenship within the new unit? There were mainly two approaches. One argument was utilitarian, connecting the right to vote with the logic of "women's merits" and capabilities. Equalization should take place on the basis of "deserved rights"—with their work, women demonstrated their "capability" of being equal with men and should thus be given equality. The other argument was the natural right's argument, claiming that women had genuine political rights as human beings and did not have "to deserve" them.

Although one can find both arguments advocated by different defenders of women's rights, the utilitarian one—the more practical argument after the experience with war—dominated. Women relied a lot on the "convincing power of the roles they had played in the war, in which they did the work in all areas very successfully." They demanded to be "paid off" now: "It was proved in World War I that *a woman is worthy* and *capable of carrying out all male duties*, and therefore she *deserves* and *is able to handle the male citizenship rights* as well."[22] However, proving that they were "capable to working and carrying out duties" did not bring them corresponding rights. There was still a long way before them, a long and difficult battle, leading to formal equality; the story had just began begun. The women's vote in Yugoslavia was not introduced before the end of World War II.

With the new state women's movements began a new circle of struggles. The GSWS, for example, specified demands more precisely and a few new local offices were founded. In 1921, the GSWS declared its independence from all political parties.[23] In 1919, a new union of women's organizations in the new state was launched, the National Women's League of the State of Serbs, Croats, and Slovenes.[24]

A whole spectrum of women's organizations developed in the 1920s and 1930s. In 1919, when the electoral law was decided and the constitutional debate began, women sent several resolutions demanding votes for women to the authorities. The minister of the "constitutional assembly" (a Slovene politician) promised them to make efforts to promote "the justified demands of our women, who certainly *deserve* to be given the political equality *in our homeland.*"[25]

But it was all in vain. The new homeland did not recognize women's political aspirations. As Erna Muser put it, "already at the time of preparation for the new voting system for the national assembly representatives it became clear that women had been . . . betrayed."[26] Even the demands of the Yugoslav Social Democrats (including the Slovene Social Democrats), who had supported an equal, general, and direct voting right for women in their plans for the common state after the end of the war (1919), were withdrawn. In 1920, the strongest party in Slovenia—the Slovene People's Party—demanded the local vote for women in the constitutional debate. The Social Democrats argued against this and accused the People's Party of having the intention to "abuse the vote for women to strengthen their own influence" (under the presumption that women would vote for a clerical party such as the Slovene People's Party).[27] But in 1921, with the new constitution, it turned out that female suffrage had not yet been realized.

The constitutive efforts did not accomplish the women's movements' political demands; nor did the emergence of the new South-Slavic state bring any other improvement of the women's position—in either the social or political respect. The percentage of women within the working class had grown to 27 percent by 1923. They were the worst paid part of the working force. Women were without any citizenship rights and there was no common civil law for the whole country; early nineteenth-century codes were still in power. One would expect that such legalized discrimination would result in the same and united demands of the largest strata of women regardless of their class origin.[28] However, the cooperation of various groups was rather difficult in the whole period between the two world wars.

DIFFERENCES AND SPLITS

In many regards, there were several differences in the newly established state—different history, different stages of political and economic development or lack of development, language, religious, social and educational differences, and so on. In spite of the overall fundamental discrimination of women (and thus the potentially common interests) the great cultural, social, and customary differences were not easy to overcome in the common South-Slavic state nor "within" the Slovene nation itself. Despite numerous women's organizations, clubs, and societies, the common power was rather weak.

To give only one example: In 1922, the demand for equal treatment for children born out of wedlock became a point of dispute within the whole state, not only between women's societies and the male political mainstream but even among women themselves. In 1926, Minka Govekarjeva, the secretary-general of the General Women's Society (GWS), wrote the following on the issue: "It is well known to what an extent the spirits in Belgrade and Ljubljana were upset because of this modern and just demand and that the proposal was discussed passionately even at the congress of the National Women's League in Ljubljana in 1922."

It was not easy to find a common political language to unite the demands. In 1937, in her speech about the women's vote, Govekarjeva explicitly expressed her opinion about the main obstacle to uniting of women's political demands in Yugoslavia: the prevailing patriarchal subjection of women in all areas of life and their readiness to subject themselves also in the future. There were, she said, "thousands and thousands of women all over Yugoslavia . . . who are not ashamed of the fact, that we are treated as convicts and lunatics. . . . These women are our greatest shame."[29] Her opinion was probably also the impetus for the assessment that "the resolute women were confronted with rather unprogressive standpoints in the National Women's League, especially at the beginning."[30]

For this reason, the more radical representatives of women's societies founded the Feminist Alliance in 1923. The meeting of Serbs, Croats, and Slovenes was held in Ljubljana and was organized by the GWS. The Feminist Alliance of the Kingdom S.H.S. (later, after 1926, the Women's Movement Alliance) saw its mission above all as a "cultural movement."[31] Feminism was defined as a "form of political, social and cultural work for socialist and humanist ideals."[32] The main criterion for associations to join the alliance was their demand for the women's vote. With the new organization, the radical-conservative split in the women's movement became apparent.

Still, many women's organizations and individuals cooperated and demonstrated together on different occasions. Inasmuch as the split between Liberals, Social Democrats, and Catholics (Slovene People's Party) in Slovenia was deeply rooted, it was almost a tradition that especially non-Catholic women's organizations cooperated in actions for a better social and political position of women.[33] Such occasions occurred in the 1920s, as well as in the 1930s; in 1925, the "united women of Slovenia" (thirteen women's organizations) held public meetings "regardless of party and class" against the extension of the Serbian patriarchal family law to the whole state. The organizers were members of the Slovene section of the National Women's League and its member societies (the GWS). Meetings were organized in Ljubljana and other places. The participants demanded equality for women and children (including those out of wedlock) in the Inheritance Law, the woman's right to vote, and campaigned against alcoholism, prostitution, and for peace.

Some new organizations were launched at the beginning of the 1920s: the first Slovene Social Democratic Women's Society, and the Association of Working-Class Women and Girls (1924), which edited a newsletter *Ženski list* (Women's paper). This organization was banned in 1935 after falling under the revolutionary influence of the Communist Party, which was forbidden under King Alexander's dictatorship. Meanwhile, some new Catholic organizations were established as well: the Slovene People's Party, for example, founded Slovenska Ženska Zveza (the Slovene Women's Alliance) in 1922.[34]

In 1933, only the non-Catholic organizations demonstrated against paragraph 171 of the penal code legalizing abortion in cases of social indication (*Sozialindikation*). In 1935, there was a large demonstration for women's right to vote again. The pressure for political rights—especially for the vote for women—became stronger at the time before World War II. In 1939, the 67 women's and 185 mixed societies signed a special document on national cooperation in which they declared that Slovene women "want to work together for common interests and forget conflicts from the past." But in fact, all women's organizations never succeeded in cooperating. The black-white presentation of women's position, the split between the bourgeois and the proletarian bloc, started to be even more apparent in the 1930s. The Communist Party enhanced its attitude toward the so-called woman question which at the same time deepened the already existing gap.

There is one significant text, "Feminizem in borba delovne žene," from which I would like to quote to illustrate the growing ideological differences between "bourgeois" and "proletarian" women's activists. Published in 1934, the text shows clearly the communist-proletarian standpoint and is actually an attack on "bourgeois" (apparently "feminist") ideas. It also reveals the foundation and the contradiction of the later socialist state's attitude toward the so-called woman question that was practiced in the third Yugoslavia and other socialist states after the World War II.[35] Milena Mohorić, one of the proletarian activists, writes:

> Diverse class positions result in diverse women's movements. . . . The bourgeois women's movement emerges earlier. Since they are not trained for professional work, bourgeois women have to fight for the "right to education and work." Proletarian women do not have to struggle for the "right to work" since labour is their duty, stemming from their class position. . . . Therefore, the goals of the two movements are different. . . . The bourgeois women's movement is also called feminism, inasmuch as the "independent" women's organization, regardless of its political belief (Weltanschauung), considers about the women's problem as the central problem—without reflecting its connection with the economic progress. . . . Different kinds of women's actions show their class differentiation in our region, too. On the one hand, the struggle of proletarian and working women for a piece of bread, for the right to work, for the human and social equality, for a new society, on the other hand the "samaritaniarism, body culture, esthetics and glamour." Development of the society we have to live in demands a sharp distinction between women's movement's fronts and a clear definition of the struggle.[36]

But in fact, there were many more complex differences and many more similarities at the same time. In fact, the declared feminists (the radicals) became the real outsiders. The political "alternative" between the Catholic-conservative mainstream and the class-social essentialist claims of the Communist Party made most radicals join the radical left or sympathize with the Communist Party's antifascism in the time before and during World War II. Some of them were typically accused of feminism or some other "deviation" later. The feminist-oriented part of the GWS membership was therefore faced with the same kind of problems and dilemmas as other radical bourgeois feminist societies in other countries at the turn of the century. They were sympathizers of the left, they saw common points and wanted a joint struggle of proletarian and bourgeois movement for the political rights, but the attempts at cooperation failed.

In feminist circles of the 1920s and 1930s, criticism of the Yugoslav situation resembled the criticism of the old Habsburg monarchy—except that the disappointment with the existing state which had come after 1929 dictatorship, such an obvious nondemocratic regime, was much deeper. In the resolution, written on the occasion of a political rally for women's suffrage in 1927, women claimed the following: "Our politicians and statesmen always present our state as democracy, but real democratic principles demand unconditioned equality of all citizens, regardless of sex and class."[37]

Deep social, political, and national discrimination was an overwhelming pattern in the Yugoslav state before World War II. Women's activists were aware of this situation and of the deep crisis in the state. They felt the danger of the coming war. They emphasized the inability of politicians to act in favor of both the general interest and women's interests. The critique of the male notion of and practice in politics was inexorable. Women had "no reason to feel inferior in comparison to the male genius" if only they would look around and saw "all the mess, created by politicians who have brought the world to the edge of destruction." In fact, women "do not want such abilities. . . . We want to build in politics, to create, but not in order to destroy the results later."[38]

CONCLUSION

The women's movement in Slovenia has still not been well explored from the historical point of view. Especially the existence of the bourgeois women's movement between the two world wars was neglected in the decades of socialism and has not been examined critically yet.

A radical feminist and researcher of women's history, who was not particularly popular in the socialist time (she was, on the contrary, marginalized), Erna Muser, wanted to write a general history of women's movement in Slovenia in her lifetime but never succeeded. Nevertheless, she left us some important studies, fragments, and comments, from which I would like to quote one, in my opinion, very interesting thought, namely, that the history of Slovene women's movement cannot be compared to the history of women's movements of the big, politically independent and economically strong nations, as we usually do. Whilst experiencing social discrimination, the movement for defending national interests unavoidably prevailed in the public appearances of Slovenian women, being crucial for the Slovene people.

I think that this important factor can be traced through the whole development of the women's movement in Slovenia; it can be discussed and understood only from the above-outlined perspective of the state framework and stateness. The history of the (national) women's movement (illustrated by the Slovene case) in earlier multinational states does not show (as Muser stated) that the national interests prevailed because they were crucial but that the power of essentialist ideologies was so strong that women's political demands, although they played one of the roles within that ideologies, were mostly overwhelmed by them. This was the case with the right to vote in the first Yugoslavia in 1918. Until the 1990s, women's movements could not get rid of the common cultural and national issue and develop their own political strategy.

In comparison to many other European states where women's suffrage was introduced after World War II—and a certain decline of women's movement activities had to be noticed—the condition in the region of Slovenia gave a full swing to women's movements. In the second half of the 1930s there were fifty-four different societies in Slovenia (one society per 11,000 female inhabitants and in Ljubljana one society per 1000). Nataša Budna claims that a numerical comparison with other states of that time (the 1920s and 1930s) shows that women in Slovenia would be "entitled only to 6 or 7 societies of their own."[39]

In spite of this, their power was rather weak. Neither the GWS initiative for a united women's front at the beginning of the 1920s nor the idea about establishing a women's party was successful. Only on certain occasions—when women in fact defended their already existing rights—did they protest together (during the danger of an extension of the Serbian patriarchal family law to the whole state in the mid-1920s).

This circumstance persisted in the history of women's movements until the beginning of 1990s. Slovene women acted in solidarity only in cases when their customary rights were endangered: within the first Yugoslavia in the case of the Inheritance Law. At the time of the emergence of the independent Slovene state at the beginning of the 1990s, they were united to keep their reproductive rights. In both cases, they did not really contribute to the expansion of their rights but rather to the preservation of the "old rights." However, neither in the past nor at the time of the emergence of the independent Slovene nation-state in 1991 did they succeed in really putting forward either their claim to political equality (in the 1920s) or equal chances and equal representation (the 1990s) as a constitutive part of democratic legitimacy of the state itself. Both the first Yugoslavia (1918–41) and independent Slovenia (since 1991) arose as states that could but did not have to deal with or legitimate themselves with political rights of women (the time between the two world wars) or equal political participation of women (the time after the Velvet Revolution).

5

WOMEN IN THE YUGOSLAV
NATIONAL LIBERATION MOVEMENT

Barbara Jancar-Webster

Previous analyses of women's role in the Yugoslav National Liberation Movement (Narodno-Oslobodilački Pokret [NOP])[1] and the Civil War of 1941–45 have focused on their role and functions in comparison with men's role in the same conflict. In my earlier study on women and revolution in Yugoslavia,[2] I, too, focused my analysis on roles: women fighters, women in the Yugoslav Communist Party, women in the rear. My conclusions were expected. Women could and did fight as bravely as men. By comparison with male achievement, women achieved lower military rank. Women held lower office in the communist partisan organization. Where women excelled and exhibited the potential to become a political and organizational force in their own right, the communist-founded Anti-Fascist Front of Women (Antifašistički Front Žena [AFZ]), they were exposed as elitist, their leaders asked to admit their mistakes, and transform the AFZ into a "truly" mass organization.

These findings supported a hypothesis formulated from earlier research on the status of women under communism:[3] Authoritarian revolutionary regimes can liberate women only insofar as they understand liberation as a tool to serve their purposes. Initially, when women are moving out of the domestic environment of traditional society, the command nature of communist movements can produce changes in their status with relative efficiency because the kinds of change involved are susceptible to rule-making and administrative action. In the context of the Yugoslav National Liberation War (Narodno-Oslobodilački Vojna [NOV]), the partisans were the only group of combatants to introduce such changes. These included organizing a woman's antifascist front, recruiting women into the armed partisan movement, admitting women into the Communist Party, giving women the right to vote, and assigning or electing them to important administrative tasks and functions. However, the further advance of women toward equal status in society brings into question the whole structure of the male political hierarchy and hence is something that can only be won by women through their own efforts.

War is a liberating environment that has the potential to attack established hierarchies and democratize participation. The gun knows no class, sex, or ethnic distinctions. But those who lead the war seek victory with a certain desired outcome. History has no recent examples of women initiating or organizing a war. Women who become participants in a war are thus subordinated consciously or unconsciously to the requirements and shape of the outcomes demanded by the leading combatants. The women who joined the partisan-led National Liberation Movement in the former Yugoslavia are no exception, as this chapter will attempt to demonstrate.

BACKGROUND TO THE WAR

The Yugoslav theater was one of the most vicious, bloody, and vengeful arenas of World War II. The war was fought simultaneously on three fronts. It was fought against the country's four invaders: Germany, Hungary, Italy, and Bulgaria to resolve the nationality issues that had led to the crumbling of the Yugoslav state in 1939. It was also fought between three contending political ideologies: fascism, represented by the invading armies and the Ustaše regime in Croatia, the largely Serb-Chetnik vision of a return to the prewar status quo ante, and the little-understood but attractively equalitarian, multiethnic, worker-oriented communist proposal for postwar Yugoslav society.

While women's liberation was only at issue in the contest between political ideologies, their role in the conflict was a key element on all three fronts. In line with Naziism, the German proxies, the Ustaše government in Croatia and the Bulgarian occupiers in Macedonia, promoted the children, Church, and kitchen (*Kinder, Kirche, Küche*) ideology of the Nazis. Both groups tried to organize a women's organization sympathetic to their cause. Neither succeeded in creating a self-sustaining women's movement. In Macedonia, the best-known fascist associations for women were Carica Joana, Nadezhda, and Maria Luisa. Communist women proved successful in penetrating and subverting some of these groups, notably in Strumica and Veleš.[4] Available research makes no mention of the organization of women's activities among the Chetniks. On the contrary, the main thrust of Chetnik propaganda against the partisan women was the immorality of their giving up home, family, and God to fight like men alongside men. One leaflet for distribution among peasant women asserted that the partisans killed all who married in the Church, while another claimed that the partisans had fathered four thousand illegitimate children in Montenegro. The Chetnik leader Draža Mihailović is reported to have told the quisling Yugoslav prime minister in 1943 that women communists either were prostitutes before they joined or became such afterward.[5]

There are many explanations for why the partisans were the only combatants able to generate a self-sustaining women's organization. One reason is that women's liberation was an integral part of communist ideology. Not only was it a major plank of the socialist and communist platforms during the interwar period in Yugoslavia but it served as a rallying cry for all Yugoslav women's groups prior to World War II. A second explanation is that, given the numbers massed on all sides of the conflict, a victory required winning over as large a segment of the population as possible. The communists correctly took advantage of the fact that women represented a good half of the population. The more complete and integrated into the partisan war effort women's mobilization was, the more likely were women to opt for a communist victory. A third reason was the demands of the war itself. With all available partisan manpower committed to the front, women by necessity had to assume the procurement and requisition functions in the rear.

The war demanded an enormous human sacrifice. It is estimated that 5.7 million people or around 12 percent of the prewar Yugoslav population joined the National Liberation Movement (NOP). The official figure for women's participation is 2 million. Of these, 100,000 fought as soldiers in the partisan forces, of whom 25,000 died in battle action and 40,000 were wounded. Approximately 2,000 women achieved officer's rank. An estimated 282,000, or 14 percent, of the women participants in NOP are believed to have died or been killed in concentration camps. The death toll for both men and women in the war was high. Only one out of every three partisan soldiers could expect to see liberation. When one factors in all the 1941–45 losses, the Yugoslav civil war cost the country 10.8 percent of its prewar population.[6] Only the Soviet Union and Poland suffered a more severe depopulation than did Yugoslavia during this time period.

Violence was no stranger to the Balkans in 1941. It is easy to brush off its cruelty and brutality with the assertion that the region has always been a cauldron of conflict. Few would disagree, however, that violence attained new heights during World War II. The extent of foreign and interethnic terror in Yugoslavia may never be completely and accurately known. The Yugoslav war of 1941–45 let loose a wave of killing and retaliation upon helpless and defenseless people that was probably unequaled elsewhere in Europe, except in the Nazi death camps for the Jews. In the Sandžak region between Montenegro, Bosnia, and Serbia, Chetniks and the Serbian guerrillas associated with them, murdered over 9,000 Muslims, raped their women, and, according to some reports, roasted their victims alive. The Croatian Ustaše massacred some 60,000 Jews, 26,000 Gypsies, and 750,000 Orthodox Serbs living in what has become known as Krajina, the old Austrian-Hungarian military borderland along the Sava River. According to Western sources, only 800 of the 7,000 Serbian inhabitants of Mostar survived. In the border village of Glamoc, all but 1,400 of the town's 7,000 Serbs were murdered or sent to concentration camps.[7] In Bulgarian-occupied Macedonia, the Bulgarians pursued their own brand of terror. Women prisoners were first placed in *internati*, or holding camps, and then deported to Bulgaria or sent to concentration camps. Vera Vesković-Vangeli's account of Macedonian women's role in NOV is full of tales of Bulgarian atrocities not only against individual women but against whole villages. The Germans were no less eager to cleanse Slovenia of its Slav population. According to Yugoslav sources, at the beginning of the occupation, the Germans attempted to deport some 250,000 Slovenians from the "annexed" territories and resettle them elsewhere in the Reich.[8]

If the West is appalled by the ethnic cleansing, rape, and mass atrocities that have occurred in Krajina and Bosnia during 1991–94, the sober truth is that all this has been experienced as déjà vu. The similarities between the wartime statistics and those from the region's latest civil war are striking, prompting the hard question of whether the most significant legacy of the National Liberation War (NOB) was the 1991–94 war.

The current reinterpretation of the National Liberation War as primarily an ethnic struggle demands that we take a fresh look at the role of women in the war. First, we must recognize and insist that only a minority of women joined the partisan cause. The vast majority of women took no specific documentable side in the conflict. In the mountains of Bosnia-Herzegovina, Serbia, and Montenegro, which bore the brunt of the battle and where the front shifted daily, a woman's prime role was sheltering, feeding, and clothing her family, and attending to the injuries of the wounded. In the cities and the occupied areas, women generally kept a low profile and, like women in all of conquered Europe, stoically endured. Wartime statistics contain gaping holes.

However, summary data gathered on the participation of 854 Croatian and Serbian women in the National Liberation Movement listed in the two-volume Croatian study on women in the National Liberation Struggle is revealing. The list contained no information on age, occupation or wartime career for 36 percent of these women. Given the military inexperience of the younger women and the vulnerability of the old, we may hypothesize that this sizable group was made up of the extremes of the age cohorts. War's prime targets are the very young and the very old. Of the women whose age was identifiable, only 3 percent were over 45, and 10 percent were between 35 and 45.[9] Within that significant age group from 25 to 35, we find the plurality of professional activists, women with higher education, such as doctors and members of the intelligentsia, teachers, and blue-collar workers. Within the age group from 15 to 24, we find the plurality of white-collar workers, peasants, and, naturally, students.[10] While we must be careful not to read too many conclusions into these data, I think we can assume that women in the National Liberation Movement were drawn from the young and idealistic, and primarily from the young women in the peasant households disrupted or destroyed in the course of the war.

Analysis of the data portrays the typical women mobilized for the partisan cause as young, peasant, and uneducated, but sturdy, independent, and hardened by the rough conditions of peasant life in the rugged up-country of Bosnia, Serbia, and Montenegro. Her female superiors were

the educated urban women who formed the core of the leftist revolutionary movement in the interwar period when they themselves were students
in high school or university. By 1941, they had advanced to the twenty-
five-year-old generation, the "ladies" generation they decried in their
teens. The task of these women leaders was to imbue the young recruits
with zeal for a postwar communist state. The data cannot tell us what
vision the twenty-five-year-old generation of women participants might
have had of the postwar Yugoslav state. Most had little idea of the realities
of Soviet communism, but, given the break-up of their country and the
social discrimination against women in interwar Yugoslavia, they were
eager for national and social change. We will return to this theme later.

WOMEN SOLDIERS

On the front lines of the war, women obtained firsthand experience of
the perils and exhilaration of military camaraderie. Except in higher
Communist Party circles, there was little chance of intermingling among
women of different nationalities. The first partisan military units were
formed by *srez* or *kotar*, the basic administrative district, and operated
with a specified area under national command. The majority of partisan
soldiers fought in these territorial units. In December 1941, Tito formed
the First Proletarian Brigade, and a year later in November 1942, the
First Proletarian Division. These forces were given a higher level of
training and were prepared to go into operation anywhere where the
fighting demanded greater discipline and professionalism, on the orders
of the central command. In January 1945, the proletarian divisions were
formed into four armies and renamed the Yugoslav Army. At its head,
were the officers of the Proletarian Divisions who had been loyal to Tito
and the partisan cause throughout the war.

   The two types of forces were kept organizationally distinct throughout the war, although together they formed the National Liberation
Army from 1942 on. Women were initially recruited into women's units,
or *čete*, but later these units were broken up and incorporated into the
male units. The rank-and-file woman soldier recruited from the peas-
antry served in her local brigade under national command. The women
promoted up the officer's ladder to serve in the proletarian divisions appear to have been drawn primarily from the medical and nursing staff.

Of the ninety-two women national heroes of the National Liberation War, thirteen attained rank in the partisan forces as indicated in their official biographies. Of these, only three had military rank. Danica Milosavljević rose to the rank of second lieutenant, and Milka Kerin and Milka Klajic both were promoted to *vod* commander.[11] The other women who obtained military rank obtained it in their function of party commissar. Of the ten who became commissars, five obtained a commissar rank equal to captain.[12]

The *partizanka* with gun in hand, commanding troops and joining with her Slav brothers to bring about a new federal Yugoslavia, must be seen largely as a myth of partisan creation. The reality is that young girls uprooted by the passage of the fighting through their village were given a gun and told to join the village partisan unit. If they were lucky, they received some military training. If they survived the first months of fighting, their life expectancy dramatically increased. Most did not survive. As the partisans became more organized, training courses were offered which the women recruits could take. But there were no courses specifically directed toward women. If a woman had any training or volunteered for training, she would more likely than not be given a very short nursing course and was sent to tend to the wounded. Some might be put in service in the bomb factories. Some would serve as couriers, and the most educated would be used in the propaganda sections of the various partisan units, staffing the printing presses, or sent to the villages to recruit women to the partisan movement. Women also were involved in the entertainment programs for the troops. In whatever capacity they served, however, few were taken from their local environment. Only the leading women partisans were able to understand the meaning of the war in a wider perspective.

The inference is that despite the communist message of national equality, women partisans by and large fought with their own people at the local or regional level. Although subjected to Party indoctrination, they had little occasion to fight side by side with women of other ethnic groups. Because they were all subject to the same propaganda message, they had no opportunity to come in contact with or validate for themselves different ethnic points of view or experiences. The memory the Serbian partizanka retained from the war was the massacre and deportation of Serbs from the Krajina. But she was told that the Ustaše were fascists and thus enemies of the new Yugoslavia. Women partisans belonging to other ethnic groups in Macedonia and Slovenia had virtually no association with women outside their immediate area. The role of partizanka was not structured to break down ethnic parochialism.

WOMEN IN THE COMMUNIST PARTY

Of all the women actively engaged in the NOP, the Party members might be expected to have had the most access to the diverse nationalities of Yugoslavia. They alone were more likely than not to belong to one of the three mass partisan organizations, the Anti-Fascist Front of Women (AFZ), the National Liberation Councils (NOO), or the Union of Communist Youth of Yugoslavia (SKOJ). My study of the biographies of the 854 women in the National Liberation Movement given in the Croatian account of the war suggests that Communist Party members on average constituted one-third of the membership in these organizations. The highest percentage of representation was in the communist youth organization; the lowest, as might be expected, was in the partisan army.[13] More than half the Communist Party members belonged to at least one additional organization, roughly 30 percent belonged to two, and around 4 percent belonged to as many as three additional organizations. By contrast, non-Party women tended to belong and work primarily in their home based-organization, with the exception of women serving in the National Liberation Council system and SKOJ, where more than half of the women members were communists.

The assumption of greater responsibilities does not necessarily carry with it increased travel and service outside one's home base. All Communist Party members were subjected to the strictest Party discipline and went where they were ordered. In general, the communists were highly successful in utilizing their women members in the cities, where the first partisan units were composed of Party and SKOJ members who had had experience in sabotage and underground warfare in prewar Yugoslavia. While women preferred to get out of the cities and escape "to the woods," those who stayed tended to be experienced cadres who had served in the women's commissions established before the war. These women were the core of the special women's commissions founded under the aegis of the Liberation Front in 1941 with the aim of mobilizing the mass of women for the partisan effort. These women took the initiative in forming new urban women's groups through the establishment of initiatory committees They were effective in getting male comrades in and out of the heavily guarded urban areas and in establishing the networks of underground reading and training of younger women for the partisan cause.[14]

Secrecy was of primary importance. Party cells were composed of up to ten people, all with noms de guerre, who reported to the chief of the next higher cell, who in turn reported to their superior in the city district. Women communists moved about the city, moved to the woods or elsewhere only at the command of their superiors. The net effect of the wartime experience was to strengthen ethnic segregation on the national level and promote strong ties of loyalty among women and Party comrades at the local level, where all were dedicated to the same cause.

With the containment of the German attack in 1942, Yugoslavia became effectively divided into liberated and occupied territories. If the Communist Party was to win the war, it had to develop a disciplined organization in the liberated territories that were highly rural and mountainous. There, the military effort preceded political organization. To achieve control of regions where the war seesawed back and forth, the Party had to enhance the recruitment of rural women into the partisan movement and develop a women's support system in the rear that could sustain the partisan effort. SKOJ was its instrument to achieve the first goal. The sending of communist women into the villages to establish local units of the Anti-Fascist Front of Women (AFZ) achieved the second goal.

The arrival of urban women in the villages was not always welcomed. The organizer's task first was to form a hand-picked initiatory committee of women. The group had then to be approved by the regional Party committee after consultation with the Party committee or Party members of that village. Committee meetings would be held in a safe house and great care was taken to assure loyalty to the partisan cause. The initiatory committee would go on to form an AFZ council. If the territory was occupied, the council would be appointed, with the initiatory committee making recommendations. If the territory was relatively secure, the committee would seek members rather openly and eventually proceed to an election where interested women could be elected to the council. From first to last, the Communist Party of Yugoslavia (CPY) directed the development of the local AFZ council.

Once the council was established, its main task was to convince ordinary women to join the National Liberation Front. In Slovenia, Dalmatia and Istria, and Macedonia, the partisans were the only organized resistance force, and women readily volunteered. The main battles of the war, however, were fought in western Serbia, Montenegro, and the mountains of Bosnia-Herzegovina, all of which were highly rural. As the region was divided in its loyalties between the Chetniks and the partisans, the woman organizer had to convince local women of the merits of the partisan cause. Even though the Chetniks had no resistance program for women, the organizer had to combat powerful latent traditional attitudes, not to mention the religious customs of the indigenous Muslim population. Given the urban bias of the AFZ organizer, there was a deep cultural gap between the older urban women, who were at least one generation distant from the village, and the village women they were trying to organize, especially the older peasant women.

Not all communist women leaders were successful. In an interview, Milka Kufrin, a Croatian women National Liberation Movement leader, attributed her success to the fact that she was a peasant by birth and a newcomer to the city. She had not yet lost her knowledge of peasant speech or the village way of life.

A final important factor inhibiting the work of the communist woman organizer was a deep national suspicion held by the villagers. "Why should you, a Croat, come to our village?" the Serbian village women would ask Milka Kufrin.[15] They did not want a Croatian in their resistance movement. Serbs encountered similar distrust among Croats. Croatian villagers would refuse to join a council organized by a Serb, unless their friends and fellow villagers also committed to join.

Clearly, the women leaders in the Communist Party were an exceptional group of women bound together by ties of marriage and loyalty to the men in the partisan command. Marija Šoljan, for example, was the wife of Vladimir Bakarić, and Mitra Mitrović, the mind behind the wartime women's journal, *Žena danas*, was the wife of Milovan Djilas. In interviews held with six women national heroes and ten other leading women partisans in December–January 1985, I asked them what were the important factors influencing their decision to take an active role in the liberation movement.

The first reason for all of them was national recognition and dignity. The role of Russia in the Serbian struggle for independence and Russia's promotion of pan-Slavism in nineteenth-century Austro-Hungary had induced a greater receptivity toward things Russian than toward things German. The Yugoslav idea promoted by Tito was the liberation of the

South Slavs from German and Hungarian occupation (a throwback to the old empire) and the formation of a state based on national recognition and equality. The Slovenian women partisans not only talked of their struggles against the Germans but constantly stressed the better organization, discipline skills, and knowledge of Slovenian women as compared to the women "in the woods" on the other side of the Slovenian border.

One of the high points of the war for the women I interviewed was the establishment of a health or epidemiological boundary between Slovenia and its neighboring provinces where the war was being fought. Lack of sanitation and hard living conditions had brought typhoid, typhus, and pneumonia to Bosnia-Herzegovina and parts of Serbia and Croatia. The Slovenian women were able to stop the epidemics from spreading into Slovenia by stopping everyone trying to cross the Slovenian border. By contrast, Serbian doctor and woman national hero Saša Božavić was strong in her praise of the courage of the partisan army in surviving the horrible living conditions, and spoke movingly of the devotion and tireless work of the few doctors in the battle areas who had to tend to the wounded, the sick, and the dying. Before the war, she noted, there were few doctors in the whole of Yugoslavia. Many of these were Jewish and left the country before the occupation. Others were sent to concentration camps. Whenever the partisans arrived at a village, the doctor was much in demand. The first day of work for the medical personnel would frequently bring them to the point of exhaustion.

Again, the Slovenian women praised Tito for his federal solution to the South Slav question because it gave each nationality its own republic with considerable jurisdiction to promote its own culture. For the Macedonian women, the high point of the war was the Second AVNOJ Conference when Tito promised that Macedonians would have their own republic in the postwar Yugoslav federal state.

Equal rights for women was a second factor influencing the active role of the communist women leaders in NOP. Saša Božavić was one of the few women to receive a higher education in the interwar period. One of the last organized women's movements in prewar Yugoslavia was a demonstration organized in 1939 by the Alliance of the Women's Movement and the woman's magazine *Žena danas* for the right to vote.[16] Massive demonstrations were held all over the country, and the magazine claims to have collected thirty thousand signatures on a petition for women's franchise. The demonstration indicated the strength of women's commitment to the civil rights issue. Significantly, one of the first acts of the partisan government, organized as the National Liberation Council of Montenegro, Boka, and Sandžak, was to give women the right to vote.[17]

A third reason for the women communists' participation was an instinctive horror at the massive suffering of the population and a desire to alleviate the pain. Taken altogether, these reasons can be accepted as the general reasons why those women who supported the partisans did so. The Party message for women downplayed national differences and stressed women's solidarity in war work and in suffering. The women's journals, edited by such well-known women partisans as Soljan and Mitrović, placed great emphasis on the twin themes of the equality gained by women in the war and the sisterhood of all Yugoslav women in binding up the war's wounds and tending the sick and the orphaned.

At the same time that the Party demanded absolute obedience, its message played on women's idealism and empathy for human suffering. In the words of Mitrović, "We were dogmatic, but the moment you become skeptical, you cannot take strong action." For the women communist leaders, the dominant impetus to work for the Party came from childhood and student perceptions of national and social injustice juxtaposed against the horrors of the fascist occupation. The conviction that the Party had the answers increased through the war years as victory came within grasp. All the women interviewed were convinced of the rightness of Tito's war and his immediate postwar policy. To quote Mitrović once more: "Ideology gives direction. Only when you are liberated from dogmatism do you start to realize how dogmatic you were. . . . Once the process of liberation begins, you are eager to enter the real world by reading and questioning everything."[18] In sum, the women communist leaders tended to be confirmed believers in the communist program because of its promise to right wrongs. They were yet to experience the reality of the Stalinist system.

WOMEN IN THE AFZ

The Anti-Fascist Front of Women (AFZ) is a fascinating experiment in what happens when women, organized for one purpose and under one sponsorship, inject their own needs and goals into the operation. After Tito's famous appeal to "Serbs, Croatians, Montenegrins, Macedonians and others" to take up the fight against the "unbearable and hated fascist slavery,"[19] the Communist Party organizations then in existence started to organize women's commissions under the aegis of the National Liberation Front. Commissions sprang up in the large cities, Ljubljana, Zagreb, Skopje.

The aim of these commissions was to recruit women for the partisan movement. In Macedonia and elsewhere, the commissions were active in establishing tailor, shoemaker, and other workshops, as well as make-shift hospitals and health care.[20] The published national republican studies of women's role in NOP indicate that these first commissions were extraordinarily spontaneous, with their number expanding throughout 1941. With the partisan declaration of the first liberated republic in 1942, the Party leadership decided to give a more formal form to the women's effort.

The first federal conference of the AFZ was convened in December 1942 at Bosanska Petrovać in Bosnia. There were 166 delegates representing women's groups from all over Yugoslavia. In the words of communist activist Dušanka Kovačević, "The women's groups were not set up to deal exclusively with women's problems, but rather to serve the movement of women ready and willing to take party in the war and revolution, and thereby make their contribution to military and political victory."[21] The conference resolution ended with calls to Serbian, Croatian, Slovenian, Montenegrin, Muslim, and Macedonian women to join the fight. "Long live the unity of the women of Yugoslavia. Long live the Soviet Union Long live our National Liberation Army. Death to Fascism—freedom to the people." The resolution adopted at the conference, among other things, stressed the AFZ's role in all-round assistance to the army, organization of the home front, participation in the national liberation authorities' work, care for refugees and children, sabotage of the enemy, mobilization of manpower and procurement of supplies, boycott of the enemy markets, and participation in the armed struggle.[22]

From its beginnings as a disparate group of women's commissions to its organization at the federal level, the AFZ was seen as women's contribution to the partisan war effort. However, the ferocity and vicissitudes of the war made it difficult for the Party to maintain control of the AFZ local council's day-to-day work, and in some areas, where most of the men had gone to the front or, in other cases, had been deported by the enemy, the women's councils were the sole representative of partisan authority in the village.

During the first phase of AFZ activity, 1942–44, communist women were in control of the organization from the local to the federal level. The federal executive committee is a "Who's Who" of important communist women.[23] In typical communist fashion, the AFZ was designed to be managed as a hierarchy, with the local councils subordinate to the regional councils that were subordinate to the republican councils that answered to the federal executive council. Republican councils, however, could only be organized as a particular territory was liberated. The largest of the AFZ organizations was in Croatia, which in January 1943 numbered some 9,348 workers in 1,667 councils; 629 of these councils, with 3,130 workers, were located in occupied territory.[24] Given such vitality, it is not surprising that the first Croatian AFZ conference was held in January 1943, immediately following the federal AFZ conference, while the first Slovenian AFZ conference was only organized in the summer of 1943, and the first Macedonian conference was not established until December 1944. Thus, many regional councils answered directly to the federal executive council.

Money collected at the local level by local AFZ councils was distributed to the units higher up the hierarchical ladder in an approved manner, making the entire organization financially independent. During this period, the AFZ leadership also imposed its own membership criteria. Given the shifting character of the wartime front, the governmental units organized by the partisans had to disband or go underground when the opposing side recaptured a "liberated" village. The AFZ council had no such problems. Organized as a semi-underground unit and responsible only to its superior organization, it could continue operations. The effectiveness of the local councils depended upon the energy and intelligence of their members. As noted above in the case of Macedonia, many AFZ councils virtually took over governmental functions in the first critical years of the war.

Given the unstable circumstances of the initial war years and the high probability that the partisans would fail, the organizer's selection of an initiatory committee and the subsequent formation of a local AFZ council became extremely important and the responsibilities laid on the AFZ Central Council were considerable. Understandably, the organizers chose women at the local level whom they considered reliable and with whom they shared the same views. Women who shared the AFZ views doubtless self-selected themselves or volunteered for the local councils. The AFZ had a job to do, and for it to be done well, like-minded, capable women had to fill the local council positions. Consciously or not, the

AFZ evolved into a virtually autonomous organization that set its own rules, and within the framework of winning the war for the partisans, determined its own tasks and functions.

By 1944, communist victory seemed assured. The National Liberation Council system was effectively and efficiently expanding as more territory was "liberated." The communist leadership's thought turned more and more to the postwar period and its control of the postwar political process. In January 1944, the CPY Central Committee brought the full force of its disapproval to bear on the AFZ. The CPY CC wrote the AFZ Executive Committee a letter accusing it of elitism, exclusivity, and bureaucratism.[25] The Communist Party asserted that the AFZ leadership had distanced itself from the "the rest of our political life and struggle," while the AFZ councils had "often developed into narrow parochial women's organizations."

To remedy these "mistakes," the Party broke up the centralized AFZ structure and subordinated the local councils to the local NOOs. The local councils were then assigned the specific function of making the AFZ accessible to all women through its "penetration into the rank and file, still uncommitted women," and "its discovery of methods for stronger recruitment of the backward women's masses." Political attitude, religious affiliation, and nationality were seen as obstacles to be overcome. The aim was to bring all women into the women's organization. By 1945, the AFZ had become a typical Stalinist mass organization.

Why was the AFZ so easily and quickly downgraded? The answer can never fully be known. But the primary reason certainly is that its leaders were communists first, who owed their position and rise to power to the communists. A second explanation may lie in the criticism that the Central Committee leveled at the organization. Until 1944, the AFZ was selective, picking those women who committed to their ideals and discipline. Very few Muslim women joined the AFZ. At first, the organization was not trying to include all women no matter what their nationality or religion wherever they happened to live. On the contrary, in each national area, AFZ members came overwhelmingly from the dominant ethnic group.

As noted above, Croat mistrusted Serb or Slovene, and Serb mistrusted Croat. After 1944, the objective of the partisan leadership was to recruit women, any women anywhere, to the partisan cause to support the coming partisan victory. This policy change altered the results very little. Again, women from the dominant ethnic group in a specific locality tended to constitute the majority of AFZ joiners in that area. Neither under the old hierarchically structured AFZ organization nor in its Stalinist transformation was there a specific program designed to sensitize or develop horizontal communication between women at the local or regional level. What communication occurred took place prior to 1944 at the command of the AFZ (with Party backing), and after 1944, only at Party command. Interethnic communication at the top was probably the most open, but it was based on the camaraderie of commitment to Tito and the communist leadership, not on the deliberate operalization of the Yugoslav ideal.

The AFZ was first and last a Communist Party tool to educate and mobilize women for its side of the conflict. The AFZ was never meant to be an organization of women representing women. Its hierarchical structure was from the top down. Once the Central Committee had dismantled the AFZ centralized organization and subordinated the local councils to the local NOOs, communication between local women leaders in the various regions became even more difficult. The formation of the five national republics set up the final barrier to open and free communication.

WOMEN AND THE YUGOSLAV MYTH OF NATIONAL EQUALITY

The very fact that each postwar republic published its own study of the role of women in that republic, one primarily of that republic's majority ethnic group, is an indication of the communist failure to give more than lip service to international integration. Rereading the republican studies of women in the National Liberation Movement, one cannot help but notice that every republic celebrates the courage, ingenuity, and loyalty of its heroes. There is no cross-republican discussion or comparison. In my interviews with the women partisan leaders, they were eager to tell me how women in their ethnic group fought, resisted, or organized in the rear. The only example of cross-ethnic cooperation they mentioned and spoke of with pride was the First and Second Anti-Fascist Women's Conferences. But these conferences were totally organized and managed by women Party leaders under Tito and the Central Committee's direct supervision. And we cannot emphasize enough that the purpose of the AFZ was to mobilize women for the partisan cause.

I certainly would not want to downplay or underrate the contribution of women to the partisan effort in Yugoslavia during 1941–45. But the record shows that all their bravery, resourcefulness, and self-sacrifice was in the last analysis under communist direction. Like all political animals, whether parties, movements, or simply individuals, the communists' main goal was to win the civil war. To win and maintain their popular acceptance, they had to formulate a broad appeal and make promises that could be partially fulfilled in wartime and then adjusted to the peacetime process of consolidation. The communists did just that. At the first AVNOJ conference, the Party gave women the right to vote and proclaimed a federal postwar Yugoslavia. The evidence shows, however, that the wartime experience promoted sexual and national equality primarily in the sense that all were welcome to join the partisan movement and help the partisans win. The development of tolerance demands the development of insight and understanding of the other point of view. The communists made no effort to foster such a process. For them, the Chetniks and the Ustaše were fascists like the occupation forces. It was a black-white world. While dogmatism may give direction in an armed struggle, it does not solve interethnic or interpersonal conflict.

In terms of education for a multinational state, the communist message was not ethnic diversity and mingling but territorial nationalism and mass solidarity. When peace came, the women in NOP returned to their homes and villages. Women who had distinguished themselves in the war quickly rose up the republican ladder to be put in places of high visibility in the republican administrations amid proclamations of national unity and women's solidarity. But the war had accomplished little in counteracting the interethnic suspicion and distrust carried over from the interwar period. Serbian women who returned from the camps to pick up the pieces of their lives in the Krajina region would remember the war for the Croatian Ustaše persecution. The failure of the AFZ to reach out to Muslim women meant the continuation of the cultural gap between what the Communist Party termed the "most backward women" (read Muslim) and the Serbian Orthodox or Croat Catholic believer.

Many women touched by the war either as innocent victims or as volunteers for NOP were able to generalize from the horror in their region to the horrors of war for all people whatever their nationality or faith. Young Croatian nurses may have tended Serb soldiers and vice versa. Both groups of young women must have realized that the other nationals were human beings as they were. This understanding may have extended to those fighting on the same side. How many of those in the partisan movement believed that the Ustaše and the Chetniks were human beings? The events of 1991 to today suggest that the strongest memories of the war were those of Serb victims and Ustaše fascists, of Serb Chetniks and Muslim backwardness.

CONCLUDING THOUGHTS

At the Fourth U.N. Conference on Women in Beijing in September 1995, thousands of women joined hands at an evening musical happening and sang: "If every woman stood up for peace, there would be no more war." Earlier that same day, some Georgian women had shown a video of their White Scarf Movement. In 1992, Georgian and Abkhazian women joined hands to go to the front lines of the Georgian civil war. In the face of protest by the generals on both sides of the conflict, together the women threw down their white scarves, challenging their men to observe an old Caucasian tradition of not treading on a white scarf when a woman threw it down. For two days, the fighting stopped. There was even an agreement on a cease-fire. Unfortunately, the cease-fire lasted only until the women had returned to their homes. The White Scarf Movement is a symbol of what women can do to mitigate a conflict. The peace song may not be pure idealism.

During the 1941–45 war most women in Yugoslavia were only on the first rung of the women's liberation ladder. They were willing to join the communists to fight against an identified and identifiable enemy to save their homes and families. However, the communists' main enemy was not the Germans but the Chetniks and prewar Yugoslavia. It is a long psychological jump from fighting against an identified enemy to realizing that there is no enemy. We are all belong to the same human family. If every woman in Yugoslavia had stood up for peace among the Chetniks and the communists, would the Germans have stopped their advance? Would the Italians, Hungarians, and Bulgarians stayed within their borders? Surely not. The invasion and occupation had their own logic and momentum.

Yet, there is no doubt that the communists' vision of the world was divisive. They wanted victory on their own divisive terms. While some of the women who joined NOP accepted the partisans' simple dogmatic vision of a divided world; the majority kept silent. The consequence was that there was no independent women's movement in postwar Yugoslavia to speak out on issues of civil, national, or women' rights until the end of the 1970s with the rise of the neofeminist movement.[26]

In summary, a review of the record indicates that the women's participation in the Yugoslav National Liberation Movement was mobilized, organized, and directed by the Yugoslav Communist Party leadership. For a while, women communists experienced the power and responsibility that derived from creating and turning the AFZ into an effective service and procurement organization in the rear. When they were called to account and told to turn the organization into a communist-style mass organization, they did as they were told. The women who sacrificed their lives to defeat the invaders and protect their homes were in a very real sense victims of the Party that called them to its standard. Women's participation played a critical role in the partisans winning the war. It was helpless in establishing an intellectual and power base from which women could have an impact on the policies of postwar communist Yugoslavia. As a result, when the second civil war began in 1991, women once again became the tragic victims of ethnic cleansing, rape, pillage, and torture. One legacy of the partizanka is that sisterhood can be powerful, but only when women reach out to other women directly, not through male power-brokers.

A second legacy derives from the neofeminists' reinterpretation of women's participation in the partisan movement. A leading advocate of neofeminism, Lydia Sklevicky, argued that the women's program adopted at the Fifth National Congress of the Communist Party of Yugoslavia in 1938 was virtually identical to the demands made by the so-called bourgeois Alliance of the Women's Movement in the 1930s. The Party's incorporation of these demands indicated to Sklevicky not only the validity of the Alliance of Women's Movement tactics but also its political strength at the time. Like good politicians everywhere, the communists had to co-opt issues with transnational appeal. But women's right to vote and women's right to equal treatment on the job and in education, had been brought to the forefront of the country's consciousness primarily by the organizational tactics of the prewar women's movement.[27] The communists' 1944 reduction of the Anti-Fascist Front of Women to an organization subordinate to the broader partisan movement put an end to any attempt by women to maintain continuity between the prewar women's movement, the AFZ experience in the national liberation movement and the nascent communist regime in Yugoslavia. The consequences of the partisan leadership's action were still visible in 1991 in the inability of women in any of the former republics of federal Yugoslavia to organize in sufficient strength to influence the male leaderships to consider a solution to the country's problems other than war.

The third legacy is also based on the neofeminist reinterpretation of NOP. Most women joined the movement for reasons other than to fight for the victory of the socialist revolution. Women's participation reflected a spontaneous, largely personal, and patriotic response to national catastrophe and personal tragedy and in this sense, differed only in numbers of dead, wounded, and homeless from the participation of women in other European countries in World War II.[28] Women's response to the 1991–94 war, or any war that affects them directly, may be expected to be similarly spontaneous, rooted in fear of personal and national annihilation.

What then can be learned from the experience of Yugoslav women during the National Liberation War? First and foremost, their participation was vital to the communist victory. Over and over again, I heard in my interviews, "We could not have done it without the support of the women in the villages." Women provided the vital support behind the lines. Whatever their ethnic origin, women in the former Yugoslavia can take pride in having played such a critical role at one of the twentieth century's most significant moments.

Second, through their participation in a movement they never completely understood, the women of postwar Yugoslavia, like American women after World War I, earned the right to male jobs and the right to elect and to be elected in turn. In other words, participation in the war won them the primary demands many of them had made before the war. These economic and legal gains probably would not have been realized if the conditions in Yugoslavia had remained as they were before the war and the Communist Party had not had to mobilize popular support to win power. They certainly would not have been realized as quickly.

The gains were significant at the time. They had been won by few women in few countries before World War II. French women did not achieve equal political rights until 1945. German women had to wait the fall of the Third Reich and the Allied occupation to gain their rights. American women did not achieve any significant degree of equal economic opportunity until the Civil Rights Act of 1964. Most of the developing world has yet to accord women even a modicum of civil and economic liberties. The gains made by Yugoslav women in the National

Liberation War moved them in five years from a "feudal" condition of dependency to "modern" legal and civil equality.

Third, no further improvement in Yugoslav women's status occurred after the war. Most Yugoslav women were not prepared to push further, and for many, the gains may have been seen as sufficiently revolutionary in and of themselves. Victory came to be associated with official appreciation of the value of woman's traditional economic and social functions in the private sphere as these were translated into the public sphere during the war. Once the war was over, these functions remained "socialized" and gradually were institutionalized into women's "industrial place." The feminization of jobs progressed no differently in Yugoslavia than in any other industrializing country.

Last and sadly, participation in the war did not give Yugoslav women a common sense of identify that transcended family roles and ethnic distinctions. This absence of a common identity made women especially vulnerable to the authoritarian dictates of the communist regime and the neonationalist rhetoric of the post-communist successor states.

It may be the nature of war—the violence, killing, rape, and push to survive—that robs women of the time and opportunity to focus on their identity and their needs. Strong, vital women's organizations appear to grow in peacetime not during a war. War for its duration transcends human categories. But war is quintessentially patriarchal in its goals and modus operandi. The economic and civil rights accorded Yugoslav woman during and after the National Liberation War, impressive as they looked at the time, were in the last analysis, a reward bestowed by the male victors for favors performed.

6

Sabrina P. Ramet

The Tito era lasted thirty-seven years—from 29 November 1943, when the Anti-Fascist Front for the Liberation of Yugoslavia proclaimed the creation of a provisional government with Tito as Prime Minister, later President, until his death on 4 May 1980. The era of Titoism lasted another ten years, withering away after Slobodan Milošević's seizure of power in Serbia at the end of 1987 and finally expiring with the disbandment of the League of Communists of Yugoslavia in the course of its Fourteenth (Extraordinary) Congress in January 1990. During those years, the promotion of greater equality between the sexes figured as an explicit plank in the socialist platform.

The following extract is typical of writings from the Titoist era:

In the course of the socialist revolution, significant results were achieved in advancing the socioeconomic position and role of woman in our society. This is indicated by data concerning the number of educated and employed women, analyses of their suc-

cessful pursuit of professional, leadership, and socially responsible
careers, everyday actions for the resolution of problems traditionally connected with women . . . etc. . . . [But] the battle for the
complete emancipation of women is not yet over.[1]

One of the keys to success in realizing gender equality was inclusion of
women in politics on equal footing with men. But progress here was slow,
as Tito-era spokespersons conceded. As Stipe Šuvar put it in 1980, "Our
ideal is that woman should be the architect of society on an equal basis
with the man. Woman's contribution to the development of society is
much greater than indicated by female presence in decision-making positions."[2]

My purpose in this chapter is to assess the nature and success of the
socialist program for gender equality in Yugoslavia, emphasizing the
years up to 1980, setting this discussion in the context of an understanding of the system established by Tito after World War II.

THE SOCIALIST CONTEXT

Josip Broz Tito and his comrades in arms were heirs to a tradition reaching back to Marx and Engels. But they inherited that tradition indirectly,
as mediated by Stalin. When they revolted against Stalin, they discarded
some elements of the Stalinist system (for example, the Soviet system
of management of enterprises, formal censorship, and, after 1964, the
anathematization of all nationalism); but they retained more than they
discarded, even if adapting these elements to local conditions and modify-
ing them according to their proclivities.

The Titoist system was famous for its contradictions. It was a one-
party state, and yet the federalization of the party sometimes allowed
behaviors which seemed to hint at an eight-party (or six-party) system. It
was a socialist system, and yet it was the first East European country both
to take profitability into account in investment policies and to permit
small-scale private enterprise. It had no censorship office, and yet censorship activity continued. And it allowed nonparty members to criticize
party policies within certain limits, but frowned on criticism of official
policy by party members, thus suggesting that party members had fewer
rights than nonmembers.

But to speak of contradictions is not to speak of the nature of the system, only to say something of its spirit. To get at its nature, one might begin by observing that as a one-party system, it had a legitimacy problem. To address this problem, it relied on three formal pillars and (more informally) on the mythology of the Partisan struggle against fascist occupation, 1941–45. The three pillars were self-management, nonalignment, and brotherhood and unity. Self-management, originally conceived narrowly as referring to the network of workers' councils which were to administer factories and other enterprises and thereby initiate the process of the withering away of the state came, in time, to be construed much more broadly, meaning worker-oriented, free, self-actualizing, and progressive all at the same time. Nonalignment was the policy of equidistance between the Soviet and American blocs and of active cooperation with other "nonaligned" countries within an institutionalized forum. Brotherhood and unity referred to the policy of promoting harmony between the sundry nationality groups that constituted socialist Yugoslavia, a country in which even the largest group, the Serbs, remained, with a mere 38 percent of the total, a minority.

Moving from this high level of abstraction one level down, one may identify several key programmatic features. These include an organizational monopoly which criminalized the organization of labor unions or youth groups, for example, which were not registered as part of either the LCY or its transmission belt, the Socialist Alliance of Working People of Yugoslavia (SAWPY); the recognition of religion as the "private affair" of the individual (a recognition which excluded any legitimate public activity on the part of religious associations); the requirement that the leading news organs (such as *Borba*, *Vjesnik*, *Oslobodjenje*, and so on) support party policy, satisfy concrete topic quotas, and advance specified party goals; the maintenance of a state monopoly in primary, secondary, and higher education; and the affirmation of parallel policies of advancing the economic level of the underdeveloped republics and Kosovo, as well as of advancing the social, economic, and political position of women. The last two of the aforementioned policies were pursued in the interests of achieving greater levels of equality in society.

At the very heart of the party's thinking, whether about gender equality or about anything else, was that all progressive forces should work within the program of the LCY, whether by joining the LCY itself or by affiliating with SAWPY or other party transmission belts. In other words, the party did not recognize the autonomy of the question of gender relations any more than it recognized the autonomy of any other sphere of policy.³ And if the issue lacked any autonomous status, then it could not be considered legitimate to organize autonomous bodies or activities to promote gender equality. Insofar as socialism promised to solve all basic social problems, working outside party channels could be interpreted as unnecessary, indicative of a lack of faith in the party, counterproductive (by dividing energies), and potentially counterrevolutionary (by adopting a line that ran counter to the party line). It followed that any activity that could be described as counterrevolutionary (or, in Tito-era Yugoslav jargon, anti–self-management) worked against the *entire* party program, including its policy of promoting gender equality. And hence, feminists were described as working *against* the achievement of gender equality—in essence, of promoting patriarchy.

ORIGINS

The struggle to assure the rights of South Slav women began in the latter half of the nineteenth century, even before the birth of Yugoslavia. Inequality was extreme: in Serbia, for example, the civil code of 1844 (para. 920) equated women with children and the feeble-minded and denied them any right to autonomous decision making.⁴ Among Serbian women, feminist activism got underway in the late 1860s, after nearly a century of grassroots efforts to provide education for Serbian girls. The works of Svetozar Marković (1843–75), a socialist active in the 1860s and 1870s, pointed out the disadvantages suffered by women in the patriarchal family and called for the solution of gender inequality within the framework of the socialist project. His works influenced emerging Yugoslav socialist activists. Early Serbian feminists included Draga Dejanović (1840–71) and Katarina Milovuk (1844–1909).⁵ An early landmark in the region was the publication in 1871 of a Serbo-Croatian translation of John Stuart Mill's book, *The Subjection of Women*, only two years after its original publication in London.

One of the earliest strikes by working women took place in the Slovenian town of Trbovlje in 1876. Later, in 1895, the Social Democratic Party of Croatia (itself founded only the preceding year) set up a party-affiliated women's organization. In Serbia, the Women Workers' Society was set up in Belgrade in 1903, also within the framework of the SDP.⁶ "Working women's societies began to be formed within social democratic labour organizations and they dissociated themselves from the bourgeois feminist and suffragette movement, because the latter did not want to participate in their programmes and demands for an end to the exploitation of workers."[7]

In 1919, the Social Democratic Party of Yugoslavia split in two, giving birth to the Communist Party. The CPY established a unified women's socialist movement (on 20 April 1919) within the framework of its organization. The statute adopted by the CPY women's section in 1919 declared, in unambiguous language, "Women socialists . . . reject any separate organization of women and consider themselves to be a technical-administrative committee in agitation and the organization of women."[8] Throughout the interwar period (1918–41), socialist advocates of gender equality had to compete with nonsocialist feminists ("bourgeois feminists" in socialist terminology). But in addition to working within their own organizations, socialist women also infiltrated nonsocialist women's organizations.[9] At its Fourth Party Congress (in 1928, held abroad in Dresden), the CPY leadership called for more vigorous efforts to draw women into political work and organize women workers in labor unions. Amid much fanfare (albeit underground, in its own press), the CPY launched the periodical *Žena danas* (Woman today) in 1936.

But it was war which gave the CPY its chance at power. It was also the war which gave the partisan generation the experience of fighting together and which began the process of resocializing the population of Yugoslavia along communist programmatic lines. Partisan forces are said to have numbered some 800,000 troops; of these, 100,000 were women. Sixty percent of all women in Tito's partisan army were killed or seriously wounded; 282,000 partisan women died in Axis concentration camps.[10] Eighty-seven women were awarded the highest decoration for military valor.[11] It was in the course of the National Liberation Struggle of 1941–45 that, in December 1942, the Anti-Fascist Front of Women of Yugoslavia (AFWY) was created; its first national conference, attended by 166 women from combat units and villages in liberated territory, was held in Bosanski Petrovac, electing Kata Pejnović, a peasant from Croatia and a national hero in her own right, as president.

The Anti-Fascist Front of Women continued, for several years after World War II had ended, to play a role in cultural and educational work among women—for example, in the spheres of medical care, health counseling centers, the organization of such facilities as restaurants, school cafeterias, collective laundries, dry-cleaning services, and so on. It was abolished in 1953, however, on the argument that the goal of gender equality could be better promoted via party agencies which were not gender-specific.[12] As an apologetic text dating from 1965 put it,

> At that time, the achievements of the Revolution had already been notably consolidated, human rights sanctioned and affirmed, political life enriched by many new forms. . . . Awareness of the fact that equality of women is a general social problem and is included in the programme of the two strongest social-political organizations in the country . . . gradually rendered a separate women's organization superfluous.[13]

In its place, the CPY created the Union of Women's Societies (UWS). There were about two thousand such societies, organized at federal, republic, provincial, district, and communal levels in functional domains (such as child welfare). There were also women's committees within the SAWPY, though these would be merged with the UWS in 1961 to form the Conference for the Social Activity of Women.

In the meantime, the new communist regime issued formal guarantees to women. The Program of the People's Front of Yugoslavia, the predecessor of SAWPY (7 August 1945), pledged:

> The People's Front has always actively promoted the equality of women. Today, when that equality has been achieved, the further consolidation [of that equality] and the complete participation of women in all areas of political and social life must be one of the basic assignments of every adherent of the Front.[14]

And socialist Yugoslavia's first postwar constitution (1946) included this guarantee (Article 24):

> Women enjoy equal rights with men in all spheres of state economic and social life. Women are entitled to a salary equal to that of men for the same work, and enjoy special protection in the labour relationship. The state particularly protects the welfare of mother and child by the establishment of maternity hospitals, children's homes and day nurseries, and by ensuring the right to paid leave before and after confinement.[15]

On paper at least, Yugoslav women seemed to have made significant strides forward. Moreover, according to socialist thinking, the structures and programs of the CPY were so effective that they were assured of success quite independently of the good will of individual persons.

ECONOMIC GAINS, PROFESSIONAL STAGNATION

From a theoretical standpoint, the difference between socialist and feminist understandings of the problem may be expressed as follows: Whereas feminists believe that patriarchy resides and abides *in the first place*, though not merely, in values, attitudes, suppositions, and modes of discourse which are manifested and reinforced in the culture and media, as well as in associations such as Churches, socialists, even while recognizing the patriarchical patterns pervasive in such values and attitudes, nonetheless trace the problem back to *the structural needs of pre-socialist society* (whether feudal or capitalist). (Any other analysis would require that women's inequality be treated as an autonomous problem.) It follows that upon changing the structures of society, the CPY could rather automatically realize a change in values and attitudes in the wake of those structural changes.

When this did not happen, socialists began to treat "reactionary attitudes" as a problem in their own right, in effect accepting the point of departure of (bourgeois) feminism. That left the socialists applying structural remedies to problems of belief systems. It is true, of course, that the communists did make considerable propaganda in favor of gender equality, whether in films or the periodical media or programmatic statements at party forums, and that the communists, by any measure, did more than any other political party, holding office, in the twentieth century, to highlight the importance of gender equality. But the communists failed ultimately, in Yugoslavia as elsewhere, to take up the task of using the educational system to reshape people's thinking about gender differences. Hence, when the Zagreb feminist group Women and Society began meeting in the 1970s, its members spent much of their time critiquing LCY-approved school texts, pointing out elements of sexism.

There were, to be sure, some striking advances made in the early postwar years, even if it was not always entirely clear whether the same could not have been achieved under some other system. In 1931, for example, 54.4 percent of the female population over age ten (versus 32.2 percent of the male population over age ten) had been illiterate, and in Bosnia-Herzegovina and Kosovo, the comparable figures for women's illiteracy were even higher (84 percent and 93.9 percent, respectively).[16] In 1961, illiteracy among Yugoslav females had been reduced to 28.8 percent of the number over age 10, and almost 75 percent of these were over age 35.[17] In 1921, women constituted only 16 percent of those attending institutions of higher education, and even as late as 1939, this figure had crept up only slightly to 19 percent.[18] During the years 1945–77, by contrast, 239,194 women (representing 36.5 percent of the total) graduated from Yugoslav institutions of higher education.[19] Moreover, within this thirty-year period one can identify a trend toward a steady increase in female enrollment at universities, with women accounting for 29.4 percent of university students in the 1961–62 academic year, for example, but 40.3 percent of university students in the 1973–74 academic year.[20]

Parallel trends characterized the work force, where the female proportion of the work force grew from 18 percent in 1940 to 23.7 percent in 1953. The rates of growth in the employment of women were particularly high in the years 1952–65, and over the years 1954–74 averaged 6 percent annually as compared with 3.8 percent annually for males.[21] By 1978, women accounted for 34.7 percent of the Yugoslav labor force (varying, by region, from a high of 44 percent in Slovenia to a low of 20 percent in Kosovo).[22]

Liberal policies with regard to divorce and abortion were introduced, together with generous policies of maternity leave. At first the Yugoslav communist authorities clamped down on abortion, prohibiting the practice in 1951. The law adopted that year provided for the prosecution of the person performing the abortion but not for the woman undergoing the abortion. In 1952, however, federal authorities legalized abortion for medical, legal, social, and related reasons; legislation adopted in 1960 spelled out conditions in more detail. Later, on 25 April 1969, the Assembly of the SFRJ adopted a resolution on family planning, establishing that families enjoyed the right to determine for themselves how many children they wished to have.[23] Yugoslavia's fourth constitution (1974) confirmed the liberal policy, guaranteeing (in anomalous wording) "the right of *man* to freely decide on the birth of *his* children. This right can be restricted only for the purpose of health protection."[24]

Implementing legislation was subsequently passed in Yugoslavia's constituent republics. In Socialist Republic of Croatia, for example, a law was passed in 1978, guaranteeing (Article 5) the availability of means to prevent unwanted pregnancy, whether through contraceptives or permanent sterilization; Article 16 of the same law provided for abortion to be granted when the continuation of the pregnancy would threaten the health of the woman.[25] In general, under legislation associated with the 1974 constitution, abortion was available on the demand of the pregnant woman up to ten weeks into pregnancy. The number of abortions rose for Yugoslavia as a whole but at variable rates. Thus, as of 1981, the largest number of abortions relative to live births was found in Serbia-proper and Vojvodina, while the lowest proportions were found in Kosovo and Montenegro, with the Slovenian and Croatian rates corresponding closely to the Yugoslav average.[26]

But despite these changes in the social position of women, and accompanying changes in the image of women presented by officialdom, Yugoslav scholars began to point out that two central *structural* problems remained unresolved: first, women tended to be concentrated in certain professions (textiles being the classic example) and all but excluded from other professions (such as court judges); second, women remained severely underrepresented in leadership bodies, whether within the party hierarchy, or the delegate system, or even the self-management councils.

Taking up the first problem first, women tended to be concentrated in services, sales, health care, and culture. The figures given in Table 6.1 are indicative.

Taking up the figures from 1980, one finds that nearly 80 percent of employees in social services and textiles were women in that year, while nearly 75 percent of health care personnel were women. Women were also significantly overrepresented in the leather industry, hotels and tourism, and elementary schools.

On the other hand, women were underrepresented among journalists, professors, administrators, and judges. In 1957, for example, women accounted for only 8 percent of regular court justices, 5.7 percent of commercial court judges, and 2.3 percent of lawyers.[27] Yugoslav researchers set about investigating why women tend to get channeled into lines of work typecast as "women's occupations." They found that although employers typically reported no difference in the efficiency of women versus men at the workplace, employers suggested that employing women risked putting men out of work, that the employment of women provoked conflicts within the family, and that, in any case, they simply preferred to hire men.[28] Yugoslav academics led the way in confronting the problem honestly and directly. As Suzana Djurić and Gordana Dragičević pointed

Table 6.1   Percentage of Women in Certain Sectors of the Yugoslav Work Force
(by sector)

	1970	1975	1980
Social services	71.0	74.5	79.4
Healthcare	68.0	71.1	73.7
Textiles	66.3	68.4	78.4
Finance and insurance	61.5	65.5	N/A
Social insurance	58.4	64.5	N/A
Leather industry	52.6	59.4	69.9
Hotels	56.6	47.8*	60.4
Tourism	47.0		54.7
Schools	52.8	54.9	56.6
Cultural institutions	51.4	53.2	N/A
Tobacco industry	49.7	48.0	49.7
Foreign trade	45.5	48.2	52.8
Graphics	46.2	45.2	44.8
Science	43.0**	43.8	44.0
Retail trade	41.4	46.3	53.2
Wholesale trade	37.7	40.9	32.2
Yugoslav average	31.1	34.0	35.5

* In 1975, figure was reported for "Hotels and Tourism."
**Figure for 1973.

Sources: Olivera Burić, "Položaj žene u sistemu društvene moći u Jugoslaviji," in *Sociologija* 14, no. 1 (1972): 64; "Savezni zavod za statistiku," *Statistički Bilten*, no. 980 (Belgrade, October 1976), p. 21; and *Statistički godišnjak Jugoslavije 1981* (Belgrade: Savezni zavod za statistiku, August 1981), pp. 128–29.

out in 1965, the enrollment of young rural women in vocational and higher schools, and thus their advancement in careers, was repeatedly obstructed by the resistance of husbands and fathers to see "their women" abandoning what they (the men) thought was woman's proper role: housewife.[29] Or as Žarana Papić put it in 1980, in a particularly forthright passage, "We still remain within the confines of traditional, largely conservative suppositions about gender—in categories of the traditional (patriarchal) man and, at his side, the 'solidary' woman, in their 'proper,' basically unequal and retrograde roles."[30]

POLITICAL STAGNATION

The party could, perhaps, plead that its control of the economy was only indirect, and that changes in the education of women, in their advancement in careers, and in their economic position over all, would require more time. It was more difficult for the party to make such claims when it came to the participation of women in the party itself and the representation of women in party leadership bodies. Here the trends proved to be, from the beginning, largely negative.

Whereas many women had taken an active role in the National Liberation Struggle of 1941–45, there was a marked decline in female activism immediately after the war, as the Fifth Congress of the CPY (21–28 July 1948), the first postwar party congress, was forced to admit. Despite that congress's preoccupation with the crisis provoked by Stalin, its delegates found time to express and confirm the party's commitment to a policy of full equality between the sexes. But in spite of this formal commitment to gender equality, among the 468,175 members of the CPY in 1948, only 93,604 (or 19.99 percent) were women. One might expect that, in order to demonstrate its commitment to gender equality, the party might have assured that women were represented in greater proportions at the congress and among the members of the Central Committee. But, in fact, quite the contrary was the case. While women constituted 19.9 percent of the party membership, they represented only 9.7 percent of the delegates to the Fifth Congress, and when the list of members to be elected to the Central Committee was drawn up, only three women (4.8 percent) were included.[31] That same year, only 4 percent of the deputies to the federal Assembly were women.[32] The Sixth Congress of the CPY (held in Zagreb, 2–7 November 1952) has come down in history as the congress at which the CPY restyled itself the League of Communists of Yugoslavia (LCY). The Sixth Congress also spelled out a theoretical and moral-political critique of Stalinism, adding that the advancement of gender equality could not be successfully carried out in a system of state socialism (that is, Soviet-style Stalinism) any more than it could be in a capitalist system. Figures from 1952 reveal that women were taking an active part in elections. Some 80 percent of women took part in local elections, while 90.29 percent of women voted in the 1950 elections for the FNRJ People's Assembly. Moreover, women constituted 52.8 percent of registered voters in that year.

But for all that, women's representation in the organs of power fell between 1948 and 1952. Female representation in local administrative committees, for example, fell from 19.01 percent in 1948 to 13.07 percent in 1952. Moreover, there were only 6 women among the 109 Central Committee members elected at the Sixth Congress. Meanwhile, women's representation in the Federal Assembly had inched up marginally from 4.1 percent in 1946 to 4.8 per cent in 1950, reaching 5.1 percent in 1953.[33] These discouraging figures prompted Tito to warn the congress that the underrepresentation of women in political life was "contrary to our principles concerning the equality of women."[34]

With the Seventh Congress (held in Ljubljana, 22–26 April 1958), the Yugoslav system came into its own. The LCY issued a lengthy program that boasted of its achievements in self-management, and held up the Yugoslav system as a model for the world. By that point, the Yugoslav economy had not only attained but even surpassed the living standard known to prewar Yugoslavia, and congress participants spoke of having "new" insights into the problem of gender inequality. In spite of these new insights, the party was making very slow progress in equalizing the participation of women and men in party and government bodies. In 1958, for example, there were only forty-one women holding seats in the Federal Assembly (6.8 percent of the total), while in 1960, fifteen years since the communists came to power, women constituted only 16 percent of the total membership of the LCY.[35] The issue remained unresolved.

By the time the Eighth Congress was convened (Belgrade, 7–13 December 1964), female membership in the LCY had increased from 16.4 percent in 1957 to 17.2 percent at the time of the congress. The congress admitted that the increase was "insignificant" and concluded that "efforts directed toward increasing the number of women in the LCY have met with objective difficulties . . . , with still potent conservative views of the [proper] role of woman in social work and life."[36] This was an important admission because with it the LCY was conceding, whether consciously or unconsciously, that the feminist analysis of the problem had been correct, and that special work directed toward overcoming conservative prejudices would be needed. Even so, the congress did not take any steps toward overcoming these "objective difficulties," and, on the contrary, elected a Central Committee among whose members only 8 percent were women. Needless to say, the same theater was played out at the Ninth Party Congress (Belgrade, 11–15 September 1969), where Tito admitted the disjunction between the steadily increasing employment of women in the social and economic sectors, and the stagnation or even decline in the number of women in self-managing organs or occupying leadership positions. At the time of the Ninth Congress, only 6.6 percent of the deputies to the Federal Assembly were women.[37]

The Tenth Congress of the LCY (Belgrade, 27–30 May 1974) took place as the country's fourth postwar constitution was being passed. It was, in many ways, a time of optimism, even though the oil price shock of the preceding year was already taking its toll on Yugoslavia's fragile and none-too-efficient economy. Tito told the congress that the party had brought about "great changes" in the position of women in society. By then the female portion in LCY membership had increased to 19.9 percent, and Tito's reference to "great changes" notwithstanding, the LCY leadership felt constrained to admit that after thirty years of communist rule, this figure did not correspond to the way things should be.[38]

The Eleventh Congress (Belgrade, 20–23 June 1978) was the last congress attended by Tito. But the representation of women remained low. Women constituted 23.3 percent of party membership in 1977, 26.3 percent of the delegates electing delegates to the communal assemblies, 33.6 percent of delegates elected by basic organizations of associated labor, 18 percent of delegates in the communal assemblies, 19.5 percent of deputies in the assemblies of the republics and autonomous provinces, and 17.2 percent of the deputies in the Federal Assembly.[39] Tito, addressing the congress, held to the line that gender inequality was a "class question." But the assembled delegates ignored this formulation in their final program, and blamed continued gender inequality on "primitivism, religious beliefs and other conservative prejudices."[40] Titoism, despite its professed ideals, had reached a dead end.[41]

AFTER TITO, TITO

When Tito passed away in May 1980, ending a four-month-long death watch, party officials were psychologically unprepared. Although there was a broad consensus that there should be no strongman stepping into Tito's shoes (a consensus which seemed to be directed primarily against Slovene Stane Dolanc),[42] there was little concept as to how to proceed. The general disposition was "Don't rock the boat"—a principle which, in practice, seemed to promise something along the lines of Hua Guofeng's "two whatevers."[43] In symbolic embodiment of this principle, the party promulgated the motto, "After Tito, Tito," a reassuring motto which probably helped many people cope with the psychological uncertainty that accompanied Tito's passing. With a few exceptions (above all media policy and cultural policy), the party tried to continue Tito's policies after Tito, learning all too soon that without the helmsman's power to resolve otherwise insoluble interrepublican disagreements, the federation was starting to disintegrate, as the republics seized steadily more and more power.

As figures from the mid-1980s show (Table 6.2), the policy of "After Tito, Tito" had predictable effects.

After forty years of promising equality, the LCY granted women less than 15 percent of the seats in the Central Committee. While communist Yugoslavia might look good, when it comes to gender inequality, in the context of a comparison with quite a number of other countries, it was damned by its own principles, by its own moral agenda. On the eve of the Thirteenth Party Congress (Belgrade, 25–28 June 1986), the last congress held under "normal" circumstances, the party membership consisted of 31.4 percent women.[44]

Partly in response to criticism from local feminists concerning the continued low representation of women in higher party echelons, Milka Planinc was elevated to the presidency of the LCY Presidium in the mid-1980s. But as late as 1986, women accounted for only 15.6 percent of deputies to the Federal Assembly, 19.3 percent of the deputies to the Assemblies of the Socialist Republics, 24.4 percent of the deputies to the Assemblies of the two autonomous provinces, and 17.1 percent of the deputies to communal assemblies.[45] By this point, a generation of articulate women had given up on the party's formulae and had begun organiz-

Table 6.2   Women in Leadership Bodies of the LCY (1985)

	% of women in party membership	% of women in the CC or PC
LCY	27.0	14.1
LC Bosnia-Herzegovina	29.2	19.5
LC Montenegro	26.1	13.2
LC Croatia	27.5	21.6
LC Macedonia	23.0	21.9
LC Slovenia	32.1	20.5
LC Serbia	27.5	17.8
LC Kosovo	13.5	14.7
LC Vojvodina	31.6	23.5

CC = Central Committee (at federal level and in the six republics)
PC = Provincial Committee (in the two autonomous provinces of Kosovo and Vojvodina)

Source: Jasna A. Petrović, "Žene u SK danas," Žena 44, no. 4 (1986): 7.

ing various independent associations and groupings, sometimes registering them as supposedly "official activities" of the local SAWPY organization.[46] They rejected what they called the "vulgar reductionism" by dogmatic Marxism of the question of gender inequality to a question of class inequality, arguing that this reduction effectively erased the gender question from the agenda.[47] Blaženka Despot spoke for many when she wrote (in 1987),

> The political articulation of 'women's' interests in diverse forms of 'combative feminism' is a negation of the 'woman question' as a class question and, as such, abandons the possibility of a theoretical foundation within Marxism. . . .
>
> A Marxist theory of society, naturally, cannot base itself on a gender struggle as a class struggle, or on a gender struggle which replaces the class struggle. But the reduction of the 'woman question' to a class question makes it impossible for women to be aware of its real essence in their everyday lives.[48]

But voices such as Despot's came up against firm party opposition. In 1982, for example, at a forum organized by the publishers of *Žena* journal, Despot crossed swords with Stipe Šuvar, a high-ranking figure in the Croatian Communist Party. Where Šuvar insisted on construing feminism as "a form of conservative social consciousness,"[49] Despot distanced herself from Šuvar's formula, qualified her acceptance of the party's reduction of the question of gender equality to the so-called class question, and called for the resurrection of a high-level organization, on a par with the youth organization, devoted to advancing gender equality.[50] But Despot and her allies made no headway and four years later, at the Thirteenth Congress of the LCY (25–28 June 1986), delegate Nadežda Gerasimovska-Hristova could still reiterate the standard party formulae that "the solution of all questions of the social position of women in essence demands a class approach" and that "one cannot approach questions of the position of women apart from, and isolated from, general social tendencies."[51]

CONCLUSION

The record of Titoism is simultaneously inspiring and deflating. It is inspiring insofar as the promises it made and the vision it sketched held the promise for achieving all-encompassing equality across all levels, in-cluding gender. There is no difficulty in enumerating governments so lacking in any sense of social justice that they make no commitment to working toward gender equality at all; indeed, since 1989, most, if not all, of the governments of Central and Eastern Europe have pointedly de-clared that gender equality is no concern of theirs, and have put into effect policies which have widened the economic and social gap between male and female.[52] The record of Titoism is ultimately deflating, how-ever, because the Titoist governments failed to make good on their promises. Take, for example, a study by Rajka and Milan Polić (published in 1979). They found that in third-grade school textbooks, 68 percent of the main characters in stories were males, while only 32 percent were females, and that 73 percent of the persons depicted in the schoolbooks were males. Moreover, the schoolbooks seemed to promote rather differ-ent values for men and women. Males were encouraged to be strong, courageous, warriorlike, and creative, with little encouragement to males to be good (future) fathers or to care about their looks. Females, on the other hand, were portrayed as maternal, beautiful, and indecisive, thereby giving encouragement to women to be weak objects of male conquest.[53] Since the schoolbooks came under the authority of the Communist Party (albeit at the level of the republic), the failure to cultivate more equal images and aspirations for girls and boys was, in the final analysis, a fail-ure of the Party.

To say that socialism failed women is not to praise capitalism, which has generally done even worse for women. The point lies not in a contrast between these two systems but in an identification of the nature of social-ism's failure. For that matter, no one is surprised that capitalism, which does not make any promises of gender equality or social justice, fails to achieve either of these. But the failure of self-managing socialism to achieve these twin goals, which it had set for itself, invites the question as to whether the radical feminists are right, that is, whether only a struggle which prioritizes the achievement of full gender equality can have any prospects of success. The roots of gender inequality are deep, entangled with all the advanced socioeconomic systems on the planet and under-pinned by the religious presuppositions of all major religious systems.

But if socialism failed to solve the question of gender inequality, it accomplished, at least, this much: By its very failure, socialism showed that the reduction of the question of gender equality to some more gen-eral question risks not merely the subordination of women's inequality to other concerns but its scuttling. In other words, socialism's failure—unlike the failure of capitalism—is singularly instructive, in that, with its failure, there can be, or so it seems to me, no question but that the achievement of gender equality requires a frontal assault on the cultural, psychological, religious, social, economic, and political bastions of patriarchy.

PART THREE

POST-SOCIALIST REPUBLICS

7

WOMEN IN POST-SOCIALIST SLOVENIA:
SOCIALLY ADAPTED, POLITICALLY MARGINALIZED

Vlasta Jalušič

My task in this chapter[1] is to reflect upon the condition of women in post-socialist Slovenia. I will do this by questioning the relationship between women and the social and the political spheres (especially the state) in the period of the so-called transition from the previous system—a one-party system and planned economy—to the new one—a multiparty system and market economy. I deal with the recent past (the 1980s and 1990s) and I try to show how important an understanding of state and the image of politics can be for the condition of women in a post-socialist situation.

In the first part, I shall analyze the rise of women's movements within the socialist system during the 1980s. The second part deals with the struggle for abortion rights as a battle for equal citizenship and a "women-friendly" state at the beginning of the 1990s. The third part is

Work on this chapter was supported by the Research Support Scheme of the OSI/HESP, Grant No. 1465/ 1997.

dedicated to the question of politics, participation, and female antifeminism in post-socialism.

INTRODUCTORY REMARKS:
WOMEN'S MOVEMENTS AND THE STATE

The exploration of the political and social condition of women in Slovenia is interesting for several reasons. The new statehood is one of them: Slovenia as an independent state has a very short history. The ex-Yugoslav republic (20,251 sq. km) officially declared its independence on 25 June 1991. After that the military actions of the Yugoslav People's Army and the war in Slovenia and later in different parts of ex-Yugoslavia began.

Slovenia has a population of 1,965,986. Along with the majority of Slovenes, there are officially recognized Italian and Hungarian minorities as well as a perceptible number of inhabitants from the ex-Yugoslav republics. The recent GDP was $9,210 (US) per capita (OECD data). Life expectancy at birth for men is 69.4 years; for women 77.3 years. The population growth is 1.1 per 1,000. The female share of total employment is around 47.2 percent; the unemployment rate is between 11 and 14 percent. Among various religious groups registered in Slovenia, the Roman Catholic Church claims 70 percent of the population as members; approximately one-third of this percentage is active within the Church.[2]

Immense political and social changes, connected above all to the fall and rise of several states, are a feature of this area and its population in this century. An accurate presentation of women's condition, of women's movements, initiatives, and struggles for equal rights in Slovenia can hardly be provided without consideration of this changes. The rise, life, and disintegration of diverse states that have been the political framework of women's movements have been of particular importance. Women "made it through" and were active in different circumstances: within the Austro-Hungarian empire (1861–1918), in the Kingdom of Serbs, Croats, and Slovenes (1918–29), the Kingdom of Yugoslavia (1929–41), in the battles of World War II (1941–45), within the Socialist Federated Republic of Yugoslavia (second Yugoslavia, 1945–91) and—at last—Slovenia (after 1991).[3]

These different circumstances were among the main reasons why, as Erna Muser points out,

The history of Slovenian women's movement cannot be compared to the history of women's movements of the big, politically independent and economically strong nations, as we usually do. Whilst experiencing social discrimination, the movement for defending national interests unavoidably prevailed in the public appearances of Slovenian women, being crucial for the Slovenian people.[4]

There is no need for us to agree with the essentialist assumption in this quotation (that women's interests were unavoidably subordinated to the national issues crucial for the "Slovenian people") in order to grasp the factual trouble of "small nations (non)feminisms" in multinational states or see the problem of the nonexistence of feminisms in the societies without a (modern, based on civil rights) state. This trouble marks all the developments and trends in women's movements in Slovenia until the 1990s, and it is even now not yet overcome. The history of women's movements (in particular, in the Slovenian case) in the predeceasing multinational states shows not (as Muser states) that national interests were crucial but that the interests and demands of women's movements were mostly overwhelmed by national or other "essentialist" interests, such as the right to vote in the first Yugoslavia in 1918.

In spite of their entitlement, expectations, and struggle for Yugoslavia, women did not gain the right to vote until the socialist system appeared in 1945.[5] Until the 1990s, women's movements mostly could not get rid of the "common" cultural and national issue and develop their own political strategy. Moreover, they have always appeared parallel with the other political movements—either in times of revolution or as contemporaries of other modern national-political upheavals. The elements of the modern women's movement in Slovenia are to a large extent connected with the crisis and disintegration of the Austro-Hungarian empire with respect to the rise of the common political aspirations of the (south) Slavic part of the former monarchy.[6]

The questions I put here are the following: How significantly different from the past was the time symbolized by the fall of the Berlin Wall (the time of changes from socialism to a multiparty system and market economy plus new nation states in the whole of Eastern Europe)? What was the relationship between women's movements and the state at that time?

The new women's groups and initiatives in Slovenia in the 1980s grew out of resistance to both the Communist Party and the emerging ethnonationalisms within Yugoslavia after Tito's death in 1980. As political initiatives, they did not aim at ethnonational "political" space but at a political legitimacy of feminist initiatives as such. At the same time, they wanted to build the political "space of appearance"[7] for (different) women and for different women's initiatives in the whole state of Yugoslavia. Paradoxically, the result was an obsolete but, under the given conditions, the only achievable framework: with all its modern paradoxes, namely, the nation-state, which can and does instrumentalize women for the national imagery. Despite this, as the experience of the nineteenth century shows, the state is the only framework that can express the demands and instrumentalize the legitimization of feminism in terms of citizenship.

OLD SYSTEM AND NEW MOVEMENTS

The project of women's emancipation in socialist Yugoslavia (including Slovenia) as a "concept" did not differ very much from that in other East European countries. It was a project of liberation of women qua animal laborans[8] and not women as political beings, that is, as citizens. Indeed, the "implementation" of "communist women's lib" in Yugoslavia was much "softer" and more liberal than in other East European countries. This has been especially the case in the northern areas with the old nineteenth-century tradition of women's employment in the textile, leather, and tobacco industries. The circumstances of "soft communist" development and the awareness in some urban women's circles during the second half of the 1970s that even the legal rights given to them (including a liberal abortion law solution from the mid-1970s) did not guarantee their equal position were the starting point for the emergence of diverse feminist groups and activities in the 1980s.

Various forums within Yugoslavia (starting from the first nonofficial international feminist meeting organized in Belgrade in 1978 and the first "academic" women's group in the 1979 in Zagreb) shaped the rise of feminist groups in the republic of Slovenia as well. The new feminist initiatives grew, as Lydia Sklevicky put it, out of "the generation without its own tradition of organized women's activism."[9] New groups demanded active involvement in issues such as domestic violence toward women and children, lower wages for female workers (approximately 20 percent lower then males), and the political marginalization of women despite formal female representation in the socialist assembly (in Slovenia 25 percent of members in the assembly were female) and general legal equality.

Several groups, among them rape crisis centers and academic groups, appeared at the beginning of the 1980s, mostly in urban centers (primarily Belgrade, Zagreb, and Ljubljana). In Slovenia, the first initiatives appeared simultaneously with the so-called new social movement groups that were active under the umbrella of the Socialist Youth Organization. In some regard, we could consider them a "part" of the so-called civil society movement, developed and articulated under the influence of East European ideas of antipolitics and civil society as an antistatist parallel oppositional organization.[10]

Feminist initiatives in Slovenia developed from two basic interests. The first has been the need for a critique of the dominant "state feminism" that declared the women question a nonexistent problem and feminism obsolete in conditions of socialism.[11] The second was to build a space for a separate identity, a consciousness-raising, women-only space for sharing the experiences, above all, of patriarchal repression.

The first group (The Women's Section at the Sociological Society) from 1984 was a result and a mixture of both needs. It undertook the first study of gender equality in postwar Slovenia[12] and, at the same time, became the first "consciousness-raising new feminist" group in Slovenia. The members were younger educated women, some scholars or students. Later on, after the founding of the Lilit group in 1995, the initial common interest faded and gradually alternative approaches emerged within the feminist circles.

Already in the 1980s, research and published works which one could call "women's studies" had become visible: few projects compared to the West and, of course, not institutionalized, but they were either a kind of female scientist's "housework" or put into the form of "hidden" courses at the university.[13] Mostly they were connected to the "women's only initiatives." The theoretical impact of existing Western women's studies (due to the open borders and, hence, access to the feminist literature) could be observed. At the same time, however, there was also the impact of our own socialist experience that made the thinkers critical toward some so-called radical ideas of Western feminism and its essentialisms. The first independent publications emerged in 1982 (some emerged before 1982 in the form of literature). Some translations and introductory studies were published,[14] as well as two women's issues of the quarterly

Problemi/Eseji and many separately published articles in a few different periodical publications.[15]

THE WOMAN QUESTION POLITICIZED

Early in 1985, Ljubljana's first "women-only" public happening since World War II was organized as an expansion of the "academic" discussions which started at the Women's Section of the Sociological Society. The Lilit section, founded on that occasion, functioned as a kind of "incubator" for many other groups that appeared later. Lilit became a society (with women-only membership) with different activities: events, meetings, and lectures. The questions opened by Lilit were various: women's identity, women in media, the question of domestic violence, abortion rights, and so on. Some independent publications as well as translations of feminist texts came out. Despite its editor's ambiguous attitude, feminist texts were also published in the magazine *Mladina*.

Due to the considerable liberalization of the political and cultural climate in the beginning of the 1980s after Tito's death, diverse groups of so-called new social movements first appeared as a youth punk subculture[16] and young intellectual discussion circles. From the beginning of the 1980s, there existed a few other independent new social movement groups: a peace group, an ecological group with quite a number of female members, and a gay group. The first women's activities were partly connected to those groups. But as I argue elsewhere, feminist activities cannot be seen as a united phenomenon of Slovene civil society.[17] Due to specific and important Yugoslav feminist networking (there was no similar case with the other alternative groups) and the latent uneasiness and discomfort with feminism among Slovene alternative circles,[18] women's activities should be treated as a separate phenomenon.

The groups were above all trying to organize "women's space" and an appropriate atmosphere for group work, socialization, and solidarity among women. To a certain degree, they had to remain more or less self-sufficient. In spite of this, they claimed the "re-politicization of the woman question"[19] and considered the right to be equal yet different at the same time as one of main conditions for the democratic system. The groups had small numbers of members with many personal differences and differences in principles among them. In 1986, the Working Group for Women's Movements and Women's Research at the Socialist Youth

Alliance was founded but the group failed to survive. While the Socialist Youth Alliance gained semi-autonomous status in the 1980s and became an umbrella for many alternative activities, the peace movement was welcomed much more than the feminists.

As a result of the attempt to build cooperation among the groups there have been two successful campaigns. The first one (organized by Lilit, together with the peace movement working group) was directed against the obligatory military training for women proposed in the secret document of the Yugoslav People's Army in 1985. The action elicited a reaction in the Yugoslav media and has been understood as one of the "Slovenian attacks" on the federal institution of the Yugoslav People's Army and showed one of most difficult problems (leading to the escalation of ethnonationalisms) regarding "new social movement's" active in Slovenia: the fact that any step within "the democratization process was described by its antagonists in national (actually ethnic) terms. It became the Slovene national deviation."[20]

The second common public action of feminists with other new social movements was the demonstration for a moratorium of the nuclear power stations in Yugoslavia organized by the Working Group for Women's Movements and Women's Studies, the ecological group and the Working Group for Peace Movements, in April 1987, one year after Chernobyl accident. The number of participants has been estimated at around four thousand, among them many present day politicians.

However, political campaigning and sporadic organized mass actions were only one part of the activities of some more established groups. The liberalization and opening of the public space allowed other groups to organize. Lesbian women founded a subgroup of Lilit in 1987,[21] while a splinter group against violence against women began a hotline for raped women in 1989.

Two of the four Yugoslav feminist meetings were organized in Ljubljana: one in December 1987 and another in January 1991. The first meeting showed the variety of feminist initiatives in the territory of Yugoslavia (a wide spectrum from "radical" feminists to "academic" and "socialist" feminists). The Common Document Feminists of Yugoslavia proclaimed by the meeting of Yugoslav feminists in December 1987 asserted the legitimacy of feminism as a political movement. It declared that the "various feminist initiatives and groups in Yugoslavia are legitimate and legal," which was partly the sign of their difficult position in socialism as neither being directly forbidden nor encouraged and supported. The meeting appealed to women "to join the existing feminist groups or establish new ones" and opposed population politics of any kind, which has been very important in the face of the very intense public discussions about the "too high birth rate of the Albanian population" in Kosova. At the same time, there was a demand that "lesbians should became publicly evident" and for the "constitutional equality of all citizens irrespective of sexual orientation."[22] The last common meeting of feminists of Yugoslavia in 1991 in Ljubljana (after the second one in 1989 in Zagreb and the third one in 1990 in Belgrade) was the last organized meeting by any alternative Yugoslav network before the war started.

The period of 1987–88 was the most lively activist period. Women's groups responded to all kinds of problems and tried to involve a larger number of activists with the work of the groups. Some female members from the League of Communists of Slovenia even joined in feminist actions and discussions. In 1988, the League of Communists invited oppositional feminists to speak about the importance of the women's movement and tried to start dialogue with them. In the same year, the first Yugoslav lesbian camp took place on the island Rab in Croatia, organized by the LL section (the lesbian subgroup of Lilit) and by Magnus (the gay society from Ljubljana). Several lesbian publications came out, such as *Lesbozine*. A lesbian and gay disco started was organized once a week. Later on, the common periodical *Revolver* was initiated from both groups.

This was also a time of national homogenization. In the spring of 1988, three civilians and one army officer were accused of stealing a secret military document on martial law in Slovenia. The civilians were closely connected to new social movements circles and the arrest of two of them incited powerful protests and solidarity within these circles. The years 1989 and 1990—at the time of and after the military trial against "the four" (as the accused civilians and the army officer were prevalently named)—were under the sign of mass protests and movements (which resulted in the referendum on independence where 88 percent of the population voted for the independent state of Slovenia). Simultaneously, once it became clear that the Serbian political leadership had a "intransigent negative stance . . . on the question of the rights guaranteed to the republics in the Constitution of 1974,"[23] the federal system started to be seriously questioned.

But the feminist groups, which were among the first protesting against the military trials of civilians in Slovenia, did not join the "rush to independence" of some cultural and civil society circles, which saw the problem of the language in which the trial was held as the top priority rather than the question of civil rights. Neither before 1989 nor later did these groups become a part of the nationalist civil society movement;[24] on the contrary, they strongly criticized some tendencies within national-cultural circles. The fact that, at the Third Meeting of Yugoslav Feminists in 1990 in Belgrade, the representatives of the Lilit group did not support the idea of an umbrella organization with the name Yugoslav Women's Alliance is no proof of their nationalism but rather the result of the anti-power monopolization sentiment and grassroots consciousness of the new feminist groups within socialism.[25]

THE CAMPAIGN FOR CONSTITUTIONAL REPRODUCTIVE RIGHTS

One of the few common points within the process of disintegration of the Yugoslav federal state in the 1980s (not in the 1990s; the overall disintegration and war were only a consequence of the earlier processes) was a certain ideological shift in the official attitude toward the so-called woman question within self-managed socialism. This shift was marked by an awakening of the discussion about the Yugoslav birth rate in the mid-1980s.

The main question put forward was the "problem of the high Albanian birth rate" in Kosova (the ex-autonomous province with the largest Albanian/non-Slavic population) and the supposedly by too-low birth rate in Slovenia, Serbia, and Croatia. The discourse about the allegedly too-low birth rate of Serbs, Croats, and Slovenes encouraged discussion about abortion and reproductive rights. The population policy question was one of the few points of agreement among groups of dramatically different orientations: the Slovene Communist Party, the Slovene national opposition (self-proclaimed cultural dissidents), the Serbian Communist Party and so on. In Slovenia, demographers started with catastrophic projections of the national future if the birth rate of Slovenes did not increase. They spoke about the "dying out of Slovenian nation," there were article titles in the newspapers as "Two Children Are Not Enough," "Less and Less Slovenians," and so on.

At the same time, the Catholic anti-abortion campaign started. In 1987, the bishop's regional conference for Slovenia highlighted the alleged decline of births in the Slovene nation as reported in the Catholic students' press. The bishops connected the decline of births with a sup-posed overall "demoralization" and irresponsibility for unborn life. The U.S. anti-abortion film *The Silent Scream* has been shown since 1985 in every parish all over Slovenia. These were the foundation for the later, much larger anti-abortion campaign, beginning at the time of the self-determination (referendum) in 1990, and continuing to the first multi-party elections in 1990 and the discussion about the constitution of the new Slovenian state.

I think that the discussion of population politics in the mid-1980s precisely encapsulates all the ethnonational fantasies that were connected to the traditional picture of women and the public/private split of women. These fantasies and myths not only contributed to the escalation of hate and war later but also inspired the many atrocities which were perpe-trated in the war in Bosnia and Croatia. The demographers' campaign (with its points common to pro-Slavic population politics and the attempt to control "our" women) had fatal effects on the situation in Kosova and the process of national homogenization in Serbia, Slovenia, and Croatia.

Socialist Solution

There was an unique solution in the area of reproductive rights within the socialist Yugoslavia. Since 1974, there has been a paragraph in the federal constitution that guaranteed reproductive rights.[26] It was defined as a "human right to decide over the birth of one's own children" which included abortion rights and the duties of the state to provide the facilities (the opportunities) for the implementation of this right. In the republic of Slovenia, for example, the right included not only abortion rights (on demand until the tenth week of pregnancy) but also, first of all, the avail-ability of social, health, and other facilities to enable women to give birth to wanted children. These facilities included the whole network of wom-en's health centers, accessible (free) contraception, abortion on de-mand—to be paid out of the health insurance—plus health care for mothers and children, as well as other social facilities.[27]

I was born at the end of the 1950s and experienced times of liberal attitudes vis-à-vis contraception and abortion, where reproductive rights were not questioned by the state or politicians. To be entitled to decide over one's own body was considered "natural." But this was only one side of the coin. Since the old socialist legislation came "from above," and the mass of women had inherited rights without having to participate actively in the struggles for them, there existed the feeling among many women, that one did not have to fight for these rights. When the anti-abortion campaign started, nobody really believed that these long-lasting rights could be taken away. Because "democratization" promised so much for everybody, no one thought that the new-born democrats could put reproduction rights seriously into question.

The Response to the Anti-Abortion Campaign

As a result of the first multiparty elections in Slovenia in 1990 (still within the Yugoslav federal state) very few women were elected into the Slovenian parliament (11 percent). In spite of the early reformist approach of the Slovene Communist Party in the 1980s, the reformed socialist and communist parties lost their influence and power. The Christian Democrats were the leading party within the winning right-party coalition of Demos (with 53 percent of seats). The emancipation of women ceased to be an automatic part of the system's legitimization. The legitimization of special social politics, connected to the presupposed special women's role in socialism, became "useless" once the new concept of a market system was introduced. All the changes in the direction of a market economy and democracy were closely connected to the growing ethnonationalism in the whole Yugoslavia, which reflects how fragile women's rights and formal equality can be if there is no long tradition of women's movements or independent women's political forums and little public political consciousness among women about the meaning of these rights.

After the process against "the four" in 1988–89 (the Yugoslav People's army military trial against three Slovene civilians and one army officer), everything was mobilized for "our Slovenian boys." Well before the first multiparty elections in 1990, when the members of a few parties (Christian Democrats, Green Party, People's Party) started the anti-abortion campaign, a number of new women's initiatives emerged. They were both independent and party groups[28] and became the main protagonists in the campaign for constitutional abortion rights.

The boiling point in the discussion about the new Slovene constitution[29] was reached exactly with the quarrel over the paragraph on reproduction rights. Since reproductive rights remained the only nonconsensual point of the constitutional proposal,[30] there was a threat that Slovenia as a new state would remain without a constitution even on the eve of the second multiparty election; therefore, there was a danger

that the paragraph would simply be left out in favor of the "whole constitution." If this happened, the fundamentals of all existing legal solutions
would be ruined and the possibility of abolishing abortion on demand
would remain open. Since the parliament had to decide this question with
a two-thirds majority and only 11 percent of the representatives in the
parliament were women, the chances of retaining this paragraph in the
constitution seemed rather small.

In spite of perceptible differences in opinion, ideology, and structure
among existing women's groups (whether feminist or nonfeminist) they
decided to start a common action—before the parliamentary decision on
the paragraph was made. After the publication of a book on the abortion
issue by the group Women for Politics, there were several roundtable
discussions organized in autumn 1991. As became clear, such actions
were not enough; therefore, the decision to hold a large demonstration
was natural, despite much hesitation and doubt about how women would
respond to such an action. But once the decision had been made, one
could feel the massive support of women, as well as men. Thousands of
signatures to support the action called "the right to choose" were gathered. The anti–anti-abortion campaign was one occasion where the
"smallness" of the emerging state of Slovenia became a kind of advantage: almost nobody was left untouched by the discussion, and almost
everybody expressed opinion.

Demonstration

The demonstration took place on 11 December 1991 in the front of the
parliament, despite the fear that very few women could come. It was actually the first time in almost forty years that women held their own demonstration. The parliamentary session was interrupted. A large number
of representatives joined women and many men on the street. Twenty-
four out of twenty-five women representatives in the parliament made
the common statement that opposed the omission of reproductive rights.
Women on the street held placards and shouted slogans such as: "Women
into the parliament!" "We want a women's ministry!" "Abortion without
compromise!" and so on. Because the women protested with much imagination and their slogans were radical and without prejudice, the prime
minister (a Christian Democrat) declared them "nasty" and "tasteless."
But one daily newspaper rightly called it the "first civil demonstration
after the elections in spring 1990."[31]

It was quite obvious that nobody—not even the government or the parliament—expected such strong opposition to the omission or reduction of the paragraph on reproductive rights. The demonstration was a success for independent and party women's groups, and although a slight compromise was made later in the very conservative constitutional commission (the word "right" was changed to "freedom"), the foundation for the existing legislation was left unchanged; therefore, abortion on demand was left as a legal constitutional solution.[32]

Troubles with Legitimization

When the post-socialist societies started to legitimize themselves with their inner "democracy," it was seen, above all, as a majority rule within the parliament (with some corrections; for example, with a quota for national minorities). Women's rights and participation in politics were not important questions. Even worse, they were ignored. Since these questions were the legitimizing principles of the old system, the main tendency was to declare such efforts illegitimate or, as I have already mentioned, as "totalitarian vestiges." Every good or bad inheritance from the old, socialist system, including abortion rights, was declared to be suspicious . This was the point where an up-to-date populistic legitimization for the anti-abortion campaign was very successful against everything old, including women's rights, which had been gained under socialism.

One of the most trivial arguments by opponents to the paragraph about the reproduction rights (section 55) was that "no other European constitution inherited such a right" and that Europe would "really laugh at us" if "we were quarreling over such a marginal problem." On the other hand, there was the defenders' argument that Slovenia had very good experiences with the existing legal solution and that throwing the paragraph out of the constitution would mean that the law could be changed by the whim of the simple majority in parliament. In other words, democratic majority decision making brought about a situation where certain rights could be "democratically" abolished. No wonder many women used the natural rights argument for their intimate right to choose against such a democracy.

However, Catholic circles probably really believed that a large part of the female population saw the forty years of socialism as some kind of "forced emancipation through work" and that they could hardly wait to "return to the household." They described the complete corpus of socialist legislation—including the constitutional reproductive right—as some kind of "totalitarian vestige." Therefore, the discussion took place, on the one hand, as a discourse about the "care" for women, nation, and health,. On the other hand, the abortion issue began to cover all other problems connected to the political and social position of women in the time of transition, from the self-managed economy to the market system and the one-party system to the multiparty parliament. Partly, it was during the pre-election campaign, in the interest of different parties, that this question was opened in order to arouse public interest and to mobilize the supposedly most antipolitical part of the election body.

In this context, the logic behind the anti-abortion rights campaign was to create a "real," "big problem" behind which all other problems such as social policy, employment, the impact of market, political representation, and so on, could be hidden. Simultaneously, there was a common East-European "transitional" situation which enabled similar anti-abortion campaigns all over Eastern Europe.

Why, in spite of this, were reproduction rights in Slovenia retained? There were several reasons. First, the so-called transition in Slovenia was a slow, long lasting process which had started at the beginning of 1980s, when the first "new social movement groups" began appearing. Since the reforming process started within the Communist Party itself as well, no strong anticommunism developed as it had in some other East-European states. Although the demands that "everything should be changed," for a complete turn around of the old system were present, they were not the majority.

Second, separate new feminist groups existed long before the fall of the Berlin Wall and were somehow a part of the democratization forces. After the first elections in 1990, both the Parliamentary Commission for Women's Politics and The Office for Women's Politics were founded as a result of the work of these groups.

Third, there already existed some consciousness among female party members that they should act in solidarity if basic rights are endangered. Besides, the independent and party women's groups decided to go public in the largest sense, to go to the street and break the fear of showing public solidarity among women by this powerful means. Last, but not least, the small political space enabled the demands of women to be heard well.

In my opinion, the experience of the transitional period shows that the parties which were opposed to free abortion lost rather than gained influence since 1990. Two examples prove this thesis. One is the leading Liberal Democratic Party (with the prime minister Janez Drnovšek in the last six years) which has and "tolerates" its own women's faction (Minerva) with an active pro-choice orientation. The other example is the extremely nationalistic Slovene National Party (with the leader Zmago Jelinčič) which had an articulate pro-abortion position in the election campaign 1992 and gained almost 10 percent votes (many of them women) from a relatively marginal position and returned to the parliament in the 1996 elections. This shows that the nationalistic-liberal combination is the most successful combination to govern in Slovenia. On the other hand, the leader of the Christian Democrats Lojze Peterle (who, as a prime minister, declared the pro-abortion demonstrations in 1991 "tasteless") replied with a rhetorical question when, in the 1996 election campaign, he was asked whether Christian Democrats wanted to put a ban on abortion. "I did not hear your question well," he replied to the television journalist.

ANTIFEMINISM AND WOMEN IN POLITICS IN THE FIRST FIVE YEARS OF INDEPENDENCE

After the breakdown of Yugoslavia and the end of the socialist system, women in Slovenia lost many of the social benefits they had had in the last period of socialism[33]—in spite of having successfully retained and built some "old rights" (including abortion) into the new state. It took some time before they became aware of this fact and began protesting against it. After five years of liberal-oriented government[34] (until recently functioning with some social corrections demanded from the ex-communists and female lobbies in the Liberal Democratic Party), they were faced with all the "classic" troubles of the so-called transition to the multiparty system and market economy with the democratic legitimization.

On the one hand, their everyday lives are exposed to growing social insecurity. The market economy discriminates against them by its own logic: they must work several jobs or work sometimes without social and pension security; there are difficulties in finding jobs or better paying jobs. On the other hand, they were faced with attempts by the new post-socialist but traditionally oriented parties such as Christian Democrats and People's Party to win the political popularity by trying to "protect" women against "exploitation" with proposing three (!) years of maternity leave.[35] Women are affected by the processes of building the new state institutions and integration into the European institutions as well. Higher budgets for sectors such as national security, the military, and foreign politics means at the same time minimizing the role of the state in the areas of social facilities. This causes the new phenomenon that I would call the "redundancy" of whole strata of people who become unemployed[36] or otherwise unsecured and are not able to "adapt" themselves to the market and social competition. There exists no serious awareness about the possible social and political consequences of this phenomenon. The social and personal conflicts caused by it are mostly "mediated" within families. Women are therefore not only directly affected by the new situation (by their own unemployment and insecurity) but also through changes and additional conflicts within the family life due to the insecurity of their partners; they perform very well known additional "therapy" within the family. Hence, the existing transition practice and theory of liberal democracy, as Hana Havelkova puts it, ignores, but at the same time assumes, the given and unchanged private-public relationships, gender division, and patriarchal family.[37]

There is still no data about the effects of privatization of the economy and social housing on the condition of women (there is no data about the sex of the new owners). Some research suggests that there are more male owners of land and housing, but emerging poverty among women, especially among emigrant women (from ex-Yugoslav republics, refugees from Bosnia, who are mostly still not allowed to work legally in Slovenia).

In any case, the statistical data (especially employment data) shows that despite the problem of unemployment, the decline of wages in the "feminized" branches,[38] more domestic violence connected to the unsecured situation, the high cost of sending children to kindergarten, and chronic problems with the health and social system, women are still more flexible and ready to adopt to the new system and market economy. The question remains, however, whether women do feel this as a new possibility or rather as a question of mere necessity.

WOMEN IN POLITICS

I have already mentioned that with the first multiparty elections female membership in the parliament declined by more than half (from 24 percent to 11 percent).[39] During the second elections, in 1992, no special campaigning for votes for women was made, but brought (despite the presence of fewer women candidates on the lists) a slightly better result (13.3 percent). At the third elections, in November 1996, the percentage of women in the parliament decreased to 8 percent.[40] The reasons for the decline are diverse.

Above all, there is the fact that from the beginning of the 1990s no party had actually systematically built the quota system or any other useful means of empowering women in politics (despite the positive public opinion on this question). On the other hand, after the second elections, almost every party founded its own women's faction,[41] and due to the efforts of both party and independent activists the need for positive discrimination has been at least partly recognized. However, there still exists a perceptible degree of antifeminist sentiment in the consciousness of women themselves and a kind of aversion toward party and state politics. Among the newly formed parties, in the public opinion and even among the women fractions within the parties, a general opposition to the introduction of legal measures for the equal opportunity politics (quota and similar) seems to predominate.

Empirical research into the images of democracy (within the political elite which is, for the most part, composed of men), in Slovenia as well as in Eastern and Central Europe, shows that, in their evaluation, the political elite put freedom above equality and that, in contrast to the social-democratic visions of Swedish or Austrian political elite, the prevailing values are those of capitalism and competition.[42]

Antifeminist attitudes in women are a reaction to the past, present, and future possible images of women's participation in public affairs and politics, and a reaction to their general and individual situation. Female antifeminism in Eastern and Central Europe is, on the one hand, a reaction to stigmatization. Experience tells us that in many cases it is mainly women—politicians, reporters, and so on—who proclaim themselves to be nonfeminists. Thus, the rejection of feminism can also mean a certain defense strategy, showing us a different starting point for post-socialist Central and Eastern European countries. In any case, women in Slovenia, as well as in other Eastern European countries, mostly try to avoid "feminist conflicts" and try to build their public promotion above all as good professionals and experts, not as "token women."

The second problem in the majority of Eastern and Central European countries involves the rejection of both the institutionalization of women's interests and the quota system as a means of political participation, as well as a strong aversion toward "state involvement" in their lives, and their cooperation with the state.[43] All of this is in spite of the fact that the post-socialist state interferes strongly in people's lives through its reforms.

It is interesting that at the beginning this aversion was not so strong in Slovenia: Many feminist activists became active within the parties and the state apparatus and became the new "state feminists." Women and women's groups (independent and party) in Slovenia realized very early that they did need the state and party influence if they wanted to push their interests through so that the nation state would not be able to instrumentalize them if they were active in the politics.

Despite this, the pressure of the liberal and national temptations were too strong. Most party women's sections rejected the quota system in the lively discussion of autumn 1995 and spring 1996 about the obligatory quota for women candidates on the election lists for the election 1996. The proposal came from the ex-Communist Party–Women's Section (United List of Social Democrats).[44] Liberal democratic women who were supposed to support the law on the quota remained parvenus and did not want to break with the male parties mainstream.[45] It was very interesting to follow how the arguments, pro and con, were made. It seemed that the most important question was not so much whether or not such a law would pass through parliament. The sole discussion became about the possibilities of women in politics, about positive discrimination, which makes opinions on the issue political. The surprising result of the few weeks of discussion was the shift in the public opinion—it showed the preference in favor of "positive discrimination" of (competent) female candidates.

However, within the new, more or less liberal, development in the last years, the power of both party women's sections and the new and old independent groups diminished. Party women did not succeed in taking advantage of the power and influence of the independent women's groups from the 1980s. Some of the more politicized "civil society" groups, such as Women for Politics (Initiatira delle donne), were not strong enough to develop at least some institutionalized power. They either dissolved into the nonofficial pressure groups or were largely depoliticized by much of the humanitarian work they have done in the time of war and later.[46]

The existing groups still have personal contacts with the other ex-Yugoslav groups. Some of them participate in the discussions organized by the Bureau for Women's Politics but their influence is much weaker than in the years of the so-called civil society movement in the 1980s. As of this writing, they are treated as a part of a large number of rather nonpolitical, nongovernmental organizations, trying to provide welfare and legal help for depriviledged groups, women among them.

The main characteristics of the women's nongovernmental organizations (NGOs) are problematic. They are concentrated primarily in the capital city of Ljubljana. Having an antipolitical orientation and being more interested in solving social problems, they tend to be autarchic and do not receive enough publicity. Above all, they act in a unstable climate of competitiveness instead of one of solidarity which is the result of inadequate funding.

There are some constant trends and relative stability, however, in the work of groups which persist for more than four years. Under their influence, progress has been made regarding the public and institutional treatment of violence against women; some public strength has been gained in the defense of the constitutive abortion solution. There exist some successful long-term projects, such as the SOS Hotline, the Women's Shelter Project, and some socialization and lesbian projects through the Women's Center (where cultural events also take place). Gender studies projects exist in some areas but are fragmented and disorganized.

The main problem that I want to emphasize is that the influence of these groups is, in general, very small. There exists almost no continual, organized political efforts for the improvement of the position of women. There is some *circulus viciosus* present: There is a small number of women in politics, so the few and depoliticized NGOs do not succeed in forming a women's agenda; because there is no agenda, there are few women in politics. Above all, as a consequence of the war and the dissolution of Yugoslavia, most women's groups in Slovenia were left out of (primarily funding) networks on the assumption that Slovenia is developed enough to not need such systemic help. The resulting backlash was unexpected: the total lack of political influence of women in Slovenia in comparison with countries which would be expected to have much worse opportunities.

The political participation of women did not become a constitutive part of the political agenda. Among the main parties, there dominated a viewpoint that men could represent women as well (if not even better) than they could represent themselves. The standard statements of diverse parties were that it was (it would be) appropriate to increase the number of women in politics, though in fact none of them supported any serious political measure to do this. There were demands to finance the parties, to some extent, in correspondence to the percentage of women on voting lists. This proposal failed in parliament. The only concrete step within one party (done after the strong pressure of the Women's faction within the United List of Social Democrats), namely the 40 percent female quota on the candidate lists for the election in Autumn 1996, did not have any factual consequences for the representation. The arguments which were used by some women's factions in favor of increased political partic- ipation of women were refused by the populist-oriented parties and poli- ticians (also women) as a ghetto-ization of women.[47]

If women were the losers of the first multiparty elections in 1990, the election in autumn 1996 represented a real backlash in their political representation. It obviously became a part of tradition in the women's movements and their demands for gender equality in Slovenia, that "more important issues" prevailed over them; namely, despite many ac- tive and successful women at the level of economic and lower political levels (consultants, advisers and similar nonpublic functions and prepara- tory positions within the state and party apparatuses) they were not repre- sented at all at the highest public political level. The fact that only seven women were elected to parliament (no political party has had more than one women representative in the parliament) and there was no women minister in the government showed their sad "realistic" position within politics.

Despite the party quota of 40 percent of women on the candidate lists, not even one woman from the United List of Social Democrats was elected, which explains how all parties put the female candidates (regard- less of their number) on the lists within those electoral units where the electoral possibilities for the party were smaller.[48] In addition, explana- tions, from both inside and outside the party, for the defeat of the United List of Social Democrats in the election (down from 14 percent in 1992 to 9 percent in 1996) blamed scapegoats, namely, the many women on the lists.

CONCLUSION

Liberal-democratic institution- and elite-building, along with economic reforms, were the main activities and relevant political and research issues of the so-called transitional period to democracy. The main problem I see in connection to this process is that women, in spite of their men- tioned readiness to adapt, were not politically active in this period. Even more, the new institutions were mainly built under the assumption of nontransformed traditional social-political divisions: private and public relationships and presupposed gender divisions within the family and their functions for the state and economy. In this sense, the shift from the socialist paternalism that built huge social facilities for "solving" the housework problem to the liberalism that relied on the "good old family" (without factual equality measures) shows that, without the efforts to change traditional partner relationships, family conditions, and daily life, there is no serious chance for the active political participation of women. In a time of overall transformation and hyper-legislation, which is con- nected to many legal obscurities, the new institutions automatically pro- duced gender-hierarchic structures. Political institutions are the core of this process and it seems that there is no additional sexism needed for the progress of this pattern, only a powerful gender-neutral ideology of freedom.

8

WOMEN IN CROATIA: FEMINISTS, NATIONALISTS, AND HOMOSEXUALS

Tatjana Pavlović

Post-communist Croatia is marked by a radical redefinition of all of its "values." National identity, the concept of family, motherhood, and the cult of masculinity are all inscribed with new meanings. But, above all, the central contested issue in Croatian media and politics is that of the family. During the 1997 Croatian elections, the streets of Zagreb were saturated with posters encouraging Croatian people to vote for the party in power, the Croatian Democratic Union (HDZ). One poster depicted a jovial and exemplary Croatian family of six with the father as the central figure. He is talking on the phone while his whole family is gazing at him. Everyone is smiling. In this family, as in Croatia, there is no space for discontent. The poster's slogan reads: "For a peaceful, safe, and rich Croatia."

The family, which once occupied a private space, has been aggressively pushed into the public realm. The family unit has become essential for the newly born narratives of national destiny. An analogy has emerged between the new state and the patriarchal family. Croatian President Franjo Tudjman has often repeated in his speeches that "our State is a big family." After his speech in Knin,[1] Istrian pop-star Marinela sang to the president:

> Heavenly voices are heard on high
> Across the sea and mountains of Croatia
> O, homeland, you are our mother
> Wise father, you are our leader!

In this big, newly founded family, the president is our "wise" father and the homeland is our mother. The concept of motherhood obtains its sacred place in Croatian national discourse. If Croatia itself becomes the mother, it is only logical that the Croatian woman herself is reduced to a reproductive function. In her article "From Reverence to Rape," Vesna Kesić notes that one of the first notions to be reconceptualized in post-communist Croatia was that of the "socialist woman." Woman became "homeland-mother, woman-soil, and mother-Croatia."[2]

The father metaphors were also radically reconceptualized in the postwar period. The father in the HDZ campaign poster occupies the central position in the family, President Tudjman is the wise father of the Nation, and the rest of the country's popular imagination is filled with father-warriors (defenders both of their families and the newly created nation). The defenders also become the decision makers. At a press conference in 1992, President Tudjman said that "just as in any other family, in Croatia, someone always must have the last word, someone that will make a decision in case of conflicts."

The HDZ campaign poster tells us a lot about the homogeneous and rigid vision of the Croatian family and national identity. Its emphasizes the three most important political issues: demographics, national identity, and gender roles. This newly envisioned Croatian family (monogamous and patriarchal) illustrates the return to the most traditional and oppressive values. Its conventional gender roles convey a certain sense of stability. In post-communist Croatian narratives, stability is constructed in terms of a return to conservative values. This stability also depends on the national identity of the members of the family. The success of the HDZ poster is derived partially from an assumption that the members of the family depicted on the poster are ethnic Croatians. It is clear that their nationality is not one of any other national group living in Croatia. In an ethnically mixed space, this "exemplary" Croatian family excludes many other families living in the Nation. The family on the HDZ poster consists of six members. However, in Croatian postwar economic reality, it is almost impossible to imagine such a large family. The politics of demographic renewal clash with the economic situation of the country. Economic realities notwithstanding, large families, rigid gender roles, and national identity are portrayed as a foundation for "peaceful, safe and rich Croatia."

The HDZ poster states certain unwritten laws about gender, sex, and the Nation. The problematic of family, gender, and Nation is indissoluble in contemporary Croatian society. After all, Nation-ness is conceived as an invisible boundary.[3] The new Croatian state was simultaneously formed with its post-communist national boundaries. At that moment both the Croatian state and the family established themselves and their boundaries. The regulation of the family paralleled the regulation of its national borders. Croatia needed to separate itself from any elements of Otherness. "Pure" ethnicity became its sole identity.

Anxieties about the Nation and the family are inseparable from anxieties about masculinity and femininity. The climate of war made gender roles even more rigid than before. In post-communist Croatia women lost and are still losing the "privileges" they enjoyed earlier. Their new identity and the identity of the Nation became inseparable. They are not just women, they are reduced to the category of *Croatian* women. They are tied to their home and their nation. The usual confinement of women to their domestic spaces is intensified through this forced connection.

The domestication of women goes hand in hand with the creation of a new male category: hypermasculinity. There is irony in the fact that hypermasculinity is precisely an element that successfully traverses national borders. Rambo-like characters spring across national boundaries.[4] As Croatian novelist Dubravka Ugrešić notes in her article "Because We Are Boys," the war strengthened the unmistakable traits of *homo balcanicus*. Ugrešić describes a typical Saturday morning in the Croatian capital of Zagreb, where groups of men are hanging about leisurely. "Men are scattered, some with newspaper in hand, smoking, chatting, walking about the street with purpose, exchanging smiles, pats on the back, friendly nudging and embracing" and women loaded with their market groceries "with austere expressions hurry home to prepare Saturday's lunch."[5] This scene comes straight out of the mythologized concept of Yugoslavia, "the Yugo-imaginary, regardless of whether it is tied to Zagreb or Belgrade, urban or rural, catholic or orthodox, 'western' or 'eastern' milieu." Women and men of post-communist Croatia live in different and separated spheres. Ugrešić points out that another crucial trait of *homo balcanicus* is his conception of "woman as the lower being." In colloquial Croatian-Serbian the term for woman is *pička* (cunt): "Woman trapped in a male linguistic jargon is reduced to her sexual organ."[6]

Since a woman is only a cunt, *homo balcanicus* is not threatened by her. However, *homo balcanicus* is obsessed by its own, more threatening Other: the homosexual. The homosexual occupies an important space in the Croatian national subconscious. For *homo balcanicus*, homosexuality provokes anxieties, obsessions, feelings of contempt, and a fear of being effeminated. War jokes, political jokes, and satire are filled with homosexual connotations. There is currently a saturation of homosexual caricatures that are mocked and devaluated. From time to time, political magazines portray two naked, male politicians together in degrading homosexual poses. Even the president himself was not spared such a portrayal. During the peace talks, President Tudjman and Serbian President Slobodan Milošević were very often depicted naked, holding hands and touching each other's body parts.

Serbs are another target of this Balkan homophobia. This is especially evident in ultranationalistic publications.[7] Both Serbs and homosexuals "betray" the Nation. Ethnic and sexual scapegoating go hand in hand and are justified by imaginary, arbitrary borders. The homosexual/Serb exemplifies the creation, reification, and expulsion of the Other. It is an undesirable element in both family and national rhetoric. On the level of the family, the homosexual is a dark counterpart of the hypermasculine father/defender/warrior. On the national level, its signification is fluid and often used to mark Serbian elements. Both are elements that are expulsed from national culture and national identity.

When President Tudjman was asked about homosexuality,[8] he said: "Homosexuality has been present since the very first human communities. Therefore, there would not be any sense to either forbid it or accept it, since it is always present anyway. From a humanistic point of view it would be better to accept it and to keep it discrete (invisible)." In a deeply ironic sense, by uttering this comment on homosexuality, Tudjman quite exactly simulates the role of the wise father. He is wiser than his nation, which calls for the expulsion of homosexuals. The new masculine wisdom is satisfied by silencing expressions of homosexuality, thus driving it "into the closet." Post-communist Croatia admits only silenced difference. Vesna Kesić observes that "Croatian identity would have been better articulated if it recognized difference (Otherness). That would have been a more creative way of forming Croatian culture, identity, and political visions than having this pure ethnic space with the phantasm of the State."[9]

Therefore, the idyllic depiction of the Croatian family on the HDZ campaign poster is a pure fantasy (a national dream) which tries to hide all the elements which may disturb it. The family which appears as the source of continuity, nurturance, and social stability hides multiple conflicts and turmoil beneath its ideality. These unwanted elements are manifest as the creation, reification, and expulsion of the Other. Sameness is a prerequisite for living in Croatia. Ironically, the need for strong boundaries (both in ethnic and sexuality terms) is, in a Freudian sense, "the narcissism of small differences."[10]

In post-communist Croatia, there is a very clear attempt to regulate and promote certain narratives and sexualities and prohibit others. The sexual body becomes primarily the national body. On one hand, there is the regulation of this sexual body; on the other hand, there is the regulation of critical thinking accompanied by a proliferation of nationalistic rhetoric. Very few people have refused to be plotted in the narratives of national revival proliferating throughout Croatia and the other republics that once comprised socialist Yugoslavia. Croatian nationalism is mostly unquestioned and justified by the war situation, aggression against Croatian borders, precariousness of national identity, and so on. The aim of this chapter is to defamiliarize this nationalism through analysis of discourses on motherhood, masculinity and homosexuality.

MOTHERHOOD: "CROATIAN STORKS, WHERE DID THEY GO?"

Marija Bajt, a member of the ruling party in one of the sessions of Assembly showed a great preoccupation over the sudden "disappearance of storks" from Croatia. She entitled her speech "Kamo lete hrvatske rode?" ("Croatian storks, where did they go?"). By asking herself that question, she articulated one of the most important issues in today's Croatia, that of motherhood and demographic renewal. Bajt's preoccupation is closely linked with conservative policies of prohibiting abortions and placing women only in their reproductive context.

Her question inspired waves of response and comment. The progressive feminist groups immediately started demystifying Bajt's arguments by pointing out its profoundly antifeminist assumptions. It also drew a heavy response from conservative political parties and women's groups. Petar Zilnik, a fifty-eight-year-old lawyer from Varaždin and deputy of the Croatian Peasant Party, said that Bajt's question inspired him because it was posed from the woman's point of view. This is precisely the most disturbing trend in Croatia: the alliance between the conservative political parties and conservative women groups.

The alliance of one wing of Croatian feminism with the government and its ruling party is all the more troubling in view of Croatian nationalism's patriarchal cast. Another pervasive HDZ slogan "Uredimo naš dom" ("Let's put our house in order") applies as much to the domestic sphere (in the sense of "a woman's place is in the home") as it does to the public sphere (the metaphor of Nation as a whole as a home). In Croatian nationalist ideology, where the patriarchal nuclear family becomes the pillar of the Nation and the center of spiritual values, there is a strong need for radical and independent feminist thought.

While Croatian conservative women's groups are supported by the government, radical feminists are vilified and destroyed. The most disturbing case, that of "the five witches," happened in the beginning of the 1992 war. On 11 December 1992, Zagreb's popular weekly *Globus* published an article entitled "Croatian Feminists Rape Croatia." The article claimed to be exposing Croatian feminists' "lies" to the Croatian people. It accused five "feminist witches" (Jelena Lovrić, Rada Iveković, Slavenka Drakulić, Vesna Kesić and Dubravka Ugrešić) of "dissimulating" the rapes of Bosnian and Croatian women. They were guilty, the article said, of "covering up the truth," because they had analyzed these wartime rapes in terms of gender instead of seeing rape solely as a consequence of Serbian aggression. They also linked it to the general position of women in war, and to the masculinization of wartime Croatian society. *Globus* further insisted that Croatia's prestige in the world community had been seriously damaged by these five women writers. The "five witches" were accused of undermining their country by writing in the foreign press not only about the position of women in Croatian post-communist society but also about press censorship, media manipulation, and restrictions on freedom of speech in Croatia. In all-too-typical irony, the five feminists were vilified for airing dirty laundry in public by publishing their criticism abroad, precisely when no one dared to publish them within Croatia.

The most outrageous thing in the *Globus* article was a chart, classifying the five women by nationality, marital status, political affiliation, home, occupation, age, number of children, travel abroad during the war, and suspect opinions—this aforementioned issue was based on statements taken out of context. The chart's crude characterization of the five women's politics and professional work was virtually an open invitation to public harassment. In addition, its mixing of the public with the personal was designed to play directly into traditional antifeminist stereotypes. The article asserted:

> Since most of these ladies had serious problems in finding male partners as well as real and serious fields of intellectual interest, they chose feminism as their own "destiny," ideology and profession. . . . The few among them who, despite their theoretical position and physical appearance, did succeed in finding marriage partners, chose according to the official Yugoslav standards: a Serb from Belgrade by Iveković, a Serb (two times) from Croatia by Drakulić, and a Serb from Croatia by Lovrić.[11]

In the same vein, another article in *Globus*, several months later, alleged that Western feminists were taking up collections in order to improve their Zagreb sisters' appearance by buying them cosmetics.

Through the attacks on these women and their position on rapes in the Bosnian war, the entire tradition of Croatian and Yugoslav feminism is being denounced by the government-sponsored press. Feminism is portrayed by the Croatian media as being both crudely equivalent to hatred of men and a part of the old Marxist/communist/Yugoslav political milieu. This is particularly ironic since, in the times of socialism, the group Žena i društvo (Women and Society) to which Iveković, Drakulić, and Kesić belonged, was denounced by Communist Party leaders as "an anti-Communist and anti-Marxist element, which drags into Croatia the bourgeois and decadent ideology of the West."

But the more things change, the more they remain the same; the categories of political opprobrium are different but the paranoia and the antifeminist rhetoric continue unaltered. Now the very same feminists were being denounced as leftist, Marxist, and Yugoslav elements. They were accused of nostalgia for the communist past when, supposedly, "reds, homosexuals, Maoists, and lesbians" led lives of comfort and privilege. And they were charged, on this basis, with organizing to discredit the future Croatian state. "Everyone who remembers those fairly unhappy and frustrated women can call themselves witnesses of the birth of one of the organized centers of international defamation of the Croatian war of self-defense. . . . Worried about their comfort, they spread lies in conspiracy against Croatia abroad.''[12]

If Croatian nationalism, like communism before it, has attacked feminism from without, it has also co-opted it from within. The most radical wave of Croatian feminism crested in the late 1980s with groups like Tresnjevka, Lilit, SOS-telefon, and the lesbian group Purple Initiative. These groups formed part of a feminist network within the rest of Yugoslavia, but such links were destroyed by the break-up of Yugoslavia and the beginning of war. The movement toward national homogenization (in both Croatia and Serbia) did not leave any space for alternative modes of organization, especially ones which sought to unify women from different parts of the former Yugoslavia.

Within Croatia, one large group of feminists adopted a patriotic, nationalistic stance and subordinated women's issues to the so-called national interest. The nationalist feminist groups Kareta and Bedem Ljubavi allied themselves both with the HDZ and, internationally, with antipornography crusader Catherine MacKinnon. These groups have even joined the government in attacking the "five witches"; at the same time that they see the rapes of Croatian women in Bosnia exclusively in national terms, they have denounced Vesna Kesić for allegedly writing for pornographic magazines.

These groups are also very vocal in issues surrounding motherhood and demographics. They are involved with other conservative organizations and individuals working in this direction. Marija Bajt, Petar Zilnik, Don Anto Baković, and Ružica Cavar are just a few of the names on the Croatian scene now. The most influential conservative organizations are the HPP (Croatian Population Movement) and the Zavod za zaštitu materinstva, obitelji i djece (Institute for the Protection of Motherhood, Family, and Children). The Institute for the Protection of Motherhood, Family, and Children is led by a women's organization Hrvatska žena (Croatian Woman) and its goal is the negation of traditional and Catholic moral values. The Croatian Population Movement is headed by Don Anto Baković and Ružica Cavar. Its monthly publication, in which Don Anto Baković is very vocal in presenting his views, is called *Narod* (People). In Baković's article "Contemplation on Spiritual Renewal" (in his *Spiritual Renewal of Croatia* [Zagreb, 1992]), he wrote that "in terms of abortion we still live in Serbo-communism."[13] Once again the national identity becomes inseparable from motherhood and gender problems. The place of women in society is conceptualized as the space of national being. Without her nationality a Croatian mother ceases to be a mother. Her very identity is her nationality, which is the precondition of her motherhood.

Motherhood is one of the most important issues for Petar Zilnik. He has expressed his nostalgia for some "past, imaginary, pre-communist" Croatia, lamenting the "disappearance" of the cult of motherhood: "I would love if the cult of motherhood, that was once so well developed, returned. With women's emancipation it was watered down significantly."[14]

Popular culture is saturated with these themes as well. One recent Croatian film to dwell on these motifs is Branko Schmidt's melodrama *Vukovar se vraća kući*, the story of father and son bonding over their lost city (Vukovar), their lost Nation, and their "lost" mother. The father returns from the war where he has lost a leg. Their loss creates all sorts of psychological and emotional problems which culminate in his sexual impotency. The mother of the family is the only functional character. She is trying to earn some money translating for foreign humanitarian aid workers in the area. She is mistreated by her drunken and abusive husband but finds solace in friendship with a German humanitarian worker. She is immediately labeled a whore and the rest of the film centers on pathological feelings that the father of the family develops for his wife, country, city, and son. However, the viewer is supposed to sympathize with the father figure. Gender problems are completely overlooked and overshadowed by the national cause. The theme of mother-betrayal is recurrent in the film. There is another boy in the film who lost his father in the war. Blaming the loss of his father and city on his mother, he takes out all his aggression and frustration on her, calling her a whore and mistreating her repeatedly. In this case, the son replicates the character of abusive father from the first family. All of the male characters have fantasies of an "ideal" mother and if those fantasies are not met they become abusive to their "fallen" idols.

Vukovar se vraća kući is not the only example of misogyny and nationalism in recent Croatian film. Bogdan Žižic's film *Cijena života* centers on a "Rambo"-type soldier whose mission is saving a Croatian mother and son stranded on the enemy side. The film centers on the male hero whose hypermasculinity dominates most of the scenes. The narrative of nationalistic revival has religious overtones such as sacrifice, loyalty, strength, courage. The mother in the film is constructed as a passive entity. Her destiny is conceived as inseparable from that of her son. This film is a "masterpiece" on the two discourses mentioned before: motherhood and the cult of masculinity.

Dubravka Ugrešić has remarked that Yugoslav films of the last fifty years have been directed almost exclusively by male directors who incessantly "explored" the character of the whore who was "often brutally raped or beaten." Ugrešić points out that "a scene that was repeated a thousand times in Yugoslav film involved women's clothes being ripped off, a hairy male hand on naked woman breast, and blows of the male hand falling upon women's cheeks."[15] Contemporary Croatian film replaces brutality toward women with reverence and idealizes the mother figure, at least as long as the mother does not rebel against the attributes that are ascribed to her in the narratives of new Croatia.

Zilnik and his obsessions with the cult of motherhood prompted him to envision an elaborate system of "rewards" for deserving mothers.[16] Mothers with three children get a silver pin, mothers with five children get a gold pin, and mothers with ten or more children get a diamond pin. He emphasizes that "the diamonds would have to be real even if they are very little." On top of that Zilnik, suggests that mothers with more than three children get their groceries at a 10 percent discount and those with more than five children get free visits to cultural and art shows. "I am from Varaždin, we all know each other here and I know women with large families who never miss one single theater performance or concert. Of course, not all women have these interests, but those who do have it should have a free access to it." Fathers would also get small pins that would get them into football games for free. Zilnik also suggests that all the "deserving" mothers place their pins in visible places so "whoever sees such a pin will recognize a deserving mother."

Zilnik's obsession with motherhood is derived from his unfounded fear for his Nation. He claims that "we are in danger of becoming a national minority in Croatia." On the contrary, the Croatian problem is precisely tendency to obliterate or silence any other national minority living on its territory. Because of all of this and other outrageous claims, it is surprising that Zilnik does not advocate the prohibition of abortion. His view on abortion is that it should not be prohibited because abortion proves to be a very unsuccessful method. Instead Zilnik proposes the "mandatory consultation of pregnant women with their husbands, psychiatrists, parents and priests."[17]

It would be an easy task to see Zilnik, with his political views, as an extremist. Many dismiss the influence of people like Zilnik and other conservative groups as trivial and exaggerated. However, if one compares carefully Zilnik's views with the direction in which the legal status of women is moving there are astonishing conclusions. In Croatia, many doctors already recommend that women seeking abortions should make an appointment with a so-called abortion committee.[18] These committees do not have a legal status in Croatia and they are basically appointed by themselves. However, many women are pushed into consulting with the abortion committee. Several of these committees consist of pro-life doctors and even some priests. Dafinka Večerina, a lawyer interested in questions of women in Croatia, observes, "How could a woman who is atheist be forced to talk to a priest about her most intimate problems? The priest could be both nice and smart, but he should not force upon the women his worldview. That is completely inappropriate in our times."[19]

Vesna Kesić points out that conservative organizations are much closer to the state than we think and warns us against dismissing their connections. For example, Don Anto Baković and his HPP (Croatian Population Movement) were initially closely connected with the party, but in time Baković dissociated himself from the HDZ, even though he continued working in similar directions. The Program for Demographic Development passed by the Croatian Parliament stated that "due to a higher deathrate than birthrate" there was a huge and general threat of extinction of the Croatian Nation. They called for stopping the "national hemorrhage."[20] Increasing the national birthrate is described as "demographic renewal of Croatian people and family." Demographic renewal should be backed-up by a "positive spiritual atmosphere and protection of the family as a basic society unit" which is the "headquarters of the renewal of nation and state." The speech and behavior of public persons "will incorporate respect toward life from conception until natural death, as well as respect toward women, marriage and family."[21]

They also conceived of "positive" measures for population policy for women with several children, such as prolonged paid maternity leave, tax reduction, child support, health, and social security for parents with three or more children, and so on. The Labor Act, which took effect in January 1996, recognized women with four or more children as "Mother Educators" and proposed to give them a professional status with salary. Unfortunately, the Croatian state does not fulfill its existing laws and the state budget can not cover these expenses.

The outrageous ideas of Don Ante Baković, Petar Zilnik, Marija Bajt and others are promoted while the concerns of feminist "witches" are ridiculed, silenced, and obliterated. Alternative narratives are disappearing and what is left are fewer and fewer options for women to "plot" themselves into a new Croatian (his)tory. There is a popular Croatian song in which a girl is singing for her sweetheart in the army:

> Moj je dragi u narodnoj gardi tjera dušmane
> A ja molim Boga da se vrati slobodu donese
> Kad se vrati bit će svatovi
> A na krovu barjak pravi crven, bijeli, plavi.

> (My darling is in the army pushing back the enemy
> And I pray to God he returns and brings with him our freedom
> When he returns, we will wed
> And on the roof will wave our homeland's flag, red, white and
>   blue.)

Army, enemy, God, freedom, wedding, and flag are prominent in the narrative of both this song and of Croatia today. Dafinka Večerina sums up brilliantly the status of woman in post-communist Croatia: "Woman in the war can only be a wife of the dead hero, or a mother of the dead hero, or a daughter of the dead hero."[22]

THE CULT OF MASCULINITY: "BE A MAN."

While motherhood depends on remaining within one's nation and its national boundaries, the creation of (hyper)masculinity cuts across national boundaries. In Belgrade, Rambo Amadeus declared: "Neću da budem intelektualac, oću da opalim Vesnu Zmijanac" (I don't want to be an intellectual, I want to fuck Vesna Zmijanac). When Amadeus was accused of sexism, Vesna Zmijanac herself came to his defense: "Let the boy do his work, after all it is a propaganda for me as well."

Ugrešić recounts another episode where, in Priština, Kosovo, three rowdy youngsters burned the skirt of a young gypsy girl who was walking down the street with her child. When asked if she would sue them she replied, "They were only kidding."[23] One could continue giving similar examples from other states of former Yugoslavia. All of these incidents are closely linked with *homo balcanicus* and its conception of masculinity and femininity. These incidents demonstrate that woman indeed is conceived in terms of her sex organ. For *homo balcanicus* she is a cunt and little more. But the most interesting thing is the way in which word "cunt" is used to signify other things, and the way in which it is used within male groups. To threaten someone one can say, "Dobit ćes po pički"; to indicate then someone is a coward, "Šutio je kao pička"; and to demonstrate one's superior masculinity, "Prebio sam ga kao pičku."[24]

A poster recruiting for Croatian army reads, "Be a man." A piece of Zagreb's antiwar propaganda reads, "The hand is better off on the cunt than on the gun." The second statement is only the flip side of the first one. The HPT (Croatian Post Office and Telecommunications) issued phone cards with different motifs. On the front of one of the cards there is a slogan, "One more child for the State"; and on the back, "Children are Croatia's blessing." The image on the card is of smiling children's faces against the background of the Croatian emblem. The central space of the phone card is reserved for a boy in uniform.

The creation of this new, hypermasculine *homo balcanicus* is accompanied by songs that glorify him. These songs are called "folksies."[25] Their style is erotico-gastronomic: "You left me to cry, you didn't try my apple pie"; erotico-accommodating: "When at last my mother goes, I can live here with my Rose"; and erotico-cultural: "On the sheet two red drops appear, proof that you were the first, my dear."

Folksies more than ever permeate the space of post-communist Croatia. A popular tape from the beginning of the war was entitled *Cro-Army: Ready for the Homeland.* Some argue that it was an extremist, nationalistic tape and that it was not representative of the Croatian situation as whole. However, several songs on that tape were major hits on most of the radio stations in Croatia (for example "Čavoglave, My sweetheart is in the Army"). The cover of *Cro-Army: Ready for the Homeland* depicts a man in tight black army fatigues; his muscles are exaggerated, and his right hand is raised above his head as he holds a big machine gun. He wears black gloves, dark glasses, and an army hat. The soldier's straightened body seems to emerge from the mine fields that are exploding behind him. Looking at this image one can not help but associate it with Rambo, one of the most visible icons of masculinity in North American culture. The body of the Croatian soldier—strengthened with the Rambo-like signs of masculinity—projects the image of invincibility. His body is objectified and aestheticized and he becomes a sign of masculinity par excellence.

Cro-Army: Ready for the Homeland is full of songs that perfectly illus-

trate the cult of hypermasculinity in today's Croatia. One of the most
interesting songs is "E, moj druže Beogradski" (O, my Belgrade friend
[comrade])

> Beautiful Belgrade girls, you really knew how to kiss.
> I still remember my little blond darling from Novi Sad.
> Her villages, too, I came to love, riding through Dunav and Sava.
> O, I was so happy then.
>
> O, my Belgrade friend,
> We knew all the Serbian songs.
> And once we sang "Hail Mary, queen of Croatians."
>
> O, my Belgrade friend,
> We will meet again near Sava.
> And you will know me and you will shoot.
>
> I will not even aim and will pray to God that I will miss you.
> But in the end, I will not miss.
> I will mourn you and close your eyes.
> Oh, I was so sad because I lost my friend.

This is a song about male bonding and separation. Both emotions are
based on ambiguous feelings of rivalry and hate. In this rivalry, sexual
power has a crucial place. A Croatian soldier, the main character of the
song, is lamenting the end of his friendship with his Belgrade comrade.
He recalls with nostalgia the times when both Serbs and Croats lived
together because of "[b]eautiful Belgrade girls . . . [their] villages, too, I
came to love, riding through Dunav and Sava. . . . O, I was so happy
then." His lament is centered on the Serbian girls he used to kiss and
love and that he may not kiss or love any more.

In this folksie women are not important per se. They are merely a
vehicle for male bonding and rivalry. As Gayle Rubin points out in "The
Traffic in Women," woman is only a replaceable object in the relationship between the two men.[26] This song also "relives" the rivalry from the
times of the Yugoslav army, which was a place for articulating myths of
masculinity in the former Yugoslavia, such as "Postojao je mit kako Hr-
vati, eto, *ne mogu* kao što *mogu* Srbi i Crnogorci" (There was a myth that

Croats *can't* the way Serbs and Montenegrins *can*).[27] *Can't* and *can*, of course, refer to sexual potency of all the mentioned parties.

The song's ending sums up the dynamics between the two male subjects. After nostalgically recalling the good old times, the Croatian soldier tells us of his fantasy of the re-encounter with his former friend and Belgrade comrade. In sum, this song is a lament over the killing of a former friend with whom the killer had shared women and song. It is hypermasculinity at its most raw, most naked form; it is simply about annihilating a rival male.

The masculinization of Croatian society in conditions of nationalism heated up by war created two types of men. These men are visible in every segment of society and are exemplified in the main characters of Žižić's film *Cijena života* and Schmidt's film *Vukovar se vraća kući*. Žižić's Rambo-like hero saves a Croatian mother and her son and who defends his country. The other type is a father figure from Schmidt's film. This character loses his leg, his sexual potency, his city, and his wife. Both characters are examples of the triumph and failure of men and the impossibility of creating an identity outside of the parameters of the Nation.

HOMOSEXUALITY: "COME ON, DON'T BE A FAGGOT!"

In the previous section on hypermasculinity, we have seen that to express cowardice one can say "Šutio je kao pička" (He was quiet as a cunt). However instead of saying "Šutio je kao pička," one can also say "Baš je peder" (He is such a faggot). Both expressions are used almost synonymously. Therefore, a coward is a man who acts like a woman or like a homosexual. One can often say "faggot" when one wants to offend someone. However, there are various popular uses of "faggot" which sound so familiar in the Croatian language that they have even lost their offensive meaning. One person can say to another "Ne budi peder" (Don't be a faggot) or "Pederčino" (You big faggot) almost in an endearing way. "Ne budi peder" can translate simply as "Oh, come on," or "Don't be like that." Therefore, the phrase "Don't be a faggot" has quite an extensive use. Izabela Albini, in her article "Život i svijet dostojan covjeka," points out that " 'FAGGOT' really sounds familiar and Croatian."[28]

Hence, the word faggot permeates all of the spaces of popular culture. But whenever homosexuality is brought up as a serious political or social issue, it is shrouded in silence. The very first Croatian gay magazine was published as a supplement to *Arkzin*.[27] It was called *Speak Out* and was published thanks to a gay activist from the somewhat invisible group LIGMA (Lesbian and Gay Men Action) from Zagreb (founded 1992). The photograph that accompanies the introduction to this first issue is of two gay men each with a bandage over his eyes, holding hands. One is wearing the T-shirt, with the text, "I'm not gay, but my boyfriend is"; the other one's shirt says "boyfriend." The bandages over their eyes is the metaphor of "silenced" homosexuality in Croatia. In certain ways, President Tudjman's wish that homosexuality should be "as unnoticeable as possible" is actually the reality.

The discourse on homosexuality is only vocal when it is used as the means of designating the Other as an unwanted element of Croatian society. A homosexual is defined by a different ethnic background and by feminization. A homosexual is not one of us. By that very logic he is anyone who is not Croatian. Homosexuals have a very precarious social position. In a certain sense, they render visible what is rendered unspeakable.

Unorthodox forms of desire and sexual experimentation are unacceptable in the times of anxiety that accompany the formation of the Nation. However, this silencing articulates the emergence of certain types of homosexual practices. Croatian homosexuals are extremely closeted. In the Croatian capital city of Zagreb, the only public space in which homosexuals gather is the disco *Aquarius* on Saturday nights. Needless to say, it is really a regular dance club with a corner reserved for the "gay" crowd. It is impossible to use visual codes of recognition which one would use in any other cities. One can meet other homosexuals only through one's network of friendships and connections.

In Zagreb, on 8 January 1995, Klub 88 organized one of the first big gay parties, called a "balloon party." The balloon party promised to feature "craziness in a multiplicity of balloons." There were a couple of go-go boys and some stripping, as well as projections of gay male pornographic films. However, many people felt disappointed at the lack of transgressive and intense performance. Boris Raseta called it "decently Victorian male striptease," lamenting a lack of Visconti's, Fassbinder's, and Almodovar's sensibility. He also notes that the only couple passionately kissing and caressing at the "balloon party" was a heterosexual one. Therefore, even the bit of space open for homosexuals is invaded.

Societal homophobia also translates into self-censoring. In some ironic sense, we can say that every Croatian lesbian is a "lipstick lesbian" since codes of femininity seem to give a women a guarantee not to be mistaken for a lesbian. The fear of being labeled a lesbian is not surprising considering the fierce Balkan machismo. The depiction of lesbians is as stereotypical as the popular imagination's conception of male homosexuals. Ugrešić notes that, in the former Yugoslavia, any posters with women on them were already defaced by the next morning. "For Yugo-men there is nothing funnier than a woman with a mustache attacked by a multitude of penises."[30] Ugrešić notes that posters with men on them do not attract such behavior.

There is a striking difference between the private and public lives of Croatian homosexuals. In Zagreb, one can find homemade Croatian gay videos, drag queen parties, and cruising spots, but only if one penetrates the invisible world of the gay underground. One drag show features two drag queens dressed as butterflies (with green and blue see-through dresses); one video stars a drag queen as an innocent village woman who comes to the big metropolis (Zagreb) and is forced to prostitute herself. Famous cruising spots are renamed after famous Western gay hangout places (Central Park, Broadway, Miami Beach). It is interesting to study official changes in street names[31] in Croatia as a mean of obliterating a certain "unwanted" history, and of the simultaneous creation of invisible, yet real, homosexual spaces.

These "invisible" scenes and discourses form a private space that co-exists with a much harsher reality. Gay-bashing is a silenced issue. After a soccer game which Croatia lost to Germany, a group of soccer fans went to a park where male homosexuals socialize and beat up several of them. Soccer, nationalism, and masculinity were all brought together in this act. It is a drastic example of Balkan intolerance. But even analyzing "gay-friendly" articles shows a similar kind of mental framework.

One of the very interesting "gay-friendly" articles is an interview with Croatian writer Predrag Raos, a somewhat controversial (offbeat) figure in Zagreb's literary circles. He was interviewed after translating Jay Green's book *Chico*, which was the first gay novel published in Croatia. The assumption of the interviewer was that Raos, by translating a gay novel, is somehow in danger of being perceived as homosexual. Therefore, the whole article is full of double entendre questions. It wants to appear transgressive by interviewing someone who might have had some kind of experience or insight into homosexual circles. However, the article ends with a clear indication of Raos's heterosexuality. It is clear that the *Chico* interview expresses the unease and anxiety of certain writers and

intellectuals when confronted with homosexuality. Raos and his interviewer are both trying to be liberal and accepting of homosexuality but
their conversation is full of the worst clichés about homosexual (sub)cul-
ture. The interview opens with following dialogue between Raos and Desnica:

> DESNICA: It seems that as many others you were also charmed by
> Chico. Did you like men before as well? Translating *Chico*, how
> did you feel? I mean physiologically?
> RAOS: Great. It was a pleasure to translate it.
> DESNICA: Why?
> RAOS: Because of the tongue, very lively tongue.[32]
> DESNICA: Are you referring to the English language or all of those
> tongues that were bringing Chico to ecstasy?

The title of the interview is "Pederluk je zakonom propisan" (Faggotism
is prescribed by law). The image that accompanies the article is a photograph of Predrag Raos gazing seductively at the reader and holding
tightly a small black cat. In the background, we see his computer and
telephone. The interviewer is Vladimir Desnica who took the photograph as well. In the introduction, Desnica writes, "The reader who
opens this book will probably start reading it in order to be introduced
to the life of a young homosexual. If he closes the book with the conviction that he read the story of a young man's tragedy, then we can say that
the book was worth publishing." Raos has a similar opinion: "I think that
it is absurd to speak about the rights of the homosexuals, that is a stupid-
ity. The only thing that exists are universal human rights."

Both of these observations pinpoint the status of homosexuality in
Croatia. Both Raos and Desnica are much more liberal and accepting of
homosexuality than the conservative majority that wants to silence and
destroy it. But these "liberals" negate homosexual rights in the name of
"universal" human rights. On the one hand, they want to appear transgressive by dealing with a controversial subject and on the other hand
they are distancing themselves from any real connection with homosexuality as a political or social issue. Raos even adds: "Homosexuals do not
smell good or bad. I have no problems with them as long as they do not
bother me with their uninteresting sexuality."

Another interesting theme that Desnica discusses with Raos is that of
the right to privacy (in terms of one's sexual orientation) and gay "out-

ing." It is striking that they discuss and try to explain their stances on the right to sexual privacy in terms of notions of a right to ethnic privacy. Ethnicity and sexuality are once again inseparable. To make their point, they bring up an incident which happened in Šibenik, a small Croatian coastal town. There was a scandal in Šibenik because the "International children's festival" was opened by a Serbian child. The party officials (HDZ) made this child's nationality public and in the process stigmatized him. Raos observed that that should not have been done. He sees the HDZ's "outing" of the child as the violation of his privacy. He emphasized that he holds the same opinion on publicizing the sexual preference of homosexuals. Then Raos added: "For example, if that boy started to say 'I am Serbian and this is Serbian Šibenik and the International day of a Serbian child,' then everyone would have had right, or even duty to react. It would be the same if for example some homosexual wanted to be a gym teacher."

The interview both shows the connections between sexuality and nationality and displays some incredible beliefs about homosexuals. Raos posits an analogy between the "aggressive" Serbian child (one who displays his nationality in unacceptable ways) and a potentially "child-molesting," homosexual gym teacher. He explains his theory, adding that if a "heterosexual (gym teacher) cannot work with girls, then the homosexual should not be allowed to work with boys."[33] I am personally unaware of any situation in which male gym teachers are not allowed to teach classes to girls. There are plenty of male gym teachers who are not accused of an a priori tendency to "child-molestation." Raos's explanation has both elements of paranoia (certain professions are unsuitable for homosexuals) and a sense of injustice (somehow there is a fear that homosexuals would be privileged over the rest of citizens).

In today's Croatia, there is an abundance of slips and obsessions about gays and lesbians found in many different discourses. Ksenija Urličić, a famous television announcer, discussed a political fight between television and the postal service. In her article in *Globus* on 9 February 1996, she writes:

Through postal phone service you can get anything that you need . . . from tax advice to hot, sexy lesbian entertainment. And underage kids have an access to these services. Croatian postal services encourage, luckily verbal, but still sick impulses of our citizens and youth, while there is no money for science that would really be useful for the youth.[34]

In this curious article, she lumps together pornography and lesbian entertainment as the sick impulses of citizens and youngsters, and sets them against science and knowledge, which could be useful and meaningful for Croatian youth. She is a bit relieved that these sick impulses are at least only verbal. For some reason, she conceives lesbianism and science as mutually exclusive. And in her version, the lesbian situation in Croatia seems to be flourishing. In reality, there are no lesbian clubs, bookstores, bars, or other public places; in terms of law, the homosexual relationship (act) is only conceivable (and punishable) between two men in Croatia. Lesbians are even more invisible than gay men.

The social imagination concerning queers results also in a quasi-scientific discourse on homosexuality. The perfect example of this is an article by Robert Roklica, "Where Do Croatian Homosexuals Fondle?" The author saturates the readers with pseudoscientific facts about Croatian homosexuals. He emphasizes "the rapid growth of agencies specialized in finding partners for homosexuals." He notes that "in the last five years the average age of the first homosexual contact has declined from 22 to 16 years," and he is shocked by the "fact" that "those young homosexuals are usually high school sophomores or juniors and most often they are A students." It is interesting to note that Roklica's and Urličić's "scientific" data directly contradict each other.

Roklica also uses a sensationalist approach to discuss the subject of homosexuality. He is "shocked" by the estimated number of Croatian homosexuals (7 percent). "Homosexuals gather daily in famous bars and restaurants throughout the country, and in Zagreb alone there are around fifteen of those places where men and women come if they want to be entertained with the same sex partners." His description drastically departs from the fact that there are only few places in Zagreb where homosexuals can gather semi-openly.

Another topic covered in Roklica's article is gay marriages. This topic lends itself as a perfect target for authors gripped by homophobia. Roklica mocks Amir Hanusić, the ex-president of LIGMA who married Marko Ungar, a Columbia University professor of political science: "Their marriage took place in San Francisco and the 'bride' Hanusić Ungar is obtaining all the needed documents in order to join his husband Marko." This citation shows that the author cannot possibly conceive of same sex unions outside already existing gender relationships. He assumes that Amir would be a "bride" and Marko a "husband."

The next topic of Roklica's article is Zagreb's homosexual street scene. Once again Roklica shows his need for an "anthropological" excursion into Otherness. He pretends to be looking for some "action" and roams the streets of Zagreb.

> "Youngster, would you like some action for $100?," I was asked by a rough looking macho type.
>
> "There is lots of choice here, I hope to find something cheaper." I tried to find an excuse since I did not want to take any *risks*.
>
> "I would like an underage boy," I said, trying to investigate child prostitution. They told me to go to the botanical Gardens and that visit confirmed my darkest suspicions about child prostitution in its homosexual variant.

Roklica's suspicions about child homosexual prostitution are similar to Raos's fear of gym teachers' potential pedophilia. His curiosity about the Zagreb homosexual scene verges on the unhealthy. Roklica obsessively places himself within the scene that he abhors. The tone of his article is actually similar to the tone of Desnica's interview with Raos.

Roklica ends his article with an interview of a young lesbian, Vesna V. The tone of his description is much more accepting than when he was talking about male homosexuals. It is almost as if by describing lesbianism in detail the author indulges in some private male fantasy. Roklicka's description nearly reads as porn script:

> [Vesna relates:] "Very early on in high school, . . . I had a boyfriend with whom I immediately became intimate. It would be untruthful of me to say I did not enjoy being with him; however I often imagined my best friend Jasna, kissing me and touching my naked body, while being intimate with my boyfriend Zoran. Once I admitted my fantasies to Jasna and was surprised that she was so open to them. She told me that she does not have a boyfriend and that she only loves me and that she is horribly jealous of Zoran. We started to fondle and kiss and since then we are lesbians. I broke up with Zoran and I never missed him since. I can not even imagine what male homosexuals do in bed. I am repulsed by it. With women everything is different." . . . [The] young lesbian Vesna V., . . .

judging by her good looks and feminine behavior, could have any healthy young man.[35]

The interview with Vesna V., Raos and Desnica's conversation, and the popular usage of the term "faggot," all clearly show that gays and lesbians have a clear presence in the popular Croatian imagination, but one that lacks any real social and political power. When Zdenko Radić and LIGMA invited representatives of all the major political parties in Croatia to a panel, "Za koga će glasati homoseksualci?" (For whom are Croatian homosexuals voting?),[36] only two parties attended: the SDP and the ASH. Post-communist Croatia does not accept difference. Izabela Albini observed that "the right of difference became a category of the privileged ones and the rest can only try to survive in a Balkan tavern." [37]

An entire climate of paranoia and fear of Otherness has been systematically produced in the new Croatian state. National homogenization, religious revival, and monopolistic control of the media are combined with a generalized fear of difference and Otherness. Instead of encouraging democratic diversity and openness, the post-communist government sponsors a rigidly constricted "official" culture. During the war, according to the official line, it was immoral to criticize Croatia. President Tudjman declared: "It is clear who deserves the name of intelligentsia, those who are the bearers of national spirit and self-determination. All others are Pharisees." It seems that the "war" situation continues. Sexism and homophobia are correlates of this nationalist chauvinism. During the last year of the war, the Osijek newspaper *Slavonski Magazin*, published an article entitled, "Serbs, Reds, Leftists, Feminists, and Faggots Lead a War Against the War." They only pronounced more blatantly and aggressively what was already present in contemporary Croatian culture. In such a climate, any fluidity of identity becomes impossible: you must be a Croat before all else or you will find yourself excluded. By a strange logic of reversal, feminists are accused of rape and homosexuals are transformed into Serbian aggressors.

9

WOMEN IN SERBIA: POST-COMMUNISM, WAR, AND NATIONALIST MUTATIONS

Žarana Papić

The process of social and political transformations in Central and Eastern Europe since the fall of the Berlin Wall in 1989 has been associated with a rising incidence of violence as an acute social and political problem. Some of the systems in the region initiated turbulent transformations on the path to Western-style political democracy. The problem of violence assumed the character of regional turmoil in the dissolving multiethnic states of Yugoslavia and the Soviet Union.

Although in its milder forms both ethnic and gender violence were present in all other countries of the Eastern bloc as well, these problems became the most severe, ultimately, in Bosnia-Herzegovina. Their overall persistence in post-communist regimes reveals their structural dependency, which allows one to define them as societies of highly charged ethnic, racial, and sexual politics. One could even say that in times of crisis and basic social transformation, the *deconstruction* of the previous

An earlier version of this essay was originally published in War Report, *no. 36 (September 1995) and is reprinted here with revisions by permission of the editors of that publication.*

gendered order is one of the most fundamental factors of change and an effective instrument of the global restructuring of power. Furthermore, since the most influential concept in post-communist state-building processes was the nation-state concept, the ideology of state and ethnic nationalism (based on patriarchal principles) inevitably became the most dominant building force. Various forms of hegemonist nationalism, national separatism, chauvinist and racist exclusion or marginalization of (old and new) minority groups are, as a rule, closely connected with patriarchal, discriminatory, and violent policies against women, policies subversive of women's social and civil rights which had been previously guaranteed under the old communist order.

Although some post-communist states with more or less ethnically "pure" population structures (such as Poland) were not practicing extreme ethnic violence, all of them, to a greater or lesser extent, strategically violated previously acknowledged human rights of women, in the first place the right to abortion, thus showing that the patriarchal recolonization of women's bodies was central to post-communist processes of "democratic" transformations. Because post-communist men have gained decisive political and reproductive control over women, these societies are often labeled "male democracies" or "new patriarchies" or "phallocracies."

The virtual absence of women from politics in post-communist systems also reveals the damaging effects of the communist-patriarchal legacy, which *gave* women legal rights (to work, to equal pay, to education, divorce, and abortion), but strategically prevented them from becoming active political subjects of their own destiny. As the post-communist legislatures became masculinized, East European gender relations have become more gender dichotomized and more sexualized.[1] The situation of acute economic crisis which limited women's other chances gave way to their open sexual abuse, often assuming violent forms, as well as to prostitution, sex-trafficking, pornography, and so on. The disappearance of a communist "equality paradigm" and the old-new conservative ideology of State, Nation, or Religion, in each post-communist country, was crucially based on the strategy of retraditionalization of women's identities, their social roles, and symbolic representations.

The structural connection between ethnic and gender violence is most clearly seen in the case of the breakup of socialist Yugoslavia. Yugoslavia's multiethnic and multicultural structure became the most dramatic site of virulent nationalism, resulting in war. The first post-communist pluralist elections in 1990 resulted in the victory of national and nationalist parties with more or less open xenophobic and patriarchal agendas in all of Yugoslavia's republics, except possibly Macedonia; associated with the new xenophobia were political challenges to women's right of abortion in Slovenia, Croatia, Bosnia, Serbia, and Montenegro. In Serbia, hegemonist ethnic nationalism under the despotic rule of Slobodan Milošević excluded the possibility of a peaceful transition and played the central role in instigating the war in the first place, first in Slovenia, and subsequently in Croatia and Bosnia-Herzegovina. Croatian ethnic-state nationalism also played its part, however, with its racialized project of a "pure" Croatian nation-state.

The genocidal brutality of the ethnic war in Croatia and Bosnia-Herzegovina showed how ethnic hatreds had been provoked and produced for the purpose of constructing the frontiers of *enemy-Otherness* through the fluid and mixed lines of religion, culture, ethnicity, and gender, thus reflecting the contemporary redefinition of racial hostility.[2] Furthermore, ethnic nationalism is based on a politics of specific gender identity/difference in which women are simultaneously mythologized as the Nation's deepest "essence" *and* instrumentalized as its *producer*. This allows one to conclude that the Serbian Hegemonic War could not be easily interpreted as the result of the tribal and "eternal" barbarian mentality of its peoples, but as the contemporary phenomenon of violent, post-communist strategies of redistribution of ethnic-gender power by defining new ethnic and subethnic borders *between men* and their respective (often militarized) elite structures. Also, the nationalist abuse of women sheds light on the phenomenon of totalitarian ethnic nationhood as a naturalized fraternal order, in which women are doubly subjugated: as insiders they are colonized and instrumentalized in their "natural" function as "birth-machines"; and as outsiders they are reified into the targets of destruction as mediated instruments of violence against other men's nations and cultural identity. The abuse of women and their bodies in the "pure" nation-building processes results in two interdependent forms of violence against them: highly restricted or no abortion for the insiders, and, in extreme (but consistent) cases, rape for the outsiders.

Rape became a central feature in the war in Bosnia-Herzegovina, as a systematic strategy or war against women. Mass rape committed by Serb military and paramilitary men was used as a conscious instrument with the purpose of accelerating ethnic cleansing, the destruction of culture, and genocide against the Muslim people of Bosnia. Also, to a lesser degree, there is evidence that all three sides in this war used rape as a form of punishing and humiliating the enemy ethnic group.[3] This war, occurring in "civilized" Europe, showed once more that women's bodies are an essential instrument of male war strategy as a symbolic (and actual) battlefield of men's brutal conquest of other men's ethnic domain in an endless construction of women as the universal Other.

But what has been happening to women and gender relations in Serbia? Serbian women have been close to the war area, yet distant enough not to face the real destruction, bombs, snipers, concentration camps, exile, the heatless winters, and the starving. Although Serbia "was not in the war," as it was officially declared, sociologists defined the situation in Serbia as a "destruction of society," "breakdown," "organized chaos," "disastrous shock," "general disintegration," and "societal turmoil."[4] In the effort to define the situation in Serbia, I am more inclined to characterize it as a set of dramatic social, political, economic, and ideological *mutations*, in which the society of Serbia in the 1980s went through three interconnected stages of Milošević's power: the mutation from state socialism (after he took power in Serbia in late 1987) into state nationalism (before the during the destruction of socialist Yugoslavia)[5] and finally, the mutation of Serbia into a sort of "oriental despotism" during the war and after the Dayton Peace Accords.[6]

The external destruction of one sociocultural identity system in the war is the most brutal form of deconstruction, but life in conditions of malignant internal mutations is, perhaps, equally disastrous because it systematically diminishes and humiliates the basic human values of decency, honesty, tolerance, individual morality, or even more basic assumptions, such as the concept of time (past, present, and future), and those principles assumed to be eternally valid, such as personal identity, or the simple ten commandments (Love thy neighbor and Thou shalt not kill). In Serbia, one could watch them all disappear, only to be replaced with *alien* substitutes[7] taken for the "real" thing. A son of my friend is only sorry that this war was not chivalrous enough; otherwise, everything would have been fine. Mirjana Marković, President Milošević's wife and an influential columnist in her own right, argued forcefully in print that the Serbs bore no responsibility for the violence occurring in Bosnia-Herzegovina.[8] The most that Marković was willing to concede was that "Like desert clouds from the Sahara, which brought the rain to Belgrade last night, maybe the same clouds of nationalism, hatred, violence, and war filled our sky one night, four or five years ago, coming from afar."[9]

One fascist writer engaged in the adventure of constructing the metaphysics of the Serbian "soul" stated that "being among Serbs even the dog learns to love freedom, and is deeply insulted when it is, even temporarily, deprived of it."[10]

One could adopt the perspectives of Ernest Gellner and Maurice Godelier and reflect on "our situation" as a process of "transition," a moment in history when ways of thinking, seeing, and feeling that belonged to the previous system are dismantled in conditions of widespread social anxiety.[11] Or, following Victor Turner, one could define it as an intense social drama, a liminal phase of chaotic polysemy, inversion, conflictuality, and paradox when a new image of the world, a new order of stability in process is arising.[12] Or we could comply with Michel Foucault's idea of a powerful and mysterious discontinuity between two *epistemes* that "neither in our knowledge nor in our thoughts is there anything which could remind us of the previous state of affairs."[13]

Whatever we might choose as a possible or rational interpretation, the common element in each of them is the fact that we are confronted with the phenomenon of dramatic, decisive events as "moment[s] of origination where an actor and structure meet, halfway between the past and the future."[14] Therefore, the outbreak of war in the disintegrating Socialist Federated Republic of Yugoslavia (SFRY) and consequent social processes in its successor states finds its meaning not only in the present, nor is it only an "evocation" of past ethnic conflicts. Its disruptive power, which lies in the very destabilization of the previous perception and intelligibility of the balance between past, present, and future, elevates the war to status as *the* event of the early 1990s in the western Balkans. It is a new, mutated totality of the past, present, and future, dramatically imposed on all people who lived (now expelled or dead) or are still living in the region—it is not the past we thought we knew, nor the present we thought we had been living, nor the future which we thought we could foresee and expect.

The catastrophic drama of Yugoslavia's "eventfulness" shows how the "transition" of one sociopolitical system may turn into a disaster for both humans and civilization. Being specific, even exceptional in its *softer* political, ideological, and economic features, as compared to other, more openly totalitarian regimes of "real socialism," and having an elaborated multiethnic decentralized party and state structure, socialist Yugoslavia broke down in such a brutal way that it lost both of its most specific features, namely, both its halfway position between Soviet-style communism and Western capitalism and its unique (for Central Europe) multi-cultural composition. Thus, the case of post-communist transition in socialist Yugoslavia and its successor states is not simply a case of dramatic but bearable crisis-transformation, confusion, anxiety, and tension but also a phenomenon with much deeper consequences, namely, the fundamentally turbulent transformation of the entire European area, which had previously been ideologically divided. The system breakdown in the Balkans makes more transparent than elsewhere the explosive potential of the phenomenon of *transition* in Central and Eastern Europe.

Briefly, in the last years of socialist Yugoslavia, four basic identity levels came under extreme stress: self-identity, gender identity, civic (urban) identity, and the identity of the Other. In all four dimensions, the following forces were intertwined in circular and claustrophobic ways: the Nation, Tradition, Patriarchy, closure, fear, exclusion, conflict, violence, revenge, extinction, displacement, disempowerment, brutality, insecurity, unpredictability, and impoverishment. By contrast with other war-affected areas, in which all four identity levels came under physical attack by an "outside" aggressor (whether the Yugoslav Federal Army or the "other nation" inside a newly independent republic), Serbia, "exporting" its aggression to the other Yugoslav successor states, was spared the destructiveness of war and any kind of *outside* aggression. Thus, when speaking of Serbia, one could say that all four identity levels were under stress not from any outside force but only as a result of *internal* forces of nationalist and patriarchal aggression. Although, on the surface, Milošević's regime still retains a strange mixture of nationalist and "socialist" ideas and values, the decisive process is one of peculiar retraditionalization, a tightly blended dynamics of fundamental civic disempowerment and state/nationalist/patriarchal authoritarianism which bases its power on the revival and survival of the rural/feudal/collective identity which delegates or transfers a huge power to the Leader. The Serbian word for Leader (*vožd*), whether merely coincidentally or otherwise, actually had, in the ancient Serbian language, a triple meaning, referring simultaneously to Duke/Master/Leader.

In the perspective of this fundamental social, public versus private type of *mutation* in Serbia, it is more comprehensible to explain the paradox that the most damaging, even destructive, events and trends in Serbia, such as the U.N. sanctions, instead of effecting the weakening of the Milošević government, actually strengthened the aforementioned system of power, together with its associated state/social/personal permutations.

So the whole series of events and processes which destroyed the other republics that emerged from the disintegration of the SFRY served as strategic constructive factors for Milošević's despotic power. The war in Slovenia, Croatia, and Bosnia-Herzegovina, the flight of Serbian refugees from Croatia and Bosnia, the emigration of many educated elites from Serbia, the worldwide blockade and isolation under U.N. sanctions, the economic collapse and hyperinflation, the impoverishment of the population, the disappearance of the urban middle class, the destruction of the social fabric, the instability and powerlessness of all the politicoparliamentary institutions except the institution of the president, the legal/societal/communal insecurity, and the dramatic proliferation of criminality throughout Serbia—all of these, in combination, produced the unpredictable power of the civic void as the essential precondition of Milošević's unlimited and uncontrollable power.[15]

The initial impetus of this power of the civic void started much earlier, with the Eighth Conference of the Communist Party of Serbia in 1987, the coup d'état under the guise of ideological conflict with liberal, non-nationalist communists, the centralization of personal power, and the abuse of tradition and mythologization of history for the purpose of building a new power structure. Milošević also bears primary responsibility for having deliberately destabilized the state and party structure of the Yugoslav federation, for having relativized universal moral values,[16] for having purposefully changed the distribution of resources between the public and private sectors, and for having (re)constructed a collective/authoritarian/militant patriarchy based, in part, on a "traditionally" ordered gender system. Genders are divided as *naturalized sexes* in order to make them complementary *agents* of the Nation; they negotiate between the spheres of History and reproduction, Nation and survival, battlefield and shelter, public glory and private survival, and so forth.

The feminist slogan, "The Personal Is Political," in a deeply ironic sense became part of the official, state-nationalist policy in Serbia. First of all, it translates as "the personal belongs to the state politic," but, since even before the war, politics in Serbia has been identified with the nationalist cause, national destiny, and national glory. As a result, the meaning of this slogan is actually "the personal is nationalist." In the dominant political discourse, deceivingly, this slogan does not seem to relate, on first sight, to women, since Serbian nation-building rhetoric is primarily directed toward men in deconstructing the previous communist-era concept of masculinity and reconstructing a new nationalist and war-oriented notion of masculinity.[17] Indeed, this gender reconstruction was the prime objective of nationalist homogenization and the effective precondition for catalyzing ethnic warfare in the Yugoslav region.

In every nationalism, and particularly in its aggressive fascist type, men constitute the "soul" and the "engine" of the vision and interpretation of the exclusionary, war-oriented essence of the Nation. The poetically simplified message of President Slobodan Milošević ("If we Serbs do not know how to work, we at least know how to fight") is an apt example of his active contribution to the pre-civic mythology of Serbian men as "natural" and eternal warriors. In this kind of Serbian militantly masculinist discourse, women are nearly invisible, unless they become much publicized victims of the Enemy Nation. They are not in the open and are not the constant focus of the nationalist identity construction. This invisibility may appear advantageous since at least they are not under constant pressures with nationalist slogans, recipes, and advice as to how to become "real" Serbian women. But, in fact, this situation of women's absence from the public sphere is itself a sign of patriarchy. Women are not even to be talked about in public—except in the "natural" context of bearing children for the Nation.

The most obvious example of this "silent" patriarchy was the 1995 Christmas message advocated by Patriarch Pavle, the head of the Serbian Orthodox Church. Unlike his previous messages directed "universally" to the Nation, Man, and the People, this one was particularly and directly addressed to women. The reason for his sudden change of focus in giving special attention to women was a "dangerous phenomenon" he identified as a widespread "epidemic" threatening the contemporary world including, "unfortunately," the Serbian nation, namely, a declining birthrate. Along with many Serbian nationalist demagogues, Patriarch Pavle called it a "White Plague," ascribing it to the social repercussions of industrial civilization, and warned that as the mean Serbian age increases, Serbia's most vital instrument of its present and future power, its ability to reproduce itself, is "endangered." The patriarch claimed that nothing less than infanticide had produced this situation, or more precisely, the "infanticide" committed *exclusively* by women who choose not to give birth to ever more little Serbs. This "disease," as the patriarch chose to see it, can only be cured in one way, which is by *making* Serbian women *want* to bear children, the patriarch advised. And this, he advised, could be achieved if they were told that not doing so constituted a threefold sin: toward themselves, toward the Serbian nation, and, of course, toward God himself.

> Sin one: "Many mothers who did not want *more* than one child today bitterly weep and pull their hair in despair over the loss of their only son in the war. . . . Why did they not give birth to more children and now have them as consolation?"
> Sin two: "If such a birthrate continues, the Serbs will become an ethnic minority in their own country."
> Sin three: "Those mothers who never allowed their children to be born will meet them when they come to meet God, where they will ask their would-have-been mothers, 'Why did you kill me? Why did you not let me live?' "[18]

At first sight, and for those unfamiliar with the cunning of nationalism, this Christmas message may have sounded like a rather isolated, extremely fundamentalist, sexist, so-called pro-life cry, and not part of the general "socialist" social climate, since usually there is very little talk about women anyway. Its blunt and horrific tone distinguishes it from the official, less openly biased, canons of the articulation of analyses of social problems affecting women. However, its expression of concern for an allegedly endangered Serbian nation represents only one of a series of documents which collectively amount to a Serb national program.

In October 1992, a document on demographic issues was published, under the title of "Warning," and signed by officials of Milošević's ruling Serbian Socialist Party (SSP), as well as by the representatives of the Serbian Orthodox Church, the Serbian Academy of Arts and Sciences, the Serbian Medical Association, the Republic Statistical Agency, and other "public and national institutions." In this document, drafted by nine male "reputable academics," the proposal was advanced that the State Council for the Population should be established, to be headed by either the president himself or the prime minister.

A "folk-wisdom" style of narration dominates the tone of the document: "The one who owns the flock, owns the mountain as well" and "Without kin there is no nation." Also, in strongly nostalgic overtones, as if Serbia should never have participated in contemporary processes of industrial development, this document bemoans the fatal consequences of urbanization and migratory trends. But, in spite of all the "universality" of its tone, the essence of the "Warning" lies in a very specific zone of trouble: "There is a lack of balance in terms of the growth and renewal of some nations, minorities, and ethnic groups," or, more precisely, "three ethnic groups—Albanians, Muslims, and Romas—with their high birthrates, are [reproducing] beyond rational [limits]."[19] The SSP Conference adopted this document, and the same year the Serbian parliament adopted a resolution setting out some principles on population renewal. These principles stipulated a stimulation of the birthrate in some regions and its suppression in other regions, depending on existing birthrates. This seemingly neutral language veiled a clear call for a policy of stimulating the reproduction of Serbs, while discouraging and reducing rates of reproduction among Albanians and other non-Serbs.

The problem here is not actually the idea of the dual system of stimulating versus suppressing the birthrates in different regions, for there are indeed significant differences from one region to another. According to 1994 statistics, in central Serbia (with a homogeneous Serbian population), the birthrate was −2.94 per 1,000, and in Vojdodina (with a Serbian majority) it was −3.11, while in Kosovo (with an Albanian majority), the birthrate was +17.38. But the real danger lies in the reasonings and "arguments" given to explain this disproportion. According to the "Warning" published in *Politika*, the causes of the lower birthrate among Serbs and the higher birthrate among Albanians are not social, economic, or historical but ideological, political, and naturalistic. Thus, according to this interpretation, Albanians have many children not because of the strong rural/patriarchal system and economic underdevelopment (97 percent of Albanian women are unemployed) but because it is the long-term political strategy of Albanians to outgrow the Serbian nation and, of course, because they are "so primitive" in their "natural" and unchangeable "ethnic mentality."

The same oblivion to historic, social, and economic factors and the escape to purely ideological and naturalistic explanations appear in the "Warning." Here, too, the instruments of change are not social or economic factors; on the contrary, Serbian women are held to be responsible, ostensibly exclusively, to correct the "imbalance" in growth rates. This explains why Patriarch Pavle's Christmas message was not an extremist exception but a perfectly integrated and typical expression of the nationalist climate of population renewal *only* for Serbs. Serbian women are, therefore, seen as the "natural" means of renewing the Serbian Nation. Their primary task is to bring into this world as many Serbian children as possible and, in the final consequence, it is their "national duty" to submit their very bodies to the Nation, in order to start a long-term *fertility war* against Albanian women, matching the latter in the output of descendants. Serbian nationalist body politics is thus the politics of using and abusing Serbian women's bodies as incubators in the war not only against other women's bodies (Albanian women's bodies, for example) but against the whole nation. Ironically, this idea of the political instrumentalization of Serbian women's bodies is, in fact, identical to the one ascribed to the reproductive political strategy of "primitive" Albanians.

The nationalist instrumentalization of women was also confirmed in the new abortion law adopted by the Serbian parliament in May 1993. Just like the patriarch's message, this abortion law all of a sudden introduced women into the political arena, after their long and "normal" invisibility. The version adopted by the parliament permitted women to decide on an abortion only up to ten weeks into their pregnancy, while a commission composed of a physician, a psychologist, and a social worker would be empowered to take the final decision where women sought abortions between the tenth and twentieth week of pregnancy. Also, women between sixteen and eighteen years of age (although having the right to work and to found a family) must obtain permission for both parents in order to have an abortion performed. And last but not least, the initial draft of this law did not recognize rape as a legitimate reason for abortion.

The abortion law provoked major resistance on the part of feminist groups as well as the Civic Alliance, the only major opposition party to have taken up the cause of women's rights. But, surprisingly, this law was among the few that President Milošević declined to sign, sending it back to the parliament with the explanation that "it diminishes the basic freedom to decide whether to give birth, as one of the fundamental human rights."[20] Thanks to the president's sudden generosity, the revised abortion law eventually adopted in Serbia included rape among acceptable reasons for granting an abortion, and allowed women between the ages of sixteen and eighteen to make their own decisions without parental consent. But it still did not allow personal, family, or social reasons to be considered after the tenth week of pregnancy; nor did it allow women to make their own decision after the tenth week.

Where the first draft had stipulated that raped women had to give birth, the "ameliorated" law represented only a lesser erosion of women's fundamental rights. Abolishing women's right to decide on abortion up to the twentieth week of pregnancy, grounded on personal, family, and social reasons, in fact does not represent at all a contradictory precedent in the general trend of *ideologization* surrounding the issues of fertility and population politics in the service of the Nation. Compared to the "hard" reasons accepted as the only allowable reasons for granting approval for abortion up to the tenth week (the woman's health, a deformed fetus, rape, or incest), *personal* (including family and social) reasons are the only ones that could be translated as "ideological," that is, reasons outside the realm of "natural" causes. And evidently, these very ideological reasons are out of consideration, in order to leave room for a different kind of ideological reason: *impersonal* political, nationalist reasons such as the continuation of the pregnancy for the revitalization and reproduction of the Serbian nation.

Moreover, it is exactly these impersonal nationalist/instrumentalist motifs that would be the most endangered by the social and personal arguments that women in Serbia could mention to the abortion approval committee, if permitted to do so, above all their living conditions. Only 4 percent of the members of the Serbian parliament are women, and even that represents some small progress when compared with the period 1990–93, when only 1.6 percent of parliamentary deputies were women. Not a single law was passed in this parliament concerning women's rights. Women represent the major part of the workforce that was laid off or put on a compulsory vacation. Women and rural inhabitants were the real pillars of Serbia, bearing the brunt of the burden of the U.N. sanctions from 1992 to 1996. They were the most inventive in the art of surviving under the phenomenally high inflation; they returned to the old technologies of food processing; women predominated in the endless queues, selling things on the black market, taking on several jobs at once, caring for their children, husbands, elderly relatives, and refugees. Their health and the health of their children, is under constant threat considering the worsened medical care and the deteriorated living conditions, which is indicated in the fact that in Belgrade, the deathrate among the newborn increased from 12 percent in 1992 to 16 percent in 1994.

So why should women give birth in a country which is still officially unrecognized, a country without a future for the next fifty years, where women are treated as an inexhaustible resource, not only in the everyday art of survival but as the procreative saviors of the dying Nation, and expected to sacrifice their comfort, their personal preferences, and even their very lives for the sake of raising the birthrate in Serbia? Fortunately, this restrictive abortion law did not succeed in its hidden, aggressive, and hostile agenda against the members of other nations living in Serbia. It did not introduce the "mechanism" which would, for example, have forced Albanian women to have abortions even when they did not want it, as some deputies had demanded. The day Serbian and Albanian women find legal ways of achieving full control over their bodies will, of course, be a very bad day for the so-called real Serbs as well as for the "real Serbs' " nationalist policy of abusing women's bodies.

All these social and political, public, and private nationalist permutations are provoked, produced, and instrumentalized for the purpose of the nationalist autocratic construction of the Serbian rural/militant/patriarchal mentality, personal identity, and gender formation. Although, as I have mentioned, some confusion between the private sphere and the public sphere was entailed in the project of disrupting and overthrowing the previous social order, the dichotomy between public and private is still very much controlled. Indeed, this dichotomy has become even more important since 1987, as the dominant governing structure in gender relations and as the vital precondition underlying all the permutations of the system. The public sphere is the supreme, vertical level of Great History, Manhood, Nation, state, and world politics; it is the order of the despotic masculine power with the mysterious, silent, and invisible Great Master/Leader as the omnipotent Great Savior/Father/Provider/Controller of the totally subjugated *female* Nation. On this level, everyone is equally powerless except those who belong to Master's and Mistress's suite, but they are, for all that, an extremely expendable, insecure, and endangered species. They are to serve while their services are needed, and when the need for their services passes, they disappear in silence, as is expected of dutiful, discrete, and obedient servants.

The private sphere, on the other hand, is the level of trivial horizontality, of everyday life, and real existence, the level of destructive and unglorious changes, of the breakdown of institutions as well as of the previous legal, financial, social, medical, and educational support systems and structures, as well as of the proliferation of *ad hoc* criminal forms of control over people's lives and property. Here one must talk also of the swamping of Serbian city with refugees, the chaos produced by these nationalist wars, the ever-changing immediate conditions of survival, the stress on family and other informal strategies and networks, the reduction and minimization of needs, and the precipitous drop in the standard of living accompanied by widespread shortages of basic commodities including even medicines and resulting in the rapid pauperization of the urban, hitherto middle-class population. These circumstances have increased the levels of stress in families and personal relations and have induced people to postpone higher needs in the interest of satisfying unpostponable lower needs.

More specifically: 50 percent to 70 percent of the Serbian population now lives below the poverty line; the grey economy accounts for 40 percent of registered social income; 75 percent of respondents say that their standard of living has worsened; 16 percent of Belgrade households have taken in refugees; 20 percent of families have borrowed money in order to survive; 33 percent of households have received help in goods (basic foods and toiletries) from family and friends; 62 percent of the families investigated had been exposed to up to five stressful events, 10 percent to six to ten stressful events, and only 6.4 percent had not been exposed to any stressful events (with the remaining 21.6 percent not responding); 66 percent of Belgrade families had had to deal with extreme scarcity or illness or violence; 66 percent of Belgrade families have suffered psychological-interaction stress, which, combined with the multiple existential-material stresses, leads to even more complex family and personal disturbances; and, not surprisingly, the unemployed have been among the most affected by these sundry stresses.[21]

These data clearly show the disastrous effects of Milošević's public, national, and state politics on the everyday lives and existence of the Serbian people, indeed of the destruction and disintegration of society, economy, and state. They confirm the thesis of a "general overall chaos and social disarray in Serbia,"[22] and show the social, political, public and private effects on its people.

The character of gender relations and the position of women in this global situation of disempowerment is, as expected, the intensification of the gender dichotomy and the nationalist restructuring of the patriarchy, the "naturalization" of women as breeders for the purposes of the Nation, and the ideologization of femininity in Serbia. The extreme social and economic crisis in Serbia has resulted in the worsening of women's social position in the public sphere (with whole industries, especially those feminized, stopping or curtailing production) and with the restriction of child care facilities and the deterioration of family infrastructure.

The nationalist revival of the patriarchal tradition invoked, strengthened, and formed a "new" Serbian nationalist patriarchy, one much marked by features of Milošević's rule. One could even say that Serbian nationalist patriarchy is, to some extent, self-contradictory, since Milo-šević despotically subjugated all members of the "female" Nation. More precisely, from the beginning, he has been consistently politically disempowering all political institutions, and therefore *all men* (except himself) in order to exclude any possible competition of "equals." On the other hand, the unstable social circumstances and the extremely hard living conditions in Serbia, have mobilized the enormous energy of women for sheer survival, as the hyperintensified form of their *subjugated empowerment* in vital adaptation to times of crisis, war, and violence. The insecurity in the production and reproduction of life and everyday existence, endless time and energy consumption. and the return to old techniques and technologies of domestic labor, strengthened women's patriarchal self-denial and orientation toward others and their needs but, at the same time, gave them new power and control over others through their dependency in crisis as a form of "self-sacrificing micromatriarchy."[23] By activating their "natural" survival potentials, women actually bore Serbia's heaviest burden during the social and economic crisis in the period of the U.N. sanctions, and therefore, willingly or not, actually played the part of Milošević's most faithful allies. The fact that his despotic charisma has been successful lies partly in the fact that certain types of women have faithfully adored him from the beginning. The majority of women in Serbia have, in fact, been "seduced" by One Man as their despotic patriarch and willingly surrendered themselves to the "destiny" prescribed by the nationalist program.

The overall civic void which was consistently filled with the disempowering hegemony of the nationalist collective homogenization, the constant life-in-crisis conditions, the condition of near-war, the destruction of society in Serbia, the autocratic power structure of one man who disempowered every other political institution and force, the mythologized total investment in Great History and Great Sacrifice in Serbia resulted in a specific gender dynamics which can not be seen as a one-dimensional oppression of women by men but only rather as a more complex dynamic. It is self-contradictory in part and significantly different on public and private levels, as well as in its practices and discourses. On the public level, both in practice and in the dominant nationalist discourse, women are legally, economically, and institutionally almost totally disempowered.

But, in contradiction with what they would think and declare, men are not empowered at the public levels. Only on the level of manifest ideological nationalist discourse are they the dominant, ruling, militant, and heroic actor-gender, because Milošević's despotic destruction and dissolution of the social/civic institutional/political fabric disempowered them almost to the same degree as women. They have invested, delegated, and transferred all aspects of their own public power to the mysterious, unpredictable, and uncontrolled power of One Man. He is the Master of them all, and is not even pretending to be willing to share it with anybody, not even with his close and faithful "associates."[24] Milošević's exclusive masculinized power emasculates all other men; economically and politically, Serbian men are, in fact, disempowered by Milošević, since they play no role of any importance in the fundamental decisions of state.[25]

This structural emasculation of men's power on the public level makes the gender power dynamics on the private level even less one-dimensional. The disempowerment of men renders them even more powerless privately than heretofore. The distribution of power on the level of private everyday life has lost its traditional dichotomous character, because men's power structure in everyday life has deteriorated and almost all means of their private power over women have dissolved, other than the dominant ideological discourse. The aforementioned research shows that in the private sphere, the gender dichotomy in the structure of women's and men's everyday existence, as compared to the vertical-hierarchical gender distance on the public level, is more egalitarian than ever. The dualism between genders is lessened to a considerable degree. Interdependence, solidarity, mutual respect, concern for the family are all noted by respondents in Blagojević's survey.[26] In this context, gender boundaries become blurred and the incidence of the crossing of gender boundaries in everyday life has increased tangibly; this has, in turn, challenged men to adapt and the increased rate in violence against women is, of course, an alarming sign of the difficulty experienced by some men in adapting to changing and blurred gender boundaries, which have resulted in what may be characterized, in their eyes, as an unwanted gender egalitarianism. This gender egalitarianism is, in fact, the result of one other equality—the equality of powerlessness under despotism.

In addition, there is one other factor which, in my opinion, contributed essentially to the psychological or private disempowerment of men, namely, the fact that, although Serbian discourse has been warriorlike all these years, the middle-range element for individual-collective construction of warrior masculinity has been lacking since the war was not on *her* territory and did not result in the overall militarization of society and the new "class" of militant men: "officially" the country was not at war, the "volunteers" were not public heroes but unrecognized patriotic enthusiasts, killers, robbers; on the other side, thousands of young men fled from mobilization by hiding (generally with the help of women) or by leaving the country.

Being more knowledgeable in the area of everyday strategies of private survival, women in fact used the very patriarchal stereotypes of women as "producers" of life to establish a certain "micromatriarchy," as the means of strengthening their private hold over children and men; this syndrome went beyond the "cryptomatriarchy" syndrome outlined by Andrei Simić in Chapter 2, by strengthening women in their relationships with their own husbands. Meanwhile, the public disempowerment of men deprived them of the previous economic, public, and professional means of control over women. Women have become, thus, privately more empowered at the same time as they have become ideologically more subordinated.

So, if we are to compare Serbian women's "escape into privacy," a phenomenon visible in all other post-communist countries, I would not say that their "escape," in the Serbian case, was an escape at all. In times of extreme existential insecurity, women were offered only one choice: the traditional women's strategy of strengthening their own position precisely by complying with the most "natural" patriarchal expectation of women, namely, their self-sacrifice. As so many times before, women accepted the role which was pathetically offered to them, to "save the nation," by enabling their own families to survive. In times of crisis, along with men, women returned to privacy, to retain one and only one possible area of survival that had been left to them in times of systematic shocks to life, property, and security, and to restructure their own life and health, as well as the lives and health of family members. The private empowerment of women in this process is, in itself, an extremely costly achievement, and, what is more, it actually helped the survival of the despotic nationalist political system which had caused and provoked the very crisis which they had been trying to survive. In terms of overall insecurity and the unpredictability (even after the peace settlement) of the social and political situation in Serbia, one cannot even find the possibility to hope for the future. One cannot hope for any durable gains for women in their present, limited, temporary, and deeply contradictory private empowerment.

10

WOMEN IN KOSOVO: CONTESTED TERRAINS

THE ROLE OF NATIONAL IDENTITY IN SHAPING AND CHALLENGING GENDER IDENTITY

Julie Mertus

There is no gender identity prior to the performance in which it is expressed, Judith Butler has observed.[1] Similarly, there is no national identity prior to the performance in which it is expressed. Performances of gender and performances of national identity intertwine: the boundaries of each shape the corners of the other. These processes never end, as both gender identities and national identities quickly become *contested terrains* to be won or lost, preserved, or dissolved.

Particularly when under attack, gender identities and national identities must be reconciled with each other; intersections must be examined, explained, or exploited. In his analysis of wartime propaganda, Obrad Kesić explains how political leaders in ex-Yugoslavia have manipulated gender in the struggle over national identity.[2] Conversely, political lead-

Julie Mertus wrote this while she was a fellow at Harvard Law School and the Harvard Center for International Affairs. Funding for the research for this chapter was provided by the John D. and Catherine T. MacArthur Foundation.

ers and women's groups alike have manipulated national identity to shape
and challenge gender identity.

These complex, interrelated performances include the development
of the real and imagined relationship between (1) *gender and nation-Other*;
(2) *gender-nation and state*, and (3) *gender-nation and authorities*. In defining
and defending their national identity and gender identity, all people of
ex-Yugoslavia must somehow negotiate these relationships. This chapter
explains each component in turn by using narratives from women in Kosovo, the predominantly ethnic Albanian part of ex-Yugoslavia.[3] Nation
and gender in Kosovo, as elsewhere, are works in progress, with recognizable shape at any point in time but, perhaps for the good of us all, remaining in a constant state of (re)definition. Nationalism does shrink the scope
for individual identity choice but, oddly enough, it may also open new
avenues for identity formation.

GENDER AND NATION-ORDER

The cost of one identity is often the loss of another. Tzvetan Todorov
explains: "The valorization of the group has a double aspect—it implies
turning one's back on the lesser entity (the self) as well as to the greater
entity (other groups, humanity as a whole). Attachment to the group is at
once an act of solidarity and an act of exclusion."[4] In the Balkans, especially in times of war and oppression, one's ethnonational group takes
precedence over all other claims to identity.[5] Just as Serbs are expected
to be Serbs above all else, Kosovar Albanians are expected to be first and
foremost Albanians.[6]

Serbian women activists and Albanian women activists, however, face
a slightly different array of choices in the identity process. Serbian
women who fight for the rights of women, refugees and ethnonational
minorities are labeled as traitors by their own communities. To be wom-
en's rights activists, Serbian women have had to choose their gender
identity over their identity as Serb—a tag which has become equated in
the international community with the oppressor/aggressor/war criminal.[7]
So, too, Albanian women who fight for the rights of women and speak in
broader terms of human rights for all are in danger of being called traitors
by their own people. However, the call for solidarity among Kosovar
Albanians is so strong, and the cost of breaking rank so high, that most
Albanian women cannot choose to emphasize their gender identity over

their Albanian identity.[8] And, unlike Serbs, they need not do so, as "Kosovar Albanian" is not equated with aggressor but with suffering victim.[9]

For Kosovar Albanian women, then, the cost of being Albanian is the loss of other identities, including that of "Woman." "Women here aren't living life as women, but as Albanians," J., one of the leading human rights activists in Uroševac declared.[10] Her friend, a young teacher of Albanian literature, added, "Women can't be free women when they are occupied as a nation." "After the revolution," more than one Kosovar woman has vowed, "we will have our freedom."

Even at the World Conference on Women in Beijing, Kosovar Albanian women were nearly invisible, despite their physical presence. The Kosovar Albanian delegation to the World Conference of Women in Beijing—the official delegation sponsored by the parallel Kosovar Albanian government—decorated the NGO forum with posters of Ibrahim Rugova, president of the Kosova government, and Adem Demaqi, a human rights activist known as the "Albanian Mandela" for his long prison term. The "official" Albanian handout spoke much about Serbian police violence against Albanians but omitted mention of domestic violence; it emphasized the substandard health and education system (both of which have tremendous impact on the lives of women and girls) but skimmed over the high illiteracy rates among women in villages and the lack of reproductive health education nearly every locality. The official presenters appeared more comfortable talking about the women killed by police than the alive women who are attempting to build a better society.

The image of woman as victim bolsters the larger Kosovar Albanian identity, that of the suffering people.[11] The police brutality against Albanians has been documented—people have suffered.[12] Yet an unyielding investment in perpetuating this image dissuades initiatives to improve the quality of Kosovar life. All problems lead in one direction, to the oppressive Serbian state. When village women remain illiterate, girls turn to prostitution, and women throughout Kosovo suffer from lack of medical care, the reaction becomes: "Look what they [Serbs] are doing to us."[13] Vjosa Dobruna, a doctor who co-founded the Center for Women and the Protection of Children in Priština, has seen the end result. "The woman comes [to the health care center] and says that her husband [has been] beating her for the last five years, and that he is unemployed. In this case, the woman thinks that the problem [of the beating] will be solved if the problem of employment is solved, so she keeps it quiet and sacrifices herself."[14]

As Renata Salecl has succinctly stated, "National identification with
the nation ("our kind") is based on the fantasy of the enemy, an alien
which has insinuated itself into our society and constantly threatens us
with habits, discourses and rituals which are not those of 'our kind.' "[15] A
nation knows what it is because it knows what it is not—the dangerous
stronger, the Other.[16] For Serbs, while their own cause bespeaks a moral
and historical imperative, "Albanians are understood as pure evil."[17] Similarly, Kosovar Albanians see themselves as the victims and Serbs as the
aggressors. Serbs look into their oppositional mirror and see their women
as cultured, strong, and worthy of motherhood, as opposed to the primitive, weak, and indiscriminately fecund Albanian women.[18] Albanians see
their women as the strong pillars of the family, the martyrs for the nation,
as opposed to the weak, selfish Serbian women who are misled by their
aggressive Serbian men.

For a long time, many Kosovar Albanian women have quietly confessed their doubts that all problems can be blamed on the Serbs. "If we
compare ourselves to other women's lives here in Europe, we are not
living at all," a school teacher in Uroševac stated, adding "an independent
Kosova isn't going to change all that." Only recently have a small but
growing group of women dared to speak publicly. In a widely circulated
interview, Sevdije Ahmeti, co-director of the Center for Women and the
Protection of Children, declared: "It is our duty to change the mentality,
to get out of the stagnation that has capture us [women]."[19] Although a
handful of Albanian women's groups now exist in Kosovo, those who
have publicly attempted to reexamine and redefine women's gender roles
in Kosovar society have risked being harshly criticized by their own community as undermining the Albanian national struggle. For example,
Xheri, a young women journalist, found herself lambasted by the mainstream Albanian press for writing an article about Albanian prostitutes.
Her mistake? The prostitutes had testified frankly about the poor family
conditions that had led some of them to the streets.[20] "How can she waste
time tearing down our families when we are under occupation?" older
Albanian journalists responded.

Regardless of the strong social disapprobation, some Albanian women
seek to reshape "Albanian Woman" to fit their definition of woman—to
minimize the trade-off and decrease the space between the two identities.
One group has been particularly adept at using national identity to reexamine gender identity: a group of volunteers working with village
women in the region known as Has, the most conservative corner of the

most conservative part of the former Yugoslavia. The volunteers include local women activists—mainly young women who had attended higher education in the city—a literacy and women's rights group, Motrat Qiriazi, named after the two sisters Qiriazi, who founded the first school for girls in the Albanian language one hundred years ago. Run by two sisters, Igballe and Safete Rugova, Motrat Qiriazi had been formed over six years ago and then abandoned due to political pressures. The group had not negotiated the relationship between gender and nation well. Fearing that Motrat Qiriazi had been neglecting the nation at the expense of other aims, Albanian political leaders had dissuaded women from attending their workshops. By the time I found them, the group had already worked out a different relationship between gender and nation.

We greet each man as he enters the faded green classroom and takes a seat on the scrubbed tan wooden benches—three to a bench, just as they had learned in school. The seats at the back of the class remain empty. I look out the cracked window panes at the mountains, and the square, red-roofed houses piled on top of each other across the hill behind the school, the only common building in this village of nearly one hundred houses. A few boys in muddy sandals play with cows at the edge of a dirt path lining a chin-high cement wall. "Where are the women?" I whisper to my friend, the local teacher who has been leading workshops with women in this village for the past two months. "The men wanted to see us today," she says, snapping her pencil nervously against her thigh, "they want to know what we've been doing with their women."

She needed their approval to keep meeting with "their women." A difficult task. These men were the oldest and youngest men of the village—nearly all of the men in the middle-age bracket were out of the region, mostly far out of the country, working as bakers and laborers. Catholic and Muslim, these men deeply believe that only tradition and unquestioned solidarity have kept their families alive. Their adherence to patriarchal tradition has been unwavering.[21] Most urban Albanians living in Kosovo have never been to Has and its deeply conservative ways are utterly foreign to their own way of life.

Has is the place where Muslim girls are still being "bartered" into marriage for as much as thirty thousand German marks, a price given upon engagement at a young age (around thirteen), although marriage takes place years later (around age nineteen). This is the place where women live together in segregated quarters; where some mothers give the best food and care to their sons, leaving their daughters to take care of each other; where few girls attend high school and where not a single girl has ever graduated from a four-year accredited university; where many brides are kept confined in the house for one year after marriage; where birth control is nonexistent and gynecological health care is restricted to maternity care; where girls and women wear traditional skirts down to their ankles and beautiful, colorful traditional dress—with heavy padding (Catholic women) or a wide wooden bar (Muslim women) at their waist, purportedly to help them carry things, but serving as well to hide their hips and distort their shape into a box.

But this is also the place where a handful of local women, working in conjunction with urban Albanian women, have decided to do something to change women's lives. The local women—mainly nurses and teachers who graduated from two-year colleges in the city and thus are considered immoral (what were they doing in the city?) and therefore unmarriable—hold weekly meetings in which, through informative talks, role-playing, and discussions, they simply encourage women and girls to think about themselves . . . for themselves.

And now the men want an explanation.

My friend stands in front of the men in her blue jeans and button-down shirt, questioning them: "Who takes care of your sons?" then answering for them: "Your women." "And how can they help them with their lessons if they cannot read? If they have no knowledge? Education of girls and women is good for the whole [Albanian] nation," she proclaims, "How can we advance as a nation without the advancement of women?" The men nod in enthusiastic agreement. She wins them over easily by portraying the education of women as a matter for the entire Albanian nation.

Word spreads into other villages in Has: the women are getting special attention—attention that would improve the entire nation. Men in villages which have not yet been visited by the group become angry. "Why haven't you come to see our women? When are you coming?" they demand. Nationalism becomes a powerful legitimizing force for organizing women as women.

About twenty village women sit in a circle in a single room school house. It is their first meeting. As an ice-breaker, the group leader asks each woman to say her name and something she likes. The leader uses herself as an example: "I like chocolate ice-cream," she says. The women laugh. "I like the traditional dress of the women in Has," her co-leader adds. The women laugh again. But they cannot follow these examples.

None of them can imagine something for themselves. "I like helping my family." "I would like to have a son." "I like health for my family." "Oh, come on," the leader urges, "What do *you* like for *you*?" The women shift uncomfortably. "I like working with cows," one woman volunteers, her eyes downcast. "O.K.," the leader turns to the next woman in the circle, "And you?" "I like to cook for my family." Only one fifteen-year-old girl dares to say something for herself, and even then she turns the question into what she *would like*. "I would like to continue school but my mother won't let me," she admits. The older woman stare.

They try another exercise: Make a list of three things you would want for your girl children. The leader writes, without comment or judgment, each suggestion on the scuffed green chalkboard. The group slowly gathers steam. After "I want her to have sons," "Beauty," "Wealth," and "Health," the responses became bolder and more imaginative: "Education," "To Travel," "Intelligence," "To be President or an Astronaut!" The work has begun.

If anyone had stood in front of a group of Has women and announced, "Forget about nation, from now on, think about yourselves first as women," the women would have felt challenged. The only construct that they had been taught since childhood was of national identity—Albanian Self and oppressor Other. Most women had no concept of themselves as women apart from their role as serving the nation, bearing sons and preparing them for a life of surviving against the Other. They needed to find an identity for themselves within the nation first, and only then could they begin to explore their identities *as women*. When the group leader told them, "Improving the lives of women improves the whole nation," she gave them permission to think about themselves—a necessary prerequisite to any work with women *as women*. In other words, she helped them reconcile their national identity with a broader, potentially transformative gender identity.

GENDER-NATION AND STATE

Gender identity and national identity are formed not only in relationship to each other but also in response to state oppression of them.[22] At the same time, the story of oppression is shaped and experienced by national and gender identities. All three elements—gender, nation, and state— further the goals of each other.

First, gender identity reflects the story of state oppression as mediated through the national discourse in Kosovo. Nearly all women come from families in which at least one family member has been beaten by police or imprisoned; it is the women who must take care of the family when the men are imprisoned. Many Kosovar woman have been laid off or forced out of their jobs, denied the education of their choosing, and subjected to substandard medical care; it is the women who are expected to sacrifice their own jobs, education, and health. The health effects of living under such stress are acute. In the nationalist discourse, women become the martyrs, the saints. Their accepted gender identity is limited to the bounds of national sainthood.

Second, furthering the cycle, the story of oppression incorporates and exploits these identities. The "story of oppression" refers to both the apology/explanation of the group in kin with the oppressors and the experience recounted by those on the firing line. Most Serbs believe that police harassment of Albanians is wrong but that the heavy police presence in Kosovo is justified by threats from Albanians against Serb civilians. One of the most consistent threads in their apologies/explanations are stories about Albanians raping or sexually harassing Serbs.[23] At the same time, Albanians frequently invoke gender in the telling of their stories of oppression. For example, an Albanian man who was beaten by police cries when he remembers that he was "humiliated in front of his family."[24] The extreme torture inflicted later at the police station was nothing, he says, compared to the moment the police took his manhood away by thrashing him in front of the family he was supposed to protect.

The state-influenced Serbian media pumps out portraits of Albanian women as baby makers, calling their offspring "biological bombs," labeling Albanian family life primitive and backward. In the hands of the propagandists, the strong Albanian woman martyr becomes the barefoot and pregnant village girl. The graphs and charts predicting dire population explosions become a form of oppression. The Albanian doctor attending a physicians' meeting in Belgrade must brace herself for the many people who will great her with the same stunned gasp, "You're an Albanian?!" Many Albanian women challenge the validity of the claims, pointing out that the natality rate among educated, urban women is no higher in Kosovo than in Serbia proper.[25] To complete the circle, however, some women co-opt the negative images and oppressive experiences, adding them to their mantle of martyr, victim, saint.

The interrelationship between gender, nation, and state undergoes new dimensions in cases of state-sponsored torture. The torturers choose their victims based on national identity, but they design their methods according to both national and gender identities. Men beaten on their genitals are to become women; women raped or threaten with rape are to become whores, that is, subhuman.

Survivors often say that their national identity and, less frequently, their gender identity gave them strength to endure. Men and women experience this process differently. Men have support in their communities as men, and very little can be done to harm their identity as men as long as they are suffering in the name of the nation. A man who is beaten on his genitals can say, "I knew I was a man [and] they could not take that from me."[26] In contrast, women have little support in their community as women. A woman who is raped or sexually assaulted would not say, "I knew I was a woman." Women who are raped in custody, unlike men who are sexually abused, tend to survive by hiding their sacrifice to the nation. While the man will still be acceptable to his community, the woman would be an outcast.

Male and female survivors of severe forms of physical abuse tend to reject the label of martyr, although they are forced to wear it publicly as part of their national identity—they are an *Albanian* former political prisoner, an *Albanian* torture victim. The label of martyr can become a complicated part of a former political prisoner's identity, and men and women wear the label differently. Women martyrs are some of the most public women in society. They are expected to do certain things, such as marry a male martyr, and to refrain from doing certain other things, namely escaping the country or running off with a foreigner. In this sense, men tend to have more freedom in their martyr role. Nevertheless, the role of martyr and the experience of oppression can have an indirect liberating effect on women's gender identify. Society grants the martyred woman greater latitude in breaking social norms, testing her own voice, or demanding her own silence.

L. is one such survivor. I know about her status as martyr before I know anything else about her. She is one of hundreds of small, living legends in Kosovo. I met L. over a dozen years after her release from prison.[27] She had only just begun to remember. Her story demonstrates some of the intersections between state, gender, and nation.

L. had just begun to practice medicine in 1984, when the trail of arrests from the 1981 demonstrations finally led to her door. Although L. had indeed played an active role in an underground student group advocating for an autonomous Kosova republic, the only thing police had on her was possession of an illegal newspaper. "It was the kind of paper that people passed from person to person," L. remembered, "I had passed it on to another student two years before, but police had found him and he had confessed that he got it from me."

A small group of police inspectors, which included both ethnic Albanians and ethnic Serbs, tried to force L. to tell them who had given her the newspaper. "I was shivering. It was so cold. With the first question, they slapped me. The inspector said, 'Stand up enemy. You are against Tito's Yugoslavia.' They called me an Albanian whore. They hit me two, three times and then pushed me into a chair." The police repeatedly tried to get L. to implicate her boyfriend, a fellow activist who had been arrested at the same time.

The inspectors became incensed when L. would name only one man in connection with the newspaper—a man who was already dead. They sent her into a larger room. L. had already been in police custody for over twenty-four hours without sleep, food, or water.

> They told me to stand up. There was this man there who was talking to me. He knew everything about me although I did not know him. Men stood in a circle around me, beating me. They forced me to keep standing. I think it lasted about a half an hour. Sometimes I had no power to stand up. They would lift me from the ground when my knees buckled. They were asking me about the teachers from Albania who were teaching in Kosovo, teachers at the University, intellectuals. I didn't say anything. I said I don't know anyone. They started beating me with a leather stick filled with sand. They hit me on my hands, fingers, feet.

> I was so thirsty. . . . I asked for water. They gave me a bottle and they said, "Don't drink it." They just showed it to me. "If you drink this," they said, "you will tell us everything." I laughed. I said, "Even if the water is drugged, I'll drink." I just didn't care anymore. After I drank, they brought me to my cell and I started vomiting and having diarrhea. I started to see colors and snakes and I became dizzy.

> The next day, when they beat me I started peeing on myself. I couldn't control it. They laughed, "You have to pee, hee hee."

They kept beating me in the lowest part of the stomach. When they saw that I was all wet, they told me to go to the toilet.

After three days, L. was taken to a prison in Kosovska Mitrovica (Mitrovice), and then moved blindfolded to another cement holding cell. Here, a particularly brutal regime of real torture began.

They didn't let me sleep or eat for four days. They kept teasing me all the time, teasing me about how much I didn't eat. They would make a table for me like I was going to eat. They would let me sit at the table. They would place food in front of me, and then they would take it away. . . .

One man told me to take off my tights. I refused, so he beat me more . . . I had to lie on my stomach with my knees bent, soles of feet facing upward. They put a chair over my thighs and one man sat on the chair, pinning me so I couldn't move. Two other officers held down my arms. Another one held my feet together. Someone started beating me on the soles of my feet. I screamed as loud as I could. I became an animal struggling to get free. They kept beating and beating and I was screaming and screaming.

I don't remember when they stopped. I was lying on the floor still and they told me to get up and walk to the wall. My feet were blue and swollen. I could only walk on the sides of my feet. My feet were so big that I couldn't wear shoes.

To this day, L.'s feet bear the scars of her torture. Still, according to L., the worst form of torture was "the assault on my privacy and womanhood." Although the guards never raped her, they would threaten that they could do it anytime. "They would brag to me about how many [prisoners] they had raped," she recalls, "And whenever I heard the screams of women I thought they were being raped . . . and there was nothing I could do." The guards would also watch the women prisoners when they went to the toilet. "They would search me before and then look at me through the door. I felt ashamed. I was no longer a woman, no longer a human."

Today, L. faces a difficult task in reconciling her oppression with her national and gender identity. Some of her torturers—the Albanian ones—are now in prison themselves, charged with trying to establish an illegal Albanian police force. Albanian solidarity suggests that L. should sympathize with their plight. Instead, L. says, "I think of those policemen in prison, my torturers, and I wonder if they are watched while they pee." L. dreams of going to visit her torturers in jail, "just to see them . . . and to have them see me on the other side of the living."

Four years ago, L.'s boyfriend was released from prison after serving over six years. They had only been seeing each other for three months when he was imprisoned. "There was never any dating or anything like that. We would just meet at clandestine meetings and do clandestine activities together. It was a kind of ideological love," L. laughs, comparing her relationship to many others that had formed during the student protests. "And then when you both were thrown in prison, the entire community romanticized your relationship. You were expected to get married whenever you both were free." Within a month of her boyfriend's release, they had no choice but to be married. L.'s entire life after her arrest—including her own marriage—was limited by her identity as former political prisoner, martyr for the Albanian cause.

Just as her community defines L. by her oppression, L.'s gender and national identities stem in part from her experience of oppression. Denied a passport,[28] L.'s boundaries have been physically defined for her. Her experiences in prison however, eventually opened her world, leading her to work with local women's rights activists. As a practicing gynecologist, she now sees and treats women who have been victims of all kinds of sexual abuse. Few of the women will ever admit they were abused, L. says. "I'm treating one woman, a former political prisoner, who has a torn vagina and who can't have children. . . . She denies she was ever abused. She says it must have been the cold prison floor." Unlike some doctors, L. says, she understands the silence.

GENDER-NATION AND AUTHORITIES

The relationship between gender and nation is shaped not only by relationships with the Other (the evil Albanian, the aggressive Serb) and by the state, but also with "authorities"—forces above and below the state. Identity formation today arises in a world marked by rapid globalization in markets, information and security arrangements, and shifting communal power arrangements. Global power and the reach of international law has shifted simultaneously out to international and regional actors (that is, the International Monetary Fund [IMF], World Bank, NATO), and down to, in Richard Falk's terminology, "transnational social forces."[29] Transnational social forces, from environmental and human rights NGOs (nongovernmental organizations) to communal groups that spread over nation-state lines, are "gradually shaping a very weak but still real global civil society that represents a form of globalization from below, as an alternative to the globalization from above being achieved by market forces."[30]

Residents of Europe, especially in areas of conflict, look to regional and international laws and institutions for protection, jobs, goods, and for their daily news. In turn, these regional and international forces play an important role in shaping the identities of struggling nations. In Kosovo, the development of "transnational social forces" has been stunted by the totalitarian conditions which discourage the development of a functioning civil society. While nation and state play important roles in development of identity, civil society has yet to do so. However, regional and international forces have found their way into Kosovar life, having an impact on identity formation.

The notion of international law has had a particularly profound influence. In Kosovo, 90 percent of the population formally rejects the official state (Serbian) law; yet the parallel Albanian government does not have the institutions, police, and military to enforce its own law in its place. In these circumstances, the *only* law recognized as legitimate is something above the state.[31] Just as urban kids in America might know somehow from the movies and from *their* culture that "I have the right to remain silent, I have my rights," referring in some vague way to a U.S. Constitution that they have never read, kids in Kosovo know that they have their "human rights," to culture, language, and freedom from police violence, referring to the U.N. Declaration on Human Rights and the U.N. Convention on Civil and Political Rights—documents which they are only slightly more likely to have read.[32]

A notion of international human rights "law" has thus become part of Kosovar Albanian culture. Law refers not to mere written words but to the process in which authority is *deposited* at the international, regional, domestic and subdomestic (community) levels. What matters is not just what is true as a matter of positive law, but what people think is true: authority rests not only where it is granted by positive law but where people perceive it rests.

Local and outsider women working on women's rights issues in Kosovo have been able to tap into the reserve of authority granted by Kosovars to anyone dealing with human rights. In order to persuade men who have enough money to buy VCRs for themselves to buy electric stoves for their wives, an activist could argue that "Geneva" or "New York" (code for United Nations) would *want* Kosovars to address the issue. To encourage a community to address the problem of lack of job opportunities for young women, an activist need only mention the words "human rights." Kosovar Albanians see themselves as a people that *understands* human rights. If they were in power, *they* would respect others' rights. Kosovar Albanians are incredibly invested in maintaining this part of their identity, even if it means renegotiating the relationship between nation and gender.

I found myself attempting to help four Kosovar Albanian women find a free place to stay in Vienna during one of the preparatory meetings for the Fourth World Conference on Women. It was no easy task. Finally, I secured a place for all four of them in the guest room at the Rosa Lilla Villa House, a gay and lesbian cooperative that offers tidy rooms to visitors. Not wanting them to be surprised, I called to warn them in advance.

"I found a place for you," I said.

"Oh, that's great," P. replied.

"It's, uh, well, like . . ." I stumbled, "A woman's house . . . well, more of a lesbian and gay house."

P. didn't miss a beat. "What do you think we are?" she said, "Primitives?"

I apologized, explaining that I just wanted to make sure that they would not be uncomfortable or that their surprise would not make their hosts uncomfortable. P. told the other women about the nature of the accommodations, that is all except for J., the oldest activist. She waited to tell J. on the airplane. "What do you think I am?" J. said, "I support human rights!"

When the women arrived in Vienna, they went directly to the Lilla Villa. J. and P. were to share one room, the other two women another, and the Serbian women in another—all with a shared kitchen and bath. No problem. J. and P. went into their room. On the wall, an enormous photo of a white woman kissing a black woman greeted them. "Ahh!" J. gasped, setting down her luggage.

"What?" P. quickly replied, "Are you a racist?"

"Oh, no!" J. protested. The room was just fine.

The Kosovar Albanian women could be seen every night in the small bar in the front of the Rosa Lilla. They weren't slumming, they weren't watching people like animals in a zoo. They were just enjoying themselves and their new experience. "We like this place," J. said, "It's very cosmopolitan."

Many other women at the same conference would not have dared set foot in the Rosa Lilla Villa house, although they too called themselves human rights activists. They did not have a strong ethnonational identity which depended upon a vision of human rights *for all*. Also, perhaps, those who stayed away already knew too well that the international community does not actually support rights for all. In this case, the *perceived* role of authorities served to minimize and disclaim difference.

"Different identity categories imply their own membership rules." Ethnonational identities are said to be the "hardest, since they depend on language, culture, and religion, which are hard to change, as well as parentage which no one can change."[33] Leaders of ethnonational groups may not be willing to take in members of opposing ethnonational groups, and in this sense ethnonational groups are closed. However, a group such as the Kosovar Albanians, which has embraced the concept of universal human rights, cannot afford to cast away other outcast groups. In this sense, strong Kosovar Albanian nationalism offers opportunities for expanding the notions of gender identity.[34]

CONCLUSION

The way in which gender has been constructed in Kosovo has helped solidify a particular Albanian identity, a vision of self unique to that of the powerful oppressor, whomever that may be at any point in time. However, constructed terrains based on artificial divisions flow in both directions and are mutually supporting. Gender does not only serve national identities, but also constructed national identities and their sister nationalisms, and can be used to build and challenge concepts of gender. These brief narratives show how the relationships between gender and nation-Other, gender and state, and gender and authorities all play a role in these dynamic processes.

Feminists may be uncomfortable with the notion that something with the potential to become as divisive and aggressive as nationalism is being used to improve the status of women and lay the groundwork for anything which could be seen as a "feminist" consciousness.[35] But Albanian women organizers are not the only women who have found this approach unavoidable. Many women in societies molded on national identity (or the resulting "nationalisms") throughout the world and throughout time have, knowingly or unknowingly, adopted a similar approach.

Where the starting ground is a sense of national identity, the circle of self-exploration and self-discovery may appear as follows: *national identity* (based on self as part of a nation as opposed to Other); *gender identity* (first as part of the nation, and thus still contrasted to the oppositional Other, and then eventually as part of a group called "women" and contrasted to the gender group known as "men"); *national identity with gender identity* (national identity reconstructed with an awareness as to how the gender constructs of women and men serve to promote the goals of the nation, and with possibly a desire to re-shape both national and gender identities); and then, in times of crisis, and particularly when challenged by competing nationalisms, back to *national identity* (perhaps re-shaped by awareness of gender identity).

Having seen firsthand the destructive force of nationalism, I would like to believe that women who live in nationalist societies and in societies confronting nationalisms need not move through this circle. I would like to believe that women move to the second step of developing a gender identity and then remain at this point, recognizing their "similarities through difference" with women of other national groups and refusing to move back to national identity as the basis for construction of self. Perhaps. But I have seen too well the power of nationalist discourse in shaping peoples. In deeply nationalist societies, as Serbia and Kosovo have *become*, the most realistic "best outcome" would be to rest at the third stage and to not complete the circle. If women can develop their own strong gender identity, they can hold on to it and use it to challenge and mold nationalist discourse, at the very least refusing to move back to the stage of national identity alone.

11

WOMEN AND GENDER IMAGERY IN BOSNIA: AMAZONS, SLUTS, VICTIMS, WITCHES, AND WOMBS

Obrad Kesić

> Raped and murdered women do not die
> as heroines. No monuments rise for
> them. Raped and survived women bear
> the shame. They become heroines only
> for us—women who look at the world
> with woman-identified eyes.
>
> —LEPA MLADJENOVIĆ,
> IN *OFF OUR BACKS* (MARCH 1993)

The outbreak of war, first in Slovenia then in Croatia and Bosnia-Herzegovina, ended any hope of maintaining a unified Yugoslav state. For
women, it marked the beginning of a new and much more destructive
period. The political marginalization of women began through the transformation of the political system accelerated during the wars. The impo-
sition of a separation of patriarchically defined roles between the
masculine and feminine, further isolated women and strengthened the
dominance of aggressive, nationalist male elites. Masculine roles centered
around power, strength, prowess and death, while feminine roles revolved
around passivity and helplessness.

In order to mobilize the nation for war, political leaders need to manipulate gender imagery. Deeply patriarchal in its essence, aggressive nationalism is based on warrior mythology. Sociologist Žarana Papić
describes this warrior mythology as it relates to women, referring to

> warriors mythology in which the place for women is clearly and
> strictly defined—women are there because of men, they are in

their function as breeders of new generations of brave soldiers. . . .
This kind of war-gendered-order is the most extreme example of
men's and women's separated realities, which are presented and
seen as a national, unavoidable and "eternal" (based on nationalist
mythology) state of affairs.[1]

The gender imagery which grew out of the wars in the former Yugoslavia
is not unique; it can be found in all wars. The importance of the gender
imagery which developed in the Yugoslav wars lies in the continued manipulation of this imagery to continue public support for war and to undermine any internal opposition to the war effort. This chapter will
examine the development of the different war images of women and the
feminist response to this nationalistic manipulation of women.

I have classified the most common war images of women as Amazon,
Slut, Victim, Witch, and Womb. These images tend to be interconnected
and are commonly found throughout all of the formerly Yugoslav republics. Each of these images is rooted in traditional patriarchal ideology and
has been constructed in its current form primarily through the media and
the rhetoric of official government and party statements. These images
are validated at all levels of society and through all sociocultural institutions from the Church or mosque to the schools. As a result, they will
probably linger long after the conflict ends.

AMAZONS

Even during peace, the image of women as Amazons or "Iron Ladies"
abounded. Women who sought and excelled at traditionally "male" tasks
or skills had their femininity questioned and were masculinized. Some
women eagerly embraced the patriarchal ideology of their newly found
status. During the buildup to war and during the war itself, many women
decided to support the war effort and actively participate in its conduct.
There were women in all of the militias and national armies throughout
the former Yugoslavia. Most of these women occupied noncombat positions within the military formations in administrative or support roles.
They were communication operators, nurses, doctors, cooks, drivers, and
armament workers. The small group of women who did go to the front
on all sides were converted into mythical figures, which, one feminist has
observed, confirmed that patriarchal history teaches us "that women

enter history only when they have taken on masculine roles. The media celebrate these women as heroines when they kill the enemy; when women fighters from the other side are captured they are denounced as 'monstrous women' "; and the like.

The first all-female unit of the war was a brigade formed in Glina, a Serbian-majority town in Krajina. At the swearing in of the unit in December 1991, a women shouted the oath "We will fight against all the Serbs' enemies under the protection of God."[2] Another Serbian all-women brigade, "the Maidens of Kosovo," was formed in Bosnia in 1993, and there were all-women units in the Croatian and the Muslim-dominated Bosnian armies. The media focus on these women portrayed them as patriots and warriors. They were de-feminized and portrayed as modern-day Amazons whose exploits become legendary.

The reason for this mythologization of these women soldiers is twofold. The first reason is that mythologization serves as a tool in the mobilization of the nation and the recruitment of fighters. The second reason for this celebration of women fighters is more subtle; it serves to shame men who have not lived up to their obligation of going to war for the Nation. The message to these men is simple—if these women have gone into battle willingly, you must be a coward or lower than a woman for not doing your duty. This message of shame is sometimes sent directly by the women fighters themselves. Dušica Nikolić, a member of Serbia's parliament and veteran volunteer of the war in Croatia, expressed her contempt of those men who shirked their duty to her Croat captors, who were taunting her after television images of men sitting in Belgrade cafés were shown on Croatian television. She responded, "These are not real Serbs! Real Serbs do not sit in cafés and do not live without a care in the world, not in these times. Those are not pure Serbs."[3]

Nikolić, a vice-president of the ultranationalist Serbian Radical Party (SRS), is perhaps one of the best-known women fighters of the Yugoslav wars. She was frequently featured on television and in magazine interviews. Wounded in action and a prisoner of war, she endured three months of beatings and torture in a Croatian prison. As a result, she was promoted by "Duke" Vojislav Šešelj, the extremist leader of the SRS and the Chetnik fighters, to the rank of Chetnik Lieutenant. Her popularity among nationalists attests to the power of patriarchal mythology. The warrior enjoys the highest respect and honor in patriarchal cultures. Women who attain this warrior myth are especially honored.

Interestingly, enemy women soldiers are normally demonized and singled out as war criminals. A headline in the Zagreb newspaper *Večernji list* exclaimed, "Women-Chetniks are the Most Monstrous Killers." The story cited a Croat commander in Bosnia who claimed that women members of Željko Raznjatović—Arkan's notorious "Tiger" paramilitary units—killed adults and children alike, and that they would kill the children by "grabbing them by the legs and smashing them into walls."[4] Likewise, Dušica Nikolić in her interview in *Duga* claimed that the worst torturers in the Croat prison were women, who had taken sadistic pleasure in beating Nikolić on her wounds.[5]

Although most of the stories of enemy women as monstrous killers have the ring of urban legends, there are several well-documented war crimes committed by women. The demonization of enemy women soldiers results from the need to defend the masculinity of one's own male soldiers. "Our" soldiers cannot be beaten, especially by an enemy which has women in its ranks. When "our" soldiers lose, it is either because of betrayal or as a result of the inhuman barbarism of enemy tactics. According to this logic, it is to be expected that the women soldiers on the enemy side are especially cruel and inhuman.

The women who actually commit atrocities probably differ little from the men who commit them. They may, however, be especially driven to prove themselves to their male fellow soldiers in the same way that "Iron Lady" politicians such as Margaret Thatcher and Bosnian Serb leader Biljana Plavšić are driven to prove that they are more "macho" than their male counterparts. Because women are assumed to be weak, women who embrace the patriarchal dominant order and attain positions of authority spend much of their time proving how strong they can be. Likewise, women who commit war crimes, celebrate their own escape—no matter how temporary—from being the Other and their victory over the Other through ritualistic slaughter.

Women who take on the role of Amazon tend to be extremely antagonistic to feminists, especially those involved in antiwar movements. Fully immersed in patriarchal ideology, they hold the nation to be supreme to everything else; any attack on the war is an attack on the nation. Simonida Stanković, a self-proclaimed member of the matriarchal stream of the new Serbian right and the founder of the organization Only Serbian Women Can Save Serbdom proclaims her ideology: "For me matriarchy is not an answer to patriarchy above everything else, he [patriarchy] is older. Secondly, matriarchy does not mean feminism in the militant sense, nor the domination over men. Matriarchy creates a harmony between these elements and in this way, authenticity of culture and the nation is created through women."[6]

Ironically, these "Amazons" and "Iron Ladies" unknowingly and indirectly help in breaking patriarchal gender stereotypes. Like the women partisans before them, they adopt masculine characteristics and roles, but by distinguishing themselves, despite the patriarchal manipulation of their success, they make important inroads in male-dominated centers of power in politics and society.

SLUTS AND WHORES

The image of women as sluts and whores was pervasive even in the prewar societies of socialist Yugoslavia. This image stems from the view of women as property and holds that women exist because of and for the use of men. The war has added one aspect to this image—women can do their duty in supporting the war effort by improving "morale" among the troops. Sex and sexuality are the most common morale boosters for troops coming back from the front or troops stationed in large garrison towns. The need for sexual morale-boosting is not restricted to men from the Yugoslavia successor states—as can be seen in the number of brothels, striptease clubs, and pornographic shops that have mushroomed around United Nations Protection Force (UNPROFOR) bases.

In Yugoslavia before the wars, brothels and prostitution existed mostly hidden from everyday life. Everybody knew of their existence, but most could not say where or who worked in these houses. Now the sex industry has established itself publicly in Zagreb, Belgrade, Skopje, and Sarajevo. Hard-core pornography is sold openly next to the daily newspapers, women's magazines, and children's comic books at kiosks in most neighborhoods. Although most formerly communist countries have had a similar explosion of pornography and prostitution, the situation in the Yugoslav successor states has been exacerbated by the war. One former Yugoslav diplomat joked that the sex industry had become the number one growth industry in the former Yugoslavia as a result of the war.[7]

The linkage between sex, the war, and politics can be seen in many different ways, from the posting of combat death notices next to advertisements featuring semi-clad women to the prevailing tendency of "news" magazines and papers to feature nude women or sensual images of women on the front covers and in publication inserts. Readers, who are predominantly but not exclusively men, read stories about the battle-fronts, political scandals, and business, which are set off by a profile of a semi-clad young woman, who is almost always photographed in awkward positions usually indicating submission. These young women occasion-ally "wear" military uniforms and always express their preference for "strong" men of their own nation and proudly proclaim their patriotism.

The image of these women is simply another piece in the symbolic war effort to maintain a desired level of patriotism and mobilize recruits and volunteers. The subliminal message to the recruits was: If you are a "real man," you will do your duty for your nation and country, and if you do your duty, your reward will be the gratitude and possibly the bodies of young women, like this one. The message that women love uniforms and the men who wear them is an old recruitment tactic but still an effec-tive one.

The danger of this imagery is that it may fuel the psychosis of vio-lence, rape, and destructive ritual behavior on the part of many men re-turning from the front. Many of these men lose all touch with reality and suffer from some form of post-traumatic stress disorder. They feel that society and their nation owe them an extreme sense of gratitude and that they should benefit in some way for the sacrifices that they made and the killings that they committed in the name of the Nation. This has led to an explosion of violence, murders, rapes, and robberies at the home fronts. One Belgrade journalist claimed that the number of violent crimes committed in Belgrade had quadrupled since the outbreak of fighting and most of these were crimes directed at women and could be attributed to young men either on leave or discharged from units and paramilitaries involved in the fighting in Bosnia and Croatia. This same journalist added that many women, including herself, felt extremely intimidated by men in uniform and that they felt uncomfortable in rejecting requests for dates from soldiers because of a sense of guilt that these young men may be killed fighting for them and that they had an obligation to at least go out with them.[8]

The feeling of obligation by these women is precisely the objective of this patriarchal imagery. Men are supposed to fight and die while women are supposed to bear babies and boost the men's morale by satisfying their sexual desires. To the victor go the spoils, which in this case are the bodies of enemy women and their own "grateful" women. The linkage between the whore image manufactured at the home front and rape at the battlefronts is a direct one, as can be seen in the abundance of pornographic material at frontline positions. Although this is not, as Catherine MacKinnon claims, the driving force behind the war, it does influence men's image of women and adds to the property essence of this image.[9] The creation of a slut image for women is only one form of victimization of women and contributes to the creation of an image of women as victims.

VICTIMS

Women and children make a disproportionately high number of the wars' victims, especially of the refugees. This status of victim for women and the image of women as victims produced by governments, media, and the military is extremely complex. It is perhaps the most manipulated image associated with war. It is the manipulation of women as victims and the image that is created by governments, as well as by well-intentioned feminist organizations, which is the primary focus of this section. This manipulation is another tool in the war effort and further enforces the primary patriarchal images of women as property.

The use of rape as a tool of war is, unfortunately, as common as war itself. As Susan Brownmiller has documented in her highly acclaimed book *Against Our Will: Men, Women and Rape*:

> Man's discovery that his genitalia could serve as a weapon to generate fear must rank as one of the most important discoveries of prehistoric times, along with the use of fire, and the first crude stone ax. From prehistoric times to the present, I believe, rape has played a critical function. It is nothing more or less than a conscious process of intimidation by which all men keep women in a state of fear.[10]

In war, intimidation through rape is done to spread fear through an enemy population in order to either force them to surrender or to flee. Rape in war is also a ritual act of male bonding in the most primitive sense, a ritual of marking territory and desecrating the enemy man's "property."[11] The man who is not able to defend his "property" is humiliated and his masculinity is questioned.

Rape is usually, but not exclusively, committed by victorious armies, as Brownmiller observes.

A simple rule of thumb in war is that the winning side is the side
that does the raping. There are two specific reasons for this, one
pragmatic and one psychological, and neither has much to do with
the nobility of losers or with the moral superiority of an heroic
defense. First, a victorious army marches through the defeated
people's territory, and thus it is obvious that if there is any raping
to be done, it will be done on the bodies of the defeated enemy's
women. Second, rape is the act of a conqueror. This is more than
a truism. It helps explain why men continue to rape in war.[12]

Another truism concerning rape and war is that the victims of rape will
be used to manipulate support for the cause of continuing the fight and
will be used to manipulate international public opinion with the hope of
provoking enough outrage to lead to an intervention that would change
the course of the war. All of the above elements can be seen in the wars
in Croatia and Bosnia.

One of the most damaging effects of the rapes and the manipulation
of these rapes for the war effort, other than the psychological trauma to
the victim herself, has been the fragmenting effect it has had on feminists
and women's groups within the territory of the Yugoslav successor states.
Feminists and women's groups have been split into two relatively antagonistic groups: those who see rape as a universal problem of violence
against women which needs to be identified and combated as such, and
those who see the high incidence of rape in this particular war as being
unique and the product of a contempt or hatred by one particular army
(Serbian) for the women of a particular ethnic group (Muslim or Croatian).

This split was best illustrated in two international meetings held in
Zagreb, Croatia. The first meeting, called Women In the War, was held
in October 1992 and was organized by the women's groups Kareta and
Women's Help Now. This international feminist meeting was designed
to focus on the issue of rape as a war crime and draw attention to victims
of rape from the war in Bosnia. The meeting became extremely controversial when the organizers of the meeting and the Croatian media attacked five of the most prominent feminists in Croatia for trying to
undermine the basic purpose of the conference. They claimed these feminists were undermining the conference by insisting that rape is a universal
act of violence by men against women and that, by holding this position,

these women were aiding the Serbian aggressors because they failed to single out "Croatian" and "Muslim" women as the victims.[13]

The second meeting, the International Congress of Women's Solidarity, was held in January 1993, also in Zagreb. The idea for the Congress originated with German feminist groups from Berlin, but even before it was held, given what had happened in October, there were signs that there would be problems. It created a public split between Croatian women's groups, the Zagreb Women's Lobby and associated groups who welcomed the congress, and other groups (Kareta, Women's Group Tresnjevka, and Bedem Ljubavi) who criticized the idea. Opposition to the congress centered upon its perceived neutrality; these women's groups did not want abstract discussions of rape and victims but instead wanted a public naming of the principal perpetrators and victims. The leaders of Bedem Ljubavi and the other groups favoring a singling out of the aggressors came to the congress with the hope of passing a resolution that would condemn Serbian aggression and specifically name Muslim and Croatian women as the principal victims.

When discussion at the congress did not proceed according to the wishes of these groups, Bedem Ljubavi issued an official protest. When a Serb-American, Vesna Božić, got up to speak, the Bedem-led group walked out. Božić gave a speech that was an emotional indictment of Milošević government, but when the Bedem group was told about the nature of her speech, its members dismissed it by saying "In Zagreb people do not have the right to speak if at the same time their husbands and brothers are burning, raping and bombing."[14]

The polarization of women's groups over rape and its victims plays into the nationalists ideology of creating a homogeneity of thought within the nation which equates self-identity with the nation and seeks to manipulate women as symbols of the nation's struggle. It is interesting to see a nationalist government and media rally to support "our" women at the same time it manipulates women in order to mobilize support for the war effort. Bedem Ljubavi and like-minded groups are glorified in the patriarchal culture of nationalist politics, while members of the Zagreb Women's Lobby were portrayed as disloyal and morally suspect. This manipulation of imagery overlaps into the creation of the image of "disloyal" women as "witches," which will be explored in depth later in this chapter.

The battle lines drawn between women of one nation over the politicization of rape carries into the international arena. The pressure to differentiate between types of rapists and types of victims as "theirs" and "ours" is overwhelming, the underlining meaning of this being that "they" are guilty for everything, even the crimes of "our" side. The desire to differentiate between "their" bestial war crimes and our "defensive" crimes can be seen in an article written for *The Nation* by Slavenka Drakulić, one of the best-known and respected Croatian feminists attacked at the international women's meetings in Zagreb. In the article, Drakulić struggles to differentiate the rapes committed by Serbs from those committed by Croats and Muslims.

> Of course, Croats and Muslims have raped Serbian women in Bosnia, too, but the Serbs are the aggressors, bent on taking over two-thirds of the territory. This does not justify Croat and Muslim offenses, but they are in a defensive war and do not practice systematic and organized rape.[15]

Later in the article, she adds:

> But even if the rapes were used for political propaganda, this could be justified because of the Serbian policy of exiling and destroying the Muslim population. If an entire ethnic group is systematically destroyed to the point of genocide, it is legitimate to use accounts of rape (or anything else for that matter) as a means of getting attention and influencing public opinion.[16]

This attempt to single out Serb-committed rape as being uniquely evil and horrible can also be seen in the writings of Western feminists and proponents of Bosnia's cause, such as Catherine MacKinnon and Alexandra Stiglemayer.

MacKinnon, in her article "Turning Rape into Pornography: Postmodern Genocide," argues that the origins of the wars in the former Yugoslavia can be traced to the culture of pornography that existed in the prewar former Yugoslavia and that the Serb rapes of Muslim and Croatian women are "to everyday rape what the Holocaust is to everyday anti-Semitism."[17] Stiglemayer's book, *Mass Rape: The War Against Women in Bosnia-Hercegovina*, a collection of essays from various authors, argues for the uniqueness and singular repulsiveness of Serbian rapes of Muslim and Croat women. Stiglemayer is much more cautious in her approach than MacKinnon, whose article from *Ms.* is reprinted in *Mass Rape*. Stiglemayer offers qualifiers to the number of rapes and indicates the culpability of Croat and Muslim forces as well as that of the Serbs.

Both MacKinnon and Stiglemayer, knowingly or unwittingly, are embroiled in the internal struggle between feminist groups in the Yugoslav successor states, and both rely heavily on information from these groups, such as Kareta, which want to specify the ethnicity of victims and aggressors. MacKinnon even directly attacks the feminists who had denounced the nationalist politicization of rapes in Bosnia by attacking the prewar magazine *Start*. MacKinnon describes these women, whom she does not name, but whom Yugoslav readers can immediately identify: "Select women who were privileged under the Communist regime, and who presented themselves as speaking for women."[18] MacKinnon, who prior to her interest in the rape issue surrounding the wars, probably had never seen an issue of *Start*, could only have developed this "insider's" view of the rape debate in Croatia from her Kareta sources. The fact that she joins in the politicization of rape and the polemical struggle between feminists in Croatia reflects the strong emotions and passions that are triggered by nationalistic wars.

In a response to MacKinnon's article in *Ms.*, Vesna Kesić, one of the former editors of *Start*, reveals the full implications of MacKinnon's accusations and conclusions.

Pornography is a substantial part of every militarism and warring male culture but to promote it as the primary causal element in the sexual violence which is perpetrated against women in this war means to omit all the complex historical, social and political courses of this war, especially nationalism, hate and revenge.

MacKinnon also reveals an ignorance of the current political climate and a failure to understand the implication of her accusations. We live in a society where the media serves as the principle medium for spreading propaganda against The Enemy to stir up ethnic hatred and fuel a desire for revenge. . . . MacKinnon's failure to check her facts and to be honest in her interpretations has resulted in many errors and false accusations. MacKinnon has embraced a nationalistic argument which has become a part of the war propaganda which stirs ethnic hatred and promotes revenge—fueling actions which are often expressed violently by men against women.[19]

This war of words between MacKinnon and the groups whose views she has come to represent and Kesič and her group is counterproductive. It does little to help the victims of rape and shifts attention from larger issues such as ensuring that rapes are finally prosecuted as war crimes.

Each of the governments involved in these wars has sought to manipulate and politicize rape and its victims. These efforts at manipulation and the media which eagerly cooperates with these efforts, victimizes the victims a second time. The use of inflated numbers also helps set up rape victims for a hard fall. When doubts are raised about the veracity of figures and reports, as they always are in these cases, skepticism sets in and all victims are viewed suspiciously. As a result, few women victims of rape during wars, like those victims in times of peace, ever receive justice—most end up being judged by a fickle public and media.

Furthermore, the image of women as victims as used by nationalist regimes assists in fueling the war by appealing to the patriarchal notions of women as property and the responsibility of men for protecting their property and taking revenge on those who would "pollute" this property. Women who become "tainted" by the enemy receive attention as symbols but tend to be surrounded by shame in public life. The underlying implication is that women who are raped by the enemy have in some absurd way betrayed the nation. This image of women as betrayers of their nation was briefly discussed in the previous section, and is a fundamental premise of traditional patriarchal cultures. This image of betrayal is especially pronounced in the nationalist imagery of some women as "witches."

WITCHES

The word *vještica* or *veštica*—"witch"—has traditionally been used by the South Slavs as a slur for women who are perceived to be conniving, ill-intentioned, bitter, secretive, and odd. In the nationalistic political cultures found in the former Yugoslavia, in addition to the standard connotations noted above, "witch" also implies betrayal and conspiracy against the nation.

The image of "trouble-making" women as witches can be found in the nationalistic press throughout the territory of former Yugoslavia. Outspoken women, usually antiwar activists, are often depicted riding brooms or even vacuum cleaners. The most notorious use of the witch image occurred in Croatia, as described in the previous section, when the weekly newspaper *Globus* attacked five feminists who had spoken out against the nationalistic manipulation of rape.

The initial salvo fired against the five feminists—Rada Iveković, Jelena Lovrić, Slavenka Drakulić, Dubravka Ugrešić and Vesna Kesić—was fired by the Zagreb daily *Globus* on 10 December 1992. The unsigned article not only referred to the women as witches, but it also used the emotionally charged rape imagery, as can be seen in its title, "Croatia's Feminists Rape Croatia." In addition to the charges that they had undermined the October 1992 international feminist meeting organized by Kareta and others, they were also charged with trying to prevent the 58th International Pen Congress from being held in Dubrovnik; of being concerned with the "struggle between sexes" because most of "these ladies had serious problems in finding a partner of the male sex"; that they had formed a quadrangle of feminism-Marxism-communism-Yugoslavism; and, most damning, that they were "Yugo-nostalgics" who abandoned Croatia in "her" hour of need.[20] The article was accompanied with a chart listing "vital information such as parentage, property, trips abroad during the war, attitudes on Croatia, and war aggression."[21]

Although Rada Iveković and Slavenka Drakulić had been attacked before by *Globus* and government-run newspapers, the *Globus* article of December 1992 reached a new low and began an all-out witch hunt. In an article in *Večernji list* by Milan Ivkosić on 15 December 1992, in a response to Vesna Kesić's reply to the charges in *Globus*, Kesić's Croatianhood was implicitly questioned and her ties to "friends" in America revealed.[22] Most of the articles shared a few central themes, which stressed links between feminism and communism, the connection of the women with foreign countries, and their lack of patriotism. Vesna Kesić described the atmosphere created by the media attacks: "It was a lynch mentality, by publishing personal information about us, including where we lived, they were in effort calling for a 'patriot' to rid Croatia of this dangerous coven of witches."[23] The only group to come to their defense was the Zagreb Women's Lobby, which issued a harsh denunciation of the attacks on the five women, which among other things stated, "We won't mention the degree of pervertedness of the mind which abuses even the rape of women in order to humiliate and prosecute other women. We should ask ourselves who are the people profiting from rapes of women and why?"[24]

Although the attack on the five "witches" occurred in Croatia and was triggered by a specific incident (the Pen Congress debate), the central issue involved is a common characteristic of patriarchal, nationalist cultures. The fact that during the wars in the former Yugoslavia, it was mainly women who organized pacifist movements and humanitarian actions, made them even more suspect in the eyes of nationalists. Any show of nonsupport for the militaristic policies being waged in the name of the nation immediately makes one a member of the "Fifth Column" or a foreign agent. The additional fact that many pacifists in the western Balkans identify themselves as feminists also make them suspect. For most Serb, Croat, and Muslim peasants and uneducated people, feminism is a mysterious concept which many people perceive as a men-hating, deviant, foreign concept. It is no accident that the media attacks against the five feminists directly challenged their sexuality and implicitly through the use of the word "witches" implied "deviant" sexual behavior.

The nationalistic use of gender imagery during war centers around images of "good" women, usually mother's who produce strong soldier sons, and "bad" women, usually pacifists and feminists who are single and do not fit the women as wombs image.

WOMBS FOR THE NATION

The nationalistic elections held in each of the former Yugoslav republics were highlighted by party platforms which called for an increase of births to stem the demographic threat faced by the nation. This was also a common element of elections throughout Eastern Europe in 1989 and in some cases, like that of Hungary, led to the creation of mother's national parties which upheld the paternalistic stereotypes of love for one's country (meaning nation) and the image of women as mothers. The political situation in the Yugoslav region drastically intensified, however, due to the war.

In Serbia, for most of the 1980s, nationalists were preoccupied with the "demographic invasion" by Albanians in Kosovo. This led in 1990 to a move by the ruling Socialist Party to create a law which would provide incentives to Serbian families with more than two children at the same time cutting social benefits to Albanian families with more than three children.[25] The Belgrade Women's Lobby successfully fought against this legislation, which was also supported by the Serbian Orthodox Church. Even though the law was passed, as of this writing, it remains to be applied and indications are that its enforcement will not occur anytime soon.

Similar developments occurred in Croatia, Slovenia, and Bosnia. In Bosnia, Reis-ul-Ulema, Mustafa Ćerić issued a "Fetva" (edict) in January 1994, calling on all Muslim women to give birth to five children each and condemning mixed marriages as a betrayal of one's faith and culture.[26] In Croatia, President Franjo Tudjman, in his State of the Nation speech on 22 December 1994, tasked the Ministry of Reconstruction and Development with the preparation and implementation of a demographic revival program, warning that unless immediate steps were taken the "Croatian people would face extinction."[27] In Slovenia, the Christian Demographic Union backed by the Church pushed for a ban on abortion, also warning that if such a law was not passed, the Slovenes would soon be a minority in their own country.

This image of a demographic crisis is a classic nationalist phobia which is further reinforced by deeply rooted patriarchal stereotypes of male and female roles. In times of war, the perception of threat to the nation is intensified and pressure on women to have more children increases dramatically.

The Serbs and Montenegrins have a saying that a perfect family has three sons—one for the Church (God), one for the army (state), and one for the parents (progeny). Montenegrins and Albanians traditionally celebrate the birth of a son by firing a rifle. The implications are clear, women must produce sons in order to be good mothers. If any woman balks at the notion of producing cannon fodder for the militaristic ambitions of a nationalist elite, they run the risk of being identified as traitors. Textbooks, the media, and religious leaders all reinforce the image of women as wombs. As external pressures (war, famine, disease) increase, so do internal societal pressures on women to conform to the stereotype and to do their patriotic duty.

IMAGE AND REALITIES

In this chapter I have highlighted the prevailing images of women produced by nationalist politics in the Yugoslav successor states. These images reinforce the stereotypes of patriarchal systems and enhance the culture of male dominance. Women are treated as commodities, symbols and baby factories. Any objection to these rules leads to public condemnation, suspicion, and ridicule. The nationalist paranoia and emotions which overwhelm people in times of war undermine efforts at women's empowerment and fragment feminists according to their level of patriotism.

The fact that many feminists embrace patriotism is a testimony to the power of nationalism and to the weakness of universal or supra-identities. How deeply this embrace of nationalism has taken root will be seen as post-Yugoslav societies adjust to an uneasy period of peace.

12

RAPE IN WAR: THE CASE OF BOSNIA

Dorothy Q. Thomas and Regan E. Ralph

Reports of rape in the former Yugoslavia have brought much deserved and long overdue international attention to the issue of rape in war. This attention has highlighted the abusive character of wartime rape, but it also has revealed the persistent misunderstandings regarding rape's prevalence, function, and motivation in war. Moreover, efforts to ensure that rape is prosecuted effectively by the International Tribunal established to try war crimes committed in the former Yugoslavia have underscored the difficulties in applying international human rights and humanitarian law to rape.[1] In order to overcome these difficulties and end the appalling history of impunity for this abuse, rape in conflict must be understood as an abuse that targets women for political and strategic reasons.

This chapter was originally published, under the title "Rape in War: Challenging the Tradition of Impunity," in SAIS Review *14, no. 1 (winter–spring 1994). Copyright © The Johns Hopkins University Press. Reprinted by permission.*

THE PREVALENCE OF RAPE

Violence against women in conflict situations assumes many forms: rape is often only one of the ways in which women are targeted. But, while other abuses such as murder and other forms of torture have long been denounced as war crimes, rape has been downplayed as an unfortunate but inevitable side effect of sending men to war. It thus is ignored as a human rights abuse. Then when rape *is* reported and condemned, as it has been in Bosnia-Herzegovina, the abuses are called unprecedented and unique in their scale. In fact, wartime rape has never been limited to a certain era or a particular part of the world.

During World War II, for example, Moroccan mercenary troops fought with Free French forces in Italy on terms that "included license to rape and plunder in enemy territory."[2] Nazis raped Jewish women despite soldiers' concerns with "race defilement" and raped countless women in their path as they invaded the Soviet Union.[3] The Soviets then exacted their revenge upon German women as the troops battled their way to Berlin.[4]

More recent history provides further evidence of wartime rape. Pakistani soldiers fighting to suppress Bangladesh's independence, which was declared in 1971, terrorized the Bengali people with night raids during which women were raped in their villages or carted off to soldiers' barracks.[5] Similarly, Turkish troops were notorious for the widespread rape of women and girls. In one instance, twenty-five girls who reported their rapes by Turkish soldiers to Turkish officers were then raped again by those officers.[6]

In Bosnia, countless women have been attacked and brutally raped. J., a thirty-nine-year-old Croatian woman, was detained in Omarska, a detention camp where Serbian forces tortured and summarily executed scores of Muslims and Croats. She recounted her rape by a reserve captain of the self-proclaimed "Serbian Republic." He threw me on the floor, and someone else came into the room. . . . Both Grabovac and this other man started to beat me. They said I was an Ustaša and that I needed to give birth to a Serb—that I would then be different."[7]

In Peru, rape of women by security forces is common practice in the ongoing armed conflict between the Communist Party of Peru–Shining Path and government counterinsurgency forces. In 1992, Human Rights Watch documented more than forty cases of rape of women committed by soldiers during interrogation in Peru's emergency zones or in the course of security force sweeps and massacres.[8] In the violent struggle between Indian security forces and Muslim insurgents in the north India states of Jammu and Kashmir, Human Rights Watch recorded numerous rapes by Indian security and mulitant groups. In one case, members of an army unit searching a village for suspected militants gang-raped at least six women, including an eleven-year-old girl and a sixty-year-old woman. One of these women was told by her rapist, "We have orders from our officers to rape you."[9]

Of all of the abuses committed in war, rape is inflicted in particular against women. Although men also are raped, efforts to document wartime rape reveal that women overwhelmingly are its most frequent targets. In Kenya, for example, of the 192 rapes of Somali refugees documented from February to March 1993, 187 involved women, 4 were against children, and 1 was against a man.[10]

Recently, efforts have been made to document and publicize such abuse. Although these efforts are crucial to enhancing accountability for wartime rape, they often risk isolating sexual assault from other abuse occurring in conflict against either women or men. In fact, rape of women in war almost always occurs in connection with other forms of violence or abuse against women or their families. Women are raped as men are beaten or forced into hard labor. In Burma in 1992, government troops rounded up Rohingya Muslim men for forced labor, then returned to villages and raped the women left behind. When soldiers broke into sixteen-year-old Dilara Begum's house in the Arakan province in western Burma, looking for the husband they had forced into hard labor, Dilara was gang-raped.[11] In December 1991, Jahura Khatu's husband was taken by government soldiers for forced labor from their home in the Arakan province. The soldiers returned repeatedly to the house and raped Jahura. In early 1992, soldiers forced Jahura at gunpoint to march with three other women to a nearby military camp where all four women were raped repeatedly for twenty-four hours.[12] Women who are raped are often also murdered or left to die by their attackers. "Pancho," a Peruvian soldier who had served in the security forces, recalled one rape in 1982: "The boys played her like a yo-yo. Then we wasted her."[13] It is important to place rape in this context in order to understand that it functions, as do other wartime assaults, as a human rights abuse. Moreover, the harm inflicted by rape may be compounded by other concurrent violations against either the rape victim or those close to her.

Despite the pervasiveness of rape, it often has been a hidden element of war, a fact that is linked inextricably to its largely gender-specific character. The fact that the abuse is committed by men against women has contributed to its being narrowly portrayed as sexual or personal in nature, a portrayal that depoliticizes sexual abuse in conflict and results in its being ignored as a war crime. A more accurate understanding of the political function of wartime rape and the complexity of its motivation is necessary if adequate and responsive remedies are to be applied.

RAPE'S FUNCTION IN WAR

Rape has long been mischaracterized and dismissed by military and political leaders—in other words, those in a position to stop it—as a private crime, a sexual act, the ignoble conduct of the occasional soldier, or, worse still, it has been accepted precisely because it is so commonplace. In Peru, for example, despite numerous reports of rape by soldiers, Peruvian military officers have dismissed such abuse as a "regrettable excess." Responding to reports of widespread rape of women refugees in camps in northeastern Kenya, the Kenyan government has denied that the rapes are occurring or has blamed the victims. One Kenyan official stated that the rape allegations were made solely to "attract sympathy and give the government negative publicity."[14] In April 1993, Radovan Karadžić, leader of the Bosnian Serbs, denied any knowledge of widespread rape in Serb-controlled Bosnia: "We know of some eighteen cases of rape altogether, but this was not organized but done by psychopaths."[15] Karadžić dismissed claims of mass rapes as the propaganda of "Mulsim mullahs." When confronted with evidence of rape by government troops in Kashmir, Indian authorities try to impugn the integrity of witnesses, discredit the testimony of physicians, or just flatly deny the charges. A high-ranking army officer commented, "A soldier conducting an operation at the dead of night is unlikely to think of rape when he is not even certain if he will return alive,"[16]—as if soldiers rape only when operating under safe conditions.

In fact, rape is neither incidental nor private. It routinely serves a strategic function in war and acts as an integral tool for achieving particular military objectives. In the former Yugoslavia, rape and other grave abuses committed by Serbian forces were intended to drive the non-Serbian population into flight. Serbian forces rid villages of the non-Serb population by first shelling towns, then segregating men from women and taking the men to detention centers. Women either were left to fend for themselves in towns controlled by enemy forces or were taken in groups to holding centers, where they might be raped, gang-raped, and beaten for days or even weeks at a time. B., a forty-year-old Muslim woman, remained in her home with her husband when Serbian forces began shelling Doboj. Ground troops moved through the city, forced people from their houses, and ordered the women and children onto buses. B. was taken to an abandoned high school where she was raped repeatedly for almost one month: "It began there as soon as I arrived. On [one] occasion I was raped with a gun. . . . Others stood watching. Some spat on us."[7]

In Burma, too, rape was a part of a campaign to drive the Rohingya out of the country. Eslam Khatun, wife of the village headman, was at home in the village of Imuddinpara with her children and sister-in-law, Layla, when soldiers forced open the door. The soldiers stripped Layla and began molesting her as they took her away. Eslam found Layla's body a week later; she appeared to have bled to death from her vagina. The next week, after the mutilated bodies of Eslam's husband and his brother were found, Eslam and her six children fled to a refugee camp, which then housed two-thirds of her village. Having driven more than 200,000 refugees into neighboring Bangladesh, the Burmese government maintained that the Rohingyas were illegal immigrants from Bangladesh and never belonged in Burma in the first place.[18] These refugees, however, were no more welcome in Bangladesh. An October 1993 Human Rights Watch report details the abuse, including rape, of Burmese refugees by Bangladeshi military and paramilitary forces in charge of refugee camps.[19]

Documenting where and how rape functions as a tool of military strategy is essential to counteracting the longstanding view of rape in war as private or incidental. The attention to rape's strategic function, however, has attached much significance to "mass rape" and "rape as genocide." This emphasis on rape's scale as what makes it an abuse demanding redress distorts the nature of rape in war by failing to reflect both the experience of individual women and the various functions of wartime rape.

Rape rises to the level of a war crime or a grave breach of the Geneva Conventions regardless of whether it occurs on a demonstrably massive scale or is associated with an overarching policy. Individual rapes that function as torture or cruel and inhuman treatment themselves constitute grave breaches of the Geneva Conventions.[20] Thus, even if rape occurs in an apparently indiscriminate fashion and not in the service of an overarching strategic policy and not on a massive scale, it constitutes a violation of international law. When rape does occur on a mass scale or as a matter of orchestrated policy, this added dimension of the crime is recognized by designating and prosecuting rape as a crime against humanity.[21]

Reports from Peru demonstrate the different ways in which rape, although not explicitly a matter of security force policy, functions as a tactical weapon. In Peru's Emergency Zones,[22] rape occurs in the course of armed conflict, usually in order to punish a group of civilians for perceived sympathies with armed insurgents, and to demonstrate the soldiers' domination over civilians.[23] In March 1992, Florencia lost her husband to a Shining Path execution squad and then was raped by the guerrillas. The army arrived in her village a week later and accused the villagers of collaborating with the guerrillas. Florencia was gang-raped by soldiers as the men of her village were beaten.[24] Rape during interrogation by Peru's counterinsurgency forces is committed in order to get information or frighten and intimidate an individual into complying with the wishes of her captors. Arrested and detained by Civil Guards for alleged guerrilla activity, Flora Elisa Aliaga, twenty-nine years old and pregnant, was raped by eight of her captors, once with a machine gun.[25]

Although rape is a sex-specific type of abuse, it generally functions like other forms of torture to intimidate and punish individual women. In some instances, however, it also can serve a strikingly sex-specific function, when, for example, it is committed with the intent of impregnating its victims. A Bosnian rape victim told Human Rights Watch, "It was their aim to make a baby. They wanted to humiliate us. They would say directly, looking into your eyes, that they wanted to make a baby."[26] This function of rape has never been reflected in the remedies available for rape victims. If anything, pregnancy is viewed as the "inevitable byproduct of . . . rape," rather than as a distinct harm meriting its own remedy.[27]

In some documented instances of rape, the abuse appears to serve not only strategic or political functions but also the perverse sexual gratification of the attacker. Somali women refugees in Kenya typically are raped *after* being successfully robbed. Rape in this context is thus not only a tool for frightening refugees into complying with their attackers' demands, but also inflicted specifically against women for sex. The plights of "young" and "pretty" Burmese women kidnapped by soldiers and kept at army barracks for raping[28] and of the thousands of women pressed into service as "comfort women" during World War II further demonstrate that rape's function ostensibly may be not only to achieve overt political ends but also to satisfy the sexual proclivities of the attacker. Just as rape should not be considered an exclusively sexual act, neither should it be viewed solely as a political tool divorced from the crime's sexual aspects. Doing so returns this debate to its starting point: the denial of any connection between the sexual element of rape and the political function that it serves.

Whenever committed by a state agent or an armed insurgent, whether a matter of policy or an individual incident of torture, wartime rape constitutes an abuse of power and a violation of international humanitarian law. The fact that rape functions, in most instances, as do other forms of torture or cruel and inhuman treatment makes it all the more striking that it has not been prosecuted like any other abuse. The differential treatment of rape underscores the fact that the problem—for the most part—lies not in the absence of adequate legal prohibitions, but in the international community's willingness to tolerate the subordination of women.

MOTIVATION: WHY ARE WOMEN TARGETED?

Soldiers are motivated to rape precisely because rape serves the strategic interests delineated above. But the fact that it is predominantly *men* raping *women* reveals that rape in war, like all rape, reflects a gender-based motivation, namely, the assertion by men of their power over women.[29] Men's domination of women is often deeply imbedded in societal attitudes, so much so that its role as a motivating factor is not easily discernible in every individual incident of rape. It is therefore difficult to distinguish the gender elements of a rapist's motivation from the specific political function served by the rape.

In human rights work, however, the assessment of motivation is crucial to determining the nature of the abuse and the remedy to be applied. Traditional human rights work has focused on politically motivated abuse by states. Because gender-based abuse often was not considered to be political, it was not considered a human rights issue. Recognizing gender-specific abuse requires an understanding not only of the political character of the abuse but also of that element of motivation that is particularly related to gender.

Despite the difficulties of determining motivation, documentary efforts have revealed common elements in the motives of uniformed rapists. Soldiers rape to subjugate and inflict shame upon their victims, and, by extension, their victims' families and communities. Rape, wherever it occurs, is considered a profound offense against individual and community honor. This is true for Somali women, for example, who have been raped and must cope with not only the physical and psychological trauma of rape but also the likelihood of rejection by their families. In many cases, refugee families beg U.N. High Commissioner for Refugees (UNHCR) officials to take their daughters to another camp after they have been raped because the families feel such stigma. Other women, once raped, are ostracized by their husbands and isolated from their families.[30] Similarly, a commentator reported from the former Yugoslavia that "[o]ne woman told me that if she were raped, she would kill herself, even if her husband did not reject her. She could not stand the shame and humiliation, she could not face her children afterward."[31]

Soldiers can succeed in translating the attack upon an individual woman into an assault upon her community because of the emphasis placed—in every culture in the world—on women's sexual purity and the fact that societies define themselves, in overt or less clear-cut fashions, relative to their ability to protect and control that purity. It is the protection and control of women's purity that renders them perfect targets for abuse. In Turkey, an observer dismissed as impossible allegations of rape by Turkish government forces of Kurdish women—both civilians and guerrillas—on the ground that Turkish soldiers understand that virginity and women's honor are sacred. Soldiers, it was argued, would not dare to defile women whose communities place a high social value on virginity and female modesty.[32]

In fact, soldiers do rape women precisely because the violation of their "protected" status has the effect of shaming them and their communities. Seventeen-year-old S., a Kurdish woman from southeastern Turkey, was detained by village guards and antiterror police during a night raid on her village, accused of harboring members of the Kurdish Workers' Party (PKK), raped during her interrogation, and taunted by her captors: "Now you're engaged, but after we rape you, no one will marry you." When she was released on a hillside in the middle of the night. S.'s captors warned her not to speak of the rape, "because it would be very bad for" her.[33]

S.'s story suggests that rapists may also be motivated by the likelihood that their victims will not report the assault. By virtue of being a rape victim, a woman becomes the perceived agent of her community's shame. In a bizarre twist, she changes from a victim into a guilty party, responsible for bringing dishonor upon her family or community. As a result, women victims, whether for fear of being seen this way, or because they see themselves this way, are extremely reluctant to report rape. The shame of rape may keep women, who would rather bury their "dis-honor," from seeking punishment for their attackers. K.S., a fifty-four-year-old housewife who was raped in her home by Serbian soldiers, told Human Rights Watch, "What happened to me, happened to many, but the women keep it secret. It is shameful. Thus the mother conceals it if it happened to her daughter so she can marry and if it happened to an older woman, she wants to protect her marriage."[34] Only changes in women's protected status coupled with a better understanding of rape's function as a political or tactical abuse will help communities resist sham-ing and punishing the victim and put the responsibility on the attacker where it belongs.

While it is absolutely essential that efforts to achieve accountability tease out the "gender element" of rape's motivation, an overemphasis on gender alone, at least on a narrow conception of gender, can obscure other characteristics of a woman's identity that determine *which* women are raped. In Bosnia, a woman's religion or nationality as well as her gender makes her a target for rape. In Burma, government soldiers rape Rohingya women, thus identifying their victims by their sex *and* their ethnic affiliation. Rape by the security forces in Peru is strongly deter-mined by race and class: rape victims are overwhelmingly poor and brown-skinned. And Somali women refugees report that they are asked by their rapists to which clan they belong. Women who are the same clan as their attackers may still be robbed, but often are spared rape.[35]

The tendency to focus exclusively on the gender-motivational element of rape risks playing into an understanding of women's human rights abuse that is abstracted from the reality of different women's experiences. Women's experience of rape in war, like that of women's human rights abuse more generally, is always determined by a variety of factors, includ-ing race, class, religion, ethnicity, and nationality. Efforts to focus on gen-der alone, while understandable in the context of the historical disregard of gender as a motivating factor in human rights abuse, create a different problem, that of oversimplifying the ways in which different women expe-rience human rights abuse. This not only obscures the diversity of wom-en's experience, but also may hide the need to craft remedies that are responsive to gender and the many other factors that intersect with it.[36]

A TRADITION OF IMPUNITY

The failure to punish rapists appears to be as consistent and widespread as rape itself. Only recently did the Japanese government officially admit to and apologize for forcing thousands of women into sexual slavery during World War II.[37] Even so, official statements have failed both to acknowledge the acts of the Japanese army as war crimes and to recognize the need for redress. This apology comes long after survivors—Korean, Chinese, Filipina and Indonesian women—came forward to tell their stories of being kidnapped, lured with false promises of employment, and shipped to various locations where they were forced to work as prostitutes.

Since World War II, there has been little improvement in acknowledging the gravity of rape as a wartime abuse, as demonstrated by the fact that it still goes largely unpunished. In October 1992, six Kashmiri women raped by Indian troops went to the hospital after their assaults, where doctors collected medical evidence of rape. The government inquiry of their allegations found the evidence unreliable and declared the charges "false" and an effort "to discredit the security forces."[38]

How is it that rape, a crime universally condemned, can be disregarded and trivialized when it occurs in war? Unfortunately, the answer is partly because the attitudes toward women which prompt rape in the first place and which fuel its mischaracterization as "personal" are reinforced and even shared by those in a position to prohibit and punish the abuse. Thus, for example, when the International Commission of Jurists released its 1971 report on the fighting in East Pakistan, the Commission assumed that young girls and women kidnapped by Pakistani troops were held for the soldiers' sexual pleasure. The report failed to link widespread rape with the Pakistani army's stated goal of breaking the spirit of the Bengali people during the civil war.[39] When the European Commission of Human Rights heard evidence of rape by Turkish forces in Cyprus, it pronounced the abuse to be inhuman treatment but failed to examine its function as a form of torture.[40]

The mischaracterization of rape as a crime against honor, and not as a crime against the physical integrity of the victim, also has contributed to the failure to denounce and prosecute wartime rape. This misunderstanding of rape is reflected not only in attitudes but also in the laws themselves. In many countries and even in international law, rape is codified as a crime against honor rather than against the individual victim. In Brazil, rape is a "crime against custom." In Peru, until very recently, it was codified as a "crime against honor." Article 27 of the Fourth Geneva Convention prohibits "any attack of [women's] honor, in particular against rape, enforced prostitution, or any form of indecent assault."

Thus, a matter of law, rape is often perceived as harm against the community as symbolized by the woman's honor, and not as harm against the physical integrity of the victim herself. This characterization not only contributes to women being targeted for rape, but also reinforces their unwillingness to come forward and report it. Further, it establishes the victim as responsible for the loss of community honor rather than focusing on the attacker as responsible for the violation of the victim's physical integrity.

THE RHETORIC OF RAPE

A comprehensive assessment of the obstacles to ensuring accountability for wartime rape must include an examination of the use of rape for rhetorical purposes. After the Germans invaded Belgium in August 1914, propaganda decrying the "rape of the Hun" was directed toward the United States to galvanize the country, then neutral, to come to the rescue of Belgium as symbolized by its ravaged women. Rhetoric decrying widespread rape appears to emphasize the gravity of the abuse. But, in fact, the use of rape to inflame conflict may impede efforts to obtain greater accountability for rape in war. More recently, in the former Yugoslavia, the parties to the conflict accused each other of trumping up charges of mass rape to muster international sympathy and perhaps even military support. Rather than investigating allegations of rape and punishing attackers, political leaders accuse each other of sponsoring abuse and plead innocent to charges leveled against them.

When the horror of rape is invoked to serve political ends, women victims of rape are often ill-served by the attention they then receive. First, even if rape of women is condemned, the denunciation is intended not to ensure accountability but to exploit the problem. Women are victimized again, their assault manipulated for political ends. Rape survivors in the former Yugoslavia reportedly have attempted or committed suicide and have experienced severe clinical depressions and acute psychotic episodes after repeatedly recounting—sometimes in front of a television camera—the details of their assaults.[41]

Second, the individual crimes get lost in a sea of exaggeration, which, if not substantiated, may produce doubt about the scale of abuses and the credibility of women's individual testimonies. In early 1993, reports from Bosnia of mass rape claimed that anywhere from 10,000 to 60,000 predominantly Muslim women had been assaulted. These assertions were challenged by the Bosnian Serbs as impossible to prove and denounced as propaganda. A European Community investigative mission cited 20,000 rapes in a January 1993 report but the U.N. Commission of Experts has thus far been able to collect documentation of only about 3,000 rape cases and to identify only about 800 victims by name.[42] The number of rape cases that can be proved remains to be seen. The number of rapes that actually occurred probably will never be known. In any case, the use of numbers in the course of the conflict has served rhetorical rather than remedial purposes. This is underscored by the fact that the use of numbers by the parties to dramatize the victimization of "their women" is rarely accompanied by efforts by those same parties to prosecute alleged abusers. Thus women, perhaps twice victimized, receive no redress, and no precedent of accountability is established.

ACCOUNTABILITY: INADEQUATE PROTECTION OR ENFORCEMENT?

International humanitarian law prohibits and provides the means to punish human rights abuses committed in war. Whether rape is included in these protections became a subject of debate recently when, in demanding a response to reports of abuses in Bosnia, some urged that rape be designated specifically as a war crime. A December 1992 editorial in the *New York Times*, for example, implicitly endorsed a proposal to revise the Geneva Conventions to designate rape as a war crime.[43] Such exhortations gave the false impression that without such reform, no means of prosecuting rape exist under international law. On the contrary, the means for prosecuting rape as a war crime are firmly established in international law. The problem lies not in the law but in the failure to enforce its prohibitions.

International Law

Rape itself is explicitly prohibited under international humanitarian law governing both international and internal conflicts. The Fourth Geneva Convention of 1949 specifies in Article 27 that "[w]omen shall be especially protected against any attack on their honor, in particular against rape, enforced prostitution, or any form of indecent assault."[44] Further,

Article 147 of the same Convention designates "wilfully causing great suffering or serious injury to body or health," "torture," and "inhuman treatment" as war crimes and as grave breaches of the Conventions.[45] As the International Committee of the Red Cross (ICRC) has recognized, rape constitutes "wilfully causing great suffering or serious injury to body or health" and thus should be treated as a grave breach of the Convention.[46]

The ICRC also has stated that "inhuman treatment" should be interpreted in light of Article 27 and its specific prohibition against rape.[47] This interpretation was reinforced by the U.S. State Department in its recent statement that rape is a grave breach of the Geneva Conventions and should be prosecuted as such.[48] The Conventions specify that governments are obliged to find and punish those responsible for grave breaches and to make those accused available for trial.

As with international conflicts, humanitarian law clearly prohibits rape in internal conflicts. Rape committed or tolerated by any party to a non-international conflict is prohibited by Common Article 3 of the Geneva Conventions insofar as it constitutes "violence to life and person," "cruel treatment," "torture" or "outrages upon personal dignity."[49] Moreover, Protocol II to the Geneva Conventions, which governs some internal conflicts, outlaws "outrages upon personal dignity, in particular humiliating and degrading treatment, rape, enforced prostitution and any form of indecent assault" committed by any party.[50] The ICRC explains that this provision "reaffirms and supplements common Article 3 . . . [because] it became clear that it was necessary to strengthen . . . the protection of women . . . who may also be the victims of rape, enforced prostitution or indecent assault."[51]

Grave breaches of the Geneva Conventions attract universal jurisdiction[52] and therefore can be prosecuted by an international tribunal or by the domestic courts of any country. This mechanism for holding war criminals accountable, however, is available only for crimes committed in international conflicts. By contrast, the prohibitions against rape and other abuses committed in internal conflicts are not supported by effective means for international enforcement. Current humanitarian law provides little authority to the international community to compel a state to account for its conduct during an internal conflict.[53]

Nonetheless, rape committed in internal conflicts may, in theory, be prosecuted as crimes against humanity. Crimes against humanity may arise where crimes such as murder, enslavement, or other inhumane acts are committed on a mass scale and are directed at a civilian population.[54] The concept of crimes against humanity—unlike that of war crimes—allows for the prosecution of mass crimes committed by a state against its own nationals and thus provides a means for the international community to attack mass rape where it occurs in internal conflicts.[55] Rape was recognized as a crime against humanity in the aftermath of World War II[56] and again, in 1993, in the United Nations' statute for the international tribunal to try war crimes committed in the former Yugoslavia.

Customary international law demands that crimes against humanity be punished.[57] International consensus, however, currently recognizes that the duty and power to prosecute these crimes rests only with the state in whose borders the crimes are committed and not with an international tribunal nor with the domestic courts of any other country.[58] In the absence of an international treaty or a mechanism such as the Nuremburg Charter which specifically accords the power to prosecute crimes against humanity to an international court or which provides for universal jurisdiction, crimes against humanity must be prosecuted by the nation in which the abuses occurred.

The Torture Convention offers another possible remedy for victims of rape in internal conflicts by imposing a clear duty upon states to prosecute the acts deemed criminal by the Convention.[59] The obligation to prosecute torturers extends to all states that are party to the Convention, and thus constitutes a form of universal jurisdiction.[60] This remedy, however, has not yet been put effectively into practice. Thus, in most instances, the terms of enforcement of domestic law coupled with international pressure to prosecute rapists will give victims of wartime rape virtually their only opportunity for relief.

It is unfortunate that, in many countries, the domestic laws that would be used to prosecute wartime rape classify the crime in ways that minimize its seriousness and introduce the possibility of discriminatory prosecution. As mentioned above, Peru's laws once designated rape a crime against honor; currently rape is defined as a crime against *liberated sexual* (the freedom to choose a sexual partner) and not as a physical assault. In many countries and some parts of the United States, there is no legal concept of marital rape.[61] Turkey's criminal code classifies rape as a "felony against public decency and family order" and not—as are other types of assault and battery—as a "felony against an individual." In Pakistan, evidentiary laws discriminate against women by granting no legal weight to their testimony in certain rape trials.[62] The inaccurate portrayal of rape in national laws worldwide reduces the likelihood that rape victims in internal conflicts will receive justice. Women often find that their honor, more than the rapists' actions, is on trial. Thus, in Peru, a nursing student who complained of attempted rape was asked by an assistant to the public prosecutor: "Are you a virgin? If you are not a virgin, why do you complain?"[63]

The War Crimes Tribunal

The international response to the atrocities in Bosnia presents a singular opportunity to enforce existing international law and begin to put an end to the history of impunity with regard to rape. In February 1993, the United Nations Security Council called for the establishment of an international tribunal to investigate and try perpetrators of war crimes on the Balkan conflict. The war crimes tribunal presents the only means of holding to account those who have attacked civilians and tortured detainees in flagrant violation of humanitarian law, and of achieving redress for the survivors of such abuse.

Women victims of war crimes, in particular, look to the tribunal to vindicate their right to equal protection under law through the prosecution of violence against women alongside other war crimes. By trying rape as torture, inhuman treatment, and the willful causing of "great suffering or serious injury to body or health,"[64] and not as an offense against honor, the tribunal will correct the mischaracterizations of rape that have trivialized the abuse in the past and resulted in women's attackers acting with impunity.[65]

The precedential value of the nascent tribunal is, however, at risk of being limited to rhetorical posturing by the United Nations.[66] Despite the importance of the tribunal it may go the way of many politically unpopular plans of action. The lack of financial and political support for the tribunal is demonstrated by U.N. foot-dragging that slowed the process of setting the operations of the tribunal in motion, by the continuing failure to allocate sufficient resources to the tribunal, and by the oft-repeated concern that amnesty may yet be traded for peace. This disregard for the tribunal has led many to doubt whether serious U.N. investigations of alleged war crimes will ever take place, let alone whether the tribunal will succeed in bringing war criminals to justice.[67]

Impunity for wartime rape must end. The international community's outrage in response to widespread rape in the former Yugoslavia must translate into a commitment to punish rape not only in that conflict, but also in any conflict where it occurs. The International War Crimes Tribunal must live up to its promise, prosecute rape, and reject the history of neglect of rape and sexual assault as crimes of war. National governments must hold those who commit rape in internal conflicts accountable and, where necessary, reform their national laws to reflect the substantive nature of the abuse.

The international community is responsible for ensuring that the war criminals that have destroyed so much of the former Yugoslavia are held to account. It also must take every possible step to ensure that no rapists in any conflict escape international condemnation and prosecution for their crimes.

PART FOUR

LITERATURE
AND RELIGION

13

WOMEN WRITERS IN CROATIAN AND SERBIAN LITERATURES

Gordana P. Crnković

Women writers have been present in the Serbian cultural area since the medieval era. One of the most accomplished and well-known literary pieces of the Serbian Middle Ages, *The Praise to Prince Lazar* (1399), was embroidered into a prince's shroud by the widow of another Serbian feudal lord, a woman named Jefimija. Since the renaissance, the Croatian city-state of Dubrovnik also has had women writers, as Zdenka Marković's ground-breaking work, *The Women Poets of Old Dubrovnik; from the Middle of the Sixteenth Century to the End of the Eighteenth Century* (1970), amply shows.[1] This chapter, however, deals with the literary production of the modern period (the nineteenth and primarily twentieth centuries), focusing on the Croatian scene (my main area of interest) but also mentioning some Serbian writers. Rather than make a catalogue of women writers who worked in this period, I have chosen to represent, at somewhat greater length, the work of the few who are most well known.

I shall begin this chapter with a brief overview of the work of three Croatian women writers: Dragojla Jarnević, Ivana Brlić-Mažuranić, and Marija Jurić Zagorka. Different economic and social backgrounds, as well as different focuses of their literary works, made for widely divergent receptions of these women's writings. Ivana Brlić-Mažuranić, who was born into one and married into another rich and socially prestigious family, wrote stories for children. Consequently, her work was well-received and encountered smooth publishing paths, and she could also afford to publish several pieces herself which were not taken by larger presses. Dragojla Jarnević, on the contrary, was poor, friendless, and lacked the social connections of Brlić-Mažuranić. Jarnević had to support herself, as well as fight Hungarian censorship on account of the patriotic sentiments in her work. The immensely popular Marija Jurić Zagorka (who started her work as a political journalist writing for oppositional papers), had to pretend she was a man in order to have her first articles published and fought a bitter battle to gain acceptance into the journalist profession. Zagorka's many supporters were highly-placed male journalists and politicians. She defied those who opposed the idea of a woman journalist and established herself as an exceptional figure in the history of Croatian letters.

DRAGOJLA JARNEVIĆ

Although Dragojla Jarnević (1812–75) was born and died in Karlovac, she also traveled to Graz, worked in Venice, and lived in Zagreb. Due to financial problems in one period, she worked as a seamstress; she also held the post of director of a private school near Karlovac. Jarnević was a prolific writer of stories and poetry. Her patriotic poems reflect the period of national awakening in Croatian literature and are considered to be rather stereotypical and not of considerable literary value.

Her best-known work, however, is her lengthy *Diary*, which she began writing in 1832, and which was published in 1958 under the title *A Life of One Woman*. In her *Diary*, Jarnević recounts her life as a single woman who had to struggle with financial difficulties, sickness, emotional disappointments, and various obstacles to her literary work. Jarnević began writing her *Diary* in German, only to switch to Croatian in 1841, swept up by the patriotism and national (including cultural and linguistic) awareness of the Illyrian movement. She had problems with the publication of her poems and *Domorodne povijesti* (Homeland stories) with Hungarian censors because of the texts' implied patriotic references.[2] Her *Diary* also provides a vivid picture of the political and cultural climate of her times in Croatia and abroad.[3] Jarnević's own political courage and literary persistence were striking; "she copied her manuscript of *Home-land Stories* six times, and besides proofread it all by herself and carried a huge correspondence with regard to its distribution."[4]

Jarnević's *Diary* displays not only an independent and strong intellect, keen observation skills, and an impressive writing ability but also a very honest and open approach to the author's own sexuality. Jarnević does not, for instance, censure her writing about her affair (in her forties) with a village boy whom she actually had to pay for sex. She traces her conflicting emotions in detail, giving a moving picture of inner turmoil and the clash between a strong sexual desire, on one hand, and a variety of social and emotional concerns, on the other.

March 1856. Pribiće.

26. . . . and I cry now, sitting by my table, as I did just a short time ago walking by hayfield. And why? The question is—so to say . . . it comes hard out of my pen, but faithful to myself I will describe my smitten heart, let others know what the stirred up passions are in the human being. So many times I swore I will not deal with Mika and will let him go. This lasts as long as I don't see him; but when that young flushed lively boy comes to me, when he smiles to me, kisses my hand, then—

31. . . . because it would be a terrible debauchery, I think . . . but no, no debauchery! A claim, this is an earnest claim of a nature tortured for so long, which would like to finally have its due—it is a claim of a lonely heart which would like to share its sentiments. But to share with whom, with a boy of 22 years, vulgar, dumb, rowdy, who would play with my honesty—

April 1854. Pribiće.

17. My desire for him is ungovernable . . . that I think I will get mad from the great pain of my heart! . . . but he asks . . . given that he sees how much I want him—he asks—I am ashamed to say it—he asks me to give him money. . . . Many times I said, I will not deal with him, will not communicate with him, but the devil of temptation is not leaving me in peace and thus I go astray. But now my eyes are open. . . . I will not look into this boy's eyes again and I will run away from him like from a snake—

August 1854. Pribiće.
Beautiful, wonderful goal I attained!—a goal of being embraced all
night by the village boy. . . . I am not sorry I have done that; I
am happy and a gentle pleasant feeling passes through my whole
body.[5]

Jarnević's *Diary* continues to meet intense critical interest. Moreover, it
seems as if this work had to wait for relatively recent feminist criticism in
order to be fully appreciated and explored in novel ways (see, for example,
Divna Zečević's *Dragojla Jarnević* [1985]).

IVANA BRLIĆ-MAŽURANIĆ

Ivana Brlić-Mažuranić was born in Ogulin in 1874 and died in Zagreb in
1938. She was granddaughter of the Croatian governor and poet Ivan
Mažuranić, the creator of the famous nineteenth-century epic *The Death
of Smail-aga Čengić*, whom she saw as a guiding figure in her life. Her
days were spent in the midst of families, the one into which she was born
(her father Vladimir was a well-known lawyer and writer) and the one
into which she married (her husband Vatroslav Brlić was a politician and
lawyer).

Brlić-Mažuranić grew up in an atmosphere of learning and achievement and was highly educated. She was accomplished in, among other
things, several languages, being fluent in French, German, Russian, and
English. Aside from her grandfather Ivan Mažuranić, the two men she
wrote about as being decisively influential in her intellectual formation
were the poet and aesthetician Franjo Marković and the enlightened Croatian bishop Josip Juraj Štrosmajer. Ivana Brlić-Mažuranić was the first
woman to become a member of the Yugoslav Academy of Sciences and
Arts (in 1937).

As a writer, Brlić-Mažuranić is best known for two works, the novella
Čudnovate zgode šegrta Hlapića (The miraculous adventures of apprentice
Hlapić) (1913), and the collection of stories *Priče iz davnine* (Stories from
ancient times) (1916). This second work has been translated into numerous languages and was written about by, among others, Rudyard Kipling
and Seaton Watson. These stories "were made around names and personages taken from Slavic mythology . . . [however] not one fabula has been
found in our mythology. (Anyone who studies mythology knows that un-

fortunately our Slavic mythology . . . is a cluster of almost entirely incoherent conjectures, one field of ruins, from which like vertical columns stick out only names)," wrote the author to her son in 1938.

The names around which Brlić-Mažuranić builds her stories are *Bjesomar*, a ruler of evil forces; *Svarožić*, a beautiful boy-sun; *domaći*, playful little house ghosts; *Malik Tintilinić*, the liveliest of them, and others. Imagination, archaic and rich language, plots involving mortals who encounter fantastic beings (sea kings, fairies, talking animals), the sure and simple narrative development of these stories, and their sheer poetic beauty, made them look like authentic folk fairy tales and legends. As an afterword to the 1964 edition of these stories points out, "Some [foreign] publishers have suggested . . . that these stories are people's creations by the very titles of their editions. The English edition came out under the title *Croatian Tales of Long Ago*, and the newest Italian edition . . . came out under the title *Leggende croate*."[6]

Even though *Stories from Ancient Times* and *Miraculous Adventures of Apprentice Hlapić* are primarily seen as children's literature, their simple beauty and underlying philosophical and ethical concepts make them favorite readings of adult readers as well. In the story "How Potjeh Searched for Truth," the temptations of material riches, power, or simple distractions of the colorful world are personified in the figures of small *bjesovi* (furies). Furies are the little devils which are not harmful "until a human being takes them with him/herself,"[7] and which literally come from the "outside," preventing a person from getting in touch with his or her own inner truth. Potjeh's fury does not allow Potjeh to rediscover that which is closest to him, his simple intimate truth of attachment to a loved human being, his old grandfather Vjest. Potjeh errs when he thinks that his truth is outside rather than inside himself. Thus, the god Svarožić says: "If you had only listened to your heart, when it told you . . . to get back and not leave your grandfather, you would have found the truth without some great wisdom!"[8]

In the story "Regoč," the fairy Kosjenka meets the good-natured giant Regoč, and the two of them explore the world together. Kosjenka and Regoč are entirely different but they come to love each other despite their differences, and this articulation of the possibility of love between the two opposites—the light and playful fairy, on one hand, and the slow and silent giant on the other—is a very moving one. In "Bratac Jaglenac i sestrica Rutvica" (Little brother Jaglenac and sister Rutvica), political sovereignty is not rooted in the power of arms or riches but rather in the people's commitment. "Happy is the principality, whose fortunes are not protected by the mighty armies of the firm cities, but by the mothers and children in the shepherd's little hut. Such a principality cannot be destroyed!"[9] The narrative also indicates that by abiding by the simplest ethical principles one can oppose the greatest evils. Little Rutvica and Jaglenac hold onto their promise to their dying mother, to the few pieces of advice she had passed onto them before her death, and to their loyalty to what they know is "good," which saves them from all the evil dragons and witches.

In the short novel *The Miraculous Adventures of Apprentice Hlapić*, the little apprentice Hlapić, "small as an elbow and cheerful as a bird,"[10] runs away from his evil master Mrkonja and comes upon a score of adventures and does many good deeds on his way. Master Mrkonja's hurtful treatment and the bad people whom Hlapić meets on his journey do not manage to change his basic disposition and strong ethical principles. He sustains his original attitude to the world, characterized primarily by an extreme openness to new people and new situations. In other words, his perception of new people is not colored by his past experiences, whereby he would expect disagreeable things and behave accordingly. Therefore, "Hlapić did not talk gladly about Master Mrkonja,"[11] but instead jokingly spoke about himself as being a boy sent by the emperor to help needy people. The little apprentice sees good potentials in every situation and every person, thus making others become aware of these good potentials and eventually helping their realization. He inspires the village burglar to go back to an honest life, heartens a lazy maid to help an old milk carrier, and aids his gloomy master Mrkonja in rediscovering his happy and kind self at the end of the story.

As Ivo Frangeš points out, "the artistic creation of Ivana Brlić-Mažuranić took place completely outside of the main current of Croatian literature."[12] Indeed, Brlić-Mažuranić stands out as a completely unique literary figure, one whose themes and writing style have more to do with the ahistorical realm of fairy tales and their mythopoetic speech than with Brlić-Mažuranić's own times. One should not forget that her *Stories from Ancient Times* was published in the middle of World War I—a fact which, on the surface, did not find much reflection in this work. However, precisely by withdrawing her work from contemporary political and historical circumstances, literary trends and debates, Brlić-Mažuranić managed to transcend the ephemerality of so many of her literary contemporaries. Her work is alive and well in present-day Croatia, prominently displayed in bookstores, sold as any other major national classic, studied by critics,[13] and taught in schools. The genuinely high literary quality of her stories, and the almost magical attraction which their subject matter and poetic style exert on readers, ensure Brlić-Mažuranić's influential position in Croatian literature.

MARIJA JURIĆ ZAGORKA

A genuine literary phenomenon, Marija Jurić Zagorka (1876–1957) was the first woman journalist in Central Europe, a political activist struggling on three fronts (national, social and feminist), and the creator of a huge literary opus, including some thirty-five novels. Her literary model was Croatian writer August Šenoa, the first writer who used the city of Zagreb as the setting for a considerable and very influential literary opus.

Zagorka was a political correspondent from the Pesta Parliament, working for Zagreb's major oppositional paper *Obzor* and Split's *Jedinstvo*. Introducing "a completely new way of political reporting,"[14] Zagorka did not only electrify Croatian readers on the eve of the final encounter with the hated Khuen-Hedervary regime but had also portrayed the dissolution of the whole Austro-Hungarian monarchy to an international audience. She "refused the splendid employment in Pester Lloyd," preferring to be "behind the props of her homeland" than "on the European stage."[15] In 1903, she alone edited *Obzor* and was imprisoned. In 1925, Zagorka founded the *"Women's Paper*, the first magazine in Croatia exclusively intended for women";[16] sometime before that she had worked on the organization of a women's society, "the first feminist organization in Croatia."[17] Zagorka was prosecuted by the Ustaše regime and was sorry that she was too old to join the antifascist struggle of the partisans or of Zagreb's underground. Her popularity was undiminished after the World War II, and she continued to write until her death, leaving her memoirs unfinished. Well into the 1990s, she is still one of the best-selling Croatian authors.

Zagorka is mostly known for her immensely popular historical novels, which tremendously boosted the sales of the papers in which they were published. She wrote her novels for "the people," using a simple language, intriguing plots full of suspense and unpredictable turns, intertwining of the genres of romance, crime story, and historical narrative, and pointing out of some of the contemporary political and social problems, disguised as they were in a historical context. Her novels supplanted popular German literature of the time, which promoted not only the German language but also a discursive construction of cultured Germans who need to "civilize" barbaric Slavs.

> I had in front of me a lot of material: a struggle and opposition of embittered people against power and injustice. But here is censorship like a dragon. What should I do?—I asked myself listening to the noise of . . . the city of Zagreb. That opposition cannot be conquered by the gendarmes of power, but censorship could destroy any contemporary reflection of this struggle with one strike of a red pen. And history? Yes! Let us go to history. I will find there exactly the same events.[18]

The very titles of Zagorka's novels, featuring a woman or a woman's name (*The Grič's Witch* [Grička vještica], *Gordana*, *Jadranka*, *A Revolutionary Girl* [Mala revolucionarka], *The Countess from Petrinjska Street* [Kneginjica iz Petrinjske ulice]), indicate the importance which she gave to female characters in her fiction. Although women are central characters of her prose, Zagorka's serial novels are based primarily on strong plot, not on complex psychological characterization. They also have a rather simplistic black-and-white portrayal of good and evil, making readers side with the good, and having the good win out in the end. Not being ambiguous or very complex, the positive heroines of these novels are simply good, smart, beautiful, and in love with the right men, with whom they unite after overcoming numerous intrigues, obstacles, and deadly enemies.

The happy ending of these love stories, however, is always paralleled with the realization of a politically progressive or patriotic cause supported by the heroine. Zlata, for example, the main character of *A Little Revolutionary Girl* (one of the rare Zagorka novels with a more contemporary setting), is a young woman from the family of a high-ranking Austro-Hungarian government official who turns her back on her family, joins patriotic oppositional forces, pursues a teaching career—refusing marriage as a woman's only option in life—and eventually ends up happily married to a man of high character and good looks.

Zagorka's struggle for women's emancipation also included her invaluable historical research on Croatian women who fought for their country's causes from the thirteenth century onward, which she published in her 1939 book *The Unknown Heroine*. One could argue, however, that the main figure of Zagorka's feminist project was she herself, with her unique political courage and nerve, her journalistic talent, feminist commitment, and professional excellence.

ISIDORA SEKULIĆ

Let me conclude this brief review of early women writers by mentioning the prominent Serbian writer Isidora Sekulić. Sekulić (1877–1958) was born in Mošorin (Vojvodina), studied in Sombor and Pesta, and in 1922 got her doctorate in philosophy in Germany. She worked as a teacher in girls' schools in Vojvodina and Serbia proper (Šabac and Belgrade), served as a nurse in World War I, and traveled abroad frequently. Sekulić wrote a lyrical book *Saputnici* (Co-travelers) (1913), in which she reflects on subjects such as sadness, tiredness, or headache by combining intimate memories with a pensive and elegiac tone. She is mostly known, however, for a huge body of essays in which she displays a "strong encyclopedic affinity" and "often unhidden didactic assertions," which made her resemble an "enlightening figure and encyclopedist of the eighteenth-century."[19] An heir to the enlightenment tradition which was very strong in eighteenth-century Vojvodina, Sekulić saw her mission as that of a teacher who makes her readers aware of the vast scope of otherwise often unavailable information. Her essays concern artists from all over the former Yugoslavia (such as Croatian writers Ivan Gundulić and Tin Ujević, Slovenian poet Oton Župančič, Montenegrin painter Petar Lubarda), but also French, German, Russian, and British writers like Valéry, Goethe, Pushkin, Tolstoy, Keats, and Woolf.

Sekulić wrote about national issues (language, history), but also about other countries in her travel writings such as *Letters from Norway* (1914), in which she tells her audience about a "small nation which fought against harder geographical givens from ours, against poverty, isolation and linguistic difficulties, and yet managed to achieve cultural accomplishments which were talked about by the whole world (Ibsen and other Scandinavian writers)."[20] Sekulić herself emphasizes that getting to know another little and undeveloped European country, which only recently achieved independence, should help in understanding contemporary Serbia as well. "By chance, the Norwegian national and cultural problem reminds one somewhat of the position of the Serbs in the former Austro-Hungarian monarchy."[21]

CONTEMPORARY WOMEN WRITERS

It would be an entirely separate task to examine and reconstitute the context of Yugoslav literature from the late 1970s through the 1980s. But one can point out a few aspects of the literary milieu: the prominence of so-called genre literature (for example, thrillers placed in the Yugoslav context) of the sort written by Zagreb's Pavao Pavličić, the rising importance of historical novels (Ivan Aralica), the emergence of postmodernist and experimental writings of the sort written by the internationally known Belgrade University professor Milorad Pavić, author of *The Dictionary of the Khazars* and *The Landscape Painted with Tea*. In describing the Serbian literary context of the time, Jasmina Lukić describes yet another dominant trend, that of the "new realism."

> Throughout the seventies and early eighties, the Serbian literary scene was dominated by a group of (male) prose writers who introduced a new narrative model, labeled by some critics as "the new realism." They were mostly interested in recognizable everyday reality, often emphasizing its dark side, and in socially disapproved phenomena. They insisted upon naturalistic details and developed a particular form of quasi-documentary narration. . . .
>
> Generally speaking, within "new realist" prose production much attention was given to a model of patriarchal society with clearly defined gender roles. This is not a result of the authors' willingness to deal specifically with masculinity and femininity, but rather a consequence of their choice of topics, taken mostly from a rural or suburban social milieu, where patriarchal norms persist, determining the positions of both sexes. . . . They mainly wrote about women who were abused and victimized by their families or by society. But although they created some very convincing female characters in their works, the "new realists" were not interested in women per se. Female destinies were always taken as highly significant illustrations for other points they wanted to make, and, however sympathetic toward women, the "new realist" position remained always clearly masculine. Being so distinctly marked by

gender differences, this "new realism" was quite susceptible to female subversion.[22]

According to Lukić, the work of the author Milica Mičić Dimovska created a female version of a given narrative pattern. Dimovska's works include *Stories About a Woman* (1972), novels *Acquaintances* (1980) and *Phantoms* (1987), and *Defrosting: Cosmetic Stories* (1991). In discussing Dimovska's work, Lukić points out:

> Primarily interested in what may be called the common female destiny, Dimovska recognized the existence of several irreconcilable concepts of femininity within the same cultural frame. On the one hand, it is expected that a woman will find happiness and fulfillment in performing her highly routine everyday duties. . . . On the other hand, she is expected to be happy, attractive, desirable and inspiring. Her everyday life, so hard and so dull, leaves her with strong feelings of loneliness, uselessness and abandonment. At the same time, she faces a false image, imposed through the media as an ideal to follow, of a woman who easily performs all her tasks, rich and happy. . . .
>
> In Dimovska's writings, women are practically trapped in that feeling of inadequacy, facing the gap between their aspirations, the way they see themselves, and the reality of their lives.[23]

Lukić also discusses "women-centered" narratives by Hana Dalipi (*Weekend at Mother's*, 1986) and Biljana Jovanović (*Avala Is Falling*, 1978; *Dogs and Others*, 1980). *Dogs and Others* deals with the topic of lesbian love, and thus "introduces a really taboo theme in Serbian literature."[24]

Croatia of the 1970s and 1980s also saw the emergence of a few distinctive women writers. Most well-known among those are Slavenka Drakulić, Dubravka Ugrešić, and Irena Vrkljan.[25] Slavenka Drakulić takes as the theme of her first novel, *The Holograms of Fear* (1987), her own experience of undergoing a kidney transplant. The novel starts with the narrator being informed about the appearance of a kidney donor, her arrival at a Boston hospital, preparing for the surgery, going to surgery and then recovering and leaving the hospital. The events of this brief narrative are interspersed with the narrator's reflections, taking us back and forth in time and away from the United States to the narrator's own home country.

In a situation in which the narrator's own body behaves like a foreign element, becoming out of control and unrecognizable, unpredictable and unruly on account of its sickness, the narrator attempts to reconstitute her shattered self through language. With her physical identity being drastically altered (because her body is not anymore "I" in the ways in which it used to be), the narrator attempts to forge a new identity through writing. Instead of composing a chronologically ordered account, Drakulić constructs narrative counterparts of the brain functions which are described as "holograms": three-dimensional fields of energy—our thoughts—which are made by the interference of neural waves coming from different sides.

The holograms in *Hologram of Fear* are made of the numerous narrative fragments which come from different sides (biographical past, other people's stories, fantasies), and "crash" into each other, trying to articulate the sickness, the surgery, and the memories and thoughts accompanying such an experience. These fragments produce a collage intertwining the author's "stream of consciousness" with her imminent reality. Sickness destroys any attempt to organize the narrative in a chronological way. The author tries to go chronologically forward in her narrative, but then the fear of what this "forward" will bring (the failure of the surgery? the rejection of the kidney? renewed dialysis? immanent death?) prompts her to go back in time again, reclaiming memories or speech rituals designed to fend off terror.

There is no whole. My eyes no longer see the whole. A string of images that are repeated, first slowly and then faster and faster.
    Slow down, it should slow down.[26]

    . . . "You decided that you had to put a stop to the disintegration."
    I must communicate. With the room. With things. With people. I must try to say what I feel, without holding back. . . .
    How can I retell what really happened? . . .
    They have little importance—the visible events and actions that anyone could see. . . .
    But how can the rest be told? . . .
    Fear cannot be expressed. Sickness cannot be expressed. Loneliness is a fine, rigid axis that passes through the core. . . .

. . . It spread and I was the one, not the disease, who was more and more alone, more and more cold. Finally a lump of living matter in a void: I became the disease.

Me—disease—me: there ceased to be a distinction.[27]

Drakulić's second novel, *Marble Skin*, revolves around a daughter's sexual obsession with her astonishingly beautiful mother, and the young woman's formation of her own identity through an intense love and hate relationship with her mother. Desire for incestuous contact with the mother is intertwined with the repugnance toward the mother's male lover who made the two women "[lose] each other . . . and nothing anyone could do would ever change that, absolutely nothing."[28] "Only the man's skin separates us."[29] A yearned for contact with the mother is experienced through a sexual encounter with the mother's lover and is finally achieved only many years later in the mother's old age. "There she is before me, revealed at last. Fresh scars of her former beauty are still appearing, but it is no longer relevant, neither to her nor to me. I am close to her at last."[30]

Drakulić's latest novel (as of this writing), *The Taste of a Man* (1995), revolves around the relationship among sexuality, possessiveness, and cannibalism. Being a journalist by profession, Drakulić has combined her novel writing with the rapid publication of several nonfictional works. In *How We Survived Communism and Even Laughed* (1992) she gives a glimpse of everyday life in Eastern Europe under communism, focusing on the experience of women. In *Balkan Express* (1994), she writes about the disintegration and the war in the former Yugoslavia, and about the western attitude toward it. Both these works combine autobiographical, essayistic, and journalistic genres, creating fast-paced and poignant reading. In a chapter entitled "Death Live" of her *Balkan Express*, written in June 1993, Drakulić depicts the TV presentation of the killing of a small Sarajevo girl, and asks questions about the purpose of such media documentation.

They say that a little girl was killed while eating a pie. . . . A shell went through the roof of the house and landed in the kitchen. The girl fell to the floor . . . she was dead before her parents or her grandfather had time to understand what was happening. . . .

Then a TV camera arrived on the scene. This happened perhaps only one or two hours after the shelling. . . . We see the small kitchen. . . . The camera zooms in on the roof, on the hole left by the shell. . . . The father is sitting with his arms on the table, crying. The camera gets a close-up of his blue eyes and his tears—so that we, the television spectators, can be sure they are real, that he really cried, the little one's father.

. . . The camera moves from his eyes to that pullover so that we can see a red stain on it. . . .

Looking at the blood is nauseating. Still, the camera returns to it several times. This is unnecessary. But there is no defense from pictures like this—and no one to tell us how useless they are.

Now we are in the hospital. This is the first time we see the mother, too. She lies on the kind of a stretcher, covering her face with her hands. . . .

This is the end, this has to be the end. The camera can't go any further into human suffering. . . . I don't want the camera to look under that cover hiding her small body. But someone's hand evades my thoughts and lifts the white sheet. . . . We see a close-up of death. Then cut, a little coffin in the shallow ground. The report has finished. It has lasted three minutes.[31]

Drakulić's most recent nonfiction work is a collection of essays, *Café Europa: Life After Communism* (1997). On account of her criticism of the government of the "Croatian Democratic Community," Drakulić was attacked by the government-controlled media as one of the "five witches who [were] raping Croatia." She left Croatia several years ago and has since lived abroad.

Another of the "five witches" was Dubravka Ugrešić, also critical of the government and also demonized by the media. Ugrešić is a writer and scholar of Russian literature. Her works include the collections of short stories *Pose for Prose* (1978) and *Life Is a Fairy Tale* (1983), novels *Steffie Speck in the Jaws of Life* (1981) and *Fording the Stream of Consciousness* (1988), as well as a book on Ugrešić's perception of American culture, *Have a Nice Day: From the Balkan War to the American Dream* (1993).[32] As Celia Hawkesworth states, Ugrešić "has gone further than others in combining elements of 'higher' and 'lower' literary forms."[33]

In *Steffie Speck in the Jaws of Life*, the "low" literary genres correspond to the cultural and psychological clichés of the constitution of a woman's life. These genres include a fairy tale (Steffie watches "Snow White" on TV and fantasizes herself as a heroine of a contemporary Hollywood love story, meeting a handsome, rich and famous man who falls in love with her), real-life stories communicated through the oral medium of women's gossip and focused on the subject of a woman's "getting the man," pieces of advice on mundane matters from women's magazines, sewing manuals, and so on.

Steffie's own attempts to get her life into a desired shape end up in a series of grotesque failures: her diet flounders and her dates with three men (the Driver, the Hulk, and the Intellectual) end disappointingly. The tragi-comic effects of Steffie's striving are achieved through the juxtaposition of her thoughts or actions—which follow one or the other kitchy narrative convention—and her reality, which is grotesquely out of sync with her own perception of it. For example, when an "intellectual" who was recently left by his wife visits Steffie (who sees him as a prospective boyfriend) and peacefully sleeps through the night at her place, Steffie reacts emotionally at what she thinks is his gentleness for her. In the morning,

> Steffie made coffee: softly she placed the teaspoons of sugar and coffee in the water, softly she stirred the coffee, softly she picked up the cups, softly laid a cloth on a tray, softly placed on the cloth two cups and a pot. She was completely softened by an inner warmth.
>
> She went into the room and put the coffee on the table. She opened the windows. Soft morning light filled the room. . . .
>
> The Intellectual sat there quietly, stroking his beard. He drank a mouthful of coffee, lit a cigarette, and then gazed sadly at Steffie for a long time. Steffie said nothing. ("I'm going to melt," she thought.)
>
> Then the Intellectual broke the silence.
>
> "Hey, Steff," he said, "what do you think, is there any point in my phoning . . . her [his wife who left him with a plumber] now, the plumber's woman?"[34]

Have a Nice Day: From the Balkan War to the American Dream is based on Ugrešić's stay in the United States as visiting lecturer at Wesleyan University in the spring 1992. The book takes the form of a loose dictionary of American culture, with entries such as "shrink," "manual," "couch-potato," "body," "personality," or "contact" receiving separate short chapters as their descriptive definitions. *Have a Nice Day* also con-

tains whole chapters on the many relations between the former Yugoslavia and the United States, such as the chapters on recent Yugoslav
emigrants to the United States ("Homeland"), on mail which the author
has gotten from friends back home ("Mailbox"), or on the presence of
American culture in the Yugoslav cultural space ("Yugo-Americana").

Throughout the book, the author mentally intertwines fragments of
"Americana" in front of her eyes with scenes of violence happening simultaneously across the ocean in the former Yugoslavia. For instance,
writing about the concept of "organizer," Ugrešić compares the army
which destroyed the Croatian city of Vukovar with organizers, simply
stating: "Organizers. Kill—cleanse—organize."[35] In a similar way, while
writing about the term "shrink," Ugrešić recounts how her own appointment with a New York psychologist ended unsuccessfully, the reason
being she focused too much on the war in Yugoslavia instead of her "own
personal problems."

One recurrent theme in *Have a Nice Day* is the American discursive
construction of both the war in the former Yugoslavia and the "Balkan"
cultural space. Ugrešić reveals how this discursive construction is shaped
by sheer ignorance on one hand,[36] and the forces of the market economy
on the other.[37] She also writes about the enforcement of the cultural stereotype of the "Balkans," through which Americans perceived the war in
that area.[38]

> Unpredictable reality continues its game with myths. From here I
> observe the media reinforcement of the Balkan Myth as it is gradu-
> ally built up from newspaper photographs and television reports.
> The television shots of desperate, wretched, disheveled people
> with wild eyes absolutely coincide with the Balkan stereotype. And
> no one asks how it is that many of these desperate people have a
> decent command of the English language. At the same time as the
> myth of the wild Balkans is being composed here. . . .[39]

Have a Nice Day also unveils the mechanisms by which the American
publishing industry, media, and academy shape and change the self-pre-
sentation of an "authentic" East European or Yugoslav writer so that it
corresponds to already given preconceptions.

Ugrešić refuses to write about herself and her "authentic" East European experience and the Yugoslav war in the prescribed ways. Her refusal
lies precisely in the bearing of Western mechanisms of the creation of

"authentic" East European texts. She writes about the market demands and established discourses which are forced on East European writers. Ugrešić struggles to create her own text about herself, a writer from the former Yugoslavia (now from Croatia) in the United States at the time of the war, but also a writer whose text cannot be contained by those few stereotypes: "East Europe," "war," "Balkans," and "a woman writer." Ugrešić also shatters stereotypical views about the people of the former Yugoslavia. She reproduces parts of letters or conversations of these people (her friends and acquaintances), which show them as interesting, thoughtful, spirited, and peaceful human beings, different from the wild and violent beings they are supposed to be.

Irena Vrkljan is mostly known for her autobiographical works, starting with *Silk, Scissors* (1984), followed by *Marina, or on Biography* (1986), *Berlin Manuscript* (1988), *Dora, This Autumn* (1990), and *In Front of the Red Wall* (1995). Vrkljan was born in Belgrade and then moved as a child to Zagreb, where she lived until her departure for West Berlin in the 1960s. While in Zagreb, Vrkljan wrote mostly poetry and screenplays for television; she started writing her autobiographies after coming to West Berlin. She is a writer who boldly experiments with the form of her autobiographies, and the changing form of her texts articulates the changing form of a female identity which is created through them.

In *Silk, Scissors*, autobiography is constructed as literally *my* biography; short narratives mark the chronology of the author's life from childhood to present day. Most of the text deals with the author's life in Zagreb, and the picture which Vrkljan paints of Zagreb and its patriarchal culture—bringing about many unhappy women's destinies—is not a rosy one.

> On the wall behind the kitchen cupboard there is a note: I will drown in a swamp. Nada cuts women's heads from the newspapers and magazines, tall stairs, clouds, and makes dark collages.[40]
>
> Various cafés, dreams of happiness, wrong movies of my youth, that whole slow life started to bother me, became physically foreign to me.[41]
>
> Those who can save themselves, should do so.[42]

While *Silk, Scissors* articulates an initial act of self-constitution by the articulation of an "individual woman," her autobiography, *Marina*, Vrkljan's second autobiographical work, articulates the second step of the formation of individualism envisioned by Vrkljan. In *Silk, Scissors* "I" say myself ("I am 'I,' unique and different") by pulling myself out of the collective "we are" ("'we' are equal and same"). But individualism and "I" thus created could become limited within the boundaries of solipsism and self-centeredness. The fulfillment of "I" does not lie only in this assertion of "myself." *Marina* explores a dialectic of individualism whereupon, after asserting its own distinctiveness from the "we," "I" searches for ways of again being connected with others and overcoming its own isolation. Thus, while *Silk, Scissors* makes the first move of separating "I" from the others, *Marina* reacts to the resulting closure of individualism itself—as "separateness" between "I" and the others—through its articulation of an internalized social space as the basis of an individual. *Marina* articulates individuality as a "contact zone" by the text of an autobiography—the text of an individual—which is a collage consisting of numerous short fragments from my and other people's biographies. The juxtaposition of fragments explodes the unity of one distinctive character (Vrkljan) and her distinct biography. "[N]either autobiography nor biography, but a mixture of both, with the two strands inextricably linked."[43]

> The biographies of others. Splinters in our body. As I pull them out, I pull out my own pictures from a deep, dark funnel.[44]

> I yearn for Marina. A Russian poet, born 1892, committed suicide in Elabuga, 1941.[45]

> Dora, Marina and I. Three women saying farewell. Or arriving somewhere, where the sun still shines.[46]

The montage of *Marina* intertwines fragments of many lives—including those of Irena Vrkljan, Marina Tsvetaeva, Croatian painter Miljenko Stančić, surrealist Ljubiša Jocić, German writer Rainer Maria Rilke, Italian writer Elsa Morante, Russian writers Pasternak and Belyi, and moments from various times. The assemblage of various fragments does not create a linear narrative; rather, these fragments create *my* identity as a zone of contact among others and *my*self.

> When Marina passes through the room (and she would if she still existed), she always has paper, a pencil and a notebook in the deep

pocket of her apron. And I hear her words: "I have settled completely into my notebook."

Dora sits in a house in Zagreb and says nothing any more. Her spirit left that room five years ago. And where did I move to? Was it only to another country? A divided life. a bit in Zagreb, a bit in Berlin, one part devours the other.

In *Berlin Manuscript* (1988) and *Dora, This Autumn* (1990) Vrkljan continues her experimentation with the forms of autobiography. In these later works, the voices of others increasingly take over the narrator's text and the individual ("I's") woman's identity. Vrkljan's last book, *In Front of the Red Wall* (1995), was written between 1991 and 1993 in Berlin and consists of reflections on the tragic events in Vrkljan's homeland in that period. "The text was written slowly," said Vrkljan, "because how can one express an agitation, the tragedy of those dimensions?" She added: "In front of the shapes of evil one looses one's breath, and something essential in us, some light, is extinguished. It is hard for me to live with the experience of these past days and years, and I cannot banish from my heart some images, stories of some friends."[47] As I have pointed out, "some images and stories" of the recent violence, which Vrkljan talks about, have affected the writings of Drakulić, Vrkljan, and Ugrešić. Literary production which deals with the worlds of Yugoslav successor states *after* this violence is now in the making, and it is up to future readers to behold how this current literature deals with the issues of gender.

CLOSING REFLECTIONS

When I teach the writings of Drakulić, Vrkljan, and Ugrešić, my students often ask me: Why did these writers not include any politics in their early works? How could Vrkljan's autobiographies, Ugrešić's humorous prose, or Drakulić's novels not take as one of their themes the growing political crisis in Yugoslavia, the crisis which eventually led to the war? How could they write about "rooms of their own" as if "this room can float in space, alone, separated, like a box carried on the wind, a little piece of nothing,"[48] as Slavenka Drakulić puts it in her *Holograms of Fear*? Why were they so apolitical at that stage of their work, or else relegating their poli-

tics to other aspects of their lives in the way Drakulić (an engaged journalist) did?

It seems to me that this question inadvertently strikes at the core of
the literary projects of both Croatian and Serbian contemporary writers.
By way of answering the above questions, and also as a conclusion to this
chapter, I would like to revisit some thoughts from my 1990 article "That
Other Place," considering the nature of recent women's literature.

After discussing the absence of history, discourse, and practices of individualism in the cultural context of the former Yugoslavia, as well as
the different connotations and values which the term "individualism"
might have in the Yugoslav context as opposed to a "Western" one,
"That Other Place" points out that "the political importance of the work
of these three authors . . . [lay] in the articulation of previously nonexistent notions of a woman as an individual, and of various female subjectivities." This task of the creation of female individuality precluded a
recognizable political literary engagement.

> To return to the original question of the "apolitical" nature of the
> three authors presented here: it is impossible to give a single an-
> swer to the question, but we can speculate on one of the causes of
> this apparent apoliticality. If we use Bakhtin's notion of discourse
> as "always already someone else's," we can say that Yugoslav polit-
> ical discourse (which any mention of the crisis would unavoidably
> fall into) [was] much more "someone/everyone else's" than, for
> example, Yugoslav literary discourse or, more specifically, than the
> genre of autobiography, or works by women authors. Yugoslav po-
> litical discourse is, in the hyperpolitical Yugoslav context, overin-
> habited with different voices and meanings, each of which brings
> its own complex history and its own power.
>
>   Given that the project of the the women writers presented
> below lies in the creation of women's individual voices, of some-
> thing as yet extremely fragile, their novels had to exclude, out of
> necessity, the most powerful discourse in Yugoslavia, the over-
> whelming political discourse, because this discourse would
> smother, in the noise of its many voices, the newly-born women's
> individualities. The slightest intrusion of this political discourse
> would be charged with overdetermined meaning, shifting the
> works' focus from individual and private aspects of women's lives
> to social and political aspects of these lives. . . .

One should not qualify (or criticize) these women writers as apolitical because they write about their "petty" personal problems while the whole country is "on fire." The negation of people's individualities can be taken as one of the many causes of the current Yugoslav crisis. Bringing women's subjectivities into life in Yugoslavia [was] in itself a political project of primary importance.[49]

As we saw during the period of horrible violence in the former Yugoslavia, articulating and strengthening the sphere of individual identity was indeed a political project of primary importance. If the society had followed the road of searching for and emphasizing individual rights, bearings, and desires rather than the alternative path of the loss of individuality in a group-based national identity, the violence might have been avoided. A limited domestic audience and the stunted influence of the above discussed women writers—as opposed to the state-promoted presence of some of their chauvinistically-oriented literary colleagues—was thus a tremendous loss for all. However, one can perhaps hope (though rather unrealistically, it would seem, given current developments in the area), that the postwar societies might have more appreciation for a different way out of the crisis, and that women writers' voices might help in forging this way.

14

GENDER CONSTRUCTION IN LITERATURE:
A HISTORICAL SURVEY

Gordana P. Crnković

From the beginnings of written literature in the lands that once constituted Yugoslavia, writers—most of them men—have spent innumerable pages depicting, wondering about, and imagining women. This chapter attempts to provide an abridged journey through literary history, pointing out the various periods' typical literary constructions of gender. The purpose here is not to engage in intricacies of literary criticism, discussing how a given literary work's poetic, stylistic or metatextual aspects create its multiple meanings and its multilayered realms which can be read in manifold different ways. Instead, this chapter is intended for readers who are not literature specialists, and will sketch a basic literary terrain, point out a few exemplary writers in periods from the Middle Ages to the present, and look at these writers' constructions of gender.

Regarding the literary characterization of women in specific works, I shall emphasize aspects which are typical for a given epoch and its more general worldview rather than focus on individual and irreducible specificities of any single work's gender representation. By pointing out that which is typical over that which is unique, I hope to indicate cultural, intellectual, and artistic discourses which shaped and were shaped by literature. Consequently, gender constructions of works referenced in this chapter are those constructions shared with the intellectual and discursive context of the works themselves rather than those "additional" ones irreducible to their time and space and produced by their artistic uniqueness and excellence.

FROM MIDDLE AGES TO REALISM

Serbian despot Stevan Lazarević's "A Speech of Love" (thirteenth century), in which he writes about the pain caused by the separation from his fiancée who had been captured by the Turks, exhibits the dominant religious character of the Middle Ages and the corresponding gender construction. The writer's love for his fiancée is connected with his love of God: woman is presented as a more spiritual being than man, a being which connects the realms of earth and heaven. The connection between a loved woman and God, which also characterizes Medieval literature in other pre-Yugoslav areas, produced in its wake an idealization of woman which will mark the writing in the centuries to come.

Leaping to the later Croatian Renaissance, which flourished in coastal Dalmatian areas toward the end of the fifteenth and into the sixteenth centuries, we find several high quality authors of lyrical poetry marked by the influence of Petrarch. These poets, the most famous of whom are Šiško Menčetić, Džore Držić and Hanibal Lucić, praised woman's physical beauty and its influence over the senses. They also used some of the formulaic phrases from folk poetry (such as a woman is "more beautiful than a fairy"), to emphasize their own secular and humanistic, genuinely renaissance literary perception and representation of woman.

The humanistic, bodily and sensual Italian Renaissance of Giovanni Bocaccio likewise had its counterpart in Dalmatia. Mikša Pelgrinović's carnival poem, "A Gypsy Woman" ("Jedjupka"), ends with a hymn to woman's beauty, and with the gypsy woman (a poet in disguise) advising the surrounding ladies to yield to their emotions and desire for sensual pleasures. In a merging of gender with specific ethnicity, it is a gypsy woman—a marginalized outsider—who is associated with sexuality and free morals, while the native Christian ladies can only listen to her, with their own response left outside of the scope of the poem.

The Croatian Renaissance period had also left us one of the finest

examples of the merging of gender construction with patriotic sentiments—an important *topos* which will keep reappearing in literatures of
Yugoslav nations—whereby a woman becomes an idealized symbol of an
oppressed and rebellious homeland. Marko Marulić's epic *Judita* (first
published in Split in 1521) takes as its theme the biblical story about
the widow Judith who went to the tent of Holophernus, the invader of
Jerusalem, seduced him, and later beheaded him. The character of Judith
combines the positively valued patriotism, immense courage and cunning
intelligence, as well as the aggressive sexuality which she manipulates for
her goals. As Slobodan Novak writes, "The sacred widow serves merely
as an alibi for the representation of ripe female beauty which is able to
tame the *beast Holophernus*. . . . Marulić's epic draws its lasting actuality
. . . from a successful balancing of Eros and Thanatos." Novak also emphasizes the fact that the story of Judith was "known in Croatia in the
seventeenth and eighteenth century in no less than five theater versions:
one from Zadar, two from Dubrovnik, one from Krk and one from Slavonski Brod."[1] One can only speculate on the possible effects on pre-
modern gender imagery caused by the popularity of this play—and its
deadly heroine—among a mostly illiterate general population, as well as
by the canonization of Marulić's epic as one of the founding works of
Croatian literature.

The Catholic Counter-Reformation of seventeenth-century Croatia
turns its back to pleasures of the Renaissance and professes its guilt for
having been seduced by them. Consequently, both men and women are
constructed as penitents, who are grieved by their previous sins which
they now confess and repent in hope of being accepted back into the
Church's embrace. A good example of such an attitude can be seen in the
poem "Magdalena the Penitent" by Dživo Bunić Vučić (1630). This
poem, written after a model provided by an accomplished baroque writer
Ivan Gundulić in his "Tears of the Prodigal Son," consists of three
"plaints" in which a woman repents her past. However, another swing of
the pendulum brings along the eighteenth century's Enlightenment, and
with it the concept of woman as primarily a rational being capable of
being as educated as a man. The Serbian writer and educator Dositej
Obradović (1742–1811), a native of Vojvodina (at the time under Habsburg Monarchy), thus advocated solid education of not only male, but
also female children.

Toward the end of the eighteenth century and into the first decades
of the nineteenth, Romanticism gained supremacy in European letters.

On account of the particular historical situation marked by subjugation to foreign imperial powers, however, the South Slavic romantic writers did not indulge in Goethe's "world's pain" or in a complete withdrawal into a subjective, pensive, and self-centered world characterizing, for example, Byron's "Childe Harold." On the contrary, their works were often characterized by a strong political—extroverted rather than introverted—thrust, embodied in the patriotic aspect of that literature which also affects gender imagery. In the love poetry of Serbian poet Jovan Jovanović Zmaj, one finds a constant correspondence between a poet's intimate life and national ideals—love for a woman is always intertwined with a love for one's oppressed homeland. In the same way, "The Wreath of Sonnets" by Slovenian poet France Prešeren (1800–1849) intertwines love toward one woman with love toward subjugated Slovenia. By such constant correlation between a loved woman and a loved homeland, a woman becomes an idealized figure larger than life. Indeed, most of the romantic poetry constructs woman as a projection of a male writer's desires and ideals rather than an entity in her own right.

Given such gender construction, one should note the exceptional poem "Unmarried Mother," also by France Prešeren, one of the rare pieces of this period which does not focus on the poet's relation toward a loved woman (and thus on the poet himself), but is rather written from the perspective of an unmarried young mother ostracized by societal norms. Emphasizing this woman's love toward her "illegitimate" child, the poem praises her genuine humanity and pleads for her reintegration in society.

NOT AS REAL AS THE MEN: WOMEN IN REALISM

The last two decades of the nineteenth century witnessed the appearance of literary realism, which accompanied the radical social and economic changes occurring at the time. The beginnings of capitalism produced the break-up of rural communities, the migrations of peasants into the city, the creation of the proletariat, and the decay of the old nobility. Social thematics comes to the forefront of literature now predominantly crafted in the medium of prose rather than poetry; the novels and short stories are populated with characters whose behavior and psychology are shown as socially motivated. With socially concerned literature, portraying the evils of the new times and attempting to articulate and elevate the popular conscience, women come to be seen as particularly appropriate for the role of tragic or victimized characters. In the face of social changes, women are seen as more vulnerable than men. Women's responses to the changed economic situation are more restricted than men's, and they face the double burden of social oppression on one hand (shared by their economic class or social stratum), and gender oppression on the other.

Although Slavonian writer Josip Kozarac (1858–1906) was one of the very few "who [did] not fear the negative aspects of the industrial revolution, but rather [saw] in it the guarantee of so much needed Croatian emancipation,"[2] the main character of his short story "Tena" (1894) articulates in herself the social problems connected with the destruction of rural communities in late nineteenth-century Slavonia. The corruption of a young woman symbolically represents the corruption of the patriarchal rural communities brought about by modernization. Beautiful Tena rejects both allegiance to her husband and work in the fields, and pursues her newly awakened sensuality and her lust for material goods in paid alliances with other men. " 'If all of you were as rich . . . then I would be yours.' . . . She felt more clearly everyday that she did not belong to one man alone. To belong to one man when so many offered themselves seemed to her unjust."[3]

Even though the story's narrative voice constructs Tena mostly as a symbol of sensuality and rude materialism, the inclusion of Tena's own perception of events constructs this woman as a more multilayered character. Kozarac thus creates literary gender imagery which includes complexities and contradictions of female position and subjectivity. Tena's thoughts oscillate between the desire for a "true love," material goods, or power over people, and simple naiveté and lack of experience. Although judged harshly by the moral voice of the narrator, Tena's many actions may also seem like a woman's attempts (as miscalculated as they may be), to assert her own needs and desires. Thus, in a paradoxical fashion, Tena's self-destructive lasciviousness and greed exhibit some proto-feminist stance as well.

Ante Kovačić's (1854–89) novel *In the Registrar's Office* (1888), one of the masterpieces of Croatian literature, takes as its theme one man's life destroyed by the period's often tragic migration of villagers into the city and the creation of intelligentsia from their ranks. One of the two main female characters, the villager Dora, is realistically portrayed as the victim of both social injusticies and the sexual abuse connected with them. Poor and disenfranchised, Dora is raped by a local landlord. "God, God," she whispers afterward, "this is a dream, a terror! What?! . . . Ha, ha, ha,"— she bursts into a terrible, wild laughter—"But we are nothing! But we are garbage, garbage!"[4] Dora is "nothing": her rape connects the political depravity of the rural population with the even more severe depravity of rural women. Furthermore, a violation and the ultimate destruction of a woman (Dora goes mad), is in Kovačić's novel structurally positioned as one of the main elements of the bleak world depicted in the novel, as victimization which breeds itself. Dora bears a daughter Laura, who eventually becomes a murderer and kills the village girl Anica, who in turn very much resembles Laura's own once young and innocent mother Dora.

While Dora is portrayed realistically, the character of her daughter Laura unites realistic traits with romantic ones: she is a "femme fatale" and a mysterious and bloody leader of a gang of criminals. Thus, Laura becomes more of a literary cliché and less of a real and rich character, greatly shaped as she is by the still powerful romantic constructions of a woman who is irrational, incomprehensible, moody and changeable, incommunicable, and both fatally destructive and self-destructive. Kovačić's Laura therefore remains imprisoned within past literary conventions, whereas the novel's male protagonists come off as much more realistic characters.

The previously mentioned blending of politics (in the sense of patriotism) and gender imagery can be seen in this period in the humorous novel *Parson Ćira and Parson Spira* by Serbian writer Stevan Sremac. This novel articulates Vojvodina's political position between the forces of Germanization on one hand (under Austro-Hungarian governance), and the Serbian adherence to its own national culture and language on the other hand, through the way this dichotomy reflected itself in the cultural constructions of gender and of the women's identities. The main characters of the novel are not so much the two parsons, but rather their wives and daughters. The two daughters base their understanding of themselves as women, as well as their presentation of themselves as women to significant men, on the two different prototypes—the imported "foreign" one versus the domestic Serbian one. Sremac's own political preferences are clear: "Germanized" Melania is spoiled, sickly, insincere, and melancholic according to the fashion of the times. Jula, on the contrary, is happy being Serbian, healthy, cheerful, and hard-working. She also has children, while Melania stays childless: the domestic ways of being a woman are thus shown as fertile—a huge plus in Sremac's environment—while the "foreign" fashions end up making pretentious, superficial, and sterile women.

The three above-mentioned examples of literary realism's gender construction show how the late nineteenth century portrayed women more realistically than henceforth, presenting women's social motivation and psychological turbulences, and even so far not much existent subjective complexity. On the other hand, literary women of this period are still much less "real" than their male counterparts: they are irresistible beauties provoking irrational male behavior (like Tena), semi-romantic fatal heroines (Laura), or somewhat caricatured figures whose certain traits (such as foreign pretentiousness) are exaggerated for the purpose of obtaining a comic effect and deriding politically objectionable tendencies (as in Sremac's *Parson Ćira and Parson Spira*).

MODERNA: RENEWED IDEALIZATION VERSUS THE LEGACY OF REALISM

At the end of the nineteenth century, the bourgeoisie of western Europe experienced disappointment with the industrial revolution, exact sciences, materialism, and positivism, which did not yield the expected social benefits and individual fulfillment but rather unemployment and a general feeling of dissatisfaction and alienation. The various currents of idealism and mysticism gained supremacy in literary circles, with French symbolists (Baudelaire, Rimbaud, Verlaine) emphasizing the importance of subconsciousness.

Croatian literary *moderna*, the period between 1895 and 1914, includes in itself the tendencies of symbolism, decadence, and impressionism, all of which share the refusal of realism and its literary techniques and motives. The causes of pessimism in Croatia are different from those in western Europe: even though west European influences are not negligible, Croatian cultural figures are not disappointed with the industrial revolution but rather with the lack of it in their own country and with the resulting economic backwardness and dependency. They are also dissatisfied on account of their country's politically subjugated position in Austro-Hungary.

Zagreb writer Anton Gustav Matoš (1873–1914), provides a good example of this period's literary gender imagery in his sonnet "Cognition."

In this poem, a woman becomes a symbol of cherished purity and delicacy. The poem is about the lily of the valley, a small white flower; only at the end does the poet make a parallel between the flower and a beloved woman. The woman is seen as the substance of poetry, separated from a materialistic and prosaic life. The flower/woman is modest, tiny, silent and fine, fragile and sensitive, and also innocent and clean, white and with the fresh fragrance of snow and milk. She has a premonition of a higher life and contains the secret of a soul, as well as the harmony between the nature or physical life and spiritual life or art. In his story "The Flower from the Crossroad," Matoš gives a similar image of a woman: beautiful and blind Izabela is perfectly innocent on account of being secluded in her rich house and with her family. She is "white and gentle as if she saw only white moonlight . . . as if she played only with the nocturnal, dark, satin butterflies. . . . She spoke as children do upon waking up, without any feminine acting . . . [and her love is] beautiful as a goddess, blind as a chance."[5]

Dinko Šimunović (1879–1933), considered to be the best short story writer of the period, centers his work on female characters who greatly resemble Matoš's women in their being poetic symbols of something different and better from the everyday reality. They have the unique ability, not shared by those around them, to imagine different worlds and travel in their minds to gentler and freer spaces. In Šimunović's stories, women transcend their environment with their imagination, their will to cross prescribed gender boundaries and be different, or simply with their unique joy of life. Modern in its emphasis on psychology and atmosphere over the plot, yet realistic in its perception of the influence of the environment over the characters, Šimunović's prose constructs its women as tragic characters. Their unhappy destinies are brought about by the irreconcilable difference between them and the patriarchal and materialistic social environment of the undeveloped region of Dalmatian Zagora (Šimunović's birthplace), which provides the setting for most of his works.

Šimunović's story "Muljika" is about a girl who represents such a poetic character out of sync with her environment; she has the lyrical qualities of day-dreaming and sadness. A gentle girl, Muljika is married at a young age against her will and dies shortly after the wedding. In the story "Rudica," a young girl with "some constant joy [which] flickered in her," who "would burst out laughing for the smallest thing,"[6] is given in marriage to a man who drinks and beats her, with whom she has ten children leaving her "thin and yellow."[7] In the story "The Rainbow," the young girl Srna is not allowed to swim in the river and sunbathe (because her face needs to stay "gentle and white, as it should be in well-bred girls"),[8] nor to sing loudly ("because she [is] a woman"),[9] nor to do many other things permitted only to boys. As she is "alive as fire" and "want[s] to climb the poplar tree, swim across the Glibuša river, ride a horse" and "wrestle with boys,"[10] she decides to try to run under the rainbow where legend says it is possible to change from a woman to a man. While running, she falls into a swamp and drowns.

The work of Serbian poet Jovan Dučić (1872–1943) exhibits some of the same characteristics of *moderna*'s construction of gender that is found in Croatian writers. In his "The Poem for a Woman," Dučić (who studied in Paris and Geneva and was also under the influence of French symbolists), sees a woman as a perfect and unreachable ideal. The woman of this poem is unreal and abstract, a mysterious being who cannot be expressed or described in words. "Stay unreachable, silent and distant," sings Dučić; what is important is not any real woman or any real contact with her, but solely the poet's own creation of the perfect and distant ideal. The ultimate egocentricity and self-centeredness of this construction of a woman is also unambiguously present in the lines such as "You are all woven from my vision" and "Because we ourselves have created everything we love."[11]

Belgrade poet and Yugoslav diplomat Milan Rakić (1876–1938), who was also a Parisian student, creates an image of similarly esoteric and ethereal women. However, the women of Rakić's poetry, especially from his "Kosovo cycle," are real historical personages such as the medieval Serbian nun Jefimija, known for her poem "A Praise to Prince Lazar," (1402) which is considered to be one of the finest pieces of medieval Serbian literature. In his poem "Jefimija," Rakić attributes characteristics of a woman prescribed by symbolist literary conventions—not touched by her times, separated from the surrounding reality, solitary, dignified and calm—to a nationally canonized female figure. Thus, he unites symbolist gender construction with the national cause. Like in the previous periods, one again finds the often repeated merging of patriotic and gender ideals, whereby a loved homeland is represented through an idealized female figure.

Considered the best prose writer at the turn of the century, Borislav Stanković (1876–1927) depicts women's destinies shaped by the traditional patriarchal society of his birthplace, Vranje, a city in southern Serbia which was liberated from the Turkish government in 1878. A contemporary of Dučić and Rakić, Stanković creates women characters who are radically different from the ethereal and idealized ones intimated in the poetry of those writers. Even though Stanković's work has some of the poetic characteristics of *moderna*, he is ruthlessly realistic in his detailed descriptions of the cruel customs which destroy women's lives.

In Stanković's stories and in his novel *Impure Blood* (1910), women are shown as victims of harsh social norms which not only shape their behavior but also their innermost thoughts and desires. A reader may sometimes gasp at the cruelty of some of the customs regarding women depicted in his work. A girl's marriage is arranged by her father and brothers; she can be married off to an underage boy, in which case her father-in-law might have sexual relations with her until his son comes of age. A widow who has a relationship with a man is punished by her family, which gives her a "poison to drink it voluntarily."[12] The proper behavior of a widow consists in not ever going out of her courtyard to be seen by anyone, and in not receiving any guests whatsoever in her house. Not even her family visits her, "fearing that they would thus offend the dead man, 'intrude into his house' with their arrival."[13] A woman in Stanković's prose is shown as a complete slave of not only the living men related to her but also the dead ones.

Such social and cultural environment also cripples women's subjectivities. Women in Stanković's prose are not free-minded and enlightened individuals aware of their oppressive condition and its enormous injustice. On the contrary, these women are organic elements of their surroundings, viewing themselves and their desires and behavior in the way in which their environment does. In the story "Late Man's Wife," the widow Anica gradually grows to like her imprisonment by a dead husband and finds sensual satisfaction in hysterical outbursts on his grave. "She got used to it, and she was fine."[14]

At the beginning of the novel *Impure Blood*, beautiful Sofka opposes the marriage to an underage boy arranged by her financially ambitious father, but also identifies with her father in his need to marry her off in this way. At novel's end, she identifies with her husband who now despises and tortures her, and she takes his abuse as warranted. Even though Sofka is shown as having vivid desires, dreams, and the ability to feel life without boundaries and to love genuinely, her main characteristic ends up being her rootedness in her time and place and her ultimate identification with the men who victimize her.

Situated in the near past and in the provincial areas of Serbia only recently liberated from the Turks, the work of Borislav Stanković makes the picture of literary gender imagery in turn-of-the-century Serbia much more complex than it would be if we considered only the poets who wrote under the symbolist influence. The ideal, unreachable, and unreal woman of Dučić's "The Poem for a Woman" is in Stanković's work juxtaposed with a reachable and real, vulnerable and easily destructible women. If we sketch Croatian *moderna*'s gender imagery by considering works such as Matoš's sonnet "Cognition" and Šimunović's short stories, and similarly see Serbian *moderna* throughout both symbolist poets and Stanković, we might infer that *moderna*'s gender construction in two spaces included both renewed idealization of woman, reminiscent of romantic poetics, and a more realistic and engaged approach to real women in their authentic social environment and with their genuine problems and tragedies.

BETWEEN THE TWO WARS: THE END OF THE OLD WORLD

The years preceding World War I showed a growing literary dissatisfaction with the previous poetics of aestheticism and "art for the art's sake." Instead of perfect artistic form, the political and cultural situation produced expressionists' cries, dadaists' nonsensical happenings, and futurists' embrace of the new technical world. The most accomplished Croatian expressionist poet, Antun Branko Šimić (1898–1925), appears during the World War I. His poems, considered among the best in Croatian poetry, reflect upon the mysteries of existence but also "cry out" the social injustices which are revealed in one poignant moment. In one of Šimić's poems, for example, husband and wife are shown as sitting at their dinner table, both ashamed of their poor meal, and both trying to eat as little as possible so as "not to be each other's death."

A woman, commonly present in Šimić's poems, is not an unreachable and perfect ideal but rather a loved, known, and infinitely cherished fellow human being. His poems capture a woman in the moment of silent love between her and a man: a moment of diving into the eternity of each other's eyes and souls, of precious togetherness which does not diminish social humiliation and material poverty, but is nevertheless its own separate and powerful realm. Šimić's love poems show him to be one of those rare writers who knows how to appreciate woman's separate reality rather

than project his ego on to her, and how to express this rather novel sentiment in perfectly chiseled verses.

The two major writers of twentieth-century Yugoslav literature, Miroslav Krleža (1893–1981) and Ivo Andrić (1892–1975), also began their
literary work during the interwar period. The enormous *oevre* of Croatian
writer Miroslav Krleža contains many female characters; for the purposes
of this survey, I shall attempt to classify them in three major types.
Krleža's social and socialist concerns are first articulated in the narrative
representation of victimized women of the oppressed classes. The interwar stories show, for example, young handicapped girls raped by soldiers
and laughed at by judges, or women whose successive boyfriends die in
the war or from consumption and who end up being beaten up by their
own families.

The second type of Krleža's female characters functions as an agent
which promotes the destruction of the already unstable lives and minds
of bourgeoisie men. These are Krleža's fatal women: the baroness Castelli
in the Glembay dramatic trilogy, or Bobočka Radajeva from the novel
The Return of Philip Latinowicz (1932). These women use their sexuality
and the knowledge of psychology of their targeted male objects to attain
their financial and social goals. They can also be irrational, destructive,
and ultimately self-destructive, provoking the breakout of the men's subconscious realm into otherwise orderly bourgeois life, and embodying the
irrational drives of violence and the Freudian death instinct. In *The Return of Philip Latinowicz*, it is Bobočka Radajeva who functions as a catalyst
for the psychological and physical destruction of the men around her,
whose destruction in turn symbolizes wider spiritual degeneration of pre–
World War II European bourgeois society.

As opposed to the first two types of Krleža's women, which may appear somewhat stereotypical, the third type of women in his work are
those individual characters who are created in artistically and psychologically convincing ways, and who do not simply fulfill an ideological or
structural function in the text but rather have their own irreducible presence. From the play *In Agony*, Laura Lenbach, a formerly well-off lady
who is ruined by her husband and becomes a seamstress and meets a man
who raises her hopes for a better future, is one such richly described
woman who stays with the reader. Laura's attempts to avoid confronting
the unpleasant truth about the man she loves, the self-numbing of her
own intelligence, the interplay of her desires, imagination, memories,
pride and eroticism, her seeing of herself both through her own and her

lover's eyes, and her attitude toward her own aging, are presented in psychologically penetrating and subtle ways both in the play and in the prose text with which Krleža accompanied the play.

The second of the two grand figures of Yugoslav literature, the 1961 Nobel prize winner Ivo Andrić, also started publishing in the interwar period. However, Andrić is best known for the two novels which he wrote during World War II and which were published in 1945 (marking the beginning of the post–World War II period in Yugoslav letters): *Bosnian Chronicle* and *The Bridge over the Drina*. These two novels depict Bosnian history, culture and society, as well as the attitude of Europeans toward Bosnia. Both novels display numerous female characters shaped in somewhat stereotypical ways, such as the hysterical and asexual Austrian woman Frau Miterrer, the pure and silent domestic girl Jelka, or the proud and beautiful Fata Avdagina. The complexity and vividness of these characters is far less developed than that of their novelistic male counterparts.

Regardless of the somewhat cliché-driven execution of their characterization, however, the figures of women are interesting with regard to their structural function in the narrative, that is, with regard to their positioning within the novels' overall themes. Set during Napoleon's rule and centering on the experiences and reflections of the French consul stationed in the city of Travno, Bosnia, *Bosnian Chronicle* takes as one of its themes the problematic communication among people severely divided by different cultural, political, and religious backgrounds. On assignment in Travnik, French and Austrian consuls find it impossible to counteract the almost instinctive hatred which the majority of the city's people, Muslim *raja*, shows toward them. Women, however, are able to make connections across the cultural and political divides. They connect through the existential and universally present givens of childbirth and domestic concerns. As Celia Hawkesworth writes, "The whole community takes an interest in the pregnancies of Madame Daville [French consul's wife] and in the death of one of her children. All are favorably impressed by the Frenchwoman's quiet industry and the example offered by the consulate of harmonious family life. Cultural divisions cease at this basic human level."[15] In Andrić's own words,

> It was a true family life, the kind that depended so much on the wife, a life in which the living reality of family sentiments overcame all changes and shocks, a life of births, dying, troubles, joys,

and a beauty unknown to the outside world. This life reached out beyond the confines of the Consulate and achieved what no other thing could possibly achieve, no force, no bribe, no persuasion: it brought the inmates of the Consulate closer to the people of the town, at least to some extent, and this in spite of the hate which, as we have seen, was still felt against the Consulate as such.[16]

In sync with writers' raised social and socialist interests, literature of the period between the two world wars emphasizes women's social oppression. Some of this literature also sees a woman as a catalyst for a Freudian death instinct within a dying pre–World War II bourgeois society. Ivo Andrić's historical novels, written during and published at the end of World War II, add their own portrayals of the past era's women caught within the confines of traditional Bosnian society (for example Fata Avdagina from *The Bridge over the Drina*), or show how women—adhering to their traditional tasks of care-providing and family-making—create one of the strongest links among otherwise divided peoples, links whose existence might be felt as imperative during the war.

POST–WORLD WAR II

Differing from literatures of East European countries under Soviet domination, the post–World War II literature of the now-defunct socialist Yugoslavia was not ruled by the aesthetics of socialist realism. The Tito-Stalin rift of 1948 was followed by Yugoslav attempts to find independent ways not only in politics or economy but also in the arts and literature. Miroslav Krleža and Petar Šegedin spoke out against the aesthetics of socialist realism which had influenced Yugoslav writing in the 1930s and 1940s. Interest in Western literature grew, especially in modernist writers such as Kafka, Proust, and Joyce, already known in the interwar period. In later decades (1970s and 1980s), the Yugoslav literary scene shaped itself in lively intellectual conversation with contemporary postmodernist trends, paying special attention to writers such as Borges, Barth, and Pynchon. In the post–World War II period, prose (especially the novel) asserted its dominance over poetry with writers such as Serbian Oskar Davičo, Borislav Pekić, Milorad Pavić and Danilo Kiš, Croatian Ranko Marinković, Slavko Kolar, Mirko Božić, Vladan Desnica, Bosnians Meša Selimović and Branko Ćopić, Slovenian Florjan Lipuš, Montenegrin Mihailo Lalić, and Macedonian Slavko Janevski (the author of the first novel in the Macedonian language, *A Village Behind Seven Ash-trees*), making their mark.

Literature of the post–World War II period was characterized by an increase of themes, which brought in their wake a diversification of literary gender constructions. In Oskar Davičo's fascinating novel *A Poem* (1952), for example, the main character Ana becomes a catalyst for finding the right path of revolution. Ana's main personal characteristic is her awareness of and honesty about her own internal contradictions, incomprehensible but existent aspects, and resultant desires. She challenges a young revolutionary to be honest with himself, and his newly found honesty produces a different concept of revolution—including rather than excluding the needs of an individual.[17] An entirely different female character is the mother from Danilo Kiš's novel *Garden, Ashes* (1965). In Kiš's inimitable poetic fashion, this woman is intimated rather than directly spoken about, surmised rather than known. Her life has its unique mystery which is sensed by both herself and her children, and she is an artist in her own right, interpreting the world for her children in a uniquely imaginative and loving way.

Recent Yugoslav literature (for example, Krleža, Andrić, Selimović, Albahari) has been increasingly translated into the English language, so a reader of this chapter should not find it hard to do a more detailed research into this period on his or her own. It seems to me, however, that the most interesting women characters in recent decades are created by women themselves; these are discussed in Chapter 13, which focuses on the work of the women writers.

By way of conclusion, one might state that female characters in Yugoslav letters seem to have been constructed mostly, though not exclusively, as projections of male desires or fears rather than as known fellow human beings. A common literary feature has been the merger of some sort of ideal (from God to homeland) with the idealized woman, who is thus not to be close but instead left far and unreachable. Also common is the creation of female characters as types—fatal women, woman martyrs, giving mothers, and so on, perhaps owing its existence to the continuing strength of the romantic worldview (including nationalist romantic) in these areas, and the relative weakness of the rationalist tradition. Given a situation in which male characters are less predictable and more interesting than their female counterparts, a reader appreciates and cherishes those literary works which manage to create complex women's characters who stay with us. One is struck anew every time one encounters trembling of hopes and the ultimate acceptance of defeat of Borislav Stanković's women, the melancholy musings of Miroslav Krleža's characters, or the poetic depths of women in Danilo Kiš's prose.

15

RUŽA'S PROBLEMS: GENDER RELATIONS AND VIOLENCE CONTROL IN A BOSNIAN RURAL COMMUNITY

Mart Bax

> [U]ncritically accepting an arbitrary
> male viewpoint . . . has impeded study
> of women and of private domain. . . .
> [W]e are caricaturing fifty percent of
> the Mediterranean world.[1]

PROBLEMATIC BY ACCIDENT

Ruža Vasilj, who is fifty-nine, has spent almost all her life in the village of Bijakovići, the parish of Medjugorje, near Podbrdo, the mountain where the Virgin Mary is said to have first appeared to six local children in 1981. Ever since then, turbulent changes have taken place, both in Ruža's life and in the rapidly emerging pilgrimage center. Ruža's husband, who worked as a *Gastarbeiter* (guest-worker) in West Germany for

This essay is based on literature, Franciscan archival documents, participant observation, and interviews, which were mainly conducted in Serbo-Croat, at intervals between 1983 and 1992. In the past few years, a wide range of (ex-)Yugoslav newspapers and magazines have published articles about Medjugorje. Such periodicals as Glas Koncila, Vjesnik, Sveta Baština, Politika, Panorama, Subota, Život, Problemi, Sociologija sela, Danas, Aktualnosti, Kršćanske Sadašnjosti, Slobodna Dalmacija, Nedeljni vjesnik, *and* Večernji list *have almost all written about the pilgrimage center, the visions, and the tourist industry there. Though it is quite interesting, the information they have provided is rather one-sided. Moreover, none of them have dealt systematically with what might be called the "backstage" subjects. Most of my lay* twenty years, has returned home for good. With their two sons and their daughter-in-law, they have turned their home into a small boardinghouse for the steadily growing influx of pilgrims. As a result, farming has become of secondary importance. Ruža's life has been totally changed. She is responsible for the day-to-day care of the *gosti* (guests), as the pilgrims are called, and has to look after the farm. Her husband does help her now and then but prefers to spend his time hunting in the mountains and chatting with the other men in the village square. Ruža's sons and daughter-in-law all have jobs in a nearby town.

For a number of years, Ruža has been having a very hard time of it. It is difficult for her to cope with the domestic work and she often complains of fatigue. She tends to be agitated, has unstable moods and fits of depression. She barely ventures out into the street and seems to have become afraid of people, especially of women in the village. She consulted the doctor in town, but there was nothing much he could actually diagnose. In his opinion, Ruža is overworked and ought to try and take it easy, and her husband and sons are of the same opinion. Ruža herself, however, is convinced there is something very different going on. At regular intervals, she hears voices, she foresees accidents and other calamities, both near and far away, and she has the feeling that slowly but surely she herself is being sucked in by what she calls *Crna Moća*, the Black Power.

Ruža is not the only one in the parish with experiences of this kind. She says some of her relatives and a number of other women have similar problems. All of them say that more and more women are confronted with the same kind of thing. The men call it *ženska histerija*, women's madness. They do not set much store by those fairy tales, and they are backed in this respect by the local clergy—though they do have to admit that ever more women are starting to act a bit sickly and odd (*strane*).

The first doubts about this established male perspective began to arise

informants in Medjugorje and a few of the priests prefer to remain anonymous. Therefore, I have used fictitious names for all the persons in the case. I am grateful to my informants in Bosnia-Herzegovina and in various Croat communities abroad for their assistance. For their constructive criticism, I am indebted to Vlado Borg, the late Ernest Gellner, Jadranska Gvozdanović, Petar Jelećanin, F. Komarica, L. Oreć, M. Estellie Smith, Martin Southwold, Fred Spier, Daan Meijers, Ed Koster, Matthew Schoffeleers, Bonno Thoden van Velzen, Marko Vego, Kitty Verrips, Alex Weingrod, Ineke van Wetering, and the editor of this book. Errors of interpretation are, of course, entirely mine. Sheila Gogol edited my English writing, and Sjoukje Rienks helped me with the format of the manuscript. I would like to emphasize here that I do not make any statements whatsoever as to the "truth" or "authenticity" of the apparitions. Nor do I in any way address the question of the integrity of the individuals involved. Problems of this nature do not lie within the framework of social science research. Lastly, the readers should bear in mind that the Croatian language spoken in this region is full of turkicisms.

in the "objective" mind of this male author in 1989, after a relatively unimportant incident. In the heart of the pilgrimage center, I witnessed a traffic accident. A taxi driver hit a German couple walking arm in arm along the curb. The woman was swept along by the car and banged her back against a wooden electricity pole. Bleeding and unconscious, she lay on the street while the taxi slipped off the side of the road and landed in the dry bed of the river Lukoc. Oddly enough, her husband was completely unharmed. A circle of people gathered around the unfortunate woman. When the disconcerted taxi driver, a young man from the village, came scrambling up the hill, he was stopped by an old woman perilously waving a shepherd's crook. She shrieked that this was already his fourth accident. Did he need anymore proof that the devils were now all over and were even attacking the guests? A loud discussion ensued, a shouting match of men against women. A police patrol car arrived. Witnesses were requested to come forth, and I was one of the people who complied. We were all taken away in a police van and questioned for the rest of the day at the police station in the nearby town of Čitluk. In the course of talks I had there with several women, I began to realize that "women's madness" was a complex world of representations, experiences, perceptions, and behavior patterns of the female segment of the community; a world, as I discovered during the research that followed, of devils and evil spirits that were increasingly terrorizing the women in the parish.

The following pages describe this female world and the conditions and mechanisms the women hold responsible for the outburst of the devils' activities. An effort is then made to explain this demonology and the related behavior in sociological terms. I shall argue that the psychosomatic problems of many local women constitute a present-day expression of a long-term power struggle between the sexes to keep the feuding and male physical violence, which has long been endemic in the area, within certain bounds. The description begins with some introductory remarks about Medjugorje.

PEASANT VILLAGE INTO CENTER OF HOLY GRACE

Medjugorje is located in the arid limestone area of southwest Herzegovina, some thirty kilometers from Mostar. The population of the region is predominantly Roman Catholic, with (up to the recent war) important Serbian Orthodox and Islamic minorities. Medjugorje and Bijakovići constitute the heart of the devotion center and the core of a parish which also includes the villages of Miletina, Vionica, and Šurmanici. Medjugorje, with approximately 1,300 inhabitants divided over 400 households (1991), is the largest of the villages; Bijakovići is the second largest with some 800 inhabitants.

Some fifteen years ago, Medjugorje was still a remote and unknown mountain village. Its population consisted mainly of peasants growing grapes, tobacco, and fruit. Because of an almost endemic population pressure, Medjugorje has developed a tradition of emigration. Many people left their country for America, Canada, and Australia; others migrated temporarily to work as *Gastarbeiter* in Western European countries.

In the last fifteen years, however, Medjugorje has become one of the most famous and most visited centers of pilgrimage in the whole Roman Catholic world. On 24 June 1981, the Blessed Virgin Mary, Mother of Jesus, allegedly appeared on the Bijakovićian mountain Podbrdo to six young parishioners: two boys and four girls. There have been apparitions, it is said, every day since that date. According to recent estimates, over nineteen-million pilgrims from all over the world have visited this holy place. The reasons why this devotional cult has got off the ground so quickly have to do with an old and deeply rooted controversy within the religious leadership of the area, between the Franciscan friars who have been administering several parishes (Medjugorje being one of them) and the local bishop who has been aiming at bringing these parishes into his regime.[2]

Massive religious tourism has also had a great impact upon the parish and its inhabitants. Rapid socioeconomic changes, new forms of social inequality and dependency, large-scale return-migration, and a booming building sector are among the major transformations of the last fifteen years. Internal and external pacification also belong to this category of notable changes. The southern part of Herzegovina, like Montenegro, has an impressive history of localized warfare and a long tradition of blood vengeance and other forms of physical violence.[3] As late as the 1960s and 1970s, the private use of physical force to settle disputes was still a regular phenomenon in the area; however, increasing state interference, and particularly the massive stream of pilgrims looking for peace, have brought this endemic form of self-help almost to an end.[4] But all these changes have not turned Medjugorje into a paradise. Especially for the women of the parish, life has become problematic. How and why will be described in the following pages.

MIDDLE FIELD AND THE HIDDEN POWERS OF GOOD AND EVIL

From one generation to the next, the people of Medjugorje learned from their spiritual leaders, Franciscan priests, about the "Middle Field," a concept found in many peasant societies. In this formulation, the world is constructed in three layers or fields: *Nadzemlja*, the world above where God resides; *Srednja zemlja*, the Middle Field; and *Poljana* or *Zemlja*, the field or earth surface where people live. The Middle Field is a realm of good spirits and evil ones, saints and devils, who engage in fierce battles on behalf of people, and frequently on their request, and regularly show the outcome of these battles on earth.[5] I was told that in dreams or visions people sometimes even venture into the Middle Field. The priests are said to be regular visitors there. Priests, however, have a special place: by means of the sacraments they can convey the goodness of God to people, and they can use divine powers to exorcise devils who have taken possession of innocent villagers.[6]

People say there has always been quite a lot of coming and going in the Middle Field. At regular intervals, people have also been confronted with what they view as spontaneous descendings of good and evil spirits, which are said to result from the constant battles between devils and saints. Generally, relative equilibrium is said to prevail in the relations among people, devils, and saints, but in stressful times—during wars or feuds—the Middle Field is profoundly disturbed and evil powers can easily gain the upper hand.[7] Some fifteen years ago, when there were portents that the Virgin Mary was to appear in Medjugorje, the equilibrium was disturbed, but in a positive way.

THE BLESSED VIRGIN ARRIVES

By the end of the 1970s, there was a great deal of tension in Medjugorje. The parish, which mainly consisted of women and children since more than 60 percent of the men were working abroad, was in danger of being taken over by the priests of the diocese.[8] The people of Medjugorje did not have any experience with *popovi*, as the diocesan clerics were called, but in other parishes they had not been cordially welcomed.[9] They were reputed to be arrogant and in some cases villagers had subjected them to beatings. The people of Medjugorje reacted to the danger. Women and children were said to have more or less spontaneously formed prayer groups that met regularly in the parish church. Many saints were invoked—particularly the Mother of all mothers—to ward off the menace of "evil."

Ruža Vasilj recalls about that period:

> Our priests were often at the Middle Field, and many of us felt we were there as well. It was as if the Black Power were shriveling . . . like leaves in a fire. We felt ourselves becoming stronger, less tense and more tranquil inside . . . like the dusk. Our priests—we had two of them at the time—gladdened us with the message that the Mother of God looked after us in a special way. Everything became even better, even stronger inside when *Gospa* [Our Lady] came to us. They [a reference to the secret police] were very hard on us, but *Gospa* gave us strength and she laid an impenetrable screen over us. And all those people [pilgrims] who came to look and wanted to hear what we had to say . . . that was wonderful, it gave a warm feeling. In those first few years, we had so much strength . . . we could cope with everything: the work on the land, the goats, accommodating the guests, the Holy Masses. No one was really ill and no one left [died]. The guests said we were as radiant as *Gospa* herself.

"But that much goodness could not last forever," said Janja Ostojić, Ruža's sister-in-law and next-door neighbor.

DOUBTS AND REVERSAL

The residents of her hamlet became painfully aware of that when Janja's grandson met with his tragic death. Her four-year-old grandson had come to live with her because the air was healthier here than in the mining town where his parents lived. In addition, he could be closer to the power of Our Lady. One evening, the boy did not come home for dinner. Later his body was found floating in the river Lukoc among the fish nets. The accident was interpreted in a religious sense: perhaps *Gospa* was not strong enough to counter the evil powers of the Middle Field. In the succeeding years, this interpretation was articulated by more and more villagers. The priests, however, were of the opposite opinion. They held that setbacks, tensions, and accidents were in keeping with the rapid expansion and the great attraction of the pilgrimage center. But more and more women in the parish gradually began to think quite differently.

The first reason for this change was probably a series of accidents in the hamlet of the Šivrići clan. In the early autumn of 1984, Vlado Šivrić had returned from West Germany with the money he had earned there. Despite the objections of his wife, Vlado and his sons began to convert the family home into a small boardinghouse. Vlado, a cautious man who generally avoided taking risks, fell from a scaffold and broke his ankles. His sons were later seriously injured while operating the concrete mixer. With the help of several neighbors, however, the work was completed and the men recovered. Then Vlado's wife fell ill and began to complain of devils following her around, ruining the food she was preparing, and hurting her. She was certain that the same devils who had caused her husband's and her sons' accidents were after her.

In the beginning of 1985, two virtually identical accidents occurred in a hamlet on the other side of the hill on which the Virgin Mary had been sighted. Again, men were the immediate victims, but women continued to suffer from ailments they thought were caused by devils. Ever since then, a veritable psychosis developed among women of the parish. By May 1989, the priests at the parish hall had received more than three hundred reports of ailing women and approximately the same number of requests for exorcism.[10]

Ruža Vasilj and Janja Ostojić were indignant at the ease with which the priests dismissed this growing problem as *histerija* and refused to exorcise the devils. They felt that the priests' dismissal was why a number of women had sought the help of several *kalajdžije* or "wise old women."[11] The *kalajdžije* have traditionally been consulted, much against the wishes of the local clergy, for advice on illnesses "of the head" or "of the heart." According to my informants, they were formerly the overt rivals of priests since they could also exorcise and provide amulets and protective herbs. With the founding of the communist state in 1945, the work of the *kalajdžije* became illegal and far less multifaceted, partly because the government had a monopoly on medical care. The priests call the *kalajdžije* "*gatare*," which locally means "heretics." The women themselves prefer the term *proročica*, the equivalent of the clairvoyant women of classical times.

Ruža and Janja informed me that in the past years, quite a few women of the parish have been advised by these traditional medical-religious specialists. The women received amulets and talismans to be worn on the body, and bundles and branches of herbs and pieces of metal to be attached to corners and openings of houses, placed at the heads and feet of beds, in supply cupboards, behind toilets, near the cattle in the barns, and in the gardens and fields. These objects ward off devils and break their power to prevent them from causing trouble and settling permanently in the bodies of women. Ruža and Janja also told me that various women had been advised to be careful of certain other women in the parish and, in fact, to avoid them completely, but they were not willing to reveal further details on this matter.

It was not only in dramatic ways but also in tiny everyday occurrences, my informants said, that the devils made their evil presence felt with increasing frequency. A whetstone breaking, tobacco binders splitting, a goat wandering off, milk souring, eggs spoiling, dishes breaking, and meals burning were only a few things the devils were said to have done. Yet not all domestic mishaps and accidents could be attributed to devils. As other women stressed, negligence, carelessness, and pure clumsiness were also accepted as causes of these kinds of events in the women's interpretation. It was only in case of very specific physical experiences that a devil was certain to be involved. One would hear or feel a soft rustling breeze, though not a single leaf or twig, not one hair of the dog or feather of the chicken would move, just like before a storm. Some women claimed to have then experienced a feeling of general fatigue, lethargy, or paralysis; others sensed a severe tightness in the belly and thighs; still others said their hands could not move or grew numb. Almost all the women reported breaking out into a cold sweat which lasted for some time.[12]

There is a general consensus as to what is apt to happen next. The experiences described above constitute the first stage, the duration of which can fluctuate from a quarter of an hour to perhaps several hours. Tiny little demons are thought to be involved, evil creatures that wander about quite freely, and can cause only a relatively limited extent of damage or inconvenience. Should the sensation last longer and become more intensive, this leads to the growing suspicion that a *mučan vrag* (heavy devil) might be involved, either operating independently or on behalf of some nearby human being with evil intent. Women are particularly fearful of these devils, since they cause much more damage and may also attack close relatives. (The drowning of Janja's grandson and the construction accidents are examples of demonic interventions of this kind.) There can be a transition from this stage to the last and most feared one, during which the devil permanently takes possession of someone. Women are then perpetually ill and present a continual problem for themselves, their family, and the community. Many women fear this will some day happen to them. Despite all this, none of the informants could mention one single example of permanent possession.

EXPLANATIONS: THE WOMEN'S PERSPECTIVE

Women agreed that the sharp increase in mental and physical ailments among the local females is related to the recent developments in Medjugorje. But not one of them accepts the enormous increase in the amount of work they have to do as a possible explanation. The very notion is immediately refuted with the argument that they were also very busy in the past, and that they often used to have to work even harder because the men and boys were away. The sharp and continuing rise in the number of devils is the current explanation among the women, and they mainly blame the priests and the pilgrims for this development. Ruža Vasilj's interpretation was very explicit. "When *Gospa* came," she said, "she brought a great deal of good. But wherever there is a great deal of good, there is also a great deal of evil. Our priests have taught us that themselves; where special grace is great, evil seeks its prey." And to stress the religious authenticity of this view, Ruža added:

> In her message [to one of the seers], Our Lady cautions against the devil and his sly ways . . . the Middle Field has become full, completely full. *Gospa* brought her angels—the guests left their devils behind here. They fetch milk and they leave blood, that is the way we see it here. And blood attracts more blood. More devils, the little ones and the heavy ones alike, more and more of them are out to find a place for themselves in the Middle Field. But that is full. That makes them even more vicious and angry. Now they are looking for their place in our midst; a lot of them remain here.

Ruža made it clear that she cannot actually blame the pilgrims for coming—after all, they cannot help wanting deliverance from their misery. But it certainly did not please her much that the guests were so focused on their own problems and failed to pay any attention to those of the parishioners. Her opinion on the seers and the priests was much more outspoken. She could become especially agitated and upset about the priests because, in her opinion and in that of many other women as well, in the beginning the priests could have steered the demonic forces in the right direction. Ruža told me she had gone with a delegation of nine women (one from each hamlet) to the parish house to protest and to demand a solution.

What Ruža told me one evening in the presence of several other pro-testers about the confrontation with Father Jure also reflected the differ-ent worldviews of the local peasant women and the Franciscan priests trained in contemporary theology. "Father Jure," she said,

> What happens if you see a dead goat lying in the field? Aren't more and more wolves drawn to it? And don't they attack each other, and even tear each other to bits? The cadaver and the dead wolves have to be removed. Because otherwise blood will continue to flow. And that is also the way it is with human beings and devils. If the priest does not pray and swear over the person who is pos-sessed, then the devil goes on ranting and attracting other devils and possessing other people.

In short, systematic exorcism would keep the evil forces under control. That was the opinion of Ruža and the other woman at the time.

Father Jure, Ruža said, felt it was a well-put comparison, but he did not think it applied to what was going on. He pointed out that in former times, women would be exorcised by his colleagues and the devil would thus be driven out of the community. But nowadays not one woman was really possessed—that was a point all the priests and all the men in the village agreed upon. Father Jure also said one should not look for the Middle Field outside oneself, and according to the women nowadays all the young priests feel one should seek it inside oneself. Every individual has a Middle Field where good and evil contend. And it is only by way of prayer and God's grace that good can emerge victorious. That is why women ought to go to confession more often and go to church to receive the sacrament of Eucharist. Father Jure also said that he and his col-leagues were well aware of the seriousness of the problems so many women in the parish were confronted with. They were looking for ways to more frequently bring the women close to God—in the church.

Father Jure, in recalling this conversation, said to me in 1991 that he did indeed view the women's problems as disturbing. He was of the opinion that there was increasing tension in many Medjugorje households. He saw it, however, as a kind of "growing pain." Changes in the parish were taking place extremely rapidly, and the women were having an especially hard time with them. He felt that, given sufficient time, the problems would pass. Father Jure felt that exorcism would not provide a solution. He and the other priests agreed that there were no traces of true, permanent possession by devils, and exorcism might very well backfire. The women might see it as a confirmation of their views, which would then only lead to an increase in the number of requests for exorcism. In addition, the priest acknowledged that for some time the Yugoslav Synod of Bishops had been urging local clergy to exercise the greatest restraint in connection with exorcism and other age-old customs. (He failed to mention that, additionally, the government had made exorcism punishable by law.)

Disillusioned by their confrontation with Father Jure, the women felt that their own priests had let them down. Ruža's lamentation is typical of the feelings of many women in Medjugorje: "It has been some eight years now. . . . *Gospa* and the priests are for the guests. . . . And what about us? We have to be strong, they tell us. But how? Like animals in the woods in the cold of winter? That way the wolves are certain to find us!"

ŽENSKA HISTERIJA IN A SOCIOLOGICAL PERSPECTIVE

Why do many Medjugorje women perceive their fate as described above, and why are the related experiences increasing so rapidly? Two social processes seem to be relevant in this connection: first, the sharp downward social mobility of many women, and second, the rapid growth of the pressure exerted by the pilgrims.

In the period prior to the apparitions and immediately afterward, women constituted the most prominent group in the parish. Their prayer groups and other religious activities were an example of highly esteemed piety. It was widely felt that without their effort—be it led by the priests—the Virgin Mary would not have appeared. In short, women were widely respected by the clergy and lay people alike, and they were clearly aware of their special position. However, they soon had to relinquish this high rung on the social ladder to the seers and the parish leaders, who were now in the immediate limelight all the time. The women were largely forced back into the domain of the home and had little choice but to tend to the material needs of the pilgrims.

The rapid expansion of religious tourism made it possible for many of the men working elsewhere to return home for good. They not only took command of the family and the farm work, they also engaged in economic activities related to the pilgrimage center. Women who for years had been in charge of their farm and family had to stand by and watch their position being reduced to that of a subservient housekeeper.

At the same time, there was also a rapid increase in the multifaceted pressure exerted by the pilgrims on the residents of Medjugorje. It is true that pilgrims provide the mainstay of the parish economy, but it is equally true that they thoroughly influence the social and psychological life of the population. "Everyone has to work harder and the priests insist we all do our very best to make a good impression. The guests always have to be able to see the effects of the special grace on us," was the way Ruža's fellow protesters formulated it.[13]

This pressure led to inner and interpersonal tension. Due to the constant presence of the pilgrims, however, even the slightest sign of tension always had to be camouflaged and suppressed. Various escape strategies were available to the men. Whenever they wanted, they could leave the *sveti krug* (sacred circle), a term men often use to refer to the parish. Up to the present war, the men paid regular visits to a larger town in the vicinity to get drunk and let off steam. They also went to the mountains to do some hunting, or so they claim. But escape strategies like these are not available to the women. Not only do they have to see to all the material needs of the pilgrims day in and day out, they are also expected to serve as an example in a religious sense. The conviction, reinforced by the priests in their sermons, that the women of the parish occupy a special position and perform a special task in God's Plan of Grace, is still widespread among the pilgrims.

Together with the total lack of any satisfactory regulatory mechanisms, these forms of social pressure may clarify why ever more women suffer from increasing anxiety and stress. The demonological interpretation of these feelings has been unwittingly reinforced by the conduct of the parish clergy and supported by the advice and activities of the wise old women, the *kalajdžije*.

How was it possible for such a strong preoccupation with demonic powers to develop among women, while nothing of the sort was evident among men? In circles of social scientists, the belief in devils and witch-craft is thought to be related to social tensions.[14] In this part of the Balkans, particularly in Bosnia-Herzegovina, extreme social tension has long been a structural phenomenon. In addition to wars and civil wars, this kind of tension is mainly caused by the almost endemic conflicts and feuds between and within kin groups, which easily ended in a violent vendetta.[15] Women, land, cattle, and the distribution of water constitute the most important motives. Men had the sole right to solve these conflicts by way of physical force. To a certain extent, men could thus deal with their own tension by way of outright aggression. For the women, who were often the underlying cause of the conflicts and thus had good reason to experience quite a bit of stress themselves, in this part of ex-Yugoslavia there was no similar way to openly regulate tension and let off steam. The tension accumulated and led to forms of hysteria and other psychosomatic symptoms. These symptoms were diagnosed in a demonic idiom, a system of religious representations which gradually developed into a compromise between indigenous beliefs and Roman Catholic doctrine. Popular religious specialists and their Roman Catholic counterparts both played a role in this connection. They were—and still are—thought to have the capacity to keep a check on the devils or exorcise them. This was to the advantage of both the parties involved. The women got the attention they wanted and their signal was clear: up to this point, but not further. The religious specialists, on the other hand, could thus confirm and reinforce their own positions.

Possession and exorcism also fulfilled a social function within the larger community. In this society, where the state monopoly over the means of physical force has in fact never been effectively established, the priests were the peacemakers. Urged on by the insistence of the women who were ill, the priests made every effort to bring the disputing parties closer together, after which exorcism could take place. In short, possession and exorcism were also instruments to keep the violence of the men under control.[16] It is perhaps relevant in this connection to note the saying: "A strong women is a warm cooking pot, a filled crib, and a clean cow shed; a sick women deprives her husband of his strength and his honor."

It is this combination of social and individual pressure that makes it clear why the women developed such a pronounced demonology and the men did not. It was in the women's interest to keep a check on conflicts, whereas men were forced by their code of honor to regularly engage in acts of violence. The belief in devils, however, would discourage acts of this kind. That is why the men were so unlikely to believe in any interpretation involving devils. This makes it easier to understand why, as far as the belief in devils is concerned, the men and the women live in virtually separate worlds.

CONCLUSION

A demonology can reflect tension, channel emotions into recognized patterns of expression, and serve as an instrument of power. The recent eruption in Medjugorje of the fear of devils was triggered by the influx of pilgrims, but its origins are in a more distant past and have to do with power relations between the sexes. In this male-dominated society, the possession behavior of women not only channeled the inner tension but also served to restrict men's engagement in violence. *Kalajdžije* and, even more important, local priests played a crucial role in the process as interpreters of behavior and as ritual peacemakers. In short, the physical violence of men was kept in check by women with the aid of religious and quasi-religious power and authority.

There are some indications that similar mechanisms also played a role in other Mediterranean societies with a weakly developed state monopoly on violence.[17] In Mediterranean anthropology, however, it is not unusual for micropolitics and physical violence to be discussed quite separately from such problems as the sources of religious forms of expression.[18] Should further research bear out a more general pattern, however, this would open up new perspectives on an old problem. Various researchers[19] have drawn attention to the prominence of Mediterranean women in religious practice, whereas the official Catholic doctrine only grants them a restricted formal position. In pursuit of an explanation, the authors have worked from the perspective of the clerical authorities, who make every effort to reinforce their influence on society via women, the least powerful group. This explanation is undoubtedly important, but the present case study would seem to indicate that it is only one side of the coin. Women make just as much use of the clergy to reinforce their own influence on society.

In conclusion, there is one more general, programmatic point. In the past decade or so, there has been increasing interest on the part of sociologists, historians, and anthropologists in the study of witches, magicians, devils, demons, and other evil figures and forces. There is the growing conviction that, rather than being obsolete, this "dark" problem area is in fact very topical and relevant to today's Western and Third World societies alike.[20] The case discussed here would tend to support this conviction, though it also calls for a cautiously astute approach and conscientious comparison. Witchcraft, accusations, convictions, and prosecutions are frequently mentioned in the same breath as possession by devils. The recent outburst of the fear of devils in Medjugorje and its historical manifestations bear virtually no similarity to the witch plagues and witch hunts in other parts of Europe and elsewhere. These are different phenomena with different meanings and functions. In the case of witch hunts, the interests of the "prosecutors" play a crucial role; an increase in witchcraft is not necessarily involved. In the past and the present collective Medjugorje delusion, however, it is neither a matter of accusations nor of persecution. It concerns a means of channeling emotions and of keeping a check on conflicts and violent behavior in the hands of the weaker members of society. In short, in endeavoring to develop a general theoretical perspective, ample space should be left for the formation of more specific interpretative frameworks.

POSTSCRIPT

During short visits to western Herzegovina in 1992 and 1993, several local people told me that women's madness had intensified as a result of the war problems in the area. I could not systematically investigate this since many women I had interviewed before were not responsive any longer. Moreover, many women had been evacuated and taken refuge in Germany. In addition, pilgrimage had virtually come to an end. My next period of regular fieldwork ended abruptly when a warlord, after destroying my films and written records, forced me to leave the area.

Branka Magaš

The essays in this volume deal with the role of women, and with the feminist tradition, in the lands that between 1918 and 1990 constituted Yugoslavia. They speak both about the issues that have affected the female part of the population of those lands, and about the individual and collective responses of women to the complex challenges presented to them by social and political development. It is women—their condition and their struggles—with whom the volume is directly concerned. In learning about these women, however, the reader gains an indispensable and much neglected point of entry into the extraordinary transformation their society has undergone during the present century. This has involved successive modifications of political borders, national and social revolutions, wars of state succession, and two world wars. Arguably most decisive of all for their lives has been the rapid industrialization which, under Communist Party auspices, transformed an essentially rural and illiterate society into a predominantly urban and literate one, albeit one still colored by its pre-industrial past. Women have not been mere passive objects of this history, they have taken active part in it, and in doing so they have changed not just the world around them but their own identity as well.

Reading these essays, one is indeed struck by just how impossible it is to disentangle the forms and ideology inspiring women's struggles at each stage from the wider political context within which their efforts were articulated. As often as not they were moved into action not by feminist but by national concerns, in reaction to outside threats or in pursuit of social justice—and, at times, of their communities' sheer survival. They fought for their rights, however ambitiously or modestly they defined these, as part of a broader social and political transformation, even if they often eventually came to realize that the emancipation of women must be their own work; that no one else would achieve it for them. As Sabrina Ramet reminds us in her introduction, feminist ideology and politics have been forged in a never-ending dialogue and dispute with more general political ideologies and traditions. It is this concrete interaction between feminist issues and wider political strategies, portrayed in these essays, that illuminates the importance of feminist movements for the truly dramatic transformation the former Yugoslav area has undergone during the twentieth century.

From beginning to end, this century has been dominated by the national imperative, which has managed to co-opt all other concerns, including those of particular interest to women. It would be wrong, however, to imagine that this co-option was simply imposed. On the contrary, as Vlasta Jalušič points out in Chapter 4, those Slovene women who entered active public life at the start of this century—as writers or journalists, by setting up trade unions and cultural or humanitarian societies—understood from the start that the nation-state provided the necessary framework of citizenship within which women could claim and fight for their interests. Movements for national independence and social emancipation in their different ways sought women's support, while women in turn relied on such movements to bring about gender equality, beginning with the right to vote. Thus, in 1917, Slovene women campaigned for the establishment of Yugoslavia and, encouraged by political parties, took part in a national referendum on the issue, even though a decade earlier none of these parties had supported the demand for female suffrage in the Austrian electoral reform. Following Slovenia's entry into Yugoslavia, the same parties sacrificed female suffrage to all-Yugoslav unity: women not only failed to gain the vote, but even lost some of the social and civil rights they had previously enjoyed. In Serbia too, as

Thomas Emmert writes in Chapter 3, women after 1918 demanded the right to vote as the appropriate reward for their contribution to the country's war effort, but found no support among Serbian political parties.

In the new state, women soon established common associations such as the Alliance of Feminist Societies of the State of the Serbs, Croats, and Slovenes, formed in September 1923. In tune with their country's foreign policy, they even affiliated this body to the "Women's Little Entente"! However, as its name and make-up show, the Alliance could hardly be described as an all-Yugoslav body; not only did it fail to acknowledge any other of the country's nationalities apart from Serbs, Croats, and Slovenes, but also the activity of each national group remained limited to its home ground. Slovene feminists continued to work within the framework of Slovene politics, Serbian women interested themselves in the conditions of life in Belgrade and Serbia proper—that is, not even in Kosova or Macedonia, which were then nominally part of Serbia. The virulently nationalist Kolo Srpskih Sestara (Circle of Serbian Sisters), created at the start of the twentieth century, had indeed taken active part in Serbia's territorial expansion in 1911–12. As national tensions grew following Yugoslav unification, women chose, and were encouraged to join, the side of their embattled nations. It is difficult to see how this could have been avoided. To begin with, Yugoslavia did not function as a common state or a civil society, and its early democratic potential was extinguished with the introduction of royal dictatorship in 1929. Excluded from electoral rolls, women could not participate in Yugoslav political life, while poor communications severely limited the ability of the various women's organizations to maintain contact with each other. Concentration on the most immediate surroundings, extended only by whatever information their particular national press might carry concerning events in other parts of the country, was thus inevitable.

It is against this background that one must judge the achievements of the Communist period. As Barbara Jancar-Webster writes in Chapter 5, the Communist Party's ability to draw women into the partisan war effort flowed from its ideological commitment to women's liberation as part of general social emancipation. It was the Party's attitude to the national question, however, that enabled what was essentially an urban party to recruit from the peasant population, including peasant women. Rather than preaching abstract internationalism, the Party took the nationalist bull by the horns, recognized the existence of different nationalities, and promised emancipation to each within a Yugoslavia constituted as a federation of equal national states or republics. In addition, the Party employed wholly novel techniques of education and propaganda, which reached down to the base of the partisan army and the population sustaining it. Jancar-Webster writes somewhat surprisingly—given the ethnic complexity of much of the area the partisans held at different times—that women "had little occasion to fight side by side with women in other ethnic groups." In the case of Bosnia-Herzegovina, which provided the partisans' main base for much of the time, the Party propaganda line was that Bosnia belonged equally to Croats, Muslims, and Serbs. Partisan units, whether monoethnic or ethnically mixed, often had to move through or be sustained by ethnically mixed areas. Party propaganda was addressed to a multi-ethnic audience, even when those at the receiving end were nationally homogeneous. As the author herself points out, the first federal conference of the Anti-Fascist Women's Front (AWF), convened in December 1942 at Bosanski Petrovac, ended with a call to "Serbian, Croatian, Slovenian, Montenegrin, Muslim and Macedonian women to join the fight." This was an appeal to women not just as women but as representatives of their nations. Interestingly, Yugoslavia was mentioned here only after its constituent nations had been listed individually. Far from setting up a barrier to open and free communication between women, as Jancar-Webster suggests, the formation of the five national republics precisely made such communication possible (insofar as any communication could be open and free under the new system established by the communists).

The communist experience was thus wholly different from that which was to pertain in 1990. Unable to rely on the existing state, which in any case had fallen apart, and entering into the war without an army, the Communist Party was forced to raise its own army and create new state structures from below. Its own members may have been subject to strict discipline, but the truth is that for much of the war the Party was unable to exercise control over what was happening in the country at large. This meant that not only its own branches and armed units but the AWF as well enjoyed a high degree of autonomy, furnishing considerable scope for its members' imagination.

The gulf that opened at the war's end between the subject and the object of the emancipatory process set off by the Yugoslav Communist Party was never again to be closed, despite the latter's various efforts to bridge it. The problem with the Yugoslav communist system, as Sabrina Ramet notes in Chapter 6, was that it never recognized "the autonomy of the question of gender relations any more than it recognized the autonomy of any other sphere of policy." When in 1990 the system finally fell apart, it left precious little to build upon.

How then are we to judge what Ramet calls the "Tito era"? Undaunted by the horrors of the wars of the Yugoslav succession, Ramet provides a complex and sober response by judging the system in its own terms. The Communist Party granted women the same legal rights as men, opened all levels of education to them, adopted a highly liberal policy in regard to abortion and contraception (helped by exclusion of the Churches from political life), and made women major beneficiaries of an advanced welfare system. However, she writes, the Party's belief that social change would of itself transform values and attitudes prevented it from tackling the persistence of traditional patriarchal attitudes in people's minds, attitudes which could be altered only by a radical rethinking of the forms and contents of popular education. Consequently, and despite the evident and impressive progress women made during the Tito era, the end result was disappointing: women continued to be concentrated in traditional female jobs, and to be under-represented in the free professions and in political, judicial, and state administrative bodies. Far from achieving gender equality, the communist system only reasserted gender inequality—albeit perhaps "at a higher level." Could it be, as Ramet remarks at one point, that the same could have been achieved under some other system? If "some other system" means capitalism developing in Yugoslav conditions, then the answer must be no. However, as she points out, capitalism neither achieves nor does it promise to achieve gender equality or social justice. Socialism, by contrast, does make these claims; so its failure to fulfill them is far more serious. Its failure is all the more instructive in that it demonstrates how only a frontal assault on each and every bastion of patriarchy will deliver progress toward gender equality.

As these essays show, however, gender identity is not the only identity that women possess. They are moved into action by other needs and interests as well: by a sense of national oppression, through political and intellectual engagement, as a result of workplace and social solidarity or family welfare needs, to name but a few. It is impossible, in fact, to separate the struggle for gender equality from other struggles, or to isolate achievements in the sphere of women's rights from other ideologies and movements concerned with general political or social emancipation. It is also true that a frontal attack on bastions of patriarchy is frequently not possible, however desirable it may be, and that much political wisdom is required in deciding how to proceed in a given situation. However motley the record of women's efforts in the area of former Yugoslavia has been, these essays are of immense interest precisely because they tell us how individual women or women's organizations actually coped in concrete situations.

The failure of the Tito period, as Sabrina Ramet rightly points out, was intimately related to the Communist Party's ideology. But it was also related to objective constraints within which the Party had to operate. The Party itself, after all, was a product not just of Stalinism but also of the great initial backwardness of Yugoslav society. Taking its record as a whole, it succeeded better in the more advanced than in the less developed parts of the country. What these essays reveal, however, is that whereas at first the communists' vision was in many ways ahead of the society at large, as time went on they began to lag farther and farther behind the pace of the latter's development, until by the end they were suffering from a complete failure of imagination. Such imagination now came to be supplied by ideologies outside the communist normative system, and often in direct opposition to it. The range of non- and anticommunist alternatives varied across the country as a whole; but by the late 1980s, as the common state began to fall apart, these alternatives were once again dominated by national and nationalist concerns.

In Slovenia, Vlasta Jalušič writes in Chapter 7, "the interests and demands of women's movements were mostly overwhelmed by national and other 'essentialist' interests." Paradoxically, this situation was created in part by the Slovene feminists' success in bringing gender issues to the forefront of the Slovene political debate. The "new social movements" that developed in Slovenia in the second half of the 1980s were attacked from Belgrade as a "Slovene national deviation." As a result, even though Slovene feminists were not aiming at the "ethnonational political space," they could not fail to support Slovenia's independence in the end. The nation-state, Jalušič points out, "can and does instrumentalize women for national imaginary aims"; but it also provides "the only framework that can express the demands and legitimization of feminism in terms of citizenship."

Since Slovenia's acquisition of independence took place without a prolonged war, perhaps what happened there illustrates more clearly the nature of the transition from Yugoslav communism. Two aspects are worth highlighting here, both dealing with the issue of the reproductive rights women had gained in communist Yugoslavia. These "reproductive rights were not questioned by the [communist] state or politicians. To be entitled to decide over one's body was 'natural.'" Things changed radically, however, with the 1990 election and the constitution of the new Slovene parliament, when the Catholic anti-abortion campaign acquired active supporters in the Christian Democrat deputies. And whereas in 1985, "when the anti-abortion campaign started nobody really believed that these long-lasting rights could be taken away," now that "the emancipation of women ceased to be an automatic part of the system's legitimation," this became a real possibility. The right to abortion, indeed, was attacked by many as a "totalitarian vestiges." Before, "the old socialist legislation came first of all 'from above,' and the mass of women got rights without having to participate actively in the struggles for them; there also existed the feeling among many women that one did not have to fight for them." Now, however, women realized that unless they fought they would lose their rights. And they did fight: December 1991 was "the first time, after almost forty years, that women had their own demonstration." As it happened, they won.

The second aspect has to do with the fact that, by putting up an organized resistance, women not for the first time transformed the idea of what politics is all about. Before the demonstration, democracy in Slovenia had been seen in terms of majority rule in parliament. As a result, "democratic majority decision making brought about a situation where certain rights could be 'democratically abolished.'" The women's campaign directly challenged this perception of democracy: by standing tough on the issue of abortion, they forced a general public debate on all problems connected with the political and social position of women. In this way, Slovenia learned an important democratic lesson, which is that parliamentary politics can be democratic only if it is combined with extra-parliamentary activity. Nevertheless, the real priority for Slovene women remains to increase the number of women deputies. In the 1996 elections, the percentage of women elected declined to 8 percent—from a high point of 24 percent on the eve of the introduction of parliamentary democracy. As Vlasta Jalušič concludes in Chapter 7, the new political institutions automatically produced, and continue to produce, gender-hierarchical structures. No additional sexism was needed for this to happen, "only enough powerful gender-neutral ideology of freedom." Interestingly, the women's pro-abortion campaign won considerable public support, suggesting that the communist inheritance has not been fully dissipated. This is due, in particular, to the fact that the reform process was initiated by the Slovene Communist Party itself, thus preventing the emergence of strong anticommunism and pressure to "change everything."

The "normality" of the Slovene transition stands in sharp contrast to what happened in Bosnia, Croatia, and Serbia. Tatjana Pavlović's essay (Chapter 8) describes how the current Croatian regime's dominant ideology conceives a father-dominated, ethnically pure, Croat family as the basic unit of a social order over which Franjo Tudjman—as the Supreme Father, the father of the whole Croat nation—presides. Stability in Croatia is thus construed as a return to conservative values, in which the domestic sphere is to be women's basic concern. What is offered to Croatian women as their fundamental national task is maintenance of the family, as the source of continuity, nurture, and social stability. In the official propaganda women, thus, appear not just as women, but as Croatian women dutiful to the nation and its father. No wonder, then, that feminists are vilified, denounced as "witches" and even proclaimed to be national enemies. While extolling all things Croat, the regime also encourages xenophobia, and in particular hatred of Serbs presented as the archetypal Other. Pavlović states: "An entire climate of paranoia and fear of otherness has been systematically produced in the new Croatian state. National homogenization, religious revival, and monopolistic control of the media go together with a generalized fear of differences and otherness."

Under such conditions, the critic's first impulse is simply to denounce such a policy, since resistance requires that the problem first be identified and named. However, by limiting her essay to an indictment of Tudjman's regime, Pavlović fails to question the reality that underpins it. The cult of masculinity that the official culture promotes, and of which she writes, is intended to hide the impact of the war on Croatian society and especially on its young males. In 1991, when the aggression against Croatia was at its most intense, thousands of young men, many still in their teens, were suddenly plucked out of their homes and families and sent to fight in a brutal conflict. How these young men, born and raised in a society that had been at peace for half a century, coped with their new situation, is a matter of great interest for anyone dealing with contemporary Croatia. The song *My Belgrade Friend*, which Pavlović reproduces in full, illustrates the problem of psychological adjustment involved in having to treat Serbs as mortal enemies after so many years of common life.

The song was indeed produced in the first year of the war, when the Sava and Danube became a frontline, eastern Slavonia the scene of mass carnage and an urban devastation symbolized by Vukovar. In the happy days of the past, the song recounts, Croats and Serbs knew each other's songs, and the Danube was what the Croat boy crossed to reach his girlfriend. And not only did he fall in love with the girl, but also—perhaps because of that—he came to love her village, too. Now, however, the Danube and Sava have become a battle zone and the Serb friend with whom one once shared many happy moments has become an enemy to be killed.

In this song, the Croat, contrary to what Pavlović suggests, does not appear as a hypermasculine Rambo; he hesitates before pulling the trigger. He will win the shoot-out, of course, for this is a Croat soldier's song; yet there is no rejoicing in his enemy's death. On the contrary, it only brings sadness since it means the loss of a friend: "I will mourn you and close your eyes." Tatjana Pavlović writes that in this song women are not important as such; yet there is nothing in the song that demeans women in any way (unless loving and kissing are seen as abuse). What has canceled earlier loves and happiness is war: now one has to kill or be killed. To describe this as "hypermasculinity at its rawest, most naked form, for it is simply about annihilating a rival male" is, surely, an exaggeration. Even if we are to reduce this rather complex song to the theme of male bonding and separation, it is not possible to describe the relationship between the two men as "based on feelings of rivalry and hate," since no rivalry is involved. The Croat admires the kissing skills his Serb friend showed in Belgrade; his own girlfriend lives in Novi Sad. There is no hate on display either, since most of the song has to do with love and friendship; the killing shot is fired not in hate, but in self-protection. This song, indeed, became quite popular in Belgrade, whence thousands of young men fled in order to avoid being forced to fight in Croatia. It is very difficult to grasp the contemporary reality of Croatia without inserting it into the experience of the original Serbian aggression—and also, perhaps more importantly still, into the experience of Croatia's own subsequent involvement in partitioning Bosnia-Herzegovina with Serbia.

Žarana Papić begins her essay (Chapter 9) on women in Serbia with the extremely important observation that "in time of crisis and basic social transformation, the *deconstruction* of the previous gendered order is one of the most fundamental factors of change, an effective instrument of the global restructuring of power." This is indeed what happened on the partisan side in World War II. By involving women and giving them a stake in eventual victory, the communists not only altered the position of women in Yugoslav society, they also made a first step toward pushing and pulling an overwhelmingly peasant society into the process of industrialization and modernization that was to provide the basis of their own power for almost half a century. In post-communist Serbia, as in other parts of former Yugoslavia, the communist inheritance based on the "equality paradigm" was quickly discarded.

As for the reaction of women to the regime's assault on their rights, Papić agrees with Vlasta Jalušič: the previous system must be blamed for preventing women from acquiring the necessary political experience and skills with which to defend their rights once they became endangered. In Serbia, as in Slovenia and Croatia, preoccupation with the birthrate, and with Church leadership of the ideological battle for more births and no abortions, has come to the fore—with the difference that in Serbia all this is also imbued with an anti-Western and anti-Albanian rhetoric. Serbia's low birthrate is commonly blamed on urbanization and industry-induced migrations, while the campaign for population renewal is aimed only at Serbs, becoming part of what the author calls "a long-term fertility war against Albanian women."

However, reconstruction of a gendered order, guided by state ideology and ethnic nationalism, has not merely involved relations between men and women, or the state and its female population, but has also transformed relations among men themselves. The great concentration of power in the hands of Slobodan Milošević as "the great Savior/Father/Provider/Controller" has as its counterpart a "totally subjugated *female* nation." All those not belonging to the Milošević family and political circle have become expendable and insecure: "They are to serve while their services are needed, and when the need for their services passes, they disappear in silence, as is expected of dutiful, discreet and obedient servants." By removing all power from political institutions, Milošević has also disempowered Serbian men. One consequence of this has been the blurring of gender boundaries in private life. The growing poverty has strengthened women's patriarchal self-denial, but has also given them new power and control over others in the family, producing what the author calls "a self-sacrificing micro-matriarchy." Indeed, by having to bear the main brunt of the social and civilizational crisis that has engulfed Serbia since the start of the war, Serbian women have willy-nilly played the part of Milošević's most faithful allies.

We are faced here with a real paradox. By excluding women from the public domain and simultaneously portraying men as the soul and the engine of a "war-oriented essence of the Nation" (in what Žarana Papić calls "the mythologized total investment in Great History and Great Sacrifice in Serbia"), the current Serbian regime has intensified gender dichotomy in the visible, public sphere. However, by reducing men to the state of powerless objects of autocratic rule, their power over women in the sphere of private life (which has become the only real one) has also been drastically reduced. Moreover, unlike in Croatia where (as Tatjana Pavlović so forcefully reminds us) the regime has encouraged the display of an aggressive image of masculinity, and where the army has become an untouchable institution, Serbia's official posture of noninvolvement in the wars in Croatia and Bosnia-Herzegovina has denied its generals and soldiers alike the status of public heroes. Papić might have added at this point that Serbia has nevertheless seen a widespread veneration of paramilitary leaders recruited and used by the regime for "ethnic cleansing" in Croatia and Bosnia-Herzegovina: men like Bokan, Captain Dragan, Vojislav Šešelj and most notoriously, of course, Arkan, whose spectacular wedding represented a very public validation of warrior masculinity. As the fortunes of war changed to Serbia's detriment, however, and "ethnic cleansing" came to be denounced by the world at large as genocide, public displays of affection for these "Serb heroes" diminished—albeit without ever being entirely switched off; witness the continuing popularity with the Serbian electorate (and indulgence from the regime) enjoyed by Šešelj and his Radicals.

If in Serbia, Croatia, and Slovenia the post-communist state has used its political and administrative authority and instruments to reorder gender relations, things have happened differently in Kosova. Here successive interventions have reduced within a few years a well-defined political entity to little more than a geographical concept, while its Albanian population has been subjected to permanent state terror and consequently forced to withdraw into seemingly invisible recesses, crucially dependent upon national and family solidarity. Albanians have in this way become much more Albanian than Croats have become Croat or Serbs Serb, since they cannot rely on any state or public structures for the reproduction and maintenance of their national identity. In this situation, the demands that the nation imposes on its members are if anything even more burdensome, since any admission of problems and differences can be presented as a threat to its very survival. What is more, in the present circumstances Kosova's rural majority, with its strongly embedded patriarchal social order and tradition, can no longer be kept involved in the process of modernization by reliance on the cities, as it could before when state authority and intellectual leadership (the power to structure the imagination of all the national parts) radiated from the urban centers into the countryside. For the cities have in the meantime become Serbian army and police garrisons. Hence, the task of educating new generations is now a matter of civic initiative, even though the Kosova shadow government has managed to organize a skeleton structure for the basic functioning of Albanian society.

As Julie Mertus shows in Chapter 10, through the example of a female literacy project undertaken by a group of women activists in the Has region, a frontal attack on the patriarchal order—in the basic sense of women talking and working with women without male mediation—proved impossible. It was only when the women activists presented the advancement of women as an integral part of national emancipation that male resistance was lowered. Reading about the story of the Has literacy project, one is transported back to partisan times, when liberation from foreign occupation demanded organization of women as women. There is, in fact, no contradiction between the national and the gender identification of Albanian women, notwithstanding the potential for conflict between these: as Mertus writes, gender identity and national identity are formed not only in relationship to each other, but also in response to outside oppression.

Kosova's specificity in relation to the other former Yugoslav federal units lies also in the way in which international forces—or rather international human- and civil-rights treaties (U.N. Declaration on Human Rights; U.N. Convention on Civil and Political Rights)—have come to replace an absent civic society in shaping Kosovar individual and collective identities. Their impact is not mediated through the state, as part of a bureaucratic or diplomatic procedure, but rather through the perception of individuals that these conventions codify their personal experience of living in conditions defined by absence of basic civil and human rights. And since these declarations and conventions are couched in universal terms, by accepting them as their own the Albanians of Kosova have accepted, at least in principle, that similar rights pertain also to others. Here is a potential for escape from the confines of ethnonationalism and the traditional perception of gender identity, Mertus writes—though she is not sure that this will indeed be achieved. In an area in which the process of state formation has not yet been completed, the power of nationalism to impose its priorities over all others cannot be underrated. Nevertheless, the intimate relationship between state, nation and gender identity is not a static one: as these essays show, it involves a permanent mutual questioning. The real break occurs with the understanding of one's own nation as a complex unity. After that, there is no going back.

Identification with one's nation is an act of solidarity; but, as Tzvetan Todorov reminds us, it is also an act of exclusion.[1] The strength of identification, however, is not necessarily in proportion to that of exclusion: love of one's nation need not involve hatred of another. As nation-states acquire popular roots, they also create conditions for nationalist imagination and mobilization. But not all nationalisms are equally aggressive; some indeed are produced as a defensive reaction to another nation's aggression or colonization. It is important to differentiate between national ideology and nationalism, and indeed between defensive and aggressive nationalism, for otherwise one is in no position to understand what happens in the world of international relations. By investing the ideology of nationalism with mysterious and irrational powers over its members, one loses the ability to comprehend aggressive wars as carefully planned and executed exercises.

The mass rape of Muslim women in Bosnia-Herzegovina by soldiers and paramilitaries organized by Belgrade is a case in point. The observations that in times of war women get raped, or that during the war in Bosnia-Herzegovina soldiers on all sides raped women of different ethnicity from their own, should not be used to detract attention from the fact that Belgrade—and Belgrade in particular—deliberately included rape in its war plans, as part of its effort to remove non-Serbs from areas intended for incorporation into Greater Serbia. Thus, the mass rapes in Bosnia were not just a sporadic product of war-induced anarchy but part of a strategic plan to destroy Bosnia-Herzegovina as a state and its Muslim component as a nation. They were, in other words, the product of a political intent. Consequently, to charge those who protest against this with "politicization of rape," as Obrad Kesić does in Chapter 11, is rather like shooting the messenger. It is true, of course, that this aspect of the war has been used for political propaganda which sometimes does not have the victims' interest at heart. It is also true that all rapes, and not just Serbian rapes, are to be condemned and punished. The main issue here, however, is not which ethnic group supplied the soldiers who committed the rapes, but rather the use as such of rape as an instrument of war.

In their essay on rape in war (Chapter 12), Dorothy Q. Thomas and Regan E. Ralph have cited numerous instances in which rape has been perpetrated against vulnerable minorities, used as a tactical weapon in the course of civil conflicts, or employed to drive out national minorities. They warn that emphasis on rape's strategic function can detract attention from both the experience of individual women and the functional variety of wartime rape. Notwithstanding their warning, however, it is vital that due weight indeed be accorded to the use of rape for strategic purposes, if only in order to conceive appropriate preventive instruments and ensure appropriate punishment. In view of this, the task of the War Crimes Tribunal cannot be reduced, as Thomas and Ralph claim, merely to "holding to account those who have attacked civilians and tortured detainees in flagrant violation of humanitarian law" and "achieving redress for the survivors of such abuse," but must above all incriminate political projects that use mass rape, concentration camps and summary execution of civilians as instruments of war. The actual perpetrators, after all, have committed their crimes on orders from, or with the permission of, people like Radovan Karadžić and Slobodan Milošević. Even if these ultimate instigators may not themselves have killed, tortured or raped, it is only *their* punishment that can create conditions for the return of two million displaced persons and the healing of Bosnian society. For various reasons Bosnia has become a prime test of the international community's determination to punish and prevent genocidal projects: only if the latter passes the Bosnian test can we expect it seriously to prosecute collective or individual sexual assault and rape as crimes of war.

The 1991–95 wars of succession have come to overshadow all of Yugoslavia's past. In their light, the past appears different from what it looked like when it was happening. Writing about women writers in Serbian and Croatian literature in Chapter 13, Gordana P. Crnković tries to answer the question, put to her by her students, of why Croatia's foremost contemporary women writers—Slavenka Drakulić, Irena Vrkljan, and Dubravka Ugrešić—failed to include politics in their early works. As the author points out, this question "though inadvertently, strikes at the core of the literary project of both Croatian and Serbian contemporary writers." Her answer shows great sensitivity toward the emergence in the 1980s of female subjectivity as an object of literary concern and construction: "The political importance of the work of these three authors [lies] in the articulation of previously nonexistent notions of a woman as an individual, and of various female subjectivities." The task "of creation of women's individual voices, of something as yet extremely fragile" could, in fact, be pursued only by their excluding themselves from the powerful and unremitting political discourse that engulfed the country after Tito's death. Articulating and strengthening a sphere of individuality separate from the national collectivity, and in collision with its permanent claims upon the individual, should thus be viewed not only as a political project of primary importance but also as an investment in a more humane and peaceful future. With this in mind, one is better prepared to follow the process of gender construction in the literatures of Croatia and Serbia. Reading Crnković's essay, one wonders whether and to what extent Yugoslavia's break-up will divide what was once a common literary tradition.

One wonders also to what extent the overall development of the former Yugoslavia's constituent parts will diverge in the future. Andrei Simić's essay (Chapter 2) on machismo and cryptomatriarchy illustrates the extent to which rural family tradition has continued to hold sway in many areas, even in such large cities as Belgrade. As Simić points out, this is partly due to material scarcity: the acute housing shortage frequently prevents the "post-marital neolocality" that is typical in much of the Western world. Of the many reasons explaining the phenomenon of cryptomatriarchy in former Yugoslavia, two seem to me of particular importance: the fact of relatively recent industrialization, and the low labor mobility caused by the life-long job security characteristic of all communist societies. An unintended outcome of this "socialist gain" was the fact that rules governing kinship in the countryside were extended to the cities—with the difference that, in the latter, matri-locality as well as the usual patri-locality became the norm. In its desire to prevent the rule of capital, the communist system thus conserved older norms of life. Mart Bax's essay (Chapter 15) on what happened to Medjugorje following the apparition of the Virgin testifies to the great power of private enterprise, not only to effect a deconstruction of the existing gendered order but also to invade the individual psyche: not only do the women have to see to all the pilgrims' material needs day in and day out, they are also expected to "perform a special task in God's Plan of Grace." The author's investigation of the psychological response of the women of Medjugorje to this situation was, in the event, interrupted by war—which changed everything, except for the spirit of private enterprise.

Gender Politics in the Western Balkans: Women and Society in Yugoslavia and the Yugoslav Successor States does not aim to present an exhaustive survey of the subject or the area. The essays do not speak with a single voice, indeed they sometimes contradict each other. They raise as many questions as they are trying to answer. None of this detracts from their exceptional interest. They represent a most valuable and in every way fascinating embarkation on a voyage into an area of social and political inquiry that has been much neglected, to the detriment of all of us— whether we come from the former Yugoslavia or study the area for some other reason—who have been trying to grapple with the complexity that was Yugoslavia and its terrible end. They go to prove that no country can ever be understood without proper knowledge of the social and political history of its women.

Chapter 1

1. Regarding the origins and development of patriarchy, see Gerda Lerner, *The Creation of Patriarchy* (New York: Oxford University Press, 1986).

2. Adrienne Rich, *Of Woman Born, Motherhood As Experience and Institution* (New York: W. W. Norton, 1976), p. 57, as quoted in Zillah R. Eisenstein, *The Radical Future of Liberal Feminism*, rev. ed. (Boston: Northeastern University Press, 1993), pp. 18–19.

3. Quoted in Claudia Koonz, *Mothers in the Fatherland: Women, the Family and Nazi Politics* (New York: St. Martin's Press, 1968), p. 180. Regarding Italian fascism, see Victoria de Grazia, *How Fascism Ruled Women: Italy, 1922–1945* (Berkeley and Los Angeles: University of California Press, 1992), especially chapters 1–4, 8.

4. Shulamith Firestone, "On American Feminism" (1970), in Vivian Gornick and Barbara K. Moran, eds., *Woman in Sexist Society: Studies in Power and Powerlessness* (New York: Mentor Books, 1971), p. 684.

5. Rada Iveković, "Women, Nationalism, and War: 'Make Love Not War,'" *Hypatia* 8, no. 4 (fall 1993): 115.

6. *Globus* (Zagreb), 11 December 1992, p. 33.

7. Marina Blagojević, "How It All Started," in East European Feminist Conference, *What Can We Do For Ourselves?* (Belgrade: Center for Women's Studies, June 1994), p. 11.

8. On gender systems, see Betty Yorburg, *Sexual Identity: Sex Roles and Social Change* (New York: John Wiley and Sons, 1974), pp. 1–2; Herbert Barry III, Margaret K. Bacon, and Irvin L. Child, "A Cross-Cultural Survey of Some Sex Differences in Socialization," *Journal of Abnormal and Social Psychology* 55, no. 3 (November 1957); and Gerda Siann, *Gender, Sex and Sexuality: Contemporary Psychological Perspectives* (London: Taylor and Francis, 1994), pp. 3, 125.

9. E. M. Forster, *A Room With a View* (1908), ed. Oliver Stallybrass (London: Penguin Books, 1978), p. 60.

10. Quoted in Francis A. Boyle, "Application of the Republic of Bosnia and Herzegovina" (29 March 1993), in Francis A. Boyle, ed., *The Bosnian People Charge Genocide: Proceedings at the International Court of Justice Concerning Bosnia vs. Serbia on the Prevention and Punishment of the Crime of Genocide* (Amherst, Mass.: Aletheia Press, 1996), p. 29.

Chapter 2

1. See Andrei Simić, "Commercial Folk Music in Yugoslavia: Idealization and Reality," *Journal of the Association of Dance Ethnologists* 2 (fall–winter 1978–79): 30–31.

2. Cf. William G. Lockwood, *European Moslems: Economy and Ethnicity in Western Bosnia* (New York: Academic Press, 1975), pp. 20–34, 47–55.

3. See Joel Halpern, *A Serbian Village* (New York: Columbia University Press, 1958); E. A. Hammel, "Economic Change, Social Mobility, and Kinship in Serbia," *Southwestern Journal of Anthropology* 25, no. 25 (summer 1969): 188–97; E. A. Hammel and Charles Yarbrough, "Social Mobility and the Durability of Family Ties," *Journal of Anthropological Research* 29, no. 3 (fall 1973): 145–63; Andrei Simić, *The Peasant Urbanites: A Study of Rural-Urban Mobility in Serbia*

(New York: Seminar Press, 1973); and Andrei Simić, "Kinship Reciprocity and Rural-Urban Integration in Serbia," *Urban Anthropology* 2, no. 2 (fall 1973): 206–13.

4. See Andrei Simić, "Urbanization and Modernization in Yugoslavia: Adaptive and Maladaptive Aspects of Traditional Culture," in Michael Kenny and David I. Kertzer, eds., *Urban Life in Mediterranean Europe: Anthropological Perspectives* (Urbana: University of Illinois Press, 1983), pp. 203–24.

5. Cf. Olivera Burić, "The Zadruga and the Contemporary Family in Yugoslavia," in Robert F. Byrnes, ed., *Communal Families in the Balkans: The Zadruga* (Notre Dame: University of Notre Dame Press, 1976), pp. 117–18.

6. Lorraine Barić, "Levels of Change in Yugoslav Kinship," in Maurice Freedman, ed., *Social Organization: Essays Presented to Raymond Firth* (London: Cass and Co., 1967); and Lorraine Barić, "Traditional Groups and New Economic Opportunities in Rural Yugoslavia," in Raymond Firth, ed., *Themes in Economic Anthropology* (London: Tavistock Publications, 1967), pp. 253–78.

7. Arnold van Gennep, *The Rites of Passage* (Chicago: University of Chicago Press, 1960).

8. Cf. May N. Diaz, "Opposition and Alliance in a Mexican Town," in Jack M. Potter, May N. Diaz, and George McClelland Foster, eds., *Peasant Society: A Reader* (Boston: Little, Brown, and Co., 1967).

9. Vera St. Erlich, *Jugoslavenska porodica u transformaciji: Studija u tri stotine* (Zagreb: Institut za znanost i književnosti, 1971), pp. 39–40.

10. Halpern, *A Serbian Village*, p. 202.

11. Related to me in Tuzla, Bosnia.

12. Bott has made similar observations about the behavior of working-class London families. See Elizabeth Bott, *Family and Social Network* (London: Tavistock, 1957).

13. Halpern, *A Serbian Village*, p. 203.

14. See Andrei Simić and Barbara Myerhoff, "Conclusion," in Barbara Myerhoff and Andrei Simić, eds., *Life's Career—Aging: Cultural Variation on Growing Old* (Beverly Hills, Calif.: Sage Publications, 1978), pp. 236–40.

15. St. Erlich, *Jugoslavenska porodica*, p. 75.

16. Ann Cornelisen, *Women of the Shadows: A Study of the Wives and Mothers of Southern Italy* (New York: Vintage Books, 1977), p. 219.

17. Personal communication.

18. For further discussion, see Andrei Simić, "White Ethnic and Chicano Families: Continuity and Adaptation in the New World," in Virginia Tufte and Barbara Myerhoff, eds., *Changing Images of the Family* (New Haven: Yale University Press, 1979), pp. 263–64.

19. For discussion, see Andrei Simić, "Management of the Male Image in Yugoslavia," *Anthropological Quarterly* 42, no. 2 (April 1969): 89–101.

20. Lorelei Halley, "Old Country Survivals in the New: An Essay on Some Aspects of Yugoslav-American Family Structure and Dynamics," *Journal of Psychological Anthropology* 3, no. 2 (spring 1980): 133.

21. See Reinhard Bendix, *Max Weber: An Intellectual Portrait* (Garden City, N.Y.: Doubleday, 1962), pp. 260–67.

22. Halley, "Old Country Survivals," p. 131.

23. John Kennedy Campbell, *Honour, Family, and Patronage: A Study of Institutions and Moral Values in a Greek Mountain Community* (Oxford: Clarendon Press, 1964), pp. 150–72; Julian Pitt-Rivers, "Honour and Social Status," in J. G. Peristiany, ed., *Honour and Shame: The Values of Mediterranean Society* (Chicago: University of Chicago Press, 1966), pp. 26, 42, 44, 45–53, 62–71; J. K. Campbell, "Honour and the Devil," in Peristiany, ed., *Honour and Shame*, pp. 150, 156–57, 170; J. G. Peristiany, "Honour and Shame in a Cypriot Highland Village," in Peristiany, ed., *Honour and Shame*, pp. 182–84; Pierre Bourdieu, "The Sentiment of Honour in Kabyle Society," in Peristiany, ed., *Honour and Shame*, pp. 224–25, 227; Ahmed Abou-Zeid, "Honour and Shame

among the Bedouins of Egypt," in Peristiany, ed., *Honour and Shame*, pp. 253–54, 256–57; and Julian Alfred Pitt-Rivers, *People of the Sierra* (New York: Criterion Books, 1954), pp. 84–121.

24. Ernestine Friedl, *Vasilika: A Village in Modern Greece* (New York: Holt, Rinehart, and Winston, 1962), pp. 87–91.

25. See Simić and Myerhoff, "Conclusion," pp. 236–40.

26. Margaret Mead, *Male and Female: A Study of the Sexes in a Changing World* (New York: New American Library, 1949), p. 223.

27. Elizabeth Fisher, *Woman's Creation: Sexual Evolution and the Shaping of Society* (New York: McGraw-Hill, 1979), pp. 7–8.

Chapter 3

1. Jovanka Kecman, *Žene Jugoslavije u radničkom pokretu i ženskim organizacijama, 1918–1941* (Belgrade: Institut za savremenu istoriju, 1978), p. 5.

2. Zorka Kasnar-Karadžić, "Ženski pokret kod nas i na strani," in *Ženski Pokret* 3, nos. 1–2 (January–February 1922): 23–24.

3. Quoted in Paulina Lebl-Albala, "Dositej i Njegoš o ženama," in *Ženski Pokret* 3, nos. 5–6 (May–June 1922): 184.

4. Kecman, *Žene Jugoslavije*, pp. 6–8.

5. Ibid., pp. 165–67.

6. Zorka Janković, "Izveštaj o radu Narodnog ženskog saveza za godinu 1921," *Ženski Pokret* 2, nos.11–12 (November–December 1921): 363.

7. Zagorka Stojanović, "Skupština narodnog ženskog saveza u Ljubljanji," *Ženski Pokret* 3, nos. 7–8 (July–August 1922): 236.

8. Alojzija Štebi, "Mišlenje javnosti i feminizam u Jugoslaviji," *Ženski Pokret* 5, no. 9 (15 November 1924): 378.

9. Leposava Maksimović Petkovićka, "Žena pred Gradjanskim Zakonom u Srbiji," in *Ženski Pokret* 2, nos. 11–12 (November–December 1921): 337–44. For a discussion of the laws pertaining to women in the various regions of the Kingdom of Yugoslavia, see Kecman, *Žene Jugoslavije*, pp. 5–63; Mira Kočonda-Vodvarka, "Žena pred Gradjanskim Zakonom u Hrvatskoj i Slavoniji," *Ženski Pokret* 2, nos. 11–12 (November–December 1921): 344–51; Alojzija Štebi, "Žena pred Gradjanskim Zakonom u Slovenačkoj," *Ženski Pokret* 2, nos. 11–12 (November–December 1921): 351–62.

10. Petkovićka, "Žena pred," p. 341.

11. Ibid., p. 342.

12. Velika Benić et.al., *Borba žena Srbije za emancipaciju i ravnopravnost i njihovo učešće u revolucionarnom radničkom pokretu, 1903–1941 godine* (Belgrade, 1969), pp. 51–53.

13. B. T., "Žensko pitanje: istorijski razvoj i značaj po društvo," *Ženski Pokret* 1, no. 3 (26 June 1920): 9.

14. Jovanka Šiljak, "Urzroci skupoće," *Ženski Pokret* 3, nos. 3–4 (March–April 1922): 93.

15. Draga Stefanović, "O nevoljama naše dece," *Ženski Pokret* 5, no. 4 (April 1924): 163–64.

16. Ibid., pp. 164–65.

17. Ibid., p. 168.

18. Zorka Janković, "Izveštaj o radu Narodnog Ženskog Saveza za godinu 1921," *Ženski Pokret* 2, nos. 11–12 (November–December 1921): 374.

19. Jovanka Šiljak, "Uzroci skupoće," p. 91.

20. Katarina Jovičić, "Uloga žene i ženskih društava u socijalnom i kulturnom preporodjaju našega naroda," *Ženski Pokret* 7, nos. 1–2 (January–February 1926): 15.

21. Hasan M. Rebac, "Pojava Muslimanke medju sestrama Jugoslovenkama," *Ženski Pokret* 1, nos. 4–5 (15 August 1920): 25.

22. Zorka Kasnar, "Program našeg roda," *Ženski Pokret* 1, no. 1 (18 April 1920): 5.

23. Alojzija Štebi, "Mišljenje javnosti i feminizam u Jugoslaviji," *Zenski Pokret* 5, no. 11 (15 November 1924): 378.

24. Alojzija Štebi, "Za novi smer u feminističkom pokretu," *Ženski Pokret* 6, no. 7 (15 September 1925): 244.

25. Comments presented in issues of *Ženski Pokret* from February to June 1926.

26. V. J. "G. Radić o ženskom pravu glasu," *Ženski Pokret* 7, no. 4 (April 1926): 140.

27. Olga Josipović, "Predavanje G. Dr. Laze Markovića," *Ženski Pokret* 7, no. 5 (May 1926): 180.

28. "Republikanska stranka i žensko pitanje," *Ženski Pokret* 7, no. 6 (June 1926): 183. Prodanović had expressed similar views on women's right to vote six years earlier. He observed that when a good civil servant sees that one part of society is denied rights, he comes to its assistance of his own accord. He asked the men of his country to consider the sacrifices of their women during the war. They did not give of themselves as they did and then come begging for the right to vote, rather they expected it to be offered to them as partners in a new society. See "Žensko pravo glasa pred narodnim predstavništvom," *Ženski Pokret* 1, nos. 4–5 (15 August 1920): 13.

29. "Republikanska stranka i žensko pitanje," pp. 178–86.

30. Jelica Nesković-Vučetić, "Higijenske prilike Beograda," *Ženski Pokret* 7, no. 5 (May 1926): 158–59. Belgrade had 80 to 85 deaths from tuberculosis per 10,000 inhabitants compared to 18 deaths per 10,000 in London, 43 in Vienna, and 60 in Zagreb.

31. Ibid., pp. 159–61.

32. Milica Krstić, "Uredjenje Beograda," *Ženski Pokret* 7, no. 5 (May 1926): 164.

33. Katarina Jovičić, "Opština i vaspitanje omladine," *Ženski Pokret* no. 5 (May 1926): 167.

34. O. J., "U ime gradjanke govori gospodja Mileva Milojević, predsednika Ženskog Pokreta," *Ženski Pokret* 7, no. 5 (May 1926): 174–75.

35. B. J., "Savez zemljoradnika i akcija Ženskog Pokreta," *Ženski Pokret* 7, no. 4 (April 1926): 138–39.

36. G. Bogić, "O radu žena i dece u našim rudnicima," *Ženski Pokret* 6, no. 2 (15 February 1925): 41–48.

37. A. Stižanin, "Kroz selo," *Ženski Pokret* 3, nos. 3–4 (March–April 1922): 103.

38. G. Bogić, "O radu žena," p. 46.

39. Darinka Lackovićeva, "Izveštaj sekcije domaćičkih tećajeva za seoske domaćice," *Ženski Pokret* 4, no. 6 (June 1923): 280.

40. Zorka Kasnar-Karadžić, "Ženski pokret kod nas i na strani," *Ženski Pokret* 3, nos. 1–2 (January–February 1922): 26–27.

41. "Rad društva za prosvećivanje žene i zaštitu njenih prava, Beograd," *Ženski Pokret* 3, nos. 1–2 (January–February 1922): 42.

42. The club also sponsored a number of lectures on a wide variety of topics. A list of lectures given from October 1922 to May 1923 included "Women in Contemporary Germany," "American Women," "The Role of Mothers in the Sexual Education of Their Children," and "Eastern Women in Ancient Times." See Vera Jovanović, "O radu društva za prosvećivanje žene i zaštitu njenih prava, Beograd, 1922–1923," *Ženski Pokret* 4, no. 6 (June 1923): 276–77.

43. Katarina Bodganović, "Moral o kome se govori i moral po kome se živi," *Ženski Pokret* 1, no. 7 (October 1920): 10.

44. Sima Marković, "Kriza ljubavi povodom smrti R. Stojanovićeve," *Ženski Pokret* 1, no. 8 (November 1920): 8.

45. Vasa Knezević, "Naša javnost i mere protivu prostitucije," *Ženski Pokret* 3, nos. 5–6 (May–June 1922): 169–73.

46. Ibid., p. 173.

47. See "Aliancija feminističkih društava," *Ženski Pokret* 4, no. 7 (September 1923): 325–27.

Ženski Pokret reported a lively discussion in Ljubljana in which one could feel the differences between extremist and moderate feminists. Nevertheless, according to the report, the disparate members of the new organization always managed to find a middle ground. In 1926, this alliance was renamed Aliancija ženskih pokreta.

48. "Mala Feministička Antanta, liga za mir i slobodu," *Ženski Pokret* 4, no. 6 (June 1923): 264–68.

Chapter 4

1. While the well-organized German-speaking women had already split themselves into two parts—the bourgeois and the proletarian women's movement—there was still a very weak Slovene women's movement at the beginning of the twentieth century within the Habsburg Empire.

2. As Linz and Stepan put it in their study of democratic transition, "Democracy is a form of governance of a state. Thus no modern polity can become democratically consolidated unless it is first a state. Therefore, the non-existence of the state or such an intense lack of identification with the state that large groups of individuals in the territory want to join a different state or create an independent state raises fundamental and often insoluble problems. In their realistic opinion, which I share, 'stateness' problems are so basic . . . that one should pay much more attention to it." Juan J. Linz and Alfred Stepan, *Problems of Democratic Transition and Consolidation* (Baltimore: Johns Hopkins University Press, 1996), p. 7.

3. Most of them were writers, "Einzelgängerinnen" (solo activists), who, similar to those in some other European countries, especially at the time of the revolution in 1848–49, independently and self-consciously declared their interests (cf. Ute Gerhard, *Über die Anfänge der deutschen Frauenbewegung um 1848, Frauen suchen ihre Geschichte*, ed. Karin Hausen [Munich, 1983]).

4. Nataša Budna, "Feministično delo splošnega ženskega društva" (Feminist activities of the General Women's Society), in *Journal for History, Literature, and Anthropology* 46, nos. 535–37 (1994): 1232–57, Engl. summary, p. 1280. This historical article has helped me enormously.

5. Alojzija Štebi, "Aktivnost slovenske žene" (The Slovene woman's activity), in *Slovenska žena* (Slovene woman), ed. Minka Govekarjeva (Ljubljana: Slovenska žena, 1926), p. 162.

6. Budna, *Feministično delo*, p. 1280.

7. Cf. Vlasta Jalušič, *Dokler se ne vmesajo ženske* (Until the women meddle) (Ljubljana, 1992), p. 114; Budna, *Feministično delo*, p. 1239.

8. Minka Govekarjeva, *Petindvajsetletnica ženskega dela* (Ljubljana: Slovenska žena, 1926), p. 186.

9. Budna, *Feministično delo*, p. 1233.

10. Minka Govekar and Mila Dobova, "Splošno slovensko žensko drustvo," in *Slovenka* (Trieste), 25 April 1901 (cited from Budna, *Feministično delo*, p. 1232, my emphasis).

11. Govekarjeva, *Petindvajsetletnica ženskega dela*, p. 186.

12. This was partly the result of the factual situation in the national and class structure of the Habsburg Empire, where the ruling nations boasted the strongest rich, capitalist class/bourgeoisie, and the other nations consisted of numerous socially and politically depriviledged members.

13. It is perhaps important to mention that the name of the General Slovene Women's Society was changed in 1922 (after the decline of the Austro-Hungarian Empire). The word "Slovene" was erased from the name, since the members were convinced that there was no need to emphasize "Slovenehood" anymore. In the new state of Yugoslavia, full national freedom was to be guaranteed (this was at least the expectation). Under Habsburg rule, on the other hand, it seemed very important for the society to unite the women's elite of the whole country under the name Slovene.

14. The national public school system played a very important role in the building of national consciousness and, therefore, also in the nation-state building. The connection between female teachers and the first demands for equal citizenship is obvious since women represented the major-

ity of teachers and, therefore, the first massive group of formally educated women. See Mirjam Milharčič-Hladnik, *Šolstvo in učiteljice na Slovenskem* (Ljubljana, 1995), pp. 12–13.

15. Budna, *Feministično delo*, p. 1236.

16. Erna Muser, *Slovenke do leta 1941* (Slovene women until the year 1941) (Belgrade: Borbeni put žena Jugoslavije, 1972), p. 190.

17. The Slovene proletarian women's movement, similar to the earlier German pattern, did not emerge until the founding of the Slovene Communist Party in the 1930s. And even then the socialist women such as Alojzija Štebi and Angela Vode, who wrote a few important books on women's condition in the 1930s, did not become mainstream proletarian ideologists.

18. Štebi, *Aktivnost slovenske žene*, p. 170.

19. Muser, *Slovenke do leta 1941*, p. 190.

20. "Old Yugoslavia" means the state that ceased to exist after the beginning of World War II.

21. Muser, *Slovenke do leta 1941*, p. 190.

22. Budna, *Feministično delo*, p. 1242, my emphasis.

23. Govekarjeva, *Petindvajsetletnica ženskega dela*, p. 192.

24. The Serbian National Women's League invited all Slovene women's societies to attend the congress in Belgrade in 1919. The newly constituted League had a Serbian president and two vice-presidents, from Croatia and Slovenia (the Slovene vice-president was Franja Tavčar, a conservative liberal and the president of the GWS).

25. Govekarjeva, *Petindvajsetletnica ženskega dela*, p. 192, my emphasis.

26. Muser, *Slovenke do leta 1941*, p. 190.

27. See Momcilo Zečević, *Slovenska ljudska stranka in jugoslovansko zedinjenje* (The Slovene People's Party and the Yugoslav Union) (Maribor, 1977), p. 317.

28. See Lydia Sklevicky, "Karakteristike organiziranog djelovanja žena u Jugoslaviji u razdoblju do drugog svjetskog rata," *Polja* (Novi Sad), vol. 30, no. 308, n.d., p. 415.

29. Budna, *Feministično delo*.

30. Muser, *Slovenka do leta 1941*, p. 192. The National Women's League was the largest umbrella organization.

31. This was probably under the influence of the "new women" concept that emerged in the 1920s. See Jalušič, *Dokler se ne vemešajo ženske*, p. 117. The "moving force" of the Alliance was the already mentioned Alojzija Štebi, who left the GWS; see Muser, *Slovenke do leta 1941*.

32. Muser, *Slovenke do leta 1941*, p. 192.

33. All attempts to found a united women's front failed (the first one in 1920, and the last one before World War II in 1939).

34. Muser, *Slovenke do leta 1941*, p. 192. Already in 1919, the Slovene Christian Women's Alliance stood for political and citizenship rights of women.

35. I analyzed this attitude in my "Troubles with Democracy: Women and Slovene Independence," in Jill Benderly and Evan Kraft, eds., *Independent Slovenia: Origins, Movements, Prospects* (St. Martin's Press: New York, 1994), pp. 135–57.

36. Milena Mohorič, "Femnizem in borba delovne žene," in *Književnost* (Ljubljana), vol. 2, no. 1 (1934): 24–31.

37. Budna, *Feministično delo*, p. 1239.

38. Ibid., p. 1241.

39. See Nataša Budna Kodrič, "Žensko gibanje na Slovenskem do druge svetovne vojne," unpublished manuscript (Ljubljana, 1996), p. 7.

Chapter 5

1. Three acronyms used throughout the chapter may cause confusion for the reader and necessitate some explanation. They are NOB, NOP, and NOV. NOB stands for *Narodnooslobodi-*

lacka borba or National Liberation Struggle; NOP stands for *Narodnooslobodilacky pokret* or National Liberation Movement; and NOV stands for *Narodnooslobodilacka vojna* or National Liberation War. NOB and NOV refer to the same process of winning the civil and international war on Yugoslav soil. NOB is slightly more comprehensive in meaning, referring to the totality of effort, including taking care of the sick, wounded and orphans, organizing the "liberated villages" for the communist cause, providing food and material to the front, and so on. NOV refers more directly to the actual fighting. NOB is used rather more frequently by the Croatians, NOV by the Serbs. NOP refers to the collectivity of persons recruited into the communist-led movement to engage in the NOB or NOV, excluding those actually engaged in fighting.

2. Barbara Jancar-Webster, *Women & Revolution in Yugoslavia 1941–1945* (Denver: Arden Press, 1991).

3. Barbara Jancar, *Women Under Communism* (Baltimore: Johns Hopkins University Press, 1978).

4. Vera Veskovik-Angeli, *Zhenata vo revolutsjata na Makedonija 1941–1945* (Women in the revolution in Macedonia 1941–1945) (Skopje: Institut za Natsionalna istorija, Zavod za unapreduvan'e na stopanstvoto na CRM, 1982), p. 287.

5. Jancar-Webster, *Women and Revolution*, p. 46; Jozo Tomasevich, *War and Revolution in Yugoslavia, 1941–1945: The Chetniks* (Stanford: Stanford University Press, 1975), p. 189. In his study of the Chetnik movement, Milazzo makes no mention at all of women's pro-Chetnik associations. See Matteo J. Milazzo, *The Chetnik Movement and the Yugoslav Resistance* (Baltimore: Johns Hokpins University Press, 1975).

6. Danilo Bulajić, ed., *Leksikon Narodnooslobodilački rat i revolucija u Jugoslaviji 1941–1945* (Encyclopedia of the national liberation war and revolution in Yugoslavia 1941–1945), 2 vols. (Belgrade and Ljubljana: IRO *"Narodna knjiga"* and IRO *"Partizanska knjiga,"* 1980), 1:624, and 2:1251.

7. Milazzo, *The Chetnik Movement*, p. 50; Ronald H. Bailey, *Partisans and Guerrillas* (Alexandria, Va.: Time-Life Books, 1978), p. 106.

8. Dušanka Kovačević and Dragutan Kosović, eds., *Borbeni put žena Jugoslavije* (Yugoslav women's militant road) (Belgrade: Leksikografski zavod, *"Svezjanje,"* 1972), pp. 195–202.

9. The list may be found in Marija Šoljan, ed., *Žene Hrvatske u Narodnooslobodilačkoj borbi* (Women of Croatia in the national liberation struggle), 2 vols. (Zagreb: Izdanje Glavnog odbora Saveza ženskih društava Hrvatske, 1955), 2:447–554.

10. See Table 2.1, Jancar-Webster, *Women and Revolution*, p. 54.

11. A *vod* is a subdivision of the *ceta*, the basic military unit.

12. Jancar-Webster, *Women and Revolution*, pp. 91–92.

13. Ibid., p. 113.

14. Veskovik-Angeli, *Zhenata vo revolutsiata*.

15. Interview with Milka Kufrin, Zagreb, January 1985.

16. *Žena danas*, no. 26 (January–February 1940), p. 12.

17. Instructions of the Provisional High Command of the National Liberation Council of Montenegro, Boka, and Sandzak, 22 July 22 1941, as published in Slobodan Nesovic and Branko Petranovic, eds., *AVNOJ i revolucija: Tematska zbirka dokumentata 1941–1945* (AVNOJ and revolution: Thematic selection of documents, 1941–1945) (Belgrade: Narodna Knjiga, 1983), p. 106.

18. Interview with Mitra Mitrović, Belgrade, December 1984.

19. As cited in Jancar-Webster, *Women and Revolution*, p. 39.

20. Veskovik-Angeli, *Zhenata vo revolutsiata*, p. 287.

21. Dušanka Kovačević, *Women of Yugoslavia in the National Liberation War* (Belgrade, Jugoslovenski pregled, 1977), p. 34.

22. The resolution is cited in full in Kovačević, *Žene Hrvatske*, 1:171.

23. Members of the AFZ Executive Committee are listed on a photocopy of the front page of the 13 December 1942 issue of *Borba*, in ibid., p. 178.

24. *Žene u borbi* 1, no. 1 (January 1943): 7.

25. The full text in English may be found in Jancar-Webster, *Women and Revolution*, pp. 198–200.

26. See Barbara Jancar-Webster, "The New Feminism in Yugoslavia," in Pedro Ramet, ed. *Yugoslavia in the 1980s* (Boulder, Colo: Westview Press, 1985), pp. 201–23.

27. See Lydia Sklevicky, "Karakteristike organiziranog djelovanja žena u Jugoslaviji u razdobju do drugog svjetskog rata" (I and II) *Polja*, part I, no. 308 (October 1984), pp. 415–17; part II, no. 309 (November 1984), pp. 454–56.

28. Miscellaneous interviews, Zagreb, January 1985.

Chapter 6

1. Franciska Jurak, "Neke pretpostavke za dalje unapredjivanje društveno-ekonomskog položaja žene u našem društvu," *Žena* 40, no. 1 (1982): 3.

2. Stipe Šuvar, "Društveni položaj i uloga žene u razvoju socijalističkog samoupravljanja," *Žena* 38, nos. 4–5 (1980): 22.

3. For the Marxist view of gender equality and inequality, see *The Woman Question: Selections from the Writings of Karl Marx, Frederick Engels, V. I. Lenin, Joseph Stalin* (New York: International Publishers, 1951).

4. Vera Vesković-Vangeli, "Report on Serbia and Macedonia," in *Women and Development* (Belgrade: Facts and Tendencies, nos. 15–16, 1978), p. 564.

5. Biljana Sljivić-Simšić, "The Beginnings of the Feminist Movement in Nineteenth Century Serbia," *Serbian Studies* 3, nos. 1–2 (fall–spring 1984–85): 35.

6. Suzana Djurić and Gordana Dragičević, *Women in Yugoslav Society and Economy* (Belgrade: Medjunarodna Politika, 1965), p. 4.

7. Vida Tomšić, *Woman in the Development of Socialist Self-Managing Yugoslavia* (Belgrade: Jugoslovenska stvarnost, 1980), p. 20.

8. Quoted in ibid., p. 21.

9. Ibid., p. 22.

10. Obrad Kesić, "Women and Revolution in Yugoslavia (1945–1989)," in Mary Ann Tetreault, ed., *Women and Revolution in Africa, Asia, and the New World* (Columbia: University of South Carolina Press, 1994), p. 240.

11. Djurić and Dragičević, *Women in Yugoslav Society*, p. 5. See also *Žene Srbije u NOB* (Belgrade: Nolit, 1975); and *Žene Hrvatske u Narodnooblobodilačkoj Borbi* (Zagreb: Izdanje Glavnog Odbora Saveza Ženskih Društava Hrvatske, 1955), 2 vols.

12. Tomšić, *Woman in the Development*, pp. 76–80.

13. Djurić and Dragičević, *Women in Yugoslav Society*, p. 20.

14. Quoted in Dušan Bilandžić, "Kongresi SKJ o društvenom položaju žene," *Žena* 39, no. 3 (1981): 32.

15. Quoted in Djurić and Dragičević, *Women in Yugoslav Society*, p. 6.

16. Tomšić, *Women in the Development*, p. 18.

17. Djurić and Dragičević, *Women in Yugoslav Society*, p. 10.

18. Kesić, "Women and Revolution," p. 238.

19. Tomšić, *Woman in the Development*, p. 114.

20. Nevenka Selimović, "Report On the Educational and Professional Advancement of Women," in Tomšić, *Women in the Development*, p. 656.

21. Slobodanka Markov, "Položaj i uloga žena u sistemu političkog odlučivanja," *Žena* 42, no. 3 (1984): 23; Djurić and Dragičević, *Women in Yugoslav Society*, p. 10; and Tomšić, *Woman in the Development*, pp. 91–92.

22. Tomšić, *Woman in the Development*, p. 92.

23. Aleksandra Beluhan, "Sociološki aspekti prekida trudnoće," *Žena* 42, no. 4 (1984): 55.

24. Quoted in Tomšić, *Woman in the Development*, p. 144, my emphasis.

25. Beluhan, "Sociološki aspekti," p. 55.

26. Dubravka Štampar, "Prekid trudnoće u svijetu i u nas," *Žena* 45, no. 6 (1987): 24.

27. Selimović, "Report," p. 656.

28. Savka Dabčević-Kučar, "Problemi društvenog položaja žene—problemi našeg samoupravnog socijalističkog društva u cjelini," *Žena* 26, no. 2 (1970): 7–9; Alica Wertheimer-Baletić, "Neke tendencije u zapošljavanju žene," *Žena* 31, no. 6 (1973): 39; and Olivera Burić, "Ozmena strukture društvene moći: uslov za društvenu ravnopravnost žene," *Sociologija* 17, no. 2 (1975): 204.

29. Djurić and Dragičević, *Women in Yugoslav Society*, p. 14. See also Željka Sporer, "Feminizacija profesija kao indikator položaja žena u različitim društvima," *Sociologija* 27, no. 4 (October–December 1985).

30. Žarana Papić, "Emancipacija u granicama tradicionalne svijesti," *Žena* 38, nos. 4–5 (1980): 75.

31. Bilandžić, "Kongresi SKJ," p. 33.

32. Markov, "Položaj i uloga žena," p. 22.

33. Bilandžić, "Kongresi SKJ," p. 34; and Djurić and Dragičević, *Women in Yugoslav Society*, p. 17.

34. Quoted in Bilandžić, "Kongresi SKJ," p. 34.

35. Djurić and Dragičević, *Women in Yugoslav Society*, pp. 16–17.

36. Quoted in Bilandžić, "Kongresi SKJ," p. 37.

37. Markov, "Položaj i uloga žena," p. 22.

38. Bilandžić, "Kongresi SKJ," p. 39.

39. Tomšić, *Woman in the Development*, p. 51.

40. Quoted in Ibid., p. 67.

41. With regard to the Tito era's record in this policy sphere, see also Olivera Burić, "Položaj žene u sistemu društvene moći u Jugoslaviji," *Sociologija* 14, no. 1 (1972); and R. Iveković, "Žena u procesu odlučivanja u osnovnoj organizaciji Saveza komunista," *Opredjeljenja* 6, nos. 3–4 (March–April 1978).

42. The Serbo-Croatian translation of Isaac Deutscher's biography of Stalin appeared during late 1979 or early 1980 and was widely displayed. As people compared Tito to Lenin, they worried as to how to prevent a Yugoslav "Stalin" from taking power.

43. The reference is to Mao Zedong's designated successor who, upon Mao's death in September 1976, obtained the posts of Party General Secretary and Prime Minister. In the endeavor to consolidate the ranks behind him, Hua Guofeng promised to honor whatever Mao had said and to continue whatever Mao had done.

44. Jasna A. Petroviž, "Žene u SK danas," *Žena* 44, no. 4 (1986): 13.

45. Kesić, "Women and Revolution," p. 245.

46. See Barbara Jancar, "Neofeminism in Yugoslavia: A Closer Look," *Women in Politics* 8, no. 1 (1988).

47. Blaženka Despot, *Ženkso pitanje i socijalističko samoupravljanje* (Zagreb: Cekade, 1987), p. 109.

48. Ibid., pp. 113–14.

49. Stipe Šuvar, "I feminizam je jedan od oblika konzervativne društvene svijesti," *Žena* 40, nos. 2–3 (March–July 1982): 71–74.

50. Blaženka Despot, "Treba li ili ne posebna ženska organizacija," *Žena* 40, nos. 2–3 (March–July 1982): 74–78.

51. Report by Nadežda Gerasimovska-Hristova, in *Trinaesti kongres Saveza Komunista Jugoslavije, Beograd, 25–28 jun 1986. magnetofonske beleške*, vol. 2 (Belgrade: Izdavački centar Komunist, 1988), p. 188.

52. For discussion, see Sabrina P. Ramet, *Social Currents in Eastern Europe: The Sources and Consequences of the Great Transformation*, 2d ed. (Durham: Duke University Press, 1995), chap. 18.

53. Rajka and Milan Polić, "Dječji udžbenici o (ne)ravnopravnosti medju spolovima," *Žena* 36, no. 1 (1979): 13–14, 16–17.

Chapter 7

1. I would like to dedicate this text to my dearest friend and never tired feminist activist Mojca Dobnikar.

2. Data: *Statistical Yearbook of Slovenia*; also Tonči Kuzmanić, "Slovenia: From Yugoslavia to the Middle of Nowhere?" paper for the project "Democratization in Central and Eastern European Countries," Sussex European Institute, April 1996, p. 13; and Evan Kraft and Jill Benderley, eds., *Independent Slovenia. Origins, Movements, Prospects* (New York: St. Martin's Press, 1994), p. xix.

3. See my "Troubles with Democracy: Women and the Slovene Independence," in Kraft and Benderley, eds., *Independent Slovenia*, pp. 137–39, where I tried to pay some attention to these different circumstances.

4. Erna Muser, "Slovenke do leta 1941" (Slovenian women until the year 1941), in *Borbeni put žena Jugoslavije* (Beograd: Leksikografski zavod, 1972), p. 90. Erna Muser was a women's movement activist and a declared feminist in the time before the World War II and in the first years of socialism. She was repressed and marginalized in socialist times. She wanted to write a general history of the women's movement in Slovenia in her lifetime but never succeeded.

5. And even then this right has not been politically legitimized with the argument of equality but with the essentialist working-class ideology argument, as well as with the argument that women "deserved rights" because of their participation in the national liberation struggle. See Lydia Sklevicky, "Emanzipation und Organisation. Die antifaschistische Frauenfront in den post-revolutionären Veränderungen der Gesellschaft (1945–1953)," *Die ungeschriebene Geschichte. Historische Frauenforschung*, Dokumentation des 5, Historikerinnentreffen, Vienna, 16–18 April 1984 (Wiener Frauenverlag, 1984), pp. 84–101.

6. See Jalušič, "Troubles with Democracy," pp. 138–39.

7. I am using here Hannah Arendt's term "space of appearance," meaning public space that would not be enlarged socialized household but would include political space. See Hannah Arendt, *The Human Condition* (Chicago: The University of Chicago Press, 1958), esp. "Power and the Space of Appearance," pp. 207–11.

8. This term, too, is used in the sense of Hannah Arendt's differentiation among the main human activities (labor, work, and political action). It stresses the genuine nonpolitical nature of liberation through work. See Arendt, *The Human Condition*, chap. 3. In connection to this, I spoke in some previous texts about the "social emancipation" of women and about the "female semi-public kingdom" created with the socialist socialization of labor and the domestic sphere. Jalušič, "Troubles with Democracy," pp. 141–42; and Vlasta Jalušič, "Zurück in den Naturzustand," *Feministische Studien* 10, no. 2, (November 1992): 12–13.

9. Lydia Sklevicky, "Foreword," in *Kultiviranje dijaloga* (Cultivating dialogue), ed. Lydia Sklevicky (Zagreb: Ženi i društvo, 1987), p. 5.

10. On this subject, see Tonči Kuzmanć, "Civil Society and Nationalism in Slovenia," un-published paper, Ljubljana, 1994; Tomaž Mastnak, "From Social Movements to the National Sovereignty," in Benderly and Kraft, *Independent Slovenia*, pp. 93–111; Vlasta Jalušič, "Politics As a Whore," paper presented at the conference "Politics of Antipolitics," Vienna Dialogue on Democracy, July 1994; and Paul Stubbs, "Nationalisms, Globalization, and Civil Society in Croatia and Slovenia," *Research in Social Movements, Conflict and Change* 9 (1996): 1–26.

11. The new groups did not criticize the indisputably important legal achievements of action

by "state feminism." Rather they criticized elitism, politics in the small, separate circles, the aversion against feminism and women's movements, and the antipluralist attitude. The problem new feminists faced was that existing socialist legislation "for women" came "from above" and that "state feminists" did not take into account the interests of actual women. They claimed the "end of politics," so to speak, while the new feminists wanted to participate actively.

12. Some ex-members of this group are important scholars in gender studies at Ljubljana University and some are active party politicians.

13. See Vlasta Jalušič, "Nove demokracije in ženske študije" (New democracies and women's studies), in Eva Bahovec, ed., *Od ženskih študij k feministični teoriji* (From women's studies to feminist theory) (Ljubljana: *Časopis za kritiko znanosti*, special edition, 1993), pp. 107–18; Tanja Rener, "Women's Studies in Slovenia," *European Journal for Women's Studies* 3, no. 2 (June 1996): 167–71.

14. See, for example: Aleksandra Kollontaj, ed., *Ženska v socialism* (Women in socialism) (Ljubljana: Krt, 1984); Mojca Dobnikar, ed., *O ženski in ženskem gibanju* (On woman and the women's movement) (Ljubljana: Krt, 1985); *Tanja Rener, ed., Ženske, družina, država* (Women, family, the state) (Ljubljana: ČKZ, 1991); Eva D. Bahovec, ed., *Od ženskih študij k feministični teoriji* (From women's studies to feminist theory) (Lujblanja: ČKZ, 1993); Dara Zviršek, *Ženske in memtalo zdravje* (Women and mental health) (Ljubljana: VSŠD, 1994); Vlasta Jalušič, *Dokler se ne vmešajo ženske: Ženske revolucije in ostalo* (Until the women meddle: Women, revolutions, and rest) (Ljubljana: Krt, 1992); Rosalind Coward, *Ženska želja* (Female desire) (Ljubljana: Krt, 1988); Mary Wollstonecraft, *Zagvor pravic ženske* (Vindication of women's rights) (Ljublanja: Krt, 1993); and Olympe de Gouges, "Deklaracija o pravicah ženske in državljanke" (Declaration on the rights of woman and citizen), in *Problemi—Eseji* 7, no. 27 (1989): 43–47.

15. The amount of original and translated feminist literature has grown enormously in recent years.

16. See Gregor Tomc, "The Politics of Punk," in Kraft and Benderly, *Independent Slovenia*, pp. 113–34; and Tomaž Mastnak, "From Social Movements to National Sovereignty," in Kraft and Benderly, *Independent Slovenia*, p. 93.

17. Jalušič, "Troubles with Democracy," pp. 145–47.

18. I can still remember quite well the discomfort of some very liberal young Slovenian intellectuals in the face of women-only meetings of the Lilit group. The weekly *Mladina* had a humorous page where jokes were made about the mainstream communist politicians and some alternative people. Since the start of the Lilit group, they published a series of fabricated "humorous reports" about the activities of the Lilit group. One reported how, when alone together, the Lilit group discussed the "scientific relationship between vaginal and clitoral orgasm." The groups' members still transfer the same "joke" to the director of the Bureau for Women's Politics. On the discomfort of Eastern intellectual opposition to feminism and the gay and lesbian movement, see Tomaž Mastnak, *Vzhodno od raja: Civilna družba pod komunizmom in po njem* (Eastern from Eden: Civil society under communism and after it) (Ljubljana: Državna založba Slovenije, 1992), pp. 17f.

19. At the Congress of the Socialist Youth Alliance in April 1986, the feminist bulletin *One Step Further, Two Steps Back* (paraphrasing the Leninist slogan) was printed, where the demand for repoliticization of the woman question may be found.

20. Mastnak, "From New Social Movements," p. 101.

21. In October 1987, "We Love Women," a special supplement of the weekly *Mladina*, and the program of the newly formed LL lesbian group (in some other weeklies) was published. See Suzana Tratnik, Nataša S. Segan, *L: Antologija lezbičnega gibanja v Sloveniji, 1984–1995* (Ljubljana: Založba ŠKUC, 1995), p. 23.

22. All quotations are from *The Common Document of Yugoslav Feminists*, December 13, 1987. (There were differences in the Yugoslav Republic's legislation concerning homosexuality. In Serbia, Macedonia, Bosnia, and Herzegovina, male homosexuality was treated as a crime.)

23. Vida Tomšič, "The History of Women's Struggle for Rights As Citizens: The Right to Vote. The Case of Slovenia," unpublished manuscript, Ljublanja, 1996.

24. See the quoted analysis of Stubbs, "Nationalisms, Globalization, and Civil Society in Croatia and Slovenia," pp. 1–26.

25. Such is the claim of one Yugoslav author in her text about women in socialist Yugoslavia. See Daša Duhaček, "Women's Time in Former Yugoslavia," in Nanette Funk and Magda Mueller, eds., *Gender Politics and Post-Communism. Reflections from Eastern Europe and the Former Soviet Union* (New York: Routledge, 1993), p. 136. The reason why feminists from Slovenia (the Lilit group on the Third Meeting of Yugoslav Feminists in 1990 in Belgrade, as well as the Women for Politics group later in the same year at the founding session of the Yugoslav Women's Alliance in Zagreb) were against an umbrella organization was not their "nationalism" but their experiences with the socialist institutionalization of the woman question. I would not like to go too deep at this point. I want to emphasize that the feminists from Slovenia could not oppose "any movement at the Yu-level" (Duhaček, "Women's Time," p. 136), since that movement had existed and had been successfully cooperating as a network and gathering under the name Yugoslav Feminist Meetings for some time. The question was about a very specific proposed organizational form and the latent conflict between younger and older feminists, and not the "YU" movement. The fact is that the last Yugoslav Feminist Meeting took place almost a year later in Ljubljana (where even some women from Bosnia, Herzegovina, Macedonia, and Kosova were present, not only Slovenian, Croatian, and Serbian women) at the time when almost no other organizations—not even social scientists—had any contact at the "Yu" level. I do not claim that there were no ethnonational problems among feminists in Yugoslavia or that they were immune to them. Especially later, it turns out, feminists were also tempted by such sentiments. I only wish to point out that the question of failed umbrella organizations was much more complex that the "nationalism" thesis argues.

26. This solution was the necessary result of the socialist ideology of women's emancipation and of the struggle of "state feminists" and liberal gynecologists within the communist party and the state. On "state feminism," see Jalušič, "Troubles with Democracy," pp. 139–43.

27. In other republics, of course, these rights were realized to different extents, not without the influence of religious differences, different traditions, and standards of living. See Vlasta Jalušič, "Zurück in den Naturzustand," p. 10.

28. Women for Politics, Initiative Society for Equal Opportunities for Women and Men, Prenner Club, Women's Initiative, Initiative Delledonne, and Women with Ideas were groups with varying members (Women with Ideas, for example, were, and remained, managers). For the first time, some groups occurred out of the Slovene capital Ljubljana.

29. This constitutional debate started in the 1980s as a discussion within the Yugoslav federation, where every republic had its own constitution. The constitutions were very similar and all were worker-class rights oriented, although they differed in some social, national, and other points.

30. The proposal has been a mixture of conservative writers, the sociologists' proposal from 1989, and the more liberal approach of the reformed Social Youth Alliance, which later became the Liberal Democracy.

31. *Mladina*, 17 December 1991.

32. In her article, "Women and New Democracy in Former Yugoslavia," in Funk and Mueller, *Gender Politics in Post-communism*, p. 124, Slavenka Drakulć comes to the wrong conclusion about the results of the constitutional debate in Slovenia, on the basis of one of the proposals. The constitution did not pass through the parliament in 1990 but in 1991.

33. These social benefits were in many regards similar to the benefits in some Middle European and Scandinavian welfare states. The difference was a lower standard, but although it was still probably the highest among the East European states.

34. Up until now, all governments were economic-liberal, regardless of their different political or ideological convictions.

35. As of this writing, the legal solution is one year of parental leave, which the partners can share.

36. The unemployment rate in Slovenia is around 14 percent, as of this writing. Although this rate has grown, the female share in the total unemployment rate has still been smaller than the male. Higher educated women are more affected by unemployment than higher educated men.

37. Hana Havelkova, "Ignored But Assumed: Family and Gender Between the Public and Private Realms," *Czech Sociological Review* 4, no. 1 (spring 1996): 63–79.

38. The female average wage is approximately 11 percent lower than the male. Especially in so-called feminized professions the wages are low (textile and leather industry, teachers, nurses, including non-specialized medical doctors).

39. See Milica G. Antić, "Ženske in volitve v Sloveniji" (Women and elections in Slovenia), in Slavko Gaber, ed., *Volilni sistemi* (Voting systems) (Ljubljana, 1996), pp. 171–89.

40. The general results of the 1996 election are the following: the position is constituted by Liberal Democracy of Slovenia (Janez Drnovšek as prime minister, with 27 percent of the votes), the Slovene Peoples Party (with 19.4 percent), and the Democratic Party of Retired Persons (4.3 percent); the oppostion by the right-oriented Social Democratic Party (16.1 percent), the left-oriented United List of Social Democrats (9 percent), the Slovene Christian Democrats (10 percent), the Slovene National Party (3.2 percent), and the two representatives of national minorities (2.2 percent).

41. Women's Forum (United List of Social Democrats, reformed communists), Slovenian Women's Alliance (Slovenian Christian Democrats), Women's Alliance (Slovenian People's Party), Social Democratic Women's Council (right-populist-oriented Social Democratic Party), and the Minerva Club (Liberal Democracy of Slovenia).

42. Jan Makarovič & Janez Jug, "How the New Political Elite in Slovenia Understands Democracy," in Gregor Tomc and Frane Adam, ed., *Small Societies in Transition. The Case of Slovenia* (Ljubljana: Družboslovne razprave, Faculty of Social Sciences, special issue, 1994), pp. 35–74.

43. This is additionally supported by many western NGO advisers. Thus most initiatives are still antistatist- and antiparty-oriented. They persist on a kind of "civil society" (NGO) ideology that mostly pushes them into specific dependent relationships with the Western sources of money and imported patterns of organization. On this very important problem, see Stubbs, "Nationalisms, Globalization and Civil Society in Croatia and Slovenia," pp. 13–22.

44. On the ideological dispersion of Slovenia's political parties, see Sabrina Petra Ramet, "Democratization in Slovenia: The Second Stage," in Karen Dawisha and Bruce Parrott, eds., *Democratization and Authoritarianism in Postcommunist Societies 2: Politics, Power, and the Struggle for Democracy in South-East Europe* (Cambridge: Cambridge University Press, 1997), fig. 6.1, p. 218. Chapter 6 also provides the most detailed critical reception of the developments in Slovenia after 1989.

45. Later, in February 1998, the Liberal Democratic Party introduced a 30 percent quota within the party.

46. Nongovernmental feminist women's groups include: the Women's Center, which includes the Prenner Media Group, a counseling group, Cassandra (lesbian group), and the Modra Group; SOS Hotline and shelter for women and children who are victims of violence; Gender Studies Group, fragmented in the universities and institutes; LL, lesbian group; *Delta*, a feminist review; and the Center for Gender and Politics at the Peace Institute.

47. Such was the argument of the second women of the Slovene National Party, Polonca Dobrajc. See the pre-election interview, "Getoizacije ne odobravam" (I do not approve ghetto-ization) in the daily *Delo*, 28 December 1996.

48. See *Položaj žensk v Sloveniji v devetdesetih* (The position of women in Slovenia in the 1990s), Urad za žansko politiko (Office for Women's Politics), Ljubljana, 1997, p. 42.

Chapter 8

1. Knin was the capital of the self-proclaimed Serbian Republic, and the "retaking" of Knin was a crucial victory for Tudjman in Croatia.
2. Quoted in Vesna Kesić, "Od štovanja do silovanja," in *Kruh i ruze*, no. 1 (spring 1994), p. 10.
3. Benedict Anderson, *Imagined Communities: Reflections on the Origin and Spread of Nationalism* (London: Verso Press, 1983).
4. Rambo iconography is essential in the popular imagination of Croatian soldiers (in Serbia there is the same phenomenon).
5. Quoted in Dubravka Ugrešić, "Jer mi smo dečki," in *Kruh i ruze*, no. 1 (spring 1994), p. 29.
6. Ibid., p. 30.
7. Even though it is mostly seen in ultranationalistic publication, it also often appears in the most mainstream publications.
8. In 1990, the magazine *Start* asked Croatian politicians several questions about five controversial issues (on the death penalty, abortion, pornography, narcotics, and homosexuality).
9. Quoted in Ivana Vucić, "Intervju sa Vesnom Kesićem," *Arkzin*, no. 71 (2 August 1996), p. 8.
10. Sigmund Freud, *Civilization and its Discontents* (London: Standard Ed., 1930).
11. Quoted in "Hrvatske feministice siluju Hrvatsku," in *Globus*, 11 December 1992, p. 33.
12. Ibid.
13. Quoted in Vesna Kesić, "Od štovanja," *Kruh i ruze*, no. 1 (spring 1994), p. 12.
14. Quoted in Mare Bulkic-Mrkobrad, "Razgovor sa Petrom Žilnikom," in *Globus*, 9 February 1996, p. 16.
15. Ugrešić, "Jer mi smo," p. 31.
16. "Deserving mother" is Zilnik's self-coined term.
17. Quoted in Mare Bulkic-Mrkobrad, "Intervju sa Petrom Žilnikom," p. 16.
18. In almost all Zagreb hospitals, there are posters on walls with moral messages against abortion, messages from the Pope on the abortion issue, and similar pro-life propaganda. This fact is very disturbing since these hospital are state and not private (Catholic) hospitals.
19. Quoted in "Intervju sa Dafinkom Večerinom," in *Arkzin*, no. 54 (22 December 1995), p. 7.
20. The text that follows is quoted from the appeal that B.A.B.E. (Women's Human Rights Group) launched to the international community on 7 February 1996 to help keep women's rights to abortion and access to contraceptives legal.
21. This indicates B.A.B.E.'s appeal to the international community.
22. Quoted in "Intervju sa Dafinkom Večerinom," p. 7.
23. Ugrešić, "Jer mi smo," p. 33.
24. Dubravka Ugrešić points out this popular use of "cunt" in her article "Because We Are Boys." It is difficult to capture the meaning of these expressions. They combine the sense of women and cunt as invitations for abuse. After beating someone severely, one can say "I trashed him like a cunt."
25. "Folksies are the new-style, 'newly-composed' folk songs. They are the glue of the nations of the former Yugo-space, a common ailment, a mark of mutual recognition, a shared reason for simultaneous sympathy and hatered. Folksies are the bared 'soul of the nation,' the heart, the

weak spot, a genetic code, collective remembrance reduced to sound" (Dubravka Ugrešić, in *Balkan Blues* (Evanston, Ill.: Northwestern University Press, 1994).

26. Gayle Rubin, "The Traffic in Women: Notes on the Political Economy of Sex," in *Toward an Anthropology of Women*, ed. Rayna R. Reiter (New York: Monthly Review Press, 1975).

27. Ugrešić, "Jer mi smo," p. 32.

28. *Speak Out*, no. 0, p. 3, published as a supplement of *Arkzin*, no. 16 (June 1994).

29. *Arkzin* is one of the few alternative newspaper in Croatia.

30. Ugrešić, "Jer mi smo," p. 31.

31. All of the streets and squares that had been named after partisan heroes became streets and squares of illustrious Croats. The best example is the change of "Square of Victims of Fascism" to "Square of Croatian Giants." There is popular graffiti on the streets of Zagreb which reads: "Square of Victims of Fascism, Communism, and Democracy."

32. "Language" is synonymous with "tongue" in Croatian.

33. Quoted in "Intervju sa Predragom Raosom," *Arkzin*, nos. 19–20 (5 August 1994), p. 19.

34. Quoted in "Intervju sa Ksenijom Urlicićem," *Globus*, 9 February 1996, p. 22.

35. Quoted in Robert Roklica, "Gdje se maze svi Hrvatski homoseksualci," in *Stil*, no. 40 (25 June 1996).

36. This event took place in KIC in Zagreb on 17 October 1995.

37. Isabela Albini borrows the term "balkanska krcma" from Croatian writer Miroslav Krleza.

Chapter 9

1. See Cynthia Enloe, *The Morning After: Sexual Politics at the end of the Cold War* (Berkeley and Los Angeles: University of California Press, 1993), p. 24.

2. See Zillah Eisenstein, *Hatreds: Sexualized and Racialized Conflicts in the Twenty-first Century* (New York and London: Routledge: 1996).

3. See U. N. Commission on Human Rights, *Rape and Abuse of Women and Children in the Territory of the Former Yugoslavia*, Report on the 49th session (New York: U.N. Publications, 1993).

4. Mladen Lazić, *Razaranje drustva* (Belgrade: Filip Višnjić, 1994), p. 1; Silvano Bolcic, *Tegobe prelaza u preduzetnicko drustvo: Sociologija tranzicije pocetkom 90-ih* (Belgrade: Institut za socioloska istrazivanja Filozofskog fakulteta, 1994), p. 141; and Andjelka Milić, "Social Disintegration and Families under Stress: Serbia, 1991–1995," in *Sociologija* (English ed.) 37, no. 4 (1995), pp. 455–72.

5. See Žarana Papić, "Nationalismus, Patriarchie, und Krieg," in Olga Uremović and Gundula Oerter, eds., *Frauen zwischen Grenzen: Rassismus und Nationalismus in der feministischen Diskussion* (Frankfurt: Campus verlag, 1994).

6. The situation, even only in its fluid democratic possibilities, has been radically changed in November 1996 in the course of the massive nonviolent protest movement lasting several months which took place in Belgrade and other towns in Serbia. The protest came in response to Milošević's annulment of an electoral victory in municipal elections on the part of the Zajedno political opposition. But, at this writing, it is difficult to be certain of the direction in which Serbian politics is evolving.

7. One columnist wrote concerning Alija Izetbegović's heart attack: "In principle, one should not wish evil to other people, but there are cases [such as this] in which God would have forgiven such thoughts." Goran Kozić, "Dragi pokojnik," in *Politika* (Belgrade), 25 February 1996. Kozić won the 1995 Journalists' Association prize for the best "individual" contribution.

8. For a discussion of fascism and the "violence of banality," see the discussion in Francine Muel-Dreyfuss, *Vichy et l'eternel feminin. Contribution a une sociologie politique de l'ordre des corps* (Paris: Ed. Du Seuil, 1996).

9. Mirjana Marković, in *Duga* (Belgrade), 31 April 1995, as quoted in "Svastalice," in *Republika* (Belgrade), no. 91 (1–15 May 1995).

10. Dragos Kalajić, in *Duga* (15 May 1995).

11. Ernest Gellner, *Nationalism* (Oxford: Basil Blackwell, 1993); and Maurice Godelier, "L'analyse des processus de transition," in *Information sur les sciences sociales* 26, no. 2 (1987).

12. Victor Turner, *Dramas, Fields, and Metaphors: Symbolic Action in Human Society* (Ithaca, N.Y.: Cornell University Press, 1974).

13. Mihel Fuko [Michel Foucault], *Rijeci i stvari*, translated from French by Nikola Kovač (Belgrade: Nolit, 1971), p. 109.

14. Mark Abrams, *Historical Sociology* (Somerset: Open Books, 1982), p. 92.

15. For discussion, see Žarana Papić, "From State Socialism to State Nationalism: The Case of Serbia in Gender Perspective," in *Refuge: Canada's Periodical on Refugees* 14, no. 3 (1994).

16. On this point, see Thomas Cushman, *Critical Theory and the War in Croatia and Bosnia*, The Donald W. Treadgold Papers in Russian, East European, and Central Asian Studies No. 13 (Seattle: The Henry M. Jackson School of International Studies of the University of Washington, July 1997).

17. For further discussion, see Žarana Papić, "Ex-citoyéenes dans l'ex-Yougoslavie," in *Peuples mediterranéens*, Special issue No. 61 (1992).

18. *Politika* (6 January 1995).

19. Quoted in "Zenski dokumenti 1990–1993," in *Feministicke sveske* (Belgrade), nos. 3–4 (1995): 34.

20. Ibid.

21. These facts are based on general statistical data and on "Sociological Investigation of New Characteristics in Serbian Society at the Beginning of the Nineties," carried out in 1994 in Belgrade and twelve provincial towns, and reported in Bolčić, *Tegobe prelaza*, passim. At the end of 1993, some 590,000 refugees were registered in Serbia with probably another 150,000 unregistered. After May 1995, another 200,000 refugees came to Serbia. 95 percent of refugees moved in with relatives and friends. Of adult refugees, 84 percent are women. As reported in Marina Blagojević, "Svadodnevica iz ženske perspektive. Samozrtvovanje i beg u privatnost," in Silvano Bolčić, ed., *Društvene promene i svakodnevni život: Srbija početkom devedesetih* (Belgrade: Institut za sociološka istraživanja Filozofskog fakulteta, 1995).

22. Milić, "Social Disintegration," p. 471.

23. Blagojević, "Svakodnevica iz ženske," p. 183.

24. The contradictory and controversial power of one woman, Mirjana Marković, is, in this regard, far less mysterious, since she is the one woman *chosen* by him, and therefore blessed and protected by his mysterious power.

25. A good example of craven subordination is Zoran Lilic, the official president of the Federal Republic of Yugoslavia 1993–96, who, as a former fashion model, served as a perfect marionette in the role of nominal executive chief of the country. Compared to Milosevic's "one man, one vote" system, even the autocratic power of Tito's communist regime looks rather "democratic," with its multilayered system of decentralized mediation of state and party power structures.

26. Blagojević, "Svakodnevica iz ženske," pp. 196–200.

Chapter 10

1. Butler writes: "There is no self . . . who maintains 'integrity' prior to its entrance into this collected cultural field. There is only a talking up of tools where they lie, where the very 'takingup' is enabled by the tools lying there" Judith Butler, *Gender Trouble* (New York: Routledge, 1990), p. 145. See also Judith Butler, "Gender is Burning: Questions of Appropriation and Subver-

sion," in Judith Butler, *Bodies That Matter: On the Discursive Limits of "Sex"* (New York: Routledge, 1993).

2. See Chapter 9 of this volume.

3. Kosovo is the Serbian spelling; Kosova, the Albanian. This chapter uses the Serbian spelling as it is the most internationally recognized in the majority of world atlases. Kosovo was an autonomous province of Serbia under the 1974 Yugoslav Constitution. In 1990, in an action called illegal and unconstitutional by Kosovar Albanians and some Serbian human rights activists, Serbian President Slobodan Milošević stripped Kosovo of its autonomous status. Ever since then, Kosovar Albanians have followed their own parallel Albanian state, complete with its own government, school system, and social welfare program. As of this writing, the Albanian Kosova government has been recognized by no country except for Albania and the "reduced Yugoslavia." On the other hand, Montenegro and Serbia (including Vojvodina and Kosovo) have been recognized by Germany and several other major world powers. The final outcome for Kosovo, however, remains undecided. For a recent survey of the debate, see Dušan Janjić and Shkelzen Maliqi, eds., *Conflict or Dialogue* (Subotica: Open University, 1994).

4. Tzvetan Todorov, *On Human Diversity: Nationalism, Racism, and Exoticism in French Thought* (Cambridge, Mass.: Harvard University Press, 1993), p. 173.

5. I use the term "ethnonational minorities" as a compromise. Europeans (and particularly people of the Balkans) would call these groups "nations." Americans would generally use the term "ethnic groups" although, with the exception of Albanians, Hungarians, Rom, and Turks, the people of the former Yugoslavia are Slavic and thus technically of the same ethnicity. To make matters more confusing, the 1974 Constitution of Yugoslavia distinguished between constituent nations—Serbs, Croats, Slovenes, Muslims, Montenegrins, and Macedonians—and minorities, such as Albanians and Hungarians. *Ustav Socijalističke Federativne Republike Jugoslavije* (Constitution of the Federal Republic of Yugoslavia), trans. Dragoljub Djurović (Belgrade and Ljubljana: Dopisna Delavska Univerza, 1974). The use of the word "minority" in this chapter does not necessarily endorse the language of the 1974 constitution but rather is meant to describe a numerical or political minority (although within Kosovo itself, Albanians are a 90 percent majority).

6. The term Kosovar refers to Albanians in or from Kosovo, thus distinguishing them from Albanians from Albania, Macedonia, and elsewhere. Unless otherwise noted, this chapter discusses Kosovar Albanians. As great differences in political and social history exist between Albanians in Kosovo and in Albania, generalizations for one group cannot be applied to the other.

7. Similarly, gay rights activists have had to choose their gender identity over their ethnonational identity. See Jelica Todosijević, "Serbia," in *Unspoken Rules*, ed. Rachel Rosenbloom (San Francisco: IGLHRC, 1995).

8. The cost of choosing the identity of Woman over a national identity is high for Serbian women as they too could be harassed by state authorities and ostracized by their families. Yet the cost for Albanian women tends to be much higher. While Serb authorities regularly dismiss women activists as unimportant and impotent, Albanian leaders tend to scrutinize the activities of all who break rank. In addition, it is harder for an Albanian woman to break rank and survive; she needs her community and no viable alternative exists. In contrast, although hundreds of thousands of Serbs have fled Serbia for political reasons, a large enough community remains to provide some sense of support to those who criticize the regime. Moreover, the extent to which Serbian women identified themselves with their ethnonational group is much lower. Many Serbs identified strongly as Yugoslav in prewar Yugoslavia; very few Albanians identified themselves as anything but Albanian.

9. The "suffering victim" plea may turn away the international community, which generally has a low tolerance for victims and quickly becomes benumbed to pain, but still the approach is more sympathetic than "aggressor/oppressor/war criminal."

10. Uroševac is the Serbian name for the town; Ferizej, the Albanian. The Serbian is used

henceforth as it appears most commonly in world atlases to date. All interviews with women in Kosovo cited in this chapter were conducted by the author during 1993–95, unless specifically noted.

11. In this respect, the identity of Kosovar Albanians differs substantially from Albanians in Albania. Instead of emphasizing their "suffering," Albanians in Albania tend to stress their lack of luck—"We have been an unlucky people," many people in Tirana can be heard to say.

12. See Julie Mertus and Vlatka Mihelic, *Open Wounds: Human Rights Abuses in Kosovo* (New York: Human Rights Watch, 1994); Sabrina Petra Ramet, "The Albanians of Kosovo: The Potential for Destabilization," *The Brown Journal of World Affairs* 3, no. 1 (winter–spring 1996): 353–72.

13. In discussing issues of illiteracy and prostitution in towns and villages with the author throughout Kosovo, many women began by blaming Serbs. After discussion, several women started to reflect on responsibility within the Albanian community itself. Author's notes from workshops and interviews, 1993–95.

14. Interview by the Club of Correspondents, Media Project, Kosova, 17 March 1996, posted to the e-mail conference "women.east-west" .

15. Renata Salečl, "Nationalism, Anti-Semitism, and Antifeminism in Eastern Europe," *Journal of Area Studies* 2, no. 3 (1993): 78–90. See also Renata Salečl, *The Spoils of Freedom: Psychoanalysis After the Fall of Socialism* (London: Routledge, 1994), pp. 20–37. For discussions of nation, gender, and "otherness," see Zillah Eisenstein, *The Color of Gender: Reimagining Democracy* (Berkeley and Los Angeles: University of California Press, 1994); Andrew Parker, Mary Russo, Doris Sommer, and Patricia Yeager, "Introduction," in Andrew Parker, Mary Russo, Doris Sommer, and Patricia Yeager, eds., *Nationalisms and Sexualities* (New York: Routledge, 1992), p. 5; Julie Mertus, "'Woman' in the Service of National Identity," *Hastings Women's Law Journal* 4, no. 1 (winter 1994): 5; Anne McClintock, "No Longer a Future in Heaven": Women and Nationalism in South Africa, *Transition* 1, no. 51 (1991): 104.

16. See Julia Kristeva, *Strangers to Ourselves* (New York: Columbia University Press, 1991).

17. Salecl, "Nationalism, Anti-Semitism, and Antifeminism in Eastern Europe," p. 80.

18. I use the terminology of Joan Cocks; see her *The Oppositional Imagination: Feminism, Critique and Political Theory* (New York: Routledge, 1989). See also Daša Duhaček "Women's Time in the Former Yugoslavia," in Nanette Funk and Magda Mueller, eds., *Gender Politics and Post-Communism: Reflections from Eastern Europe and the Former Soviet Union* (New York: Routledge, 1993), p. 131. For an example of such propaganda, see *Borba* (Belgrade), 2 June 1994.

19. Interview by the Club of Correspondents, Media Project, Kosova, 17 March 1996, posted to the e-mail conference "women.east-west" <women-east-west@igc.apc.org>.

20. *Kosovaria*, 25 December 1994, p. 10.

21. This is not to say that the village men are necessarily bound to all traditions. They have let MTV, Satellite TV, and CD players into their lives. However, many of the same men have not seen the need for gas or electric kitchen appliances.

22. Today two de facto states exist in Kosovo: the official Serbian state which rules through control over the police, military, courts, and borders, and the Albanian state, the so-called parallel government which Albanians formed in 1990, and which rules through the moral authority granted to it by Kosovar Albanians. See Isuf Berisha, "Pristina's One-Party Rule," *Balkan War Report*, February 1994, p. 12. To eliminate confusion, when referring to "the state," this chapter means the official Serbian state; use of the term "Kosovar Albanian state" refers to the parallel Kosovar Albanian government.

23. See Julie Mertus, "Gender in the Service of Nation: Female Citizenship in Kosovar Society," *Social Politics: International Studies in Gender, State and Society* 3, nos. 2–3 (summer–fall 1996) pp. 261–77.

24. Interview with author, March 1995.

25. In fact, Srdjan Bogosavljević, a Serbian academic, has found that the average number of

live births among the educated inhabitants of Kosovo is less than in Central Serbia. Srdjan Bogo-savljević, "A Statistical Picture of Serbo-Albanian Relations, *Republika* 6, special issue no. 9 (February 1994), p. 19 (published also in Serbian as "Statistička slika Srpsko-Albanskih odnosa").

26. There are very few allegations of rape of men from any sources.

27. This interview takes place in March 1995.

28. The few former political prisoners who have obtained passports are, with few exceptions, men who hold stature in the international community. The women former political prisoners are least likely to obtain a passport—the international community does not care enough to help them.

29. Richard Falk, comments in "Teaching International Relations and International Organizations in International Law Courses," *Proceedings of the Annual Meeting: The American Society of International Law Proceedings* (1993), p. 398.

30. Ibid, p. 399.

31. As a pragmatic matter, Kosovar Albanians may recognize Serbian law when it comes to such matters as taxes and registration of companies, but this does not mean that they see the law as legitimate, only as powerful and backed by the threat of force and other sanctions.

32. This insight is drawn from the remarks of Jane Collier at the New Directions in International Law Conference in Madison Wisconsin, June 1996.

33. Chaim Kaufman, "Possible and Impossible Solutions to Ethnic Civil Wars," *International Security* 20, no. 4 (1996): 141.

34. Of course one cannot predict with certainty how Kosovar Albanians would treat lesbian and gay members of their community would they be in control of the legal system. Indeed, the strong patriarchal traditions in Kosovo (as elsewhere in the Balkans) discourage same sex relationships, and tradition makes it almost impossible for all people in rural areas (but especially the women) to choose any life other than that of a spouse. However, some members of the Albanian human rights community have supported the rights of gay men and lesbians.

35. I use the terminology "potential" to become aggressive because I believe that we have not fully examined the important questions regarding the transformative potential of nationalism: Will nationalism necessarily snuff out other identities? Will it necessarily lead to segregation based on an ethnic principle and to rights based on ethnicity? To citizenship rights regardless of ethnicity? Can nationalist societies promote civic egalitarianism? See Yael Tamir, *Liberal Nationalism* (Princeton: Princeton University Press, 1994).

Chapter 11

1. Žarana Papić, "Nationalism, War, and Gender: Ex-Femininity, Ex-Masculinity, or Ex-Yugoslavian Ex-Citizens," paper presented at the working meeting, "Gender, Democracy, and Nationalism," Washington, D.C., 24–26 October 1993.

2. Staša Zajović, "The War and Women in Serbia: Partriarchy, Language, and National Myth," in *Peace News* (March 1992), p. 7.

3. Ljiljana Hebjanović-Durović, "Ja sam vojnik-četnik," in *Duga*, 16–29 January 1993, p. 31.

4. *Večernji list* (Zagreb), 20 June 1992, p. 7.

5. Hebjanović-Durović, "Ja sam vojnik," p. 31.

6. *Globus* (Zagreb), 3 September 1993, p. 35.

7. Vladimir Matić, in interview with the author, Washington, D.C., 11 September 1994.

8. Gordana Ristić, in interview with the author, Belgrade, 19 October 1994.

9. Catherine MacKinnon, "Turning Rape into Pornography: Postmodern Genocide," in *Ms.*, July–August 1993.

10. Susan Brownmiller, *Against Our Will: Men, Women, and Rape* (New York: Simon and Schuster, 1975), pp. 14–15.

11. Ibid., p. 14.

12. Ibid., p. 35.

13. *Globus*, 11 December 1992, English translation reprinted as "The Five Croatian 'Witches': A Casebook on 'Trial by Public Opinion' as a Form of Censorship and Intimidation," prepared by Meredith Tax for the International Pen Women Writers' Committee, pp. 7–8.

14. Rada Iveković, in interview with the author, Zagreb, 8 July 1993.

15. Slavenka Drakulić, "Mass Rape in Bosnia: Women Hide Behind a Wall of Silence," in *The Nation*, 1 March 1993, p. 271.

16. Ibid., p. 272.

17. MacKinnon, "Turning Rape," p. 26.

18. Ibid., 28.

19. Vesna Kesić, letter to the editor, in *Ms.*, dated July 1993, photocopy provided to the author by Kesić.

20. *Globus*, 11 December 1992, pp. 6–8.

21. See Annex I, Ibid., pp. 9–10.

22. *Večernji list*, 15 December 1992, as summarized in "Croatian Press 1991/92/93: Summaries of Articles on 'The Five Witches of Rio,' " prepared by Meredith Tax for the International Pen Women Writers' Committee, p. 17.

23. Vesna Kesić, in interview with the author, Washington D.C., 25 October 1993.

24. The Zagreb Women's Lobby, "Protest Against the Text Published in *Globus* on the 10th [of] December under the title 'Croatian Feminists Rape Croatia'," flier (Zagreb, 12 December 1992).

25. Vladimir Matić, in interview with the author, Washington, D.C., 11 September 1994.

26. *Globus*, 18 February 1994, p. 7.

27. *Slobodna Delmacija*, 14 January 1995, p. 9.

Chapter 12

1. The tribunal's formal title is the International Tribunal for the Prosecution of Persons Responsible for Serious Violations of International Humanitarian Law Committed in the Territory of the Former Yugoslavia Since 1991.

2. Michael Walzer, *Just and Unjust War: A Moral Argument with Historical Illustrations* (New York: Basic Books, 1977), p. 133.

3. Susan Brownmiller, *Against Our Will: Men, Women, and Rape* (New York: Bantam Books, 1975), pp. 46–51.

4. Ibid., pp. 64–65.

5. In March of 1971, the Bengali state—at that time officially East Pakistan—declared its independence as Bangladesh. West Pakistan imported troops to put down the rebellion. Until India's armed intervention in December 1971, Pakistani troops waged war against the Bengalis. Estimates place the death toll at 3 million, the refugees into India at 10 million, the number of women raped at over 200,000, and their resultant pregnancies at 25,000. See Brownmiller, *Against Our Will*, pp. 78–87.

6. *Report of the Council of Europe on Human Rights in Cyprus, 1974* (London: Council of Europe, 1980), pp. 121–22. The Commission ruled that the cases of rape constituted "inhuman treatment."

7. Helsinki Watch, *War Crimes in Bosnia-Herzegovina, Vol. 2* (New York: Human Rights Watch, 1993), pp. 163–65.

8. Women's Rights Project/Americas Watch, *Untold Terror: Violence Against Women in Peru's Armed Conflict* (New York: Human Rights Watch, 1992).

9. Asia Watch, *The Human Rights Crisis in Kashmir: A Pattern of Impunity* (New York: Human Rights Watch, 1993), p. 103.

10. Women's Rights Project/Africa Watch, *Seeking Refugee, Finding Terror: The Widespread Rape of Somali Women Refugees in North Eastern Kenya* (New York: Human Rights Watch, 1993), p. 2. Almost 300,000 refugees, most of them women and children, have fled the violence of war-torn Somalia since 1991 for refugee camps in North Eastern Kenya. For many of these women, rape played a role in inducing them to flee; the United Nations High Commissioner for Refugees recorded 85 cases of rape in Somalia between February and August 1992. Yet, instead of escaping the violence, Somali refugees encountered similar abuse in Kenya: UNHCR has documented another 107 cases of rape in the Kenyan refugee camps.

11. Asia Watch, *Burma: Rape, Forced Labor, and Religious Persecution in Northern Arakan* (New York: Human Rights Watch, 1992), p. 8.

12. Ibid., p. 7.

13. Women's Rights Project/Americas Watch, *Untold Terror*, p. 37.

14. Women's Rights Project/Africa Watch, *Seeking Refugee*, p. 18.

15. *Newsday*, 19 April 1993, pp. 7, 31.

16. *Times of India*, 6 January 1993, as quoted in Asia Watch, *Rape in Kashmir: A Crime of War* (New York: Human Rights Watch, 1993), p. 17.

17. Helsinki Watch, *War Crimes in Bosnia-Herzegovina*, pp. 216, 218.

18. Asia Watch, *Burma*, p. 2.

19. Asia Watch, *Bangladesh: Abuse of Burmese Refugees from Arakan* (New York: Human Rights Watch, 1993).

20. Theodor Meron, "Rape as a Crime under International Humanitarian Law," *American Journal of International Law* 87, no. 3 (July 1993): 424, 426.

21. Ibid., p. 427.

22. Under the state of emergency legislation, Peru's military is given control of a defined region and acts as the ultimate authority over civilian-elected and appointed officials. Certain rights, such as freedom of assembly and movement and the inviolability of the home, are suspended. Anyone living in a militarily controlled region, or "Emergency Zone," can be arrested without warrant and kept fifteen days in incommunicado detention.

23. Peru's is an internal, not international, conflict. Although humanitarian law prohibits rape in both kinds of conflict, it distinguishes between internal and international war and provides lesser means of redress for rape and other abuses that occur in internal conflicts.

24. Women's Rights Project/Americas Watch, *Untold Terror*, p. 39.

25. Ibid., p. 29.

26. Helsinki Watch, *War Crimes in Bosnia-Herzegovina*, p. 215.

27. Anne Tierney Goldstein, *Recognizing Forced Impregnation as a War Crime under International Law: A Special Report of the International Program* (New York: The Center for Reproductive Law and Policy, 1993).

28. U.N. Commission on Human Rights, *Report on the Situation of Human Rights in Myanmar*, 49th Session, at 16, E/CN.4/1993/37 (17 February 1993).

29. U.N. Division for the Advancement of Women, *Report of the Expert Group Meeting on Measures to Eradicate Violence Against Women* (New York: U.N. Publications), 8 October 1993, unedited version.

30. Women's Rights Project/Africa Watch, *Seeking Refuge*, p. 15.

31. Slavenka Drakulic, "Mass Rape in Bosnia: Women Hide Behind a Wall of Silence," in *The Nation*, 1 March 1993, p. 271.

32. Interview by Human Rights Watch, Istanbul, Turkey, July 1993.

33. Interview by Human Rights Watch, Diyarbakir, Turkey, 15 July 1993.

34. Helsinki Watch, *War Crimes in Bosnia-Herzegovina*, p. 170.

35. Women's Rights Project/Africa Watch, *Seeking Refuge*, p. 7.

36. The problem of oversimplification of women's experience is discussed in Vasuki Nesiah,

"Toward a Feminist Internationality: A Critique of U.S. Feminist Legal Scholarship," *Harvard Women's Law Journal* 16 (spring 1993): 189–210. Nesiah argues that privileging gender as the unifying element of the community of *all* women prevents other issues pertaining to class, nationality, race, ethnicity, or sexuality from being addressed and denies the political realities that may divide women as well as bring them together.

37. *Los Angeles Times*, Washington D.C. edition, 5 August 1993, p. A1.

38. Asia Watch, *The Human Rights Crisis in Kashmir*, p. 106.

39. International Commission of Jurists, *The Events in East Pakistan, 1971: A Legal Study* (Geneva: International Commission of Jurists, 1972), p. 41.

40. Deborah Blatt, "Recognizing Rape as a Method of Torture," *New York University Review of Law and Social Change* 19, no. 4 (1992): 843.

41. Shana Swiss and Joan E. Giller, "Rape as a Crime of War: A Medical Perspective," *Journal of the American Medical Association* 270, no. 5 (August 1993): 612–15.

42. *New York Times*, 20 October 1993, p. A1.

43. *New York Times*, 7 December 1992, p. A18.

44. *Geneva Convention Relative to the Protection of Civilian Persons in Time of War*, 12 August 1949, 6 UST 3516, 75 UNTS 287 (Geneva Convention No. IV), Article 27.

45. War crimes are violations of the laws of war that "are committed by persons 'belonging' to one party to the conflict against persons or property of the other side" (Meron, "Rape as a Crime," pp. 424, 426 n. 19). Certain war crimes are designated by the Geneva Conventions to be grave breaches.

46. Meron, "Rape as a Crime," p. 426, citing International Committee of the Red Cross, *Aide-Memoire*, 3 December 1992.

47. Meron, "Rape as a Crime," pp. 426–27 n. 21, citing Oscar M. Uhler and Henri Coursier, *Geneva Convention Relative to the Protection of Civilian Persons in Time of War: Commentary* (Geneva: International Committee of the Red Cross, 1958), p. 598.

48. Meron, "Rape as a Crime," p. 427.

49. Rape constitutes torture (as defined by the U.N. Convention Against Torture and Other Cruel, Inhuman, or Degrading Treatment or Punishment) when it is used to inflict severe pain or suffering in order to obtain information or confession, or for any reason based on discrimination, or to punish, coerce, or intimidate, and is performed by state agents or with their acquiescence. See Blatt, "Recognizing Rape as a Method," pp. 831–34.

50. *Protocol Additional to the Geneva Conventions of 12 August 1949, and Relating to the Protection of Victims of Non-International Armed Conflicts*, opened for signature on 12 December 1977, Art. 4 (2e), 1125 UNTS 609, 16 ILM 1442 (1977) (Protocol II).

51. Yves Sandoz, Christophe Swinarski, and Bruno Zimmerman, eds., *ICRC Commentary on the Additional Protocols of 8 June 1977 to the Geneva Conventions of 12 August 1949* (Geneva: Martinus Nijhoff Publishers, 1987), p. 1375, para. 4539.

52. Universal jurisdiction exists where the law recognizes the competence of any court to try an alleged offender, without regard to territorial or other traditional bases of jurisdiction. U.S. law takes the position that

> a state has jurisdiction to define and prescribe punishment for certain offenses recognized by the community of nations as of universal concern, such as piracy, slave trade, attacks on or hijacking of aircraft, genocide, war crimes, and perhaps certain acts of terrorism, even where none of the bases of jurisdiction indicated in [section] 402 is present.

Restatement (Third) of Foreign Relations Law of the United States, Section 404 (Washington D.C.: Superintendent of Documents, 1987).

53. See Françoise Hampson, "Human Rights and Humanitarian Law in Internal Conflicts,"

in Michael A. Meyer, ed. *Armed Conflict and the New Law: Aspects of the 1977 Geneva Protocols and the 1981 Weapons Convention* (London: British Institute of International and Comparative Law, 1989), pp. 55–80.

54. Crimes against humanity may also occur in the course of international conflicts and were prosecuted alongside war crimes at Nuremberg.

55. Helsinki Watch, *War Crimes in Bosnia-Herzegovina*, pp. 394–97.

56. Control Council Law No. 10, *Control Council for Germany, Official Gazette* (31 January 1946), p. 50, reprinted in Howard S. Levie, *Documents on Prisoners of War*, International Law Studies, No. 60 (Washington D.C.: Naval War College Press, 1979), p. 304.

57. Diane F. Orentlicher, "Settling Accounts: The Duty to Prosecute Human Rights Violations of a Prior Regime," *Yale Law Journal* 100, no. 8 (June 1991): 2537, 2594.

58. Ibid., p. 2593.

59. The Torture Convention obliges each State Party to "take such measures as may be necessary to establish its jurisdiction over such offences in cases where the alleged offender is present in any territory under its jurisdiction and it does not extradite him" (*Convention Against Torture and Other Cruel, Inhuman, or Degrading Treatment or Punishment*, Article 5). Article 7 of the Convention specifies that States Parties must either extradite an alleged torturer or submit the case for prosecution in their own courts. See also Orentlicher, "Settling Accounts," p. 2566.

60. Orentlicher, "Settling Accounts," p. 2567.

61. Only in 1991 did the United Kingdom outlaw marital rape. See *The Independent* (London), 24 October 1991, p. 3.

62. Women's Rights Project/Asia Watch, *Double Jeopardy: Police Abuse of Women in Pakistan* (New York: Human Rights Watch, 1992).

63. Women's Rights Project/Americas Watch, *Untold Terror*, pp. 12–13.

64. *Geneva Convention Relative to the Protection of Civilian Persons in Time of War*, 12 August 1949, 6 UST 3516, 75 UNTS 287 (*Geneva Convention No. IV*), Article 147.

65. The Statute of the Tribunal does not specifically designate rape in its list of war crimes. It does, however, rely on the terms of the Geneva Conventions which have, as discussed, been interpreted to provide for the prosecution of rape as a war crime. Further, the Statute includes rape as a crime against humanity "when committed in armed conflict, whether international or internal in character, and directed against any civilian population." *Report of the Secretary-General Pursuant to Para. 8 of Security Council Resolution 808*, U.N. Doc. 5/25704 (1993), Article 5.

66. In *Prosecute Now!*, 1 August 1993, Helsinki Watch urged the United Nations to move beyond mere discussion of setting up the tribunal to beginning its operations.

67. See *Washington Post*, 12 November 1993, p. A39.

Chapter 13

1. Marković discusses Julija and Nada Bunić, Cvijeta Zuzorić (of whom no works have been preserved), Marija Dimitrović Bettera, Lukrecija Bogašinović Budmani, Anica Bošković, and women writers among Dubrovnik's monastery (*dumne*). See Zdenka Marković, *Pjesnikinje starog Dubrovnika* (Zagreb: Jugoslavenska akademija znanosti i umjetnosti, 1970).

2. "I saw the censor today on acount of my stories. . . . He complained a lot because of my stories in which I apparently should not use the name 'Illyr.'" Quoted in Adela Milčinović, "Dragojla Jarnevićeva," in Ivo Frangeš, ed., *Ivana Brlić-Mažuranić, Adela Milčinović, Zdenka Marković: Izabrana djela* (Zagreb: Matica Hrvatska, 1968), p. 320.

3. "The crisis which took place now (April 1843) in Croatia, the investigations . . . contribute to the situation in which many are afraid. . . . O, week people! They are afraid of a handful of Hungarians and they tremble for fear of loosing their little job because of their love of a homeland." Ibid., p. 322.

4. Ibid., p. 324.

5. Dragojla Jarnević, *Dnevnik* (excerpts), in *Republika: časopis za književnost*, nos. 11–12 (November–December 1983), pp. 195–99.

6. Ivana Brlić-Mažuranić, *Priče iz davnine* (Zagreb: Mladost, 1964), p. 187.

7. Ibid., p. 9.

8. Ibid., p. 20.

9. Ibid., p. 120.

10. Ivana Brlić-Mažuranić, *Čudnovate zgode šegrta Hlapića* (Zagreb: Mladost, 1967), p. 9.

11. Ibid., p. 17.

12. Ivo Frangeš, *Povijest hrvatske književnosti* (Zagreb, Ljubljana: Nakladni zavod Matice Hrvatske, Cankarjeva založba, 1987), p. 281.

13. See, for example, the extensive bibliography of works on Ivana Brlić-Mažuranić in *Ivana Brlić-Mažuranić: The Collection of Texts on Ivana Brlić-Mažuranić* (Zagreb: Mladost, 1970), pp. 268–86.

14. Bora Djordjević, *Zagorka: kroničar starog Zagreba* (Zagreb: Stvarnost, 1965), p. 78.

15. Ivo Hergešić, "Uvod" (Introduction), in Marija Jurić Zagorka, *Tajna krvavog mosta* (Zagreb: August Cesarec, 1976), p. vi.

16. Ibid., p. xxi.

17. Ibid., p. xv.

18. Djordjević, *Zagorka*, p. 73.

19. Miodrag Pavlović, "Uvod" (Introduction), in Isidora Sekulić, *Sabrana dela* (Collected works) (Sarajevo: Svjetlost, 1967), vol. 1, p. 13.

20. Ibid., p. 11.

21. Isidora Sekulić, *Saputnici: Pisma iz Norveške* (Co-travelers. Letters from Norway) (Beograd: Vuk Karadžić, 1976), p. 198. One might also mention that *Letters* exhibits a problematic glorification of the national element over the individual or cultural one. Norwegians are criticized because they try to get "some personal liberation before achieving a national one," and because they are "struggling with problems which are not direct consequences of the totality of national life and history" (ibid., p. 197). Serbia, on the other hand, "was happier . . . because it first accomplished [national] liberation, and only then went into culture, that is, created culture" (Ibid., p. 198). The supremacy of the national cause over the individual or cultural one is often repeated and passionately asserted in the *Letters*.

22. Jasmina Lukić, "Women-Centered Narratives in Contemporary Serbian and Croatian Literatures," in Pamela Chester and Sibelan Forrester, eds., *Engendering Slavic Literatures* (Bloomington: Indiana University Press, 1996), p. 225.

23. Ibid., p. 226.

24. Ibid., p. 229.

25. Drakulić, Ugrešić, and Vrkljan seem to be the most well-known Croatian women writers in the West as well, thanks to the translated editions of their work. Given the limits of this article, I shall focus my discussion on their work, but would at least like to mention some other prominent women writers, such as the two prolific, much read and remarkable poets of the older generation, Vesna Parun and Vesna Krmpotić. The Croatian women's contemporary poetry scene is also very lively and rich with writers like Andriana Škunca, Gordana Benić, Sibila Petlevski, Milana Vuković, and Dubravka Oraić. There are young playwrights like Lada Kaštelan and Asja Todorović, and as far as post–World War II prose is concerned, Ivanka Vujčić-Laszowski, Višnja Stahuljak, Sunčana Škrinjarić, Carmen Klein, Željka Čorak and Jasenka Kodrnja should be mentioned also.

26. Slavenka Drakulić, *Holograms of Fear*, trans. Ellen Elias-Bursać (New York: W. W. Norton, 1992), p. 18.

27. Ibid., pp. 78–82.

28. Slavenka Drakulić, *Marble Skin*, trans. from the French by Greg Mosse (London: Hutchinson, 1993), p. 85.

29. Ibid., p. 107.

30. Ibid., p. 179.

31. Slavenka Drakulić, *The Balkan Express* (New York: Harper Perennial, 1994), pp. 147–50.

32. The original title of this book is *Američki Fikcionar* (The American fictionary).

33. Celia Hawkesworth, "Dubravka Ugrešić: The Insider's Story," *Slavonic and East European Review* 68, no. 3 (July 1990): 136.

34. Dubravka Ugrešić, *Steffie Speck in the Jaws of Life*, in *In the Jaws of Life and Other Stories*, trans. Michael Henry Heim and Celia Hawkesworth (Evanston, Ill.: Northwestern University Press, 1993), p. 35–36.

35. Dubravka Ugrešić, *Have a Nice Day: From the Balkan War to the American Dream*, trans. Celia Hawkesworth (New York: Viking Penguin, 1995), p. 38.

36. "When she heard that I was a writer, the young New Yorker interested in 'Eastern Europe' asked, 'So how are things now, after perestroika, I mean censorship and all that?'

'I'm sorry, but you've got the wrong country,' I said. 'Oh yes, excuse me,' she apologized. 'You're the country where there's a war on, aren't you?'

'Yes, we're the country where there's a war on.'

'I'm sorry,' she said kindly, smiling." (Ibid., p. 32.)

37. " 'The American market is saturated with East European writers,' an editor in one publishing house told me.

'Oh?' I said.

'I personally don't intend to publish a single one,' he said.

'But what has that got to do with my books?' I said, stressing the word books.

'You are an East European writer,' he replied, stressing every word. (Ibid., pp. 140–41.)

'It's a real shame you're not a Cuban writer,' the editor of another publishing house told me, with feeling.

'Oh?'

'At present, the American market is open to ethnicites, particularly Cubans, Puertoricans, Central America in general.'

'Interesting,' I said.

'Have you any connection with China?'

'No.'

'Pity. That would have helped too. The Chinese immigrant novel, that's fashionable now.' " (Ibid., p. 141.)

38. Presenting this war as an almost natural phenomenon in the "land of demons" (where irrational people simply like to "fight each other"), precluded timely identification of clearly discernible aggressors and victims. Indeed, one could say that such a discursive construction of Yugoslavs and the war there was created in order to justify reprehensible Western policies with regard to it.

39. Ugrešić, *Have a Nice Day*, p. 110.

40. Irena Vrkljan, *Svila, Škare* (Silk, scissors) (Zagreb: Grafički zavod Hrvatske, 1984), p. 47.

41. Ibid., p. 55.42. Ibid., p. 56.

43. Celia Hawkesworth, "Irena Vrkljan: *Marina, or About Biography*," *Slavonic and East European Review* 69, no. 2 (April 1991): 223.

44. Irena Vrkljan, *Marina or About Biography*, trans. Celia Hawkesworth (Zagreb: Durieux/The Bridge, 1991), p. 33.

45. Ibid., p. 13.

46. Ibid., p. 14.

47. Mirjana Dugandžija, "Irena Vrkljan: Književnost će preživjeti" (An interview with Irena Vrkljan), in *Danica* (Zagreb), no. 168, 19 August 1995, p. 2.

48. Drakulić, *Holograms of Fear*, p. 49.

49. Gordana P. Crnković, "That Other Place," *Stanford Humanities Review* 1, nos. 2–3 (fall–winter 1990): 134–37.

Chapter 14

1. Slobodan P. Novak, "Marko Marulić," in Mihovil Kombol and Slobodan Prosperov Novak, eds., *Hrvatska književnost do narodnog preporoda* (Zagreb: Školska knjiga, 1992), p. 59; my translation. Unless stated otherwise, all the subsequent translations from Croatian or Serbian are also mine.

2. Ivo Frangeš, *Povijest hrvatske književnosti* (Zagreb, Ljubljana: Nakladni zavod Matice Hrvatske, Cankarjeva zalozba, 1987), p. 202.

3. Josip Kozarac, "Tena" (excerpt), trans. Branko Mikasinovich, in Branko Mikasinovich, Dragan Milivojević, and Vasa D. Mihailovich, eds., *Introduction to Yugoslav Literature* (New York: Twayne Publishers, Inc., 1973), p. 334.

4. Ante Kovačić, *U registraturi* (Beograd: Nolit, 1965), p. 128.

5. Antun Gustav Matoš, *Pripovijetke* (Zagreb: Zora, 1968), pp. 150–54.

6. Dinko Šimunović, *Pripovijetke* (Zagreb: Mladost, 1968), p. 122.

7. Ibid., p. 127.

8. Ibid., p. 64.

9. Ibid., p. 65.

10. Ibid., p. 66.

11. Jovan Dučić, "Pjesma ženi," in *Pesme* (Poems) (Sarajevo: Svjetlost, 1969), p. 195.

12. Borislav Stanković, "Paraputa," in *Stari dani/Božji ljudi* (Beograd: Prosveta), p. 322.

13. Borislav Stanković, "Pokojnikova žena," in Vice Zaninović, *Čitanka s pregledom jugoslavenskih književnosti* (Zagreb: Školska knjiga, 1967), p. 178.

14. Borislav Stanković, "Pokojnikova žena," in *Stari dani/Božji ljudi*, p. 220.

15. Celia Hawkesworth, *Ivo Andrić: Bridge between East and West* (London: Athlone Press, 1984), p. 145.

16. Ivo Andrić, *Bosnian Chronicle*, trans. Joseph Hitrec (New York: Arcade, 1993), p. 297.

17. In the context of the times, this woman's quality of being closer to herself, as well as listening to herself rather than to externally imposed theories, becomes one of the essential prerogatives for the whole country in search of its new socialist identity.

Chapter 15

1. David D. Gilmore, "Anthropology of the Mediterranean Area," *Annual Review of Anthropology* 11 (1982): 175–205.

2. For a detailed description of this process, its causes and consequences, see Mart Bax, "The Madonna of Medjugorje: Religious Rivalry and the Formation of a Devotional Movement in Yugoslavia," *Anthropological Quarterly* 62, no. 2 (April 1990): 122–45 (also published in Eric R. Wolf, ed., *Religious Regimes and State-Formation: Perspectives from European Ethnology* [New York: SUNY Press, 1991]); Mart Bax, "The Saints of Gomila: Ritual and Blood Vengeance in a Yugoslav Peasant Community," *Ethnologia Europaea* 22, no. 1 (1992): 17–31; Mart Bax, *Medjugorje: Religion, Politics, and Violence in Rural Bosnia* (Amsterdam: VU University Press, 1995); see also Pedro Ramet, "Factionalism in Church-State Interaction: The Croatian Catholic Church in the 1980s," *Slavic Review* 44, no. 2 (summer 1985): 298–315; and Branimir Stanojević, *Crvena Gospa iz Medjogorja* (Beograd: Panpublik, 1989).

3. This region has frequently been the site of violence: on the part of the Ottoman Turks up to approximately 1870, the Habsburg troops up to 1918, and the Serbs up to approximately 1925. A civil war between Serbs and Croats raged there in the interbellum; during World War II there were German and Italian troops; and then the partisans until well after 1950. Usually the attacks were short but violent. In the hamlets, women and children would be murdered and property either stolen or destroyed. Many of the men fled into the mountains and made guerilla attacks on their enemies' home areas. In addition to these forms of warfare, vendettas, and blood feuds were endemic in the region. This makes it easier to understand the development of a violence-oriented mentality among the male segment of the population. For a survey of the literature on warfare in this region, the reader is referred to Stella Alexander, *Church and State in Yugoslavia since 1945* (Cambridge: Cambridge University Press, 1979). For other forms of violence, see Asen Balikci, "Quarrels in a Balkan Village," *American Anthropologist* 67, no. 6, pt. 1 (December 1965): 1456–69; Carlo Falconi, *The Silence of Pius XII*, trans. Bernard Wall (London: Faber and Faber, 1970); Milenko Filipović, "Cincari u Bosni," *Zbornik Radova Etnografskog Instituta* 2 (1951): 53–108; Gilmore, "Anthropology of the Mediterranean Area"; Joel Halpern and David Kideckel, "Anthropology of Eastern Europe," *Annual Review of Anthropology* 12 (1983): 377–402; Eugene Hammel, *Alternative Social Structures and Ritual Relations in the Balkans* (Englewood Cliffs, N.J.: Prentice-Hall, 1968); William G. Lockwood, "Bride Theft and Social Maneuverability in Western Bosnia," *Anthropological Quarterly* 47, no. 3 (July 1974): 253–69; Michael B. Petrovich, "Yugoslavia: Religion and the Tensions of a Multi-National State," *East European Quarterly* 6, no. 1 (March 1972): 118–35; Anthony Rhodes, *The Vatican in the Age of the Dictators 1922–1945* (London: Hodder and Stoughton, 1973); Stavro Skendi, "Crypto-Christianity in the Balkan Area under the Ottomans," *Slavic Review* 26, no. 2 (June 1967): 227–46; Jozo Tomasevich, *Peasants, Politics and Economic Change in Yugoslavia* (Stanford: Stanford University Press, 1955); Jozo Tomasevich, "Yugoslavia during the Second World War," in Wayne Vucinich, ed., *Contemporary Yugoslavia* (Berkeley and Los Angeles: University of California Press, 1969); Marko Vego, *Historija Brotnja od najstarijih vremena do 1878 godine* (Čitluk: Alba, 1981); Petar Vlahović and V. Dancetović, "Prilog proučavanju žena u krvnoj osveti," in *Glasnik Etnografskog Instituta* 9 (1960–61): 9–10; and Wayne Vučinich, "Interwar Yugoslavia," in W. Vucinich, ed., *Contemporary Yugoslavia* (Berkeley and Los Angeles: University of California Press, 1969), pp. 3–58. The provincial archives of the Franciscans in Duvno also contains a great deal of relevant and rather shocking information about the use of violence in this region. During the recent war in Bosnia-Herzegovina, Medjugorje was also the site of large-scale violence. More details are given in Bax, *Medjugorje*.

4. Cf. Mart Bax, *Medjugorje*.

5. Svetozar Koljević, *The Epik in the Making* (Oxford: Clarendon Press, 1980), provides an interesting and detailed explanation why Franciscan priests stimulated these old local beliefs and practices. See also Andrei Šimić, "Management of the Male Image in Yugoslavia," *Anthropological Quarterly* 43, no. 2 (April 1969): 89–101; and Fred Spier, "Religie in de mensheidsgeschiedenis; naar een model van de ontwikkeling van religieuze regimes in een lange-termijnperspectief," *Amsterdams Sociologisch Tijdschrift* 16, no. 4 (1990): 88–122.

6. In addition to this exorcism, in the past priests also gave their congregation advice and provided them with consecrated metal objects and herbs to keep devils at a distance and prevent them from possessing people. Later in this chapter, it will become clear that the present-day priests of Medjugorje, almost all of whom were educated abroad, have a rather reserved and ambivalent attitude to these established ideas and behavior patterns.

7. See note 3.

8. This information is from the archives of the church in Medjugorje and the *Komuna* in Čitluk. Anyone who wanted to go abroad for longer than a month had to have a visa. Priests often played an intermediary role in this connection.

9. For further details, see Bax, "The Madonna of Medjugorje"; Bax, *Medjugorje*; Pedro Ramet, ed., *Yugoslavia in the 1980s* (Boulder: Westview Press, 1985).

10. This information was given to me by one of the clergymen responsible for the spiritual care of the parishioners. A closer analysis, conducted in conjunction with a colleague of his who had a university degree in social science, showed that it was mainly married women and widows who provided accommodations for the pilgrims. The fear of possession by devils, however, was much more widely dispersed in his view, and occurred among younger women and girls as well. I was able to talk about this topic with forty-one of these women distributed over nine neighborhoods. With only very few exceptions, the girls were barely responsive, if at all. In one or two cases, the mother served as spokeswoman.

11. *Kalajdžija* (plural: *kalajdžije*) literally means coppersmith. It is a half Turkish word that, like so many other Croatian words has been Turkicized in this region. Coppersmiths often belonged to a peripheral ethnic group. Like the gypsies with their widely ramified social networks, these people also literally lived on the edge of established peasant communities. The women of these groups were said to have the gift of sight."

12. Cf. note 8. All these informants said they had learned the interpretation of this experience from their mother, grandmother, or another female relative. Many of these conceptions, they said, were then shared by the former parish clergymen.

13. This statement is inconsistent with what the women had said on prior occasions about having to do so much more work. And yet there are no traces here of an ethnographic error, but indeed of quite a normal sociological phenomenon: people say different things, perhaps even contradictory things, in different contexts. In other words, different discourses are involved.

14. Cf. Norman Cohn, *Europe's Inner Demons. An Inquiry Inspired by the Great Witch-Hunt* (London: Blackwell, 1975); Peter Geschiere and Wilhelmina van Wetering, "Zwarte magie in een onttoverde wereld," *Sociologische Gids* 36 (1989): 150–54; Max Marwick, "Witchcraft as a Social Strain-Gauge," in Max Marwick, ed., *Witchcraft and Sorcery: Selected Readings* (Harmondsworth: Pelican, 1982); R. I. Moore, *The Formation of a Persecuting Society* (Oxford: Oxford University Press, 1987); Michael Taussig, *Shamanism, Colonialism and the Wild Man: A Study in Terror and Healing* (Chicago: University of Chicago Press, 1987); Bonno Thoden van Velzen and Wilhelmina van Wetering, *The Great Father and the Danger: Religious Cults, Material Forces, and Collective Fantasies in the World of the Surinamese Maroons* (Dordrecht/Providence: Foris Publications, 1988); Keith Thomas, *Religion and the Decline of Magic: Studies in Popular Beliefs in Sixteenth- and Seventeenth-Century England* (London: Tavistock, 1971).

15. Cf. Bax, *Medjugorje.*

16. The Duvno archives clearly illustrate this, as do the parish records in Medjugorje. Eruptions of violence usually coincided with a rise in the number of requests from women for the exorcism of women. In cases where this assistance was granted, the accounts often included the words *Da bi se umirila krv* (So that the blood may be pacified). I have not yet been able to find any further details on the preparations and the actual exorcism ritual. Like the local women, the present-day priests of Medjugorje are extremely reluctant to provide any information on this subject. It is striking, though, that Serb communities had an extensive ritual, the *Slava*, for settling feuds.

17. Jacob Black-Michaud, *Cohesive Force: Feud in the Mediterranean and the Middle East* (Oxford: St. Martin's Press, 1975); Christopher Boehm, *Blood Revenge: The Anthropology of Feuding in Montenegro and Other Tribal Societies* (Lawrence: University of Kansas Press, 1984); Ernesto Cozzi, "La vendetta del sangue nelle montagne dell'Alta Albania," *Anthropos* 5 (1910): 625–87; Bette S. Denich, "Sex and Power in the Balkans,: in Michele Zimbalist Rosaldo and Louise Lamphere, eds., *Woman, Culture and Society* (Stanford: Stanford University Press, 1974), pp. 91–119; Johann Engel, *Staatskunde und Geschichte von Dalmatien* (Kroatien und Slavonien Halle-ZumTor, 1970 [1798]); Stephen Wilson, *Feuding, Conflict and Banditry in Nineteenth-Century Corsica* (Cambridge: Cambridge University Press, 1989); Ian Whitaker, "Tribal Structure and National Politics in Albania, 1910–1950," in I. M. Lewis, ed., *History and Social Anthropology* (London: Tavistock, 1968), pp. 253–87.

18. Cf. John Davis, *People of the Mediterranean: An Essay in Comparative Social Anthropology* (London: Routledge and Kegan Paul, 1977).

19. For example, William Christian Jr., *Person and God in a Spanish Valley* (New York: Seminar Press, 1972); John Davis, "The Sexual Division of Religious Labour in Islam and Christianity Compared," in E. R. Wolf, ed., *Religion, Power and Protest: The Northern Shore of the Mediterranean* (Berlin: Mouton Publishers, 1984), pp. 17–51; Joao de Pina-Cabral, *Sons of Adam, Daughters of Eve: The Peasant World View of the Alto Minho* (Oxford: Oxford University Press, 1986).

20. For example, Geschiere and Van Wetering, "Zwarte Magie"; Tanya M. Luhrmann, *Persuasions of the Witch's Craft: Ritual Magic and Witchcraft in Present-day England* (Oxford: Blackwell, 1989); Thoden van Velzen and Van Wetering, *The Great Father*; Willem de Blecour, *Termen van Toverij* (Nijmegen: SUN, 1990); Marwick, "Witchcraft as a Social Strain-Gauge"; Taussig, *Shamanism, Colonialism*.

Afterword

1. Tzvetan Todorov, *On Human Diversity: Nationalism, Racism, and Exoticism in French Thought* (Cambridge, Mass.: Harvard University Press, 1993), p. 173.

About the editor:

SABRINA P. RAMET is a professor of international studies at the University of Washington. She received her Ph.D. in Political Science from UCLA in 1981. She is the author of seven books, three of which have been published in expanded second editions. Her latest books are *Whose Democracy? Nationalism, Religion, and the Doctrine of Collective Rights in Post-1989 Eastern Europe* (Rowman and Littlefield, 1997), and *Nihil Obstat: Religion, Politics, and Social Change in East-Central Europe and Russia* (Duke University Press, 1998). She is also the editor or co-editor of twelve previous books, and author of more than seventy journal articles.

About the contributors:

MART BAX is a professor of political anthropology at the Department of Social and Cultural Studies of the Free University, Amsterdam, Netherlands. He received his M.A. and Ph.D. in anthropology from the University of Amsterdam and has conducted fieldwork in the Irish Republic, the Netherlands, Yugoslavia, and Bosnia-Herzegovina. He is widely known for his publications about the alleged apparitions at Medjugorje. He has contributed chapters to *Religious Regimes and State Formation* (1991), edited by Eric R. Wolf, and to *Antagonism and Identity in the National Idiom: The Case of Former Yugoslavia* (in press). His articles have appeared in *Anthropological Quarterly*, *Ethnology*, *Ethnologia Europaea*, *Journal of Mediterranean Studies*, *Medical Anthropological Quarterly*, and other journals. His latest book is *Medjugorje: Religion, Politics, and Violence in Rural Bosnia* (VU University Press, 1995).

GORDANA P. CRNKOVIĆ is an assistant professor of Slavic Languages and Literature at the University of Washington. She received her Ph.D. in modern thought and literature from Stanford University in 1993. She is the author of *Imagined Dialogues: East European Literature in Conversation with English and American Literature* (Northwestern University Press, 1999), and is currently preparing a second book, *Drawn from the Fire: Yugoslav Novels and the Many Faces of the Former Yugoslavia*. Her articles have appeared in *Film Quarterly*, *Vanishing Point*, *Feminist Issues*, *Stanford Humanities Review*, and other journals.

THOMAS A. EMMERT is a professor of history at Gustavus Adolphus College in St. Peter, Minnesota, where he lectures on Russian and East European history. During the 1996–97 academic year he was a visiting professor of history at Stanford University. He studied at St. Olaf College and Oxford University, receiving his Ph.D. in history from Stanford University. A specialist in the medieval Balkans, he is the author of *Serbian Golgotha: Kosovo 1389*, a major study of the Battle of Kosovo, and co-editor (with Wayne S. Vucinich) of *Kosovo: Legacy of a Medieval Battle* (University of Minnesota, 1991). He is currently writing a history of Serbia as part of Hoover Institution's series on "Nations and Nationalities of Eastern Europe."

VLASTA JALUŠIČ is the director of the Institute of Contemporary Social and Political Studies (Peace Institute) in Ljubljana, having earned her Ph.D. in political science (1996) from the University of Vienna, with a dissertation entitled, "Violence and the Political in the Theory of Hannah Arendt." Jalušič translated (into Slovene) and edited Hannah Arendt's *The Human Condition*. She is the author of *Dokler se ne vmešajo Ženske . . .* (Until the women meddle . . .). She contributed a chapter to *Independent Slovenia* (1994), edited by Jill Benderly and Evan Kraft.

BARBARA JANCAR-WEBSTER is a professor of political science at SUNY Brockport. She is the author of *The Philosophy of Aristotle* (1963), *Czechoslovakia and the Absolute Monopoly of Power* (1971), *Women under Communism* (1978), *Environmental Management in the Soviet Union and Yugoslavia* (1987), and *Women and Revolution in Yugoslavia, 1941–1945* (1990). She is also the editor of *Environmental Action in Eastern Europe* (1993), and has contributed articles to *Problems of Communism, Signs, Studies in Comparative Communism*, and other journals.

OBRAD KESIĆ is the former program coordinator of the Democratic Transitions Program of the International Research and Exchanges Board (IREX). At IREX, Kesić was responsible for Balkan programs and has traveled extensively throughout the region. Kesić also serves as a consultant on Balkan affairs for various American and international organizations and agencies and has provided analysis and briefings for U.S. government agencies and officials, at the Departments of State and Defense as well as at USIA. Kesić has also been featured as a guest on National Public Radio, CNN International, the Voice of America, and Monitor Radio. Kesić has authored many articles and essays on Balkan affairs and American policy in the Balkans. He is a member of the Atlantic Council/Woodrow Wilson Balkan Security Task Force.

BRANKA MAGAŠ is a historian and journalist, of Croatian descent, currently residing in London. She is the author of *The Destruction of Yugoslavia: Tracking the Break-up, 1980–92* (Verso, 1993).

JULIE MERTUS is a visiting associate professor at Ohio Northern University and a fellow in the Law and Religion Project, Emory University, Atlanta. Formerly Counsel to Helsinki Watch (focusing on the former Yugoslavia), a Fulbright Scholar (in Romania), a MacArthur Foundation peace fellow, and a Harvard Law School Human Rights program visiting fellow, Mertus is the author of *National Truth—Re(membering) Kosovo: The Building of Serbian and Albanian Nationalisms* (University of California Press, 1998) and co-author (with Vlatka Mihelić) of *Open Wounds: Human Rights Abuses in Kosovo* (Human Rights Watch/Helsinki, 1994) and (with Millika Dutt and Nancy Flowers) of *Local Action/Global Change* (United Nations Press, 1997). She is co-editor of *The Suitcase: Refugees' Voices from Bosnia and Croatia* (University of California Press, 1997) and has contributed articles to *Uncaptive Minds*, *New York University Review of International Law and Politics*, *The Columbia Journal of Gender and Law*, and other journals.

ŽARANA PAPIĆ teaches social anthropology at the University of Belgrade and at the Women's Studies Center, Belgrade, and has professional experience in publishing. She received her Ph.D. in social anthropology in 1995 from the University of Belgrade. A longtime activist for female equality, she has been deeply involved in feminist networks. She is the author of *Sociologija i feminizam* (Sociology and feminism) (Belgrade, 1989), and *Polnost i kultura: Telo i znanje u socialnoj antropologiji* (Gender and culture: Body and knowledge in social anthropology) (Belgrade, 1997). She also co-edited (with Lydia Sklevicky) an anthology dealing with the anthropology of women, in 1983, under the title *Antropologija žene*.

TATJANA PAVLOVIĆ is an assistant professor of Spanish and women's studies at Willamette University, Portland, Washington. She received her Ph.D. in Spanish literature and critical theory in 1995 from the University of Washington, completing a doctoral thesis about constructions of the body, sexuality, and gender in Spanish culture from the onset of the Franco era to the present. She has published articles about Croatian novelist Dubravka Ugrešić and is interested in issues of nationalism, feminism, and homosexuality in contemporary Croatia. She is currently working on a book about popular culture in contemporary Croatia and one which deals with contemporary Spanish cinema and Spanish women's fiction.

REGAN E. RALPH is the Washington director of the Women's Rights Project of Human Rights Watch, the largest human rights monitoring organization based in the United States. On behalf of the Women's Rights Project, she has investigated and reported on violations of women's human rights in Turkey, Russia, and the former Yugoslavia, and has worked with women's organizations around the world to improve the protection of women's rights. Her human rights investigations have targeted violations of women's human rights ranging from the rape of women in war to forced exams to determine women's virginity to state failure to prosecute violence against women. Ralph is also an adjunct professor of women's studies at Georgetown University, where she teaches a course on women's international human rights. She has a law degree from Yale Law School and a bachelor's degree in international relations from Harvard University. She also studied international law at the London School of Economics and Political Science and Arabic at the American University in Cairo, Egypt.

ANDREI SIMIĆ is a professor of anthropology and an associate of the Center for Visual Anthropology at the University of Southern California. He has lived and carried out fieldwork in Yugoslavia periodically since 1961, and is the author of *The Peasant Urbanites: A Study of Rural-Urban Mobility in Serbia*, as well as of more than thirty articles dealing with the Balkans published in anthropological and ethnographic journals. He produced an hour-long documentary film about Serbs in America, *Živeli: Medicine for the Heart*. His other areas of specialization include urban anthropology, social gerontology, ethnographic film, and ethnicity and ethnic groups in America.

DOROTHY Q. THOMAS is the director of the Human Rights Watch Women's Rights Project. She has conducted field research and writing on women's human rights in nearly a score of countries. Before founding the Women's Rights Project, she worked at the Washington Office on Africa and at the Lawyers' Committee for Civil Rights to monitor Namibia's transition to independence. She has a master's degree in literary theory and women's studies from Georgetown University, and in 1994, she received a Peace Fellowship at the Bunting Institute at Radcliffe College. She is the author/editor of several reports and articles on women's human rights, including *All Too Familiar: Sexual Abuse of Women in U.S. State Prisons, Criminal Injustice: Violence Against Women in Brazil*, and *Double Jeopardy: Police Abuse of Women in Pakistan*.